The Contest of Christian and Muslim Spain
1031–1157

A History of Spain

General Editor: John Lynch

María Cruz Fernández Castro	*The Prehistory of Spain*
J. S. Richardson	*Roman Spain*
Roger Collins	*Visigothic Spain, 409–711*
Roger Collins	*The Arab Conquest of Spain, 710–797*
Roger Collins	*Caliphs and Kings: Spain, 798–1033*
Bernard F. Reilly	*The Contest of Christian and Muslim Spain, 1031–1157*
Peter Linehan	*Spain, 1157–1312*
Angus McKay	*Spain: Centuries of Crisis, 1300–1474*
John Edwards	*The Spain of the Catholic Monarchs, 1474–1520*
John Lynch	*Spain, 1516–1598: From Nation State to World Empire*
John Lynch	*The Hispanic World in Crisis and Change, 1598–1700*
John Lynch	*Bourbon Spain, 1700–1808*
Martin Blinkhorn	*The Emergency of Modern Spain, 1808–1939*
Richard Robinson	*Spain since 1939*

The Contest of Christian and Muslim Spain

1031–1157

Bernard F. Reilly

BLACKWELL
Oxford UK & Cambridge USA

First published 1992
First published in paperback 1995

Blackwell Publishers Inc.
238 Main Street
Cambridge, Massachusetts 02142, USA

Blackwell Publishers Ltd
108 Cowley Road, Oxford, OX4 1JF, UK

Library of Congress Cataloging in Publication Data

Reilly, Bernard F., 1925–
The contest of Christian and Muslim Spain : 1031–1157 / Bernard F. Reilly.
    p.   cm. – (A History of Spain)
Includes bibliographical references and index.
ISBN 0–631–16913–X (hbk) –– 0–631–19964–0 (pbk)
1. Spain – History – 711–1516.   2. Christians – Spain – History.
    3. Muslims – Spain – History.   I. Title.   II. Series
                    DP99.R37   1992
                    946′.02 – dc20   91–17670
                                                        CIP

British Library Cataloguing in Publication Data

A CIP catalogue record for this book is available from the British Library.

Typeset in Garamond 10½ on 12 pt
by Graphicraft Typesetters Ltd, Hong Kong

This book is printed on acid-free paper.

To my children
who completed my education

Contents

List of Illustrations   ix
Preface   xi
Acknowledgements   xv
Abbreviations   xvi

1   The Old Order Changeth (1031–1072)   1

The Land and the Working of the Land   7
Peoples of Muslim Spain   12
Jews and Judaism in Muslim Spain   14
The Mozarab Community   17
Life and Thought in Islamic Spain   21

2   The Political Ferment in Northern Spain (1031–1073)   25

The Christian World of the North   28
A World of Change   32
Fernando I *el Magno* of León–Castilla (1035–1065)   35
The Pyrenaen Christian Realms and Zaragoza
(1031–1073)   43

3   The Emerging Society of the Christian North   50

High Culture in 11th-Century Christian Iberia   60
Iberia between Africa and Europe   64

4   The Hegemony of León–Castilla under Alfonso VI
(1065–1109)   74

The Annexation of La Rioja   76
The Repopulation of the Trans-Duero: The Reconquest
of Toledo   79
The Murābit Invasion   86

A Most Stubborn Defense   91
The End of an Era   95

5   The Murābit Empire and the Other Spains   99

Aragón and the Shadow of León–Castilla   105
The Tardy Emergency of the Country of Barcelona   118
El Cid Campeador and the Taifa of Valencia   122

6   The Dynastic Crisis in León–Castilla (1109–1126)   126

Aragón and León–Castilla at War (1113–1117)   134
The Emergence of Portugal   141

7   A New Aragón and a New Cataluña (1104–1134)   157

The New Aragón and Its Neighbors   162
Barcelona into Cataluña (1097–1131)   174

8   The Emerging Status Quo in Christian Iberia
    (1135–1143)   181

First among Equals   190
The Emergent Kingdom of Portugal   200

9   The Preponderance of the Christian North (1143–1157)   205

The *Reconquista* and the Second Crusade   211
Andalucía Fragmented and Contested   215
The New Balance of Christian and Muslim in Iberia   223

10 The Two Cultures of 12th-Century Iberia   231

Christian Iberian Society in the Mid–12th Century   238
Institutional Change and Diversification in Christian
    Iberia   242
Iberia and the Making of the Medieval Western Mind   250
Christian Iberia in Western Europe   257

Bibliography   263
Index   273

List of Illustrations

Photographs

Plate 1   Interior of the great mosque of Córdoba   23
Plate 2   Mozarabic church of San Miguel de Escalada,
          province of León   63
Plate 3   The *Aljaféria* of Zaragoza   83
Plate 4   The pilgrim bridge at Punte la Reina, Aragón   111
Plate 5   Original charter of Alfonso VII of October 12,
          1153   191
Plate 6   Castle of Leiria, Portugal   204
Plate 7   The pass of Despeñaperros in the Sierra Morena   213
Plate 8   Coinage of Ramón Berenguer IV of Bercelona   219

Maps

Figure 1   Physical and urban Iberia   10
Figure 2   Christian Iberia at the death of Fernando I in 1065   38
Figure 3   Murābit and Christian Iberia at the death of
           Alfonso VI in 1109   128
Figure 4   Christian Iberia at the accession of Alfonso VII in
           1126   166
Figure 5   Growth of the country of Barcelona to 1137   178
Figure 6   Political Iberia at the death of Alfonso VII in 1157   228
Figure 7   Avenues of French influence in 12th-century
           Christian Iberia   246

Preface

This volume has been undertaken in confidence that the time was ripe for a history of the 11th and 12th Centuries in Iberia. While it is customary to bemoan the state of archives in the peninsula generally, and, with ‘honorable exceptions, the fact that archivists are still working to repair the neglect of the 19th Century, one can easily overlook the massive publication of documents and sources which has distinguished the final three quarters of our own century. The early work of Luciano Serrano on the monastic documents of Castilla and the more recent work of Antonio Ubieto Arteta on those of Aragón are but cases in point. To them would have to be added a host of other names whose efforts have been more concentrated and somewhat less encyclopedic. The many volumes that have emanated from the Centro de Estudios e Investigación "San Isidoro" in León and those now being issued under the patronage of the Departamento de Historia of the Colegio Universitario of Burgos illustrate the growing collaborative character of these endeavors.

The same period has seen the publication of almost all of the literary sources. Most recently, the *Corpus Christianorum* series has brought out both the 13th-century *De Rebus Hispaniae* of Rodrigo Jiménez de Rada and the 12th-century *Historia Compostelana* in 1987 and 1988, respectively. One understands that a critical edition of Lucas of Túy's *Chronicon Mundi* is also in preparation. When to these most recent achievements are added the earlier editions of the *Crónica ˙Adefonsi Imperatoris*, the *Crónica Najerense*, the *Crónica del Obispo Don Pelayo*, the *Historia Silense*, and *Las crónicas latinas de la reconquista*, to mention only the most important, it becomes possible to understand the distance that has been traveled since Ramón Menéndez Pidal's pioneer work on *La España del Cid* first appeared in 1929.

Moreover, it would be grossly misleading to neglect the mention of at least some of the host of specialized studies. Julio González's two volumes on *Repoblación de Castilla La Nueva* leaps immediately to mind, as well as earlier periodical articles on repopulation elsewhere. The multivolume history of Aragón for this period of Antonio Ubieto Arteta, the many studies of Damião Peres and Torquato Sousa Soares for Portugal, and the brilliant essay of Pierre Bonnassie for Cataluña are entirely necessary additions to the list. Finally, the career-long studies of Charles Julian Bishko on the influence of Cluny in the peninsula must be cited.

In short, then, this volume has been made feasible by the more particular labors of other historians and editors of the past seventy-five years. Their work has also made obvious the lack of any coherent, overall view of peninsular history during the period between the accession of Fernando I of León–Castilla in 1037 and the death of Alfonso VII in 1157. Despite all that they achieved, no one of them has supplied the sort of comprehensive historical context within which the full significance of their own conclusions could be revealed. This latter is the intended result of the present volume.

Nevertheless, one must candidly admit that the present synthesis must be provisional. The effort must be made, at this point, precisely to clarify and identify those remaining problems which should become the focus of subsequent historical investigation. It is now necessary, in my view, not only to sum up what has been done and to evaluate it for the interested public, but also to reveal to oneself and to one's fellow laborers in the vineyard those lacunae that emerge from the comparison of the various pieces to a possible whole. That labor is a humble one, perhaps, but nonetheless imperative.

Symptomatic of what remains to be done is the fact that the royal charters of many of the political principals have not been edited. For León–Castilla, we have only partial printings of those of Vermudo III and Fernando I, and a long study by Rassow of about half of those of Alfonso VII. Consequently, we have no adequate, modern history of any of their reigns. I attempted to supply that lack for the reigns of Urraca and Alfonso VI in my 1982 and 1988 publications, respectively. To do that I first had to study the diplomas of both, which did not appear in any critical editions as such. I am now engaged in a similar study of the reign of Alfonso VII, which I hope will at some point result in another similar volume but, again, there is no critical edition of his charters.

For Portugal, we have the magnificent edition of the royal charters of the early monarchs, Count Henry, Teresa, and Alfonso Enríquez, in the *Documentos Medievais Portugueses* of Rui Pinto de Azevado, as well as the history of the reigns of the first two of these by Torquato de Sousa Soares. However, Alfonso Enríquez, the first king of Portugal, remains without a similar history.

In the case of Navarra, virtually all we have is the valuable but dated study of Pérez de Urbel on Sancho III *el Mayor*. There are no comprehensive printings of the documents of the 11th-century kings García Sánchez II or Sancho García IV, or of the 12th-century García Ramírez IV or Sancho VI, much less critical editions of their documents. Needless to say, then, we lack a modern history of any of their reigns.

Happily the situation is somewhat better for the kingdom of Aragón. In 1951 Antonio Ubieto Arteta gave us an edition of the charters of Pedro I and in 1988 another of those of Ramiro II. As mentioned above, he has also supplemented these works with his own multivolume history of early Aragón. Still, we must do without critical editions of Ramiro I and Sancho Ramírez I in the 11th Century and the all-important Alfonso I in the 12th Century. Under such conditions, Ubieto Arteta's general history itself must be regarded with some reserve.

In the case of Cataluña, none of the documents of the early counts of the 11th Century have been systematically studied or edited. The same is true for Count Ramón Berenguer III and for the count–king Ramón Berenguer IV of Aragón-Cataluña in the 12th Century. Consequently, we are still without adequate modern histories of their reigns.

If such are the conditions for Christian Iberia during the period, one can imagine those for Muslim Iberia, aggravated by the almost complete lack of documentary materials. For the history of the taifa kingdoms and the subsequent Murābit and Muwāhhid Empires, we must depend entirely upon the literary materials. Among the historians of Islam, Ambrosio Huici Miranda has spent a lifetime editing some of those materials; in addition, he has written a valuable history of the Muslim Valencia for this period as well as a political history of the Muwāhhid. Afif Turk has given us a history of the taifa of Zaragoza and David Wasserstein a general history of the taifas of the 11th Century. Beyond these, we must depend on the aging and general studies of Reinhart Dozy and, more recently, Évariste Lévi-Provençal. Studies of the Murābit Empire are scarcely begun, except for the partial work of Francisco Codera y Zaidín at the turn of the century on its decline.

There remains, then, enough work in the field of Iberian history in the 11th and 12th Centuries alone for an entire generation of scholars. That this volume should furnish them with a background and a framework to evaluate their own endeavors and discoveries is one of my fonder hopes. Certainly the present work should underscore the fact that it was precisely during this period that the peninsula became, for the first time, a society in which relations between the various political unities became virtually continuous and markedly significant. One now ignores the external events only at the risk of serious misapprehension of what is transpiring within each realm.

This particular volume should also contribute two other enduring prejudices to future historical investigation and evaluation. The first is an enhanced consciousness of the very limited resources of the central power in any of the political centers of Iberia during the period. To miss that critical factor is to misjudge the very possibilities of the times, as well as the aspirations of its actors. For this reason, I have consciously abjured any employment of the term "state" as too freighted with impossibly modern connotations. Second, it has seemed to me that the factor of geography and the difficulties of the logistics of the peninsula have entered more often into the conclusions of its historians than into the particulars of their judgments. The fashion in which the physical surface of Iberia has constricted and constrained social initiatives before our own century is central to the understanding of what our subjects could dream as well as what they hoped to effect.

However well any of these objectives has been realized by the author is his sole responsibility, of course. Nevertheless, I must acknowledge the assistance of a host of others beyond those scholars whom the bibliography will reveal. Archivists and editors of catalogs and documents reminded me daily of the extent to which my work could never be simply my own doing. Their faith bolstered mine. Their knowledge became the condition of mine. Finally, Villanova University has supplied that continuous support and aid which was essential to the completion of this book.

BFR

Acknowledgements

In the cobbling together of a book such as this the work of long years and the assistance of many persons and institutions have come into play. I think most immediately of a near generation of archivists who have yielded to my importunities and occasionally even to my impatience. In particular, the good Don Emilio Duro Peña of the cathedral of Orense comes to mind. Once, despite a fiesta in the town and again despite the fact that he was retired, he was kind enough to allow me access to the archives there when otherwise my schedule would have obliged me simply to skip them. After the archivists come the scholars whose advice over the years has saved me time, error, and sometimes I think my very sanity. While I could have spared none of them, certainly Charles Julian Bishko of the University of Virginia is outstanding for having borne with me for something like a quarter of a century.

Some of the work here was done while I enjoyed grants from the American Philosophical Society in the summers of 1971 and 1979. Other parts of it were completed while I was holder of a grant from the Comité Conjunto Hispano-Norteamericano para la Cooperación Cultural and Educativa in summer, 1987. Nevertheless, Villanova University has been my most consistent support in the fashioning of this and other works.

The Archivo Histórico Nacional of Madrid has allowed the reproduction of the charter of Alfonso VII, the American Numismatic Society that of the coin of Ramón Berenguer IV, and The Art & Architecture Collection: Ronald Sheridan Photo-Library that of the Mosque at Cordoba. Princeton University Press kindly consented to permit me to derive the first four maps from models which they had employed in the publication of my earlier books on *Queen Urraca* and *Alfonso VI*.

Abbreviations

AGWG	Abhandlungen der Gesellschaft der Wissenschaft zur Göttingen
AEM	Anuario de Estudios Medievales
AHC	Annuarium Historiae Conciliorum
AHDE	Anuario de la Historia del Derecho Español
AL	Archivos Leoneses
AU	Archiv für Urkundenforschungen
BRAH	Boletín de la Real Academia de la Historia
CHE	Cuadernos de Historia de España
DHE	Diccionario de historia eclesiástica de España
DHGE	Dictionnaire d'Histoire et de Géographie Ecclésiastiques
DMP	Documentos Medievais Portugueses
EEMCA	Estudios de la Edad Media de la Corona de Aragón
GAKS	Gesammelte Aufsätze zur Kulturgeschichte Spaniens
PMH	Portugaliae Monumenta Histórica
RPH	Revista Portuguesa de História

1

The Old Order Changeth (1031–1072)

When the Vandals, the Alans, and the Suevi crossed the Pyrenees in A.D. 409, the peninsula began a slow secession from the classical world of Rome and a gradual decline into a Germanic society of a necessarily much ruder sort. With the invasion across the Straits of Gibraltar by Tarik in 711, Iberian society experienced the abrupt demise of the kingdom of the Visigoths and sudden incorporation into the dar al-Islam of the Muslim Mediterranean. On the other hand, the disappearance in A.D. 1031 of the caliphate of Córdoba marked merely that initial tip of the old balance in the peninsula away from the prosperous and sophisticated world of Spanish Islam and toward the penurious and simpler societies of the Christian north. For roughly two centuries more the contest between these two would be undecided. Not until the great Christian victory at Las Navas de Tolosa in 1212 could one be sure that the movement away from the world of North Africa and the Near East and toward a European future was irrevocable. Nevertheless, in the approximate century and a quarter between 1031 and 1157 the waxing of the north and the waning of the south in Iberia had already proceeded sufficiently far to suggest the probable outcome.[1]

[1] The history of Medieval Spain lately is beginning to receive some attention, although medievalists all too often remain wedded to the classic trilogy of England, France, and Germany. The best single survey in English is still Joseph F. O'Callaghan, *A History of Medieval Spain* (Ithaca, N.Y., 1975). For more concentration upon the military aspect of Spain's history, one can hardly do better than Derek W. Lomax, *The Reconquest of Spain* (London, 1978). In Spanish, the single most useful volume is Luis García de Valdeavellano, *Historia de España de los orígenes a la Baja Edad Media*, Vol. 1, pt. 2 (Madrid, 2nd ed., 1955), which unfortunately only reaches the year 1212. Two more recent and brilliantly conceived surveys are José Luis Martín, *La península en la Edad Media* (Barcelona, 1976), and José Angel García de Cortázar, *Historia de España Alfaguera*, Vol. 2 (Madrid, 1973).

The deposition of Caliph Hishām III by the leading figures of Córdoba in 1031 was, if merely a signal, yet a spectacular signal of the extent to which the Ummayad society of al-Andalus was fragmenting. What shocks is the speed with which it followed the externally triumphant rule of Muhammad ibn Abī Āmír, al-Mansūr (976–1002), who in a series of campaigns had seized and looted, one after the other, those fortified hamlets which the Christians of the north called towns. Barcelona, Burgos, León, Zamora, Santiago de Compostela – all had been left smoking and in ruins. The brief rule of his son, Abd al-Malik (1002–1008), was scarcely less successful against the north. The decline of the next twenty-three years was the result of the internal weaknesses of al-Andalus rather than the strength of its rivals.

Fundamental to that weakness was the lack of political articulation, which continues to haunt Islamic society down to the present. Within Islam the only truly legitimate authority is religious authority. Supreme political control, outside the office of the caliph, has no proper institutional framework and thus remains purely personal and fortuitous. It is always, to someone's point of view, simple usurpation. The result is an instability in the secular order, which, in turn, must lead to the very usurpation of religious authority if that personal power is to be made legitimate and therefore permanent. At the same time, the absence of a priestly hierarchy within Islam, or any other religious hierarchy that would serve to regularize the transmission of religious authority, makes the caliphate itself extremely vulnerable to such attempts. The sole title of the caliph to his authority rests upon his personal holiness, but the actual road to that dignity is ordinarily hereditary. In the absence of any outstanding charisma, then, the caliph himself can appear as the mere leader of a not terribly reputable clan. Under such conditions an able and determined leader in what we would conceive as the secular sphere can always aspire to ultimate respectability if he is able to present his own program as somehow of more benefit to Islam. Religious reform is the justification of the *coup d'état*.[2]

That al-Mansūr should have manipulated the caliph Hishām II, who was but eleven years of age on his accession in 976, is hardly surprising under these conditions. More and more the caliph would

---

[2] I can think of no better introduction in English to the general history of Islam than that furnished by Gustave E. von Grunebaum, *Medieval Islam* (Chicago, 2nd ed., 1953). For Spanish Islam, the little survey by W. Montgomery Watt, *A History of Islamic Spain* (Edinburgh, 1965), is useful. The still classic study is that of Évariste Lévi-Provençal, *L'Espagne musulmane au Xeme siècle* (Paris, 1932), which, as revised, was published in a Spanish translation, *Historia de España*, Vols. 4–5 (Madrid, 1957–65), in the Espasa-Calpe series.

disappear behind the figure of his great servant as the latter loaded himself with honors and titles and, by virtue of his campaigns against the Christians and his advocacy of the reform of Islam in al-Andalus, increasingly arrogated all but the supreme authority itself. This policy was continued by his eldest son, Abd al-Malik, until the latter's own death in 1008. It was the second son of al-Mansūr, Abd al-Rahmān, or Sanchuelo, who took the logical step of having Hishām II proclaim him as heir in 1008. But this son of a Christian princess, unable to prevent an outraged rising against his presumption, was killed in 1009, and Hishām II was himself deposed. Now all factions in al-Andalus would enter frankly into the struggle for control of one or the other caliph of the moment, and the power of Córdoba over Spanish Islam disintegrated daily. The era of the "taifa" kingdoms had begun.

With minor modifications due to the character of its ethnic factions, the lines along which Muslim Spain would fracture were dictated by geography. The heart of al-Andalus had always been the rich and well-watered basin of the Guadalquivir. That great river, navigated by small Arab craft all the way from the Atlantic to Córdoba, stretches 842 kilometers into the highlands of western Andalucía draining some 58,000 square kilometers. The basin was the great prize; but the local family that ultimately established control in Córdoba after the abolition of the caliphate in 1031 lacked the resources or prestige to claim it. Power had always to be shared with the upstart taifa at Sevilla, and in 1069 the latter absorbed Córdoba itself. The ruling Abbadid dynasty of Sevilla was simply another, essentially local, Arab family. Before the conquest of Córdoba, the taifa of Sevilla had overrun the minor kingdoms in the lower reaches of the Guadalquivir basin, beginning with Huelva (1052), Niebla (1054), and Algeciras (1060), and then Arcos, Morón, and Ronda, all in 1066, and Carmona in 1067. Its ambition even stretched into the Algarve, where Mertola was taken in 1044 and Silves in 1063. In the approximate half century following the demise of the caliphate, Abbadid Sevilla gradually reconstituted the unity of the most important single geographical area of Spanish Islam.[3]

[3] To write the history of the taifa kingdoms would be a discouraging task. Their day was brief and not terribly significant once beyond the realm of intellectual history. In addition, in common with all of Spanish Muslim history, there is an almost total lack of archival materials, so that the only source of real importance is the literary material furnished by the various Arab chroniclers, genealogists, biographers, and geographers, often of a much later period. A recent example of the best that can be done is David Wasserstein, *The Rise and Fall of the Party-Kings: Politics and Society in Islamic Spain, 1002–1086* (Princeton, N.J., 1985). Spanish municipal historians are often useful in some degree; for example, see Manuel Nieto Cumplido, *Historia de Córdoba* (Córdoba, 1984), and Jacinto Bosch Vilá, *Historia de Sevilla* (Sevilla, 1984).

The second most important river basin of Andalucía was that of the Guadiana, which reaches some 840 kilometers north and east from the Atlantic and whose watershed comprises some 69,000 square kilometers. The flow of the Guadiana is much more feeble than that of the Guadalquivir so that its navigation was correspondingly less important. Nevertheless, the Aftásid dynasty, which established itself at Badajoz on the basis of the governorship held under the caliphate, was another of the most successful of the taifas. Its authority reached up the Guadiana far past Mérida to the headwaters of the river in the Campo de Calatrava. Two boundaries were formed by the Sierra de Pedroso in the south and the mountains of Toledo in the north. But west, beyond the end of the Toledan chain, the territories of the taifa ran north beyond Cáceres to Coria in the gap between the Guadarrama and the mountains of Portugal. Farther west they spread in fanshape fashion to include roughly two-thirds of what we call modern Portugal, and in the north reached virtually to Oporto before the beginning of the Christian reconquest in the 1050s. In the south they halted before the Sevillan holdings in Mertola and Silves.[4]

Geographically, the remainder of Andalucía was composed of coastal strips separated from the valley of the Guadalquivir by almost continuous mountain ranges of formidable character to their north or west. Ordinarily these areas possessed a relatively diminutive hinterland and lived off the sea and its trade. Under such special circumstances a rather small faction – the Berbers – in the case of Málaga could seize control and maintain it successfully down until the end of the taifa period; although, from 1056 to 1073 that kingdom did come under the control of the Berber kingdom of Granada. The latter taifa, too, located high in the mountains of the Sierra Nevada between the coast and the upper Guadalquivir, could be ruled by such a minority among the factions of Spanish Islam and occasionally dispute its proper borders in the north with Sevilla. It was a rich prize, but one whose geography made it hard to wrest from those who first established themselves there. No one did, in fact, before the end of the taifa period.[5]

Like Málaga in the south, Almería to the southeast was well isolated from Andalucía by an almost continuous rampart of mountains, here interspersed with near-desert. These mountains run down

[4] Manuel Terrón Albarrán, *El solar de los Aftásids* (Badajoz, 1971), is a particular study of this taifa dynasty.
[5] Rafael Gerardo Peinado Santaella and José Enríque López de Coca Castañer, *Historia de Granada: La época medieval*, Vol. 2 (Granada, 1987). F. Javier Aguirre Sabada and María del Carmen Jiménez Mata, *Introductión al Jaén islámico* (Jaén, 1979), is also useful for this city and district, often parts of the taifa of Granada.

virtually to the sea, so that Almería, with even less hinterland than Málaga, was little more than a port but with a very active trade, given often to piracy and privateering as a supplement to the former. The dynasty there was composed of those former slave mercenaries recruited from the marts of northern Europe under the later Ummayads and whose numbers had swelled still more under al-Mansūr. In absolute numbers these troops were far inferior to those Berbers recruited from North Africa in the same period. Nevertheless, Almería maintained its independence all through the taifa period.[6]

To the northeast of Almería on the coast lay the taifa of Murcia. It, too, had a slave dynasty initially, but it was less well protected either to the southwest or to the northeast. At various times it would come under the control of Almería, or of Valencia. Late in the age of the taifas it even became the object of Sevillan aggrandizement, for its lands were approachable from the northeast through the gap at Albacete. The hinterland of Murcia was more substantial, being formed chiefly by the watershed of the Segura River of some 16,400 square kilometers. The flow of that river was quite small and uneven, despite the river being 230 kilometers in length, yet it did suffice to support a considerable, although difficult, agriculture based upon irrigation.

Another dynasty was established by a former slave on the coast north of Murcia and south of Valencia at Denia, a diminutive port with a tiny hinterland and powerful coastal neighbors. Its first ruler was fortunate or talented enough to be able to quickly extend his power over the Balearic Islands. From that offshore position his descendants were able to maintain themselves, even though Denia itself was lost in 1075.

The great coastal taifa of Valencia was stabilized in 1021 under a grandson of al-Mansūr, Abd al-Azīz. This kingdom was built upon the largest of the *huertas* of the eastern coast and was partially protected to the west by the Sierra de Albarracín. Unfortunately for its kings its territories were accessible from the west by the wide gap around Albacete. Valencia was conquered by al-Mamūn of Toledo in 1065, became independent again upon his death in 1075, and submitted to his son in 1085. Most of its later history was similarly checkered. Its trade and verdant lands combined with its geographic vulnerablity to make it attractive to seize but difficult to hold.[7]

---

[6] José Angel Tapia Garrido, *Historia general de Almería y su provincia*, Vol. 2 (Almería, 1979).

[7] Ambrosio Huici Miranda, *Historia musulmana de Valencia y su región*, 3 vols. (Valencia, 1969–70), is a giant of Spanish medieval studies in this century.

To the north and northwest of Valencia lay the great taifa of Zaragoza in the basin of the Ebro River. The powerful family of the Hūddid had often been regional governors during the caliphate and emerged as unquestioned rulers there after its demise. The extent of their territories can be roughly defined as the watershed of the Ebro. That basin, 85,000 kilometers square and drained by its 928-kilometer–long river, is strictly comparable to the great basins of the Guadalquivir and the Guadiana in Andalucía. Like them it was nurtured by a river ordinarily too shallow in most of its length for navigation but useful nonetheless for irrigation. The very size of the basin also complicated its rule, although the Hūddids early annexed the taifas of Tudela to its northwest on the Ebro and Lérida and Tortosa to its east in the lower reaches of the basin. The two latter were also sometimes independent under younger brothers of the house of Zaragoza. When Lérida and Tortosa were integral parts of the kingdom, however, Zaragoza shared a border with Valencia, and the politics and fortunes of these two were rarely isolated one from the other. In addition, Zaragoza faced the full array of Christian kingdoms to the north and west. From the county of Barcelona, to the kingdoms of Aragón and Navarra, to the kingdom of León–Castilla, Zaragoza touched upon the lands of this series of hostile and interested neighbors, most of whom possessed easy access to its territories. It was best protected by geography against León–Castilla by the Sierra de la Demanda to the west, but there was an easy gap in the north leading from Burgos down to the Ebro at Logroño. Less simple but utilizable was the route from the west over the highlands of Soria and down to the Ebro at Tudela. To its southwest Zaragoza shared a border with the taifa of Toledo where the valley of the Jalón River offered a route through the gap between the eastern end of the Guadarrama and the northern end of the Sierra de Albarracín. The taifa of Medinaceli which controlled that passage had already been seized by Zaragoza in 1029.[8]

Like Sevilla, Badajoz, and Zaragoza, the taifa of Toledo was essentially a basin principality. In this case the river is the Tajo, which has a length of some 1,100 kilometers and a watershed of 81,000 square kilometers. However, such similarities are modified by its very modest flow, which made the river difficult to use for irrigation and impossible for transportation above the point at which it enters modern Portugal. In any event, the lower reaches of the river were in the hands of the taifa of Badajoz from a point which shifted between

---

[8] Afif Turk, *El reino de Zaragoza en el siglo XI de Cristo, V de la Hégira* (Madrid, 1978).

Talavera de la Reina and Coria depending upon almost momentary fortune. The upper reaches of the river began in the Sierra de Albarracín, and the interests of Toledo flowed in that direction ordinarily.

The territories of Toledo stretched northeast into the highlands past Guadalajara until they abutted Zaragozan lands at Medinaceli. To the southeast the tablelands of La Mancha presented no obstacle, and, in 1065, al-Mamūn of Toledo pushed through the gap south of Cuenca and north of Albacete to overrun the taifa of Valencia. To the south, Toledo's control ran along vaguely defined lines where it met the borders of Badajoz, here east of the mountains of Toledo, just as it did to the west of that chain. Northward, the real boundary of the taifa was formed by the Sierra de Guadarrama. Beyond that massive barrier lay the plains of the southern half of the Duero basin, then called Extremadura by the Leónese perched on its northern edge. This region formed the one real buffer between Muslim and Christian Spain, and over it neither Toledo nor León–Castilla exercised any regular jurisdiction. Power in Toledo rested in the hands of a dynasty of local origins from the time of the fall of the caliphate up until the conquest of Toledo by the Leónese in 1085.

The politics of this array of major taifa kingdoms between 1031 and 1085 are seldom of interest to the modern historian. They have been aptly described by their most recent chronicler as "petty, local, and dynastic," and their future was to be determined by essentially external forces rather than any dynamic of their own.[9] It is the larger society and economy common to Islamic Spain which formed the more enduring entity and so deserves proper attention.

The Land and the Working of the Land

Muslim Spain, like all societies of any size before the last century, was agricultural.[10] At the same time, despite the fact that most of its inhabitants were essentially subsistence farmers who lived by eating what they themselves raised, it should be noted that it was the most advanced agricultural society in Europe during the 11th Century. Of course, in Roman times, Iberia exported wheat and olive oil, but

---

[9] Wasserstein, *Party-Kings*, p. 133.

[10] Thomas F. Glick, *Islamic and Christian Spain in the Early Middle Ages* (Princeton, N.J. 1979), is particularly good on agriculture and technology. *Irrigation and Society in Medieval Valencia* (Cambridge, Mass., 1970) by the same author is marvelous on that subject. For a more particular examination of the economy, Lévi-Provençal, *Historia de España*, Vol. 5, is still basic.

even during the Muslim period material improvements had been made on the level of the Romans. Hard wheat and sorghum were introduced from North Africa, and their superior resistance to heat and drought increased both productivity and living standards. Bread and rice were the staples of the diet, supplemented above all by the olive and the grape. Again, the latter two vines were known in Roman times, but their cultivation seems to have increased under Islam, perhaps with a contraction of the land under wheat, for the same fields were suitable for either purpose. Indeed, wheat was imported from North Africa from the period of the caliphate.

Much of the change in agriculture under Islam is to be associated with the rise of irrigation. To be sure, Roman Iberia had known irrigation, but most of it had been based upon gravity flow canals, a method possible only in severely limited areas. Muslims introduced the *noria*, or water-driven wheel, which could raise the level of water flow significantly, and also the animal-driven, geared waterwheel, which could do the same and was even more adaptable to a large variety of small streams and springs.

Such innovation was responsible for the success of the new rice crop, introduced during the Muslim period. Rice took its place alongside wheat and sorghum as a staple food in areas amenable to its cultivation. But the increased efficiency in the use of available water supplies made possible a major extension of the cultivation of fruits, beyond the olive and the grape. The fig, the apricot, the lemon, the orange, and the grapefruit all came to supplement the already cultivated apple, cherry, and pear, and these newcomers were largely dependent upon irrigation in the peninsular climate. In this connection one should also mention the introduction of sugarcane, although its dietary significance was relatively minor. Rather more important than sugar were humbler new crops such as the carrot, parsnip, eggplant, and artichoke. These were further additions to the vegetable sustenance foods of beans, lentils, and chickpeas cultivated since antiquity.

During the Roman period Iberia had been an urban society in the sense that political, economic, and social life had had their seat in the cities and were directed by an essentially urban class. The new prosperity of agriculture in Muslim Spain made the urban character of society even more marked. The urban elite not only monopolized the government but also owned much of the land, especially that belt surrounding the cities and specializing in garden produce for their markets. Advantageous leaseholds, as well as the manipulation of taxes, made it possible for that class to consume cheaply the products of the countryside and also to reclaim part of the price paid for that very produce in the form of government revenue.

Under these conditions, something like 5 per cent of the population of Islamic Spain were able to reside permanently in cities of 5,000 or more. Out of a total population of some six million, the size of major cities could reach as high as 90,000, for Córdoba; 52,000, for Sevilla; 21,000, for Badajoz; 20,000, for Granada; 17,000, for Murcia; 17,000, for Zaragoza; 28,000, for Toledo; and even 24,000 in Jerez de la Frontera. By comparison, in the society of the Christian north, also agricultural if in a different sense, the sum total of the inhabitants of all of its cities over 2,000 in population in A.D. 1031 would not have equaled that of Muslim Zaragoza.[11]

These Islamic cities lived not solely from the proceeds of government and rents. They were also centers for the processing of agricultural products, for manufacturing, and for trade. If it imported wheat from North Africa, Spanish Islam also exported olive oil, raisins, figs, and almonds to the remainder of the dar al-Islam in substantial quantities. It probably exported all of the above, in addition to wine, to the Christian north during the 11th Century as well. From the fields of the countryside came cotton, silk, and flax, introduced into the peninsula from the Levant; and from the cities they went out of the peninsula as cotton, silk, and linen cloth. Even southern Iberia was then still well supplied with forests, whose timber was shipped to North Africa where it had become scarce indeed.

In the days of the Ummayad Caliphate, Córdoba had maintained fairly close contact with North Africa because of its need for Berber mercenaries. It had also acted to manipulate those tribes both to prevent them from achieving a dangerous unity and to forestall any real influence over them from being achieved by the Shiite Fatimid dynasty in Tunisia. The interests of the Fatimids were transferred east to Egypt, of course, after the latter's conquest in 969, but the Ummayad caliphs had already annexed Ceuta, Melilla, and Tangier. These were to continue as the taifa of Ceuta down until 1083. To these centers came the caravans from sub-Saharan Africa with their freight of gold, slaves, and ivory, considerable quantities of which crossed the Straits to Andalucía. The first was often coined into those gold dinars which were the real standard of coinage for the entire peninsula, and the second went into the palaces and sometimes

[11] I usually follow the figures of Josiah Cox Russell, *Medieval Regions and Their Cities* (Bloomington, Ind., 1972), p. 178, who is the most sober in his estimates on a subject that has invited the wildest speculation.

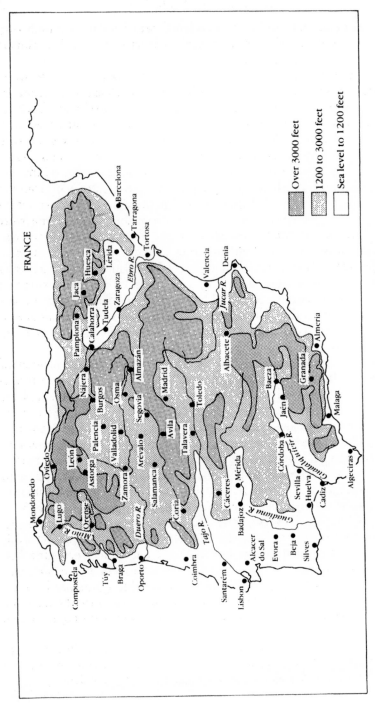

Figure 1 Physical and urban Iberia

the armies of the kings, and the third was reworked into luxury pieces of decoration and small pieces of *objet d'art* which circulated in both Iberia and the Mediterranean.

Artisanry of the latter sort was part of the larger stock of wares which kept the cities of Muslim Spain vibrant. Cloth production has already been mentioned. Pottery was widely produced for both domestic and foreign markets. Fine cabinetry of an advanced sort, various objects of worked leather, and weapons of a very good steel found an internal as well as an external market. The iron and copper ores for some of these products continued to be mined within the ambit of Spanish Islam. The leather for others came largely from the taifas of Toledo and Badajoz, whose terrain was less suited to intensive garden agriculture and where wheat and olive and vine were supplemented by stock raising on a large scale in mountain and highland areas. In general, one should remember that the farther north in the center and west of the peninsula an Islamic society was located, the simpler and more like that of the Christian world it became in its economic life. In the east, of course, the active commercial life of the Mediterranean and the more sheltered climate of that sea allowed the economy of Zaragoza and Valencia to more closely resemble that of al-Andalus proper.

Commercial life still flowed in good measure along the routes of the old Roman roads. True, Lisbon was now at the northern terminus of one such road which had run northward into Galicia, and the old "silver road" from Mérida to Zamora was no longer a great artery. After the days of al-Mansūr and his son, even Muslim armies no longer marched north along them. But the most important of these routes, that which led from Cádiz through Sevilla and Córdoba and then northeast through Toledo and Medinaceli and ultimately to Zaragoza and Barcelona, remained heavily trafficked. So did that route which led from Lisbon east to Badajoz and Mérida, then up the valley of the Guadiana and across the former artery near modern Manzanares to continue on through Albacete to the coast where it swung north to Valencia and thence ultimately to Tarragona and Barcelona. There was also a coastal road which ran east from Algeciras to Málaga and Almería and thence north to Murcia and Valencia. These were the bonds that had made of the caliphate of Córdoba a political unity and still made the world of the taifas an economic one.

The land routes were supplemented by the sea-lanes that ran from Lisbon south to Cádiz, through the Straits to Algeciras, thence east to Málaga, Almería, and north to Cartagena, Denia, Valencia, Tortosa, and the Balearics. This was coastal traffic, of course, but fairly considerable fleets operated out of Almería, Tortosa, and the Balearics in trade that reached to North Africa, Sicily, and Egypt.

Peoples of Muslim Spain

The society of Islam in Iberia at this time was fundamentally divided into three distinct parts along religious lines – Muslims, Jews, and Christians. All other divisions were superficial by comparison. The Muslim community itself was fairly homogeneous, although it did not always think of itself as being so. In strictly religious terms it was solidly Sunnite without even a tincture of Shias. Moreover, within the Sunnite tradition itself, the Malikite school of interpretation of the *hadīth* was the only one followed among the usual four variants within the orthodox Sunnite world. In the peninsula, then, Islam itself was not a source of division among Muslims but rather one of unity. Indeed, it was a relaxed sort of cult which did not even bother itself overmuch with the absence of a caliph. There were some attempts after 1031 to provide one. The Hammudid rulers of Algeciras continued to assert their own caliphal authority down until the absorption of that taifa by Sevilla in 1065, but no one seems to have paid any heed to them. In Denia, the former slave Mujāhdid supported a puppet caliph for a time, but deposed him and forced him into North African exile when the latter became ambitious. The most serious of these experiments took place in Sevilla. The Abbādids in 1035 claimed to have discovered the former caliph Hishām II still alive and duly installed him in their own city. In 1043–44, in a series of diplomatic maneuvers, the Sevillans managed to secure nominal recognition for their claimant by all of the major taifa leaders except the Zīrids of Granada. However, recognition did not include authority as well as veneration either at Sevilla or elsewhere. When the self-styled Hishām II died some years later the Sevillans did not even attempt to replace him.

The taifa kings ruled essentially independent of any religious sanction, arrogating to themselves the title of *mālik*, or *sāhib*, and sometimes that of *hājib*. Technically these were all subordinate dignities, yet they recognized no superior and their courts were replicas on a small scale of the caliphal court. When they had the resources they issued a gold coinage, whose inscription was nonetheless conveniently vague as to the authority by which it was done. Each had his own army as well and appointed and supported the traditional *qādī* in the administration of the law. The Abbasid caliphs in Baghdad as well as the Fatimid caliphs in Cairo were simply ignored.

Genealogy continued to be one of the chief amusements of good society in the peninsula, and much personal importance seemed to be attached to it. Kings and others of high station attempted to trace their lineage back to either those Syrian or Yemeni Arab tribes who had settled in the peninsula soon after the conquest in the 8th Century. To be related rather to the Berber tribes, who had probably borne the brunt of that conquest, was to be stigmatized as of inferior birth. In fact, however, the two groups had so grown together in the three centuries preceding the fall of the caliphate that they had become virtually indistinguishable except for purposes of personal invective. No political or social gulf separated the two by the 11th Century.

The same came very quickly to be true of the much newer groups of Berbers and slaves who had arrived in the 10th Century as a result of the military policy of the caliphs and of al-Mansūr. Neither of these groups were very numerous. There seem to have been no more than 10,000 of the slaves, and the Berbers were hardly more than twice as numerous in a total population of some six million. These two groups had played a major role in the process of the disintegration of the caliphate because of their practical monopoly of the military power at the time. But their mutual rivalry, the hostility of the older Muslim population, and soon the fragmentation of political authority left both groups isolated and under the necessity of having to come to terms with an essentially local elite in each of the taifas. In the course of so doing, both groups gradually ceased to be distinguishable parts of the Muslim population, except when one of them actually ruled a taifa, in which case his origins were well publicized by his rivals. Nevertheless, distinctions between Arab, Berber, and slave were not the stuff of serious politics either within or between the taifas. It was the individual family that was the unit of political activity.

The major distinctions between Muslim inhabitants were those that derived from social and economic status. The older Muslim immigrants to the peninsula had come initially as conquerors, and it was to be expected that they – and their descendants, generally speaking – would occupy the chief positions of political and economic privilege. As we have seen, the newer immigrants, whether slave or Berber, managed to find some niches in the political structure of the taifas of the littoral, and it is likely, too, that even common soldiers among them were able to translate their professional status into minor official positions in those realms, or at least into places of economic advantage such as shopkeepers, artisans, or minor proprietors of the land. As the latter, they would have merged insensibly with the great majority of Muslim themselves who derived ultimately from the converts to Islam among the native populations of Visigothic Spain.

These *Muwallad*, or new Muslims, had from the beginning a somewhat lower status in the community, which derived from the fact that they were the conquered. Initially, they had been divided even among themselves socially and economically, depending upon whether they had submitted to the conquerors peacefully or had resisted and been subdued by force of arms. By the 11th Century that political distinction had long since been transmuted into one of simple economic status. In the age of the taifas, they had become simply those relatively humble Muslim who worked the land of the countryside as proprietors of small plots, practised a trade in one of the cities or villages, or ran small shops therein. Nevertheless, evidence of the ancient origins of the *Muwallad* must have survived in one significant fiscal aspect. That is, if we are to judge by the persistence and volume of complaints lodged against the taifa rulers on religious grounds, they or their property continued to be subject to taxation in defiance of the ban in the *Koran* against the taxation of Muslim by Muslim. Still, most such levies fell upon real property in land, and those of the *Muwallad* who rose in the world to become minor officials, artisans, and shopkeepers escaped from both their historic origins and the tax collector.

Jews and Judaism in Muslim Spain

A far more significant difference separated Muslim – any Muslim – and Jew. The Jew was *dhimmi*, of course, that is, one of the subject inhabitants of the dar al-Islam who belonged to the special category of "people of the book." Like Christians, Jews were considered to possess an authentic, if imperfect and outdated, Revelation of the true God. As such, they were permitted to practice their own religion and live under the jurisdiction of their own law, insofar as that law did not conflict with the law derived from the *Koran*, which governed when conflicts at law occurred between Muslim and Jew. The authority of their rabbis over them was recognized by the Muslim rulers, and a major authority, a *nasi*, was ordinarily appointed by the taifa rulers to coordinate relations between themselves and the entire Jewish community. In relation to his coreligionists, the *nasi* exercised virtually the unlimited power of the king himself. Ordinarily, his major responsibility was the collection of that special tax which was the chief mark and duty of the non-Muslim within the dar al-Islam.

Within this general framework, Spanish Jewry flourished in Muslim Spain during the 11th Century. In subsequent years it was to be regarded by its descendants as a sort of golden age. Medieval numbers are always hard to obtain, and are rightly objects of suspicion, but a serious estimate has at least been made that the Jewish population in Muslim territories at this time amounted to about 60,000, or one per cent of the total population.[12] That population was higher in the cities, for the Jews were largely, if not exclusively, an urban group. In Sevilla they are held to have numbered 5,000 in the middle of the century. In the third quarter of the century they may have been 4,000 strong at Toledo. A small town such as Carmona held but 200. As circumstances gradually became more difficult for them in Andalucía toward the end of the century, considerable numbers migrated northward while remaining still within Islamic territories. In a place like Zaragoza, for instance, the Jewish community grew markedly and probably attained 1,200. In Tudela not far to its north was a community of another 1,000. These estimates are reached, by and large, by measuring the ancient Jewish quarter of the city, for the Jewish population usually lived within a clearly delimited district, and then calculating the probable population of the area. Clearly such a procedure has its hazards.

But if the lives, and hence the numbers, of humble Jews are most often hidden from us, the Jewish elite of the taifa states are abundantly visible. For one thing, the community existed and defined itself by virtue of its Bible, its Talmud, and its *midrash*. It was, in other words, a community of literate males by definition. As a result, the Jews were without a doubt the most literate community of the peninsula. They therefore occupy a perhaps disproportionate place in the literary remains of the age. Even when the individual was but a butcher, a tanner, a weaver, or a widow possessed of a small rural estate, he or she may appear in the legal literature. When, instead, he was a great merchant doing business the length and breadth of the Mediterranean, he may well be captured in the copious remains of the papyri of the Cairo *geniza*, or storeroom of the synagogue there. When he was a doctor, poet, philosopher, or politician of parts, he will be preserved for us in the contemporary and even subsequent literature of both Muslim and Christian.

---

[12] Wasserstein, *Party-Kings*, pp. 191–92, n. 3. For particular figures I follow Eliyahu Ashtor, *The Jews of Moslem Spain*, trans. Aaron Klein and Jenny Machlowitz Klein, 2 vols., 1966, Reprint (Philadelphia, 1973–79).

Indeed, the education and wealth of fair numbers of the Jewish population placed them among the governing elites of taifa society. Their abilities and their cosmopolitan character made them especially useful in the collection of taxes, not only among themselves but also from the population generally. Their often wide familiarity with the circles of international merchants made them useful business agents. In any age, the control of fiscal policy tends insensibly toward influence in wider areas of policy as well, and the age of the taifas was no exception. The most spectacular instance is to be found in the careers of Samuel ibn Naghrila, who became the *vizier* of the Granadan taifa in 1037 and remained so until his death in 1056, and his son Joseph ibn Naghrila, who succeeded him and held the same post until his assassination in 1065.

The incident illustrates well the peculiar position of the Jew within Spanish Islam. Although he might occasionally achieve remarkable success, such prominence was dangerous in the extreme. At law, he was never more than a tolerated inferior. That he should be invested with authority over Muslim was contrary to the *Koran* and usually widely criticized, even within the generally lax atmosphere of taifa Spain. In fact, of course, it was precisely the isolated and vulnerable position of the Jew within the Muslim elite that made him the particularly valuable agent of the king, since he was unlikely to develop independent ambitions or a following of his own. Moreover, he was the ideal scapegoat for the king if need should arise for one. The fall of such a figure was just as likely to involve his coreligionists in the community. So when Joseph was assassinated in Granada in 1065 it was in the midst of a riot that supposedly resulted in the massacre of 4,000 Granadan Jews as well. Since the total Jewish population of Granada about that time did not exceed 6,000, this figure is probably exaggerated, but it illustrates the danger.

A variety of other such figures are known, although they ordinarily held positions of *vizier* rather more briefly. They came and went in the service of their royal masters, sometimes even executing diplomatic duties among the Christians of the north, for they knew the Romance tongue spoken by Christians of both north and south. Their situation always remains exceptional, however, and not infrequently their fall from that position was accompanied by the confiscation of their goods. But that was likely to be true of all fiscal officials of the age, regardless of their origins.

In economic life, too, the Jew was often among the elite of the merchant class, sharing their life and journeys. Like the Muslim, the Jew found the Mediterranean of the 11th Century a community filled with fellows in almost every one of its ports and cities. The

Jewish community seems to have shared in the economy of Spanish Islam at almost every level, from small agricultural proprietor, to artisan, to tradesman small or large. Also, at least the elite of Spanish Jewry entered into the intellectual life of the dar al-Islam with zest and notable achievement, an aspect of their experience also best left to a general consideration of the context.

The Mozarab Community

As were the Jews, the Christians of Muslim Spain were also *dhimmi*, or people of the book. Their religion and law was tolerated, and they were allowed to live under the jurisdiction of their own bishops so long as they paid the special tax, which was the mark of their subjection to Islam, and generally did not disturb the good order of the dar al-Islam. They also had some subsidiary organization, for lay officers of individual communities, often called counts, or *comes*, are known; and even lesser, legal officials, judges, or *censors*, are sometimes mentioned. By the fall of the caliphate in 1031 they had survived for 320 years as a distinct social group and managed to maintain themselves in relatively strong numbers. They were far more numerous than the Jewish community, but also far more obscure in the surviving historical record.

Their numbers, at least relative to the Muslim majority, were important, for they constituted for Muslim Spain a major weakness in its contest with the Christian kingdoms of the north. Even in the most passive aspect of that situation, that the Mozarabs had maintained a Christian identity, which itself constituted them as an inferior group within Islam, meant that the Christian communities of the north continually acted as magnets. Almost from the original conquest of the 8th Century it is possible to trace the emigration of Christian groups from the areas controlled by Islam into those controlled by fellow Christians. In demographic terms, the constant tendency was toward a depopulation of the former and a corresponding population increase of the latter. When Christian Spain was but a pitiful remnant and Muslim Spain a great, prosperous, and united society, such a situation had little importance in determining their relative strength, but by the 11th Century the outflow of Mozarabs had already worked one substantial change.

The repopulation of the city of León by Ordóño I (850–866) may be taken as a symbol of its beginnings. From the middle of the 9th Century the old kingdom of Oviedo became the new kingdom of León, as that Christian power bit by bit proceeded to repopulate the northern half of the basin of the Duero River south of the Cantabrians. Time and again the Muslim south was to react to that continuing reality but could do no more than slow it. Still, in the time of al-Mansūr himself, in the late 10th Century, that Muslim leader was able to raid extensively and continually throughout the area. But the one achievement that was beyond his power was to occupy it, for the Muslim south had not the manpower for that. The Christian population occupying that strategic area came only in part from Asturias and Galicia. Language, place names, and agricultural innovation all testify to the importance among those settlers of Mozarab refugees from the south. By the disintegration of the caliphate, this process was already complete and was in turn about to become the springboard for a new, even more threatening one.

We shall return to that phenomenon later. The immediate question is to what extent this already-two-century-old current of emigration had depleted the ranks of the Mozarab population of Muslim Spain. There is no satisfactory answer. One basic demographic fact may profitably be remembered here, that the poorest element of any population is also that which enjoys the highest birthrate. Unless, therefore, the emigration was in overwhelming numbers, there is no need to posit any necessary absolute reduction in the Mozarab population within the Islamic area. Surely the Mozarabs were obscure, in good measure because they constituted the fundamental peasant strata of the land, a rural proletariat for the most part more humble than that of the *Muwallad* and less likely to escape that condition. They seem sometimes to have had their own villages and doubtless their own village headmen, as well as local artisans and even small shopkeepers. We also see a city population, but this must have been even more insignificant in numbers than those small proportions of the Muslim who were urban. In other words, their very social and economic condition would have conspired continually to increase the numbers of the Mozarabs relative to their conquerors, despite the clear evidence of substantial emigration.

The other relevant factor to be considered is the incidence of conversion to Islam among the Mozarabs. Clearly it was prevalent from the beginning, for the *Muwallad* component was the single largest of Muslim society. The argument has been made that the rate of conversion increased sharply during the 10th Century and that an actual Muslim minority of 2.8 million about A.D. 900 had risen to a Muslim majority of 5.6 million by A.D. 1100.[13] This hypothesis is

---

[13] Glick, *Islamic and Christian Spain*, pp. 33–35. He follows Richard W. Bulliet, *Conversion to Islam in the Medieval Period* (Cambridge, Mass., 1979). It should be noted that the later author points out that it is only the tempo of conversion that may be plotted, not the percentage of the population that converted (pp. 124–25).

based upon a very involved series of mathematical deductions using Muslim biographical dictionaries and the alleged tendency of converts to name their children in certain distinctive ways.[14] Until more detailed work is done we may remain properly skeptical. In the meantime it is interesting that the scheme entails the assumption that a very sizeable Christian majority remained within the area of Spanish Islam until well into the 10th Century.

Two further kinds of evidence should at least be considered. One is the persistence not only of Christians but of a Christian hierarchy among the Mozarabs. The bishop is the Christian official *par excellence* of course, and the perdurability of this office speaks to some continuing vigor among the cult's adherents. We may begin by noticing that of the twenty-seven bishoprics that existed within what was the stable area of Muslim Iberia during the late Visigothic period, some eight cannot be located at all after the conquest. It is true that the current resurgence of interest in the Spanish Middle Ages has hardly more than begun to renew serious work in the church history of the period. Nonetheless, the best existing evidence tells us that the most severe attrition within the Christian hierarchy, involving eight bishoprics, or roughly 30 per cent of the total, occurred at the very outset of the Muslim conquest. In the case of another six bishoprics, those which political and geographical fortune dictated would be located along the frontier between Christian and Muslim realms such as Braga and Oporto in modern Portugal, Tarragona and Lérida in modern Cataluña, or Calahorra in modern Aragón, the bishopric seems to have migrated across the border temporarily, perhaps at the insistence of the particular Christian prince. Cases such as these latter would seem to say little about the continued existence of the Christian community itself.

Only six bishoprics appear to have disappeared entirely from the Muslim areas after the first years of the conquest. Of these Córdoba and Zaragoza are the most notable, but it was true of Almería, Cuenca, Guadix, and Sigüenza as well. But of the six, only the first two seemingly perished in the 10th Century, when the rate of conversion is supposed to have risen so steeply. The other four vanished in the 9th Century. What information we have, then, indicates a rate of attrition in the Christian community which is highest at the initial conquest and which gradually tapered off thereafter. Most apposite to our interest here, a surprising seven bishoprics survived into the age of the taifas and often in the most unlikely places. Sevilla had a Mozarab bishop in 937 and again in 1144 and perhaps continuously in between, although we cannot be sure.

[14] Wasserstein, *Party-Kings*, pp. 225–32, has a critique of Glick and an associated discussion of the problem.

Valencia had one in 1090 on the eve of its conquest by the Cid. In the north of Portugal, Coimbra had one in 1018 and Viseu one in 1050. Málaga had one in 1100. A Mozarab bishop of Toledo was consecrated at León in 1058, and in 1118 a bishop of Granada attended a council at Sahagún.[15] This last case is particularly interesting, for there was no bishopric, or indeed town, of Granada, during the Visigothic period. The provincial capital of Elvira was transferred there by the Berbers after the fall of the caliphate, and the Christian bishop of Elvira seems to have migrated there as well. Something similar seems to have happened in the case of the old see of Baza, which moved to Guadix for similar reasons. The Christian Mozarab community appears to have maintained some flexibility as well as vitality.

The second set of data – at which we should look briefly here, although we will note it again in due course – derives from the policy of the Christian kings during the developing *Reconquista* in this period. On no less than three different occasions during the reign of Alfonso VI of León–Castilla we shall see him taking advantage of the fortunes of war to remove Mozarab communities from al-Andalus in order to resettle them in his own domains. He did so with those of Granada in 1094, with those of Valencia in 1102, and in 1105 with the Mozarabs of Málaga.[16] Then there is the even more famous great raid of Alfonso I el *Batallador* of Aragón through Andalucía in 1025–1026 when he is reported to have carried off no fewer than 10,000 Mozarabs to help repopulate the territories of the former taifa of Zaragoza. Even so, there remained sufficient numbers of Christians in the south to stimulate Muslim plans to remove them to North Africa for security reasons, and yet the less political emigration of Mozarabs from the south to points such as Christian Toledo remained a marked feature of the 12th Century.

At the very least, all of the above information suggests that the Mozarab population of Islamic Spain in the 11th Century was an uncomfortably large minority, perhaps something on the order of 30 per cent of the population. It had no appreciable political or even economic power of its own, to be sure. But in the new circumstances

[15] For Toledo, see Bernard F. Reilly, *The Kingdom of León–Castilla under King Alfonso VI, 1065–1109* (Princeton, N.J., 1988), p. 11, and for Granada, my *The Kingdom of León–Castilla under Queen Urraca, 1109–1126* (Princeton, N.J. 1982), p. 115. The other data comes from comparisons of that provided by Pius Bonifacius Gams, ed., *Series Episcoporum Ecclesiae Catholicae* (Ratisbon, 1873), the *Diccionario de historia eclesiástica de España*, 4 vols. (Madrid, 1972–75), and the *DHGE*, 21 vols. (Paris, 1912–).

[16] Reilly, *Alfonso VI*, pp. 244, 312, and 322.

of the times it could not be drawn upon for military purposes. In that sense, it was a handicap for Islam. But it could and would be exploited consciously by the kings of the north, who could draw upon its natural predispositions more easily to repopulate their own lands and to form an initial loyal nucleus of population in such lands as they might wrest from their weakened Muslim neighbors. More than ever, the Mozarabs of Muslim Spain weighed in the balance.

Life and Thought in Islamic Spain

For the vast majority of people, as always in an agricultural society, thought was practical and religious. It was bound up with the round of the seasons, the nurture of animals and plants, and the human cycle of birth, maturity, and death. As such, the contemporary human consciousness is not unfairly described as traditional, static, and preoccupied with its own limitations. Education was what one's father taught, or, if you were a girl, what one's mother taught. Beyond that homely wisdom, knowledge was the preserve of the faqíh, the rabbi, or the priest. So it has usually been in the countryside.

Formal knowledge and education was an overwhelmingly urban affair and hence the preserve of a tiny minority. It was also predominantly a religious and a literary learning. As the former, learning was divided, ordinarily, into three provinces corresponding to the three sacred languages of the prevailing Revelations, Arabic, Hebrew, or Latin. The language of the fields and of the streets might be that Romance which had devolved from the old, late-vulgar Latin, but the spoken language was not the language of formal learning. For the Muslim community, the home of learning was to be found in the courts of the taifa kings, who had continued the tradition of the caliphate as the patrons of wisdom and scholarship, and in the mosque to a lesser extent. The Jewish scholar was not totally unfamiliar with the court either, but his essential seat and refuge was the synagogue. Such learning as continued in the Mozarab community, on the other hand, must have found virtually its only congenial center in the episcopal cathedral. The transmission of learning, rather than its display or exercise, took place in an essentially domestic setting, the home of the individual master, who instructed his protégés there in the fashion that had long been typical and would long continue to be so.

If the three communities of learning were distinct by reason of the character of their respective scriptures and their sacred languages, nevertheless their learning exhibited an analogous typology. That is, in each community it resulted in scriptural exegesis and commentary as the major genre. Closely allied to this primary genre were the works of grammar, the dictionaries, the word lists, and the etymologies which were essential to the pursuit of the former. After all, the language of scripture, in each case, was to some extent a "school language." We are largely indifferent to this tradition of learning today, but it is necessary to realize that it formed the great mainstream of the intellectual activity of the age.

Although Muslim and Jewish intellectual traditions were distinct, one from the other, that is not to say that they went on in complete isolation. The Jewish scholars, at any rate, were fluent in Arabic and participated in its scholarship. For example, Abū al-Walīd Marwān ibn Djanah wrote his great studies of Hebrew grammar in Arabic and after the fashion of contemporary Muslim grammarians. This Jewish scholar, born in Lucena and subsequently trained in Córdoba, who migrated to Zaragoza after the end of the caliphate, also was a student of medicine and of logic, a combination not unusual in this period. But we shall come to these later. The great secular learning of the period was poetry, for the most part lyric Arabic poetry whose major themes were nature, love, the hunt, and war. The conventions were those which had been set long before in the Levant. In the age of the taifas the court of Sevilla became the center for this sort of literary exercise, and the rulers themselves, al-Mutadid (1012–69) and his son al-Mutamid (1069–1095), were avid practitioners. Even a famed theologian such as ibn Hazm (994–1064) could write perhaps the most famous single piece of this love poetry, *The Ring of the Dove*. This, too, was a genre in which a Jewish theologian, Solomon ben Judah ibn Gabirol of Zaragoza, could excel, writing in both Arabic and Hebrew.

There was also a certain development of prose as an instrument in literary studies, but it was subsidiary and largely limited to history, which, in the Arabic tradition, was what we should more properly call biography and genealogy. Prose was the instrument of the story also, but this latter was a popular rather than an erudite phenomenon.

If Arabic traditions and conventions dominated literary learning, philosophical and scientific learning derived from the classical world. Most of the Greek corpus of such writings that survive today had, in fact, been translated into the Arabic at Damascus in the 8th Century or Baghdad in the 9th, and had been more or less continuously commented upon in the dar al-Islam ever since. Muslim Spain inherited this tradition and would absorb the products of it so far as they

Plate 1   Interior of the great mosque of Córdoba

concerned the secular sciences. For example, the work of the scholars
of the Near East, such as al-Battānī in astronomy and al-Khwārizmī
in algebra, was received in Spain along with classical figures such as
Ptolemy, Galen, and Euclid. The mathematics and the numerals of
India which had been adopted in 9th-century Baghdad would also
find their way west to Iberia. The caliphs of Córdoba had patronized
learning of this sort, and al-Hakam is supposed to have collected a
library of 400,000 books. The courts of the taifa kings would continue this tradition on a somewhat more modest scale. Although the
most famous practitioners of this learning are to appear in the 12th
Century, the beginnings belong to the age of the taifas and even
earlier.

Insofar as the inheritance was to deal with the philosophical corpus of the Greeks, however, the reception was rather more hesitant,
not to say hostile. At the time, the great Muslim theologian and
philosopher ibn Sīnna (980–1037), Avicenna to the later Christian
West, was undertaking his daring attempt to rework the Greek

philosophical vocabulary and conceptual apparatus in order to make it a vehicle and envelope for the religious thought of Islam. In the west ibn Hāzm of Córdoba (994–1064) wrote somewhat in this vein although much more tentatively. In this venture he was to find no immediate followers, and, in the long run of course, Islam generally would reject such an approach as blasphemous. His works on the *Koran* and the law of Islam would prove to be the products for which he was subsequently famous.

These same currents also permeated the world of Jewish scholarship. The work of the Cordoban Hasan ibn Mar Hasan on the Jewish liturgical calendar was frankly based upon the astronomical achievements of al-Battānī. So, too, Abū al-Walīd not only studied the medical works of Galen but was also drawn to the philosophical treatises of Aristotle. However, although he might accept the Aristotelian logic and some elements of the ethics, the metaphysics were finally to be rejected as too alien. Such conceptions as the eternity of matter were simply incompatible with Revelation as he understood it. On the other hand, ibn Gabirol (1020–1058), Avicebron to the later Latin West, although familiar with both the work of Aristotle and the commentaries upon it of the easterner al-Fārābī, chose rather to employ Neoplatonic thought in *The Fountain of Life*. But, although his book seems to have been widely read, the conservatism of the synagogue would ultimately reject both it and that approach to things divine generally. Before that was finally to come about, however, Spanish Judaism, even as Spanish Islam, would see some great scholarly adventures in this vein during the 12th Century.

Formal learning among the contemporary Mozarab community must have been thinner and more closely confined to scriptural studies. What we know of it comes largely from the Mozarabic communities of the various Christian kingdoms, and there it is for the most part confined to the production of liturgical books, the recopying of collections of canon law, and the preservation of the secular legal collection of the *Liber Judiciorum*. Such activities within the world of Islam would have been at least as restricted by the end of the 10th Century.

2

The Political Ferment in Northern Spain (1031–1073)

When the collapse of the caliphate at Córdoba began in 1009 with the revolt against, and the assassination of, Abd al-Rahman, second son of al-Mansūr, the political affairs of Christian Spain were in only slightly less disarray and would long continue to be so. For many years the dynasty of the traditionally most powerful kingdom of León was to be crippled by the two minorities of Alfonso V (999–1028), who had acceded at five years of age, and then of Vermudo III (1028–1037), who acceded at nine. That kingdom would play no part, then, in the struggles which were dismembering the Muslim world.[1] The other Christian principalities were so tiny and powerless that when one or the other of them took part it was to be as little more than mercenary allies of this or that Muslim faction. In that capacity Castilian troops entered Córdoba in 1009 and Catalans in 1010. By default, then, the decline of the Muslim caliphate was to be a simply internal affair.

In the north of the peninsula that decline was contemporary to the unlikely and, one thinks, necessarily episodic hegemony of the kingdom of Navarra under Sancho García III (1000–1035), called *el Mayor*.[2] That tiny realm, then, played a role with regard to its Christian fellows of the north which it was never to repeat and which rested not only upon the talent of its king but also upon his relative longevity. The most important element in this predominance

---

[1] Beyond the basic works in English already cited, the best guide to what is known of this period remains Alfonso Sánchez-Candeira, El "Regnum-Imperium" leonés hasta 1037 (Madrid, 1951).

[2] Sancho García III is one of the few monarchs of the period whose reign is adequately treated. Justo Pérez de Urbel, *Sancho el Mayor de Navarra* (Madrid, 1950). For a standard political survey, see José María Lacarra, *Historia del reino de Navarra en la Edad Media* (Pamplona, 1975).

was to be the marriage of Alfonso V of León to Sancho García's sister, Urraca, who continued to be a real power in that kingdom after Alfonso's death. The influence of the Navarrese king in the next-largest and neighboring principality of Castilla was also assured initally by the former's marriage to the sister of the young count García Sánchez (1017–1029).[3] It was to become overwhelming when this Castilian count, barely seven years old at his accession, was assassinated in the city of León in 1029 as he was about to enter into a marriage with the sister of Vermudo III. Instead, then, of his influence diminishing in Castilla, Sancho el Mayor now found himself able to install his own second son, Fernando, as count there and to arrange that son's marriage to the sister of Vermudo III, Sancha, in 1032. In the year immediately before his own death the king of Navarra was even able to oust the unfortunate Vermudo III from the territories of León itself. In 1034 the Leónese monarch retreated into Galicia, and Sancho García III of Navarra had himself crowned in León.

Sancho el Mayor already held the string of tiny counties wedged in the high foothills of the Pyrenees between those peaks and the Muslim lands of what was shortly to become the great taifa of Zaragoza immediately to their south. Aragón, Sobrarbe, and Ribagorza were before the end of the century to overshadow Navarra itself, but, at this time, earlier marriage alliances had placed them among his domains. That left only the Catalan territories in the extreme northeast of the peninsula, themselves squeezed by Muslim territories against the Pyrenees, except along the Mediterranean where they pushed south just beyond the river Llobregat. These lands were not unified into a Cataluña as they later would be. Instead, the dominant figure among the local dynasts was Count Berenguer Ramón I (1018–1035), the client and ally of the Navarrese.[4]

Thus, during the first three decades of the 11th Century the interests of the Christian north were turned largely inward by a succession of minorities, regencies, and the tour de force of the Navarrese attempt at dominance. The fortunes of the Islam in the peninsula were left largely to its own internal dynamic. Even during the two decades after the death of Sancho el Mayor, the recovery and

---

[3] Justo Pérez de Urbel, El condado de Castilla, 3 vols. (Madrid, 2nd ed., 1969), is the reigning authority on the subject, but it must be used with care because the author was prone to exaggerate the importance of the influence of Castilla in early Spanish history.

[4] Ferran Soldevila, ed., Historia dels Catalans, 3 vols. (Barcelona, 1964), is the standard political survey.

consolidation of strength in the north took place slowly. The architect of that rebuilding was to be Fernando I *el Magno*, second son of Sancho, and the instrumentality a reunited León-Castilla.[5]

At the death of the king of Navarra, his possessions were divided among his several sons. The eldest, García Sánchez III (1035–1054), inherited not only the traditional Navarrese heartland, centering on Pamplona and Nájera, but also the territories of Alava and the Bureba which his father had detached from their ordinary dependence on the county of Castilla. This latter passed to his brother Fernando, along with the lands between the rivers Pisuerga and Cea in the west which Sancho had caused to be ceded by León. The counties of Sobrarbe and Ribagorza fell to the youngest son, Gonzalo. An illegitimate son, Ramiro, received the county of Aragón. These arrangements, like most such divisions of the age, were to prove ephemeral, however.

In the east, Gonzalo was to be assassinated in obscure circumstances in 1045. His counties of Sobrarbe and Ribagorza were then appropriated by Ramiro I of Aragón (1035–1063). That count now began to style himself a king and simply disregarded the wishes of his halfbrother in Pamplona. The history of the kingdom of Aragón may properly be said to begin with Ramiro.[6] Yet for another forty years the fortunes of that tiny realm will be of slight import beyond its own borders.

In the west rather more significant events were taking place. With the death of the king of Navarra, Vermudo III had once again taken full control of the kingdom of León and would shortly attempt as well to reclaim the lands between the Cea and the Pisuerga rivers. In that pursuit he was met, defeated, and killed at the battle of Tamarón on September 4, 1037, by his brother-in-law, Fernando of Castilla. The following spring, on June 22, 1038, Fernando was to be anointed king at León and he and his wife would rule a kingdom of León-Castilla that was utterly to dominate the north of the peninsula down until Fernando's death in 1065. This development could not be but at the expense of his older brother, García Sanchez III, in Navarra, of course. But when the latter was to try to maintain the hegemony he felt was his due, he too was defeated and would perish in battle at Atapuerca on September 15, 1054. As the price of peace, Fernando then required the cession to him of the Bureba

[5] We have no history of this most important reign. Recently a collection of the charters of Fernando I has appeared, a hopeful sign.
[6] José María Ramos y Loscertales, *El reino de Aragón bajo la dinastía pamplonesa* (Salamanca, 1961). This should now be supplemented with Antonio Ubieto Arteta, *Historia de Aragon: La formación territorial* (Zaragoza, 1981).

district on the west bank of the upper Ebro River, and his nephew, Sancho García IV (1054–1076) of Navarra, was obliged to do homage to him. A power had now arisen in the Christian north which was fully capable of intervening in Muslim Spain in the most direct fashion and which was shortly to proceed to do just that.

The Christian World of the North

The newly reconstituted kingdom of León–Castilla which Fernando had come to rule by the mid-11th Century was a realm and a society of over three centuries in the making. Geographically, historically, and sometimes politically, it was composed of three major parts. In the north, along the Bay of Biscay on the far side of the Cantabrian Mountains, lay the province of Asturias. Traditionally the first redoubt of post-Visigothic Christian Spain, it was now a backward world of mountain agriculture and abundant rain, separated from the south by passes averaging 1,500 meters in altitude. To the west was Galicia-Portugal. The two were hardly distinct as yet. This too, was a world whose traditions stretched back to the 8th-century beginnings of the resistance to the Muslim. Geography made of it a land of rivers, which ran down to the Atlantic across a narrow coastal plain, rarely more than 25 kilometers deep, the whole stretching from the modern La Coruña in the north to just beyond Oporto in the south. The region was separated from the lands to the east by a series of ranges, whose passes, where they existed, averaged 1,000 meters.

The heartland of Fernando's domains was constituted by the lands north of the Duero River and enclosed within the mountains of Galicia–Portugal, the Cantabrians, and the Sierra de la Demanda in the east. It was the northern half of the *meseta* of Castilla la Vieja, that is, the basin of the Duero, a geographic, climatic, and now political unity of approximately 50,000 square kilometers. This was the new León–Castilla, which had been in the making for the past two centuries. The older regions of Asturias and Galicia–Portugal were already, in some measure, outlying dependencies of it. What had been a colonial area had now become the new center of the realm.

This largely flat, dry, plain and forest area had been in the process of settlement – from Galicia in the northwest, Asturias in the north, and the upper Rioja region in the northeast – for over the preceding two centuries. Written records tell us little about the undertaking, but the pattern of settlement still visible suggests that the pioneers moved down the valleys of the rivers – the Balimbre, the Tuerto, the Orbigo, the Luna, the Bernesga, the Esla, the Cea, the Carrión, and the Pisuerga – by passing earlier hamlets along the way to found new ones always farther south, and at an average distance of about 5 or 6 kilometers apart, until the latest arrived finally at the northern bank of the Duero. Physical remains indicate that each village was protected by a castle or fortification so that the entire *meseta* was dotted with castles from the Duero River, back up into the mountains themselves. The Duero formed a distinct southern boundary. That river rises in the east in the highlands of Soria and flows west for more than 900 kilometers to empty into the Atlantic at Oporto. For most of that distance the northern bank is markedly higher than the southern one and forms a sort of natural rampart. By the 11th Century nature had been improved upon by the construction of a string of fortresses along the north bank from Zamora, to Toro, to Tordesillas, to Simancas, and beyond through Peñafiel, Aranda del Duero, and Peñaranda del Duero, at an average distance of 30 kilometers one from the other, which stood guard over the natural crossings.

This was the region raided by the Arab world, chiefly al-Mansūr and his son, during the latter decades of the 10th and the first decade of the 11th Century. Any one of the strongholds could be taken and the defenses breached; but by the time of final settlement the entire complex had become too interdependent and resilient to be simply destroyed, not to say resettled, from the south. There were few points in it that had not been taken and razed by the great warrior of Islam at one time or another, yet by the middle of the 11th Century it appears that the entire region had obviously recovered and was about to become the essential base of operations against the world of the taifas.

The life of the region was agriculture, based almost exclusively upon dry farming and some irrigation. The first settlers moving south from areas of greater rainfall and along the modest river valleys of the plain had come to depend upon small irrigation works to conserve river and ground water. This became more necessary as their numbers increased and they were obliged to venture farther and farther into forest or plain, which terrain separated one river from the other at an average distance of 15 to 20 kilometers. In this respect, the contribution of another flow of immigrants, the Mozarabs from the world of Islam to the south, had become critical to further development. From that quarter had come the knowledge of the *noria* and the geared waterwheel which were everywhere pressed into use.[7] Increasingly, with employment of this technology, came the cultivation of wheat and rye, the primary crops of the *meseta*. There were supplemented by the garden vegetables of the day and by the hardier sort of grape, but the climate was too cool for the olive. The northern semicircle of wetter lands around the *meseta* offered greater access to protein in the form of cattle and sheep, which could be grazed in larger numbers throughout that natural pastureland. Cheeses and butter also were abundant there, along with the apple, the cherry, and the acorn. That meant that cider was available as an alternative to wine, and that the goat and above all the pig found natural provender before becoming such themselves. This reasonably varied diet could be further supplemented with fish and shellfish on the coasts of Galicia-Portugal and Asturias. All in all, and at the level of agriculture, León–Castilla, compared to Muslim Andalucía, probably had the advantage as far as the basic standard of living available to its inhabitants. If it lacked the olive, fig, date, citrus fruits, and rice of some regions of the south, it was better supplied with dairy products and meats.

The Christian north and Spanish south were, then, in terms of basic agricultural possibilities, two different worlds, the greatest similarity being with the Muslim taifa of Zaragoza. Beyond the realm of things strictly agricultural differences were much more marked. The best estimates would give the entire Christian north a population of about one million at the beginning of the 11th Century, in contrast to six million in the Spanish dar al-Islam. Since the respective land areas of each would also roughly have been in a ratio of about 1:6 at this time, the average population density would have been about the same also. There the similarities would end. There were simply no Christian counterparts to urban centers such as Córdoba, Sevilla, or even Zaragoza. If one takes the likely population of the major episcopal centers at the beginning of the 11th Century – Santiago de Compostela, Lugo, Astorga, León, Oviedo, Pamplona, and Barcelona – and assigns them a generous average population of 1,500 persons apiece, the total will still come to barely over 10,000, which can be regarded only by the wildest stretch of the imagination as urban.[8] That would be a ratio of 1:100

---

[7] The collected studies of Santiago Aguadé Nieto, *De la sociedad arcaica a la sociedad campesina en la Asturias medieval* (Madrid, 1988), are the fundament of most of what I have to say in this regard. They do not so much revise traditional scholarship as define and sharpen it, but that process throws into stark relief the cumulative effect of many small changes.

[8] The subject has not been well studied, but the general principles of a method for

of urban to rural as against a ratio of 5:100 in Muslim Spain. Even such a comparison badly overemphasizes urban life in the Christian north, for the psychological distance between it and the countryside in a León of 1,500 people and a Córdoba of 90,000 would be immensely greater in the latter.

The reasons for the difference are varied. The inclusion of Spanish Islam in the Muslim Mediterranean network of commerce allowed it to support a mercantile elite together with an urban artisan class whose labor it directed and whose produce it distributed. These elements were scarcely present in the north at the beginning of the 11th Century. An even more important reason was that the governmental and social elites of Islam were urban in character. The caliph, the taifa kings after him, and the service and propertied nobility which served in their courts were all city dwellers even if they were ultimately supported by their landholdings in the countryside. It may be, although we cannot be sure in the absence of records, that the proportion of land worked by a dependent and servile peasantry to that worked by peasant proprietors themselves was quite similar within both societies. In the north it made an enormous difference in the tone of society that the elites were rural rather than urban. The nobility lived in the countryside and so did their kings. Unlike the taifa rulers, the Christian monarchs had no capital, but were peripatetic, moving from estate to estate of the royal fisc.

What was also true of the secular elites of the two worlds was true of their religious elites. A considerable proportion of the agricultural land in the Islamic regions seems to have been held in leasehold by the mosques, the *mezquitas*. Because their records have perished we know little of the particular arrangements, only that their property typically passed to the Christian churches which succeeded them as the *Reconquista* progressed. Nevertheless, the corporation of the mosque was a city corporation. Due to the peculiar institution of monasticism, however, the Christian church was proportionally much more a corporation of the countryside. It is true that this factor may have been overemphasized and that the bishoprics as well, as a good many monasteries were an essentially urban institution, as we shall see. Nonetheless, the great aggregations of property

making projections of town populations may be found in Josiah Cox Russell, *Medieval Regions and Their Cities* (Bloomington, Ind., 1972). Particular estimates relevant here and the special bibliography which supports them are in Bernard F. Reilly, *The Kingdom of León–Castilla under King Alfonso, VI, 1065–1109* (Princeton, N.J., 1988), p. 152.

and power that were the rural monasteries, such as Sahagún, Celanova, Silos, San Millán, and Oña, loomed larger, on the whole, than the episcopates at the beginning of the 11th Century in the north.

As a result of all this, the Christian north was much less cosmopolitan than the Islamic south. Clearly this is so in the realm of language. The Muslim world had its multiplicity of languages, Arabic, Romance, and Hebrew, with both learned and popular versions of the first and last. There may have been some Berber, but very little. But these were the languages of the whole of the world of Spanish Islam, although there doubtless were regional dialects. In the north, on the other hand, there were distinct, popular languages of the Catalan, Basque, and Gallego-Portuguese, regions, the speakers of one not understanding the speakers of the others. In addition, that language which we now call Castilian was then divided into at least the two great language blocks of Leonese, heavily influenced by the archaisms of the Mozarabic Romance, and what we may loosely style Castilian proper.[9] It is doubtful if those fluent in either one of these could understand the other, once dialectical confusions were added, and the same may be true for the language of Asturias, whatever we wish to call it.

A World of Change

It is clear from the above considerations that the world of the Christian north was a simpler, more primitive society than that of Muslim Spain at the outset of the 11th Century. Yet, in the following decades, it would prove to be a society more open to development, and even fundamental change, than its Muslim counterpart. One measure of this growth was the demographic increase, which seemed to affect Christian Spain even as it did the whole of Christian Western Europe beginning in the late 10th Century. Unfortunately, absolute numbers are impossible to obtain.[10] We must rely upon relative changes, such as the fact that, as archaeological evidence indicates, the major episcopal centers of the north seemed to grow in population by a factor somewhere between 50 and 100 per cent over the century. That leaves them still tiny in comparison with their

[9] The classic Ramón Menéndez Pidal, *Orígenes del Español* (Madrid, 5th ed., 1964), should now be supplemented with Roger Wright, *Late Latin and Early Romance in Spain and Carolingian France* (Liverpool, 1982).
[10] A valiant attempt has been made to construct a method and to reach some approximations. See Lydia C. Kofman and María Inés Carzolio, "Acerca la demografía astur-leonésa y castellana en la Alta Edad Media," *CHE* 47–48 (1968):136–70.

Muslim counterparts, but it is significant growth nonetheless. It also speaks to an in-migration from the countryside, for no city before the 20th Century had a birthrate capable of even sustaining its own population much less increasing it. The data on the countryside, documentary and physical, indicates expansion there as well. The land in the process of formation did more than furnish emigrants to those urban centers.

The growth in the rural world expresses itself in the expansion of the total area of cultivation, a *defrichement*, or clearing of the brush, analogous to what was happening in France during the same period and, indeed, generally in Western Europe. Again, one gets the sense of an increasing population pressing hard upon available land, but there is also a profound reorganization of agricultural techniques and institutions occurring. It is impossible to discern with any degree of confidence the extent to which the new pressures for land depended simply upon demographic increase or upon new techniques which increased the efficiency of the individual farmer. For example, it was during this period that the region of Asturias – and probably the whole of the northern, mountainous fringe from Galicia and the Bierzo through upper Castilla, although these have been less thoroughly studied – made the basic change from a predominantly hoe culture to a plow culture, the latter accompanied and supplemented by an expansion of stock raising.[11] In brief, agricultural society moved significantly from one that was more labor intensive to one more land intensive. One farmer could now work more land, as well as produce more from each unit of it. But the opposite side of the coin was that more land would now have been required, even if the total population had remained the same. We are not likely to sort out the respective proportions here.

During the same period the agricultural community was also becoming more sophisticated. On the individual farm, the increasing utilization of irrigation was altering the proportion of sown and garden areas somewhat in favor of the latter. The employment of the *noria* made irrigation by gravity flow feasible for the first time in a great many areas, and the spread of the animal-driven, geared waterwheel further magnified that effect. Both made the wife of the husbandman a more productive member of the farm unit since the gardening responsibilities were largely hers. At the same time it improved the average diet. But the contemporary spread of the geared waterwheel adapted to milling, and the mill powered by

[11] The argument is based upon Santiago Aguadé Nieto, *Ganadería y desarrollo agrario en Asturias durante la Edad Media, siglos IX–XIII* (Barcelona, 1983).

animal power as well, had further repercussions upon the farming unit. First of all, it encouraged even more expansion of the land under cultivation, since milling made possible the processing of far more grain by one person than had the old practice of hand grinding by quern. Second, since the new mills represented significant capital outlays for construction and operation, milling tended to become a commercial or seigneurial operation rather than a domestic one. We have clear documentary evidence of the joint-ownership of mills in this period by individual peasant proprietors. At the same time it is obvious that by virtue of their very character such construction and operation lent themselves particularly well to the lay or secular estate where large-scale operations were simpler and where small amounts of capital, in whatever form, were easier to acquire.

The combined result seems to have been a profound reorganization of northern Christian society.[12] Although it must also have radically improved the lot of the lay noble, we can best follow the development in the case of the great monasteries and episcopal establishments, for they managed to preserve much of their records as the lay nobles did not. For example, the monastery of San Millán de La Cogolla in the Castilian Sierra de la Demanda reflects a much wider pattern. A comparison by periods of its acquisitions of lands, donations, purchases, and exchanges, shows only 25 such transactions for the period A.D. 1000 to 1025, then 170 for 1025 to 1050, rising to 235 in 1050 to 1075, peaking at 340 from 1075 to 1100, and finally dropping to only 58 between 1100 and 1125. For the Castilian monastery of San Pedro de Cardeña, farther west and just outside of Burgos, maximum expansion of the monastic domain falls between 1056 and 1086, continues strong to the end of the century, and then drops off sharply between 1100 and 1150. Much farther west, in the Leónese Bierzo, the monastery of San Pedro de Montes acquired only 6 properties in the years 1050 to 1075, then 85 from 1075 to 1100, which dropped to 28 between 1100 and 1125.[13]

In brief, then, where we have detailed investigation of the evidence, the data reflects a massive increase in the mobility of land as the 11th Century proceeds, slacking off somewhat in the opening decades of the 12th Century. There are, of course, some variations

[12] Claudio Sánchez-Albornoz, *Sobre la libertad humana en el reino asturleonés hace mil años* (Madrid, 1976), was preoccupied with the social and political effects of the same phenomenon.

[13] A fair variety of detailed studies exist. José Angel García de Cortázar y Ruiz de Aguirre, *El dominio del monasterio de San Millán de La Cogolla, siglos X al XIII* (Salamanca, 1969). Salustiano Moreta Velayos, *El monasterio de San Pedro de Cardeña* (Salamanca, 1971). Mercedes Durany Castrillo, *San Pedro de Montes: El dominio de un monasterio benedictino de El Bierzo, siglos IX al XIII* (León, 1976).

that reflect more local circumstances, but the picture seems relatively uniform for the Christian north. This phenomenon, when noted, has been attributed either to an increase in piety or to the rapacity of the newly great, ecclesial organizations. Such motives were doubtless operative in some degree. Yet they should not be allowed to obscure the fact that the condition of their operation was a far-reaching reorganization of the agricultural community of the north. This latter change, together with the increase in population, would not only effect the growth of urban areas and the clearing of previously underutilised lands, but also provide the surplus of humanity needed for the conquest and repopulation of lands then held by the various taifas.

Fernando I el Magno of León-Castilla (1035–1065)

The leader of this burgeoning, restless society, who was able, in the first instance, to successfully channel its energies outward, was Fernando I of León–Castilla, the second son of Sancho III of Navarra. By eliminating Vermudo III in 1037 and García Sánchez III in l054 Fernando had effectively disposed of all possible rivals in the Christian world. Perhaps as early as 1055 he attacked the Portuguese territories of Badajoz, thus turning his attention to the world of the taifas, but the only account we have of these campaigns is sometimes confused in its chronology.[14] Those lands south of the Miño River and north of the Duero, which we think of as Portuguese, constituted a border district which León–Castilla had held for about three centuries. Entry into it from León was difficult because of the north–south mountain ranges. The best passages led from either the town of León or Zamora to Orense in Galicia and from there down the valley of either the Miño or the Limia River to the coast. The advance post of this isolated province was the town of Oporto at the mouth of the Duero River. The upper reaches of the Duero were controlled by the Muslim stronghold at Lamego, some 100 kilometers upriver. On November 29, 1057, the armies of Fernando took the town of Lamego, and the entire basin of the Duero passed finally out of Muslim hands.[15]

[14] Justo Pérez de Urbel and Atilano González Ruiz-Zorilla, eds., *Historia Silense* (Madrid, 1959), pp. 188–94. There is also an older edition, Francisco Santos Coco, ed., *Historia Silense* (Madrid, 1921), but the former will be used here. For a survey of the early history of Portugal, see Joaquim Veríssimo Serrão, *História de Portugal*, Vol. 1 (Lisbon, 3rd ed., 1979).

[15] Pierre David, *Études historiques sur la Galice et le Portugal du VIᵉ au XIIᵉ siècle* (Paris, 1947), p. 296. His edition and study of the old Portuguese annals now must be supplemented by Monica Blöcker-Walter, *Alfons I von Portugal* (Zurich, 1966).

The interests of Fernando were immediately transferred to the basin of the Mondego River just to the south. On July 25, 1058, he succeeded in capturing the town of Viseu, some 70 kilometers northeast of Coimbra, which commanded the middle reaches of the Mondego. Nevertheless, a long and grueling battle would take place for the control of the lower basin, culminating with the fall of the hilltop, fortress city of Coimbra, after a six-month siege, on July 25, 1064. Here the Christian offensive was to stall, and the basin of the Tajo River, along with Lisbon and Santarém, was to remain effectively in Muslim hands for almost a century more.

These Portuguese campaigns had far from monopolized the attention of Fernando, despite their success. In all probability, they were for the most part carried out by local troops. The king himself was at the time recovering traditional Castilian territories from, his nephew, Sancho García IV of Navarra, in the Bureba district north and east of Burgos. Fernando apparently applied diplomatic and political pressures here, since no overt conflicts are recorded, although the domains of León–Castilla had advanced to the borders of the Rioja by 1065.[16]

At the same time, these advances could not but concern al-Muqtadir, king of the taifa of Zaragoza (1046–1081). Up until this time the main problems of this taifa king had been occasioned by the combined hostilities of the neighboring taifa of Toledo and of the kingdom of Navarra. By and large, the difficult geography of his Toledan border furnished good security, but not the valley of the Ebro. In fact, the Navarrese kings had transferred their base of operations south from the old heartland of the realm around Pamplona to Nájera on the upper Ebro and in 1045 had taken advantage of disorders within the taifa to seize the stronghold of Calahorra just 135 kilometers northwest of Zaragoza. Since that time the Navarrese had begun to dispute the control of the whole of the Rioja region, one of the richest agricultural districts in the peninsula.

In those earlier conflicts Zaragoza and León–Castilla were usually allies. In fact, at some point Zaragoza had begun the payment of regular, annual tribute, *parias*, to León–Castilla as a condition of the latter's aid. In 1063 that assistance had been instrumental in the defeat and death of the Aragonese king, Ramiro I, at the battle of Graus.[17] Nevertheless, a comfortable ally is a distant ally. León–

---

[16] García de Cortázar, *San Millán*, pp. 169–70. Also, Felix Sagredo Fernández, *Briviesca antigua y medieval* (Madrid, 2nd ed., 1979), p. 99.

[17] Later literary sources attribute a prominent part in this battle to Fernando's eldest son, Sancho, and to Rodrigo Díaz de Vivar, *el Cid*, but the entire episode is unclear in the sources. For a more extended discussion, see my *The Kingdom of León–Castilla*

Castilla ensconced in the Rioja would threaten Zaragoza as Navarra never could.

To make matters worse, from the standpoint of al-Muqtadir, in or about 1060 Fernando led a strong force up the narrow valley of the upper Duero, took the fortresses of San Esteban de Gormaz, Berlanga, and Valdorrey, and then turned south to Santiuste, Huermeces, and Santamara. All of this activity put him on the western borders of Zaragoza and in excellent position to cut its communications with Córdoba and Sevilla if he chose, for the old Roman road from Andalucía to Zaragoza lay exposed before him. Finally, in August of 1064, a French army from beyond the Pyrenees fell upon the Zaragozan border fortress of Barbastro, took it, and slaughtered its inhabitants. Al-Muqtadir reacted first by breaking off payment of parias to León–Castilla, then there was a massacre of Mozarabs in Zaragoza in January of 1065, and finally the combined forces of the taifas of Zaragoza, Sevilla, and Valencia recaptured Barbastro in April of the same year, carrying out their own slaughter there of the former victors. Fernando I met this challenge with an invasion of the territories of Valencia and defeated Abd al-Malik in the environs of that city itself. The solid defeat of the taifa king of Valencia convinced al-Muqtadir that a resumption of the parias to Fernando was inevitable, however distasteful.

But the affairs of Navarra and Zaragoza no more exhausted the initiatives of Fernando than did the simultaneous concern with Portugal. His campaign in the Sorian highlands of the east in 1060 had put him in a position to menace Toledo as well as Zaragoza. In 1062 he swept around the eastern end of the Guadarrama chain into the territories of al-Mamūn. Once Talamanca north of Madrid fell into his hands he pressed south to lay siege to Alcalá. At the same time his forces were ravaging the countryside. Finally, to secure his withdrawal, al-Mamūn agreed to the annual payment of parias. There may have been some earlier payment, but we cannot be sure. It is known, for example, that Pascual, apparently the last Mozarabic bishop of Toledo, was consecrated in León in 1058.[18] He must have been at least acceptable to Fernando, who probably assumed the role of protector of the Christians in the taifa of Toledo. All of this would argue that he exacted a tribute from that taifa as well.

In any event, by 1063 the two greatest of the northern taifas were

under King Alfonso VI, 1065–1109 (Princeton, N.J., 1988), pp. 11 and 37–38. For a history of the taifa, see Afif Turk, El reino de Zaragoza en el siglo XI de Cristo, V de la Hégira (Madrid, 1978).

[18] The notice appears in a private document of the cathedral of León. AC León, Codice 11, fol. 264r-v.

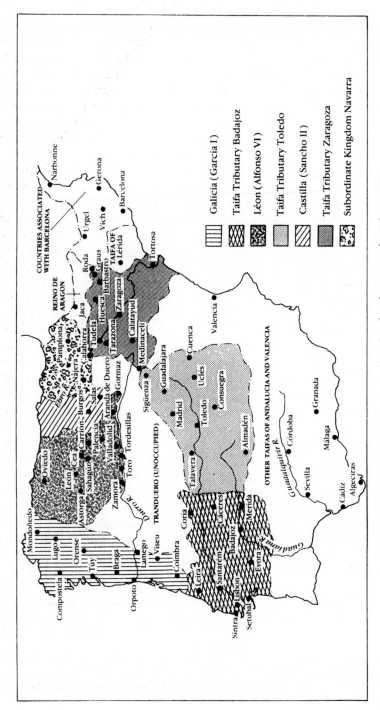

Figure 2 Christian Iberia at the death of Fernando I in 1065

tributaries of León–Castilla. In that same year Fernando would improve on that situation by striking deep into Andalucía. His armies raided and ravaged through the lands of Sevilla in the basin of the Guadalquivir and those of Badajoz in the basin of the Guadiana. As a result, both of those taifas became client-states of León and began the payment of *parias*. In the short run, the successful campaigns of 1063 undercut the ability of the southern Muslim to react against the siege and capture of Coimbra in the following year. In the long run, the annual tributes now paid by the four greatest Muslim kingdoms of the peninsula enhanced the ability of Fernando to keep in the field those very armies that ensured their progressive subjection.

With the fall of Coimbra in July of 1064 the Leonese monarch found himself in possession of two-fifths of northern Portugal. He had also humbled the taifas of Badajoz and Toledo, and was shortly to complete that process by reducing Valencia and Zaragoza to obedience. In other words, all of those powers that formed the western, southern, and eastern boundaries of the trans-Duero had been neutralized. This great 50,000-square-kilometer block of territory – comprised of those lands south of the Duero, east of the mountains of Portugal, north of the Guadarrama Mountains, and west of the Sierra de Albarracín and the Sorian highlands – had been a frontier area between Christian and Muslim for two and a half centuries. It had had little settled population precisely because it was subject to an endemic warfare of raids and counter-raids.[19] The Leonese monarch now found himself in a position to begin its annexation precisely because he could prevent such disruption. Fernando's death on December 27, 1065, was to delay that work, which would become one of the major achievements of his son, his granddaughter, and his great-grandson, in turn.

The extension of the society of León–Castilla into the trans-Duero was to be one of the major factors in the permanent alteration of the balance between Christian and Muslim in the peninsula. That its beginnings were delayed for some eight years was not due to the death of Fernando alone. In December of 1063, two years prior to his death, he had arranged for the division of his kingdom among his three sons. At the end of 1065, then, part of his realm became the kingdom of Castilla under his firstborn, Sancho II. It was comprised of the lands north and east of modern Burgos, including Asturias de

---

[19] Claudio Sánchez-Albornoz, *Despoblación y repoblación del valle del Duero* (Buenos Aires, 1966), was the first to deal exhaustively with this topic. Most of his account still stands, although he was optimistic about the results of earlier attempts at resettlement from the north.

Santillana, the lands to the south of that town as far as the watershed of the Arlanza River, and those west from Burgos to the Pisuerga River. Included in the inheritance were the *parias* of Zaragoza and some sort of suzerainty over his cousin, the king of Navarra.

To the second son, Alfonso VI, went the heart of the old kingdom and the lion's share of the rest: the territory of León itself and the *civitas regia*, Asturias de Oviedo, with the ancient center of the realm; the Bierzo in the west, but so defined as to include a good portion of modern Galicia; probably the recently conquered eastern lands along the upper Duero in the Sorian highlands; and the right to the *parias* of the taifa of Toledo. The third son, García I, received the kingdom of Galicia–Portugal, which stretched from the Bay of Biscay south to Coimbra, an Atlantic kingdom with a mountainous spine at its back. To the youngest son also went the right to the *parias* of Badajoz.

Such divisions among heirs were the commonest phenomena of the age, but then again so were the immediate and ordinarily successful attempts of the new heirs to restore the old unity at the expense of their siblings. In the post-Fernandine realms an uneasy peace lasted as long as the queen mother, Sancha, lived; that is, until 1067. As the eldest son, Sancho was understandably disgruntled with his share of the division, and the first clash between him and Alfonso came in 1068 at Llantadilla near the Pisuerga but with no great result. Rather, the very geography of Sancho's kingdom made the valley of the Ebro and the lands of Navarra and Zaragoza the preferred areas of expansion. The interests of the great houses of the realm, the Alvarez, the Ordóñez, and the Lara, also lay to the east. In 1066 Sancho seems to have campaigned around Zaragoza vigorously enough to secure the renewal of the payment of the *parias* suspended at the death of Fernando. In the following year he seems also to have fought briefly and with some success against the combined forces of Sancho García IV of Navarra and Sancho Ramírez I of Aragón – the "War of the Three Sancho's." Ultimately, however, the temptation to claim all of his patrimony was irresistible.

In that respect, if Sancho needed excuses for his subsequent aggressions, the actions of Alfonso VI would have more than furnished them. At some date in 1068 the latter had campaigned in the taifa of Badajoz and forced the ruler there to become his tributary. Those *parias* had been assigned to García of Galicia; therefore, Alfonso's action was a clear indication that he too refused to regard Fernando's settlement any longer as binding. Indeed, García I of Galicia had grave difficulties controlling his own inheritance. He had to face the revolt of some of his own nobles, and his bishop of

Santiago de Compostela was murdered during the Lenten season of 1069, it seems with impunity. Clearly some of the bishops and nobles of Galicia worked for the intervention of Alfonso VI, and in the spring of 1071 the Leónese king invaded Galicia itself. García fled south to the district around Coimbra, where he managed to maintain himself for the time being.

Alfonso now turned to Sancho of Castilla, offering the latter some sort of condominium over the former realm of García if he would accept the *fait accompli*. For Sancho, however, such an arrangement would have been farcical, given the distance between his domains and Galicia and the position of Alfonso's realm between the two. At the same time, he was little disposed to see Alfonso's, from his standpoint, already swollen dignities engrossed yet further. In January of 1072 Sancho invaded the kingdom of León and defeated and captured his brother at the battle of Golpejera. On January 12th he crowned himself in the cathedral of León. From León, Sancho marched into the old territories of García, probably to secure his recognition there as well, but subsequently moved south into Portugal where he defeated García near Santarém and forced that unfortunate to go into exile in Sevilla. Shortly afterward, Sancho also permitted Alfonso to seek exile at the court of al-Mamūn in Toledo.

The eldest son of Fernando had thus swept all before him in the field and reunited his father's domains, yet within nine months of his victory at Golpejera he would be assassinated. In the aftermath of his military triumphs, all of the evidence indicates that what Sancho could not do was to negotiate a satisfactory political settlement. The Castilian seems clearly to have been boycotted by the entire episcopacy of Alfonso's realm and by much of its aristocracy as well. That he crowned himself in León is likely less a matter of arrogance or policy than a measure of desperation since the bishop of León had refused to do so. Most serious of all, given the fact that under the monarchy all politics are dynastic politics, at least one of the royal *infantas*, his sister Urraca, refused to be reconciled to the new state of affairs. The younger sister, Elvira, seems not to have become involved. Urraca was the eldest of all of the offspring of Fernando. Sometime in the spring or summer of 1072 she withdrew with her supporters to the fortress town of Zamora on the southern edge of Leónese territory. From that point communications could be maintained with the exiled Alfonso in Toledo, a situation intolerable for Sancho. He marched south to lay siege to his sister in Zamora and there met his death outside its walls at the hand of an assassin on October 6, 1072.

News of that dramatic event was not long in reaching Toledo, and by early November of that year Alfonso was back in León, where he easily achieved recognition as rightful king. By December, Alfonso was in Burgos seeking a wider confirmation. There is no doubt that he was successful there, too, in all probability without taking the famous oath of Santa Gadea avowing his innocence of complicity in the death of his brother. That oath is supposed to have been demanded by *el Cid*, the former standard-bearer, or *alférez*, of Sancho II. The rivalry of the three sons of Fernando *el Magno* would become the subject of song and story in the late 12th Century, and much of the literary embellishment would then find its way back into later historiography.[20]

The entire subject of the murder of Sancho II is most unclear in the literature of the times. It is difficult not to suspect the *infanta* Urraca of having arranged it, but there is no real evidence that she did. Even the name of the assassin, "Velliti Ariulfi," is completely unknown to the documents. He may simply have been a madman, or an adventurer. Most likely we will never know. Also, because he gained so much from Sancho's death, Alfonso VI was naturally suspect. Here, too, we can only surmise. Still, clearly there was iron in both Urraca's and Alfonso's character where the welfare of the realm was at stake. We are better informed about García. Upon hearing the news of Sancho's death he returned to Portugal from Sevilla and attempted to reestablish himself there. Alfonso and Urraca invited him to a conference in February of 1073. When he arrived they made him prisoner, and he was to spend the remainder of his life incarcerated in the castle of Luna in the northern mountains of León.[21] In this fashion, and after a lapse of eight years, the kingdom of Fernando I was restored. Alfonso VI (1065–1109), his second son, was to prove an even more successful practitioner of the policies of his father.

---

[20] Fittingly, the modern scholar who has perpetuated this process was himself essentially a student of the language and the literature. Ramón Menéndez Pidal, *La España del Cid*, 2 vols. (Madrid, 4th ed., 1947), has been the historian of 11th-century Spain and has imposed the conclusions of his literary predilections and his Castilian nationalism on the subject for half a century. There is no good evidence that the Cid was ever the *alférez* of Sancho II, and certainly his role in the kingdom of the latter was modest, to say the least. For correctives to the older views, see my *Alfonso VI*, pp. 36–39 and 65–67, and the associated bibliography.

[21] Pérez de Urbel and Ruiz-Zorrilla, eds., *Historia Silense*, pp. 123–24. The author, writing about the period shortly after the death of Alfonso VI, intended an encomium of the latter. He was clear about García but assigned no overt participation to the royal brother and sister in the matter of Sancho.

The Pyrenaen Christian Realms and Zaragoza (1031–1073)

In the northeast of the peninsula at this time the political developments were as different from those in León–Castilla as are the respective geographies of the two regions. The great kingdom there was the taifa of Zaragoza, which encompasses most of the basin of the Ebro River and was ruled by the able al-Muqtadir (1046–1082). Al-Muqtadir was one of five sons and heirs among whom the taifa was to be divided at the death of his father, al-Mustain, in 1046. He himself held Zaragoza and its environs. Among his brothers, Yūsuf held Lérida, Lubb held Huesca, Mundir, Tudela, and Muhammad, Calatayud. Not surprisingly, al-Muqtadir set out to reconstruct his father's realm. By 1050 had subjected and imprisoned all of his brothers except Yūsuf, who maintained his independence until 1081. This latter, who took the title of al-Muzzafar, ruled the taifa of Lérida, in opposition to his brother and often in alliance with one of the petty Christian realms of the east.

Thus it was only in the very closing years of his reign that al-Muqtadir was able to completely reunite the kingdom of his father, and the enmity of his brother was forever a handicap in his dealings with his Christian rivals. Nevertheless, in 1061 or 1062 the Zaragozan was able to absorb the taifa of Tortosa, in the delta of the Ebro and to the south of his brother at Lerida, thus at least isolating the latter from Muslim help. When that had been accomplished the great bulk of the Ebro river basin, something on the order of 65,000 square kilometers of one of the most fertile territories in the Spains, was at his disposal for the purposes of either war or peace. Of all of the Spanish kingdoms, Muslim or Christian, only the sprawling León–Castilla in the north and the expanding Sevilla of the south surpassed it in size or power.

Of the Christian kingdoms with which al-Muqtadir had to contend in 1046, save always León–Castilla of course, the most formidable was Navarra. Under Sancho el Mayor, and then his eldest son, García Sánchez III (1035–1054), that kingdom had exploited the internal weaknesses of the emerging taifa to extend its hold in the Rioja basin as far south as Calahorra by 1045. Yet the strength of Navarra at that time was rather a function of the weakness of its neighbors than a natural expression of its own potential. Even including the northern Rioja region, the total area of the kingdom did not attain more than 6,000 square kilometers, less than a tenth of that of Zaragoza. This area was divided into two major parts. There was the upper valley of the Ebro River from Calahorra as far north as

Haro, perhaps with its political center of gravity at Nájera, where increasingly the Navarrese monarchs preferred to stay. Then to the northeast, beyond the heights of the Sierra de Izco, in the high plains around Pamplona, was the old center of the realm.

Relatively little has been done to date with the early history of Navarra beyond tracing its political outlines. Still, we know that both the Ebro and the Pamplona districts were by Iberian standards relatively well watered, the former by the river and the latter proportionally more by sub-Pyrenaen rainfall. As a result, both were well adapted to the sort of cereal and stock raising culture already discussed in relation to León–Castilla. Both areas, then, may be presumed to have shared the sort of rural evolution that was taking place in the latter, based upon the increasing use of irrigation and the mechanization of grain milling. Certainly both were in close enough contact with the Mozarab population of the Rioja to have assimilated the newer techniques without difficulty. We may, therefore, also presume an increasing population with an ever greater need for land as the area workable by one family alone expanded. In, addition, the growth of a more potent nobility and church in this new environment furnished a concentration of resources which could be channeled into territorial expansion.

Such factors will explain much of the brilliant, if ephemeral, achievement of Sancho III during the first three and a half decades of the 11th Century. Nevertheless, the recovery of both León–Castilla and Zaragoza were to put an end to the prospects of Navarra, as we have in part already seen. After the defeat and humbling of Navarra at Atapuerca in 1054, Sancho García IV became a client of Fernando of León. That initiated a gradual retreat of Navarrese prospects and control in northeast Castilla and increased the pressure for expansion in the valley of the Ebro. Sancho García, however, ultimately found it impossible to score major territorial advances there, even after the death of Fernando and the division of his realm in 1065 removed whatever deterrence his subordination to the Leónese may have imposed. In the War of the Three Sanchos in 1067, he joined with his cousin, Sancho Ramírez of Aragón, to limit the designs of Sancho II of Castilla, another cousin, against Zaragoza. Two years later, he entered into a treaty with al-Muqtadir, which pledged the two to cooperate against the designs, this time, of Aragón. This treaty involved the payment by the Zaragozan of some 12,000 gold *mancusos* each year to his ally. Four years later, in the spring of 1073 when a French expedition like that of Barbastro again threatened, the treaty was renewed. These diplomatic achievements, and a judicious distribution of the revenues they secured, may have relieved some of the discontent in Navarra over the failure to expand south. That they did not assuage all of it may be evidenced by the assassination of the Navarrese king in 1076.

The death of Sancho García IV of Navarra in 1076 was to lead to the very disappearance of that kingdom from the Iberian political scene for the next sixty years, and one of the major beneficiaries would be the upstart kingdom of Aragón. In the time of Sancho *el Mayor*, Aragón had been a portion of the latter's realm, and the geography of the area explains the close linkage of the two. Both belonged essentially to the western Pyrenaen configuration in which the lines of communication run east and west rather than north and south. Old Aragón lay at the foot of the Pyrenees in a relatively well watered valley which begins not far east of Jaca and stretches west to merge gradually into the *contado* around Pamplona. There are heights and relatively difficult stretches of ground near the monastery and the Sierra of Leire, which sometimes served to separate the two regions, but the barrier was slight enough that political realities often triumphed over geographical ones.

With the death of Sancho *el Mayor*, Aragón became a separate political entity, a county ruled by his bastard son Ramiro (1035–1063). Although the arrangement clearly intended that he should be subordinate to his half brother, García Sánchez III of Navarra, Ramiro seems to have ignored that implication from the first with sufficient success that he became, as Ramiro I, the founder of the kingdom of Aragón. After the mysterious assassination of Gonzalo, youngest son of Sancho *el Mayor* and half brother to Ramiro, in 1045, the former's two counties of Sobrarbe and Ribagorza were simply annexed by Ramiro. These two areas, unlike Aragón, belonged to the eastern Pyrenaen geographical configuration. That is, they were essentially composed of narrow river valleys stretching south from those mountains, and east-west communications were rendered close to impossible by the mountain spurs that flanked them. Future Aragónese monarchs would cling to them tenaciously, but their significance to Aragonese history as against Aragonese prestige was to be slight.

Aragón proper was again, one of those high valleys where a mixture of cereal culture and stock raising flourished, and we should imagine the same dynamic at work as already sketched for León–Castilla and Navarra. In the case of Aragón, however, there is an additional consideration – of the location of the town of Jaca. Jaca lay at the foot of the only practicable pass, Somport, 1,640 meters in height, between Iberia and France in the central Pyrenees. As a result, much of the growing pilgrim traffic of the 11th Century from

Western Europe to Santiago de Compostela would pass through Jaca and Aragón leaving new money and new awarenesses in its wake. The pass of Somport was also a route for a rather more secular, commercial traffic between the south of France and the Muslim emporium of Zaragoza on the Ebro, which also fertilized the town of Jaca. Finally, the same pass furnished communication for Aragón with a collection of French principalities, Bearn, Bigorre, and ultimately Toulouse, whose assistance could be solicited for a variety of political enterprises south of the mountains far beyond the capacities of that tiny kingdom with its workable heartland of perhaps 1,500 square kilometers.

In the 11th Century the options of Ramiro I were expansion either west at the expense of Navarra or south against the giant taifa of Zaragoza. He chose the latter, and to do so entered into alliance with the count of Urgel, Armengol III, to whom he married his daughter, Sancha. Urgel was the major Catalan county which lay just to the east of Sobrarbe and Ribagorza and like them comprised a river valley oriented southwest toward the Muslim Ebro basin. Urgel was a natural ally of Aragón, and its count would be killed in the course of the disastrous episode of the conquest of Barbastro in 1064 and its reconquest in 1065. That Muslim fortress controlled the passage south along the valley of the Cinca River where it debouches from the foothills of the Pyrenees onto the plain of Huesca. By the middle of the 11th Century the Aragónese had already effectively occupied the chain of sierras – Santo Domingo, Loarre, and Guara – that looks down upon that plain, but lacked the strength to move out upon the plain itself. Ramiro I was killed in 1063 in an unsuccessful attempt to take Muslim Graus, another Muslim fortress blocking the route south along the Esera River in Ribagorza.

His son and heir, Sancho Ramírez I (1063–1094), was for the next twenty years unable to score any real success in the struggle against Zaragoza.[22] He sought those allies beyond the Pyrenees that would clearly be necessary, a method which was to be brilliantly successful during the reign of his son, Alfonso I, but which produced few results in his own lifetime. In 1068, Sancho undertook a pilgrimage to Rome and also surrendered Aragón to the papacy, receiving it back as a fief.[23] One result of that initiative was that in 1073 Pope Gregory VII attempted to organize a crusade in Spain by the south

[22] This quite important monarch still requires ascholarly history of his reign. Domingo J. Buesa Conde, *El rey Sancho Ramírez* (Zaragoza, 1978), is little more than a sketch and lacks all scholarly apparatus.
[23] Paul Kehr, "Cómo y cuándo se hizo Aragón feudatorio de la Santa Sede?" *EEMCA* 1 (1945):301–04.

French. The designated leader of the expedition was to be Ebles, count of Roucy, who was both cousin and brother-in-law to Sancho Ramírez. Although the project aroused much alarm in Zaragoza, nothing more was heard of it after the spring of 1073. Sancho himself campaigned in the territories of Huesca that summer but no permanent conquests resulted. Throughout this period, all along its northern perimeter, the taifa of Zaragoza was subject to continual harassment and raids by the Christian inhabitants of that mountainous rim. The latter's mobility and ability to seize the initiative made them a nuisance to the Muslim agriculturalists of the plain. At the same time, the mountain folk could seldom muster sufficient effectives to pose a major threat.

Much the same conditions obtained at the extreme eastern end of the peninsula. There the region which we are accustomed to call Cataluña was, in fact, a congeries of counties, ruled by members of a closely related dynasty whose titles and actual powers were likely to shift dramatically as the difficult politics of the region interacted with its equally difficult geography.[24] The region was born in the high mountain valleys of the eastern Pyrenees. There, in the upper reaches of the Noguera, the Segre, the Llobregat, the Beso, the Tec, and the Tet, were located the same sort of refuges and redoubts that characterized 8th-century Asturias. The accidents of the Carolingian conquest of Gerona in 785 and Barcelona in 801 created the conditions under which the inhabitants of the latter four valleys were able, very gradually over the next two centuries, to expand down-river to the Mediterranean coast. Again we have a phenomenon roughly analogous, but on a much smaller scale, to the expansion of Asturian society southward onto the plain of the Duero in the same period.

Here, too, we see a remarkable reorganization of an essentially agricultural world in the late 10th and early 11th Centuries. That process involved the already-familiar deployment of new irrigation techniques and the spread of the mill, as well as an associated new concentration on stock raising. There were also some local variations, particularly the spread of viticulture and of fruit trees into mountain areas, only marginally suited to them at best but made more hospitable by extensive terracing. These techniques provided the most substantial returns in the Mediterranean lowlands around Gerona and Barcelona, preparing the way for the emergence of the

[24] Pierre Bonnassie, *Cataluña mil anos atrás, siglos X–XI* (Barcelona, 1988), is the latest reworking of a marvelous study first done in French in 1975 and translated into a Catalan edition in 1979. It marked the beginning of the closely documented social and economic histories of the particular areas of the peninsula. For Bonnassie, quite properly, "in the 10th and 11th Centuries, Catalonia did not really exist" (p. 21).

county of Barcelona as preeminent and the relegation of the mountain counties such as Pallars and Urgel to subordinate status. But the similarities of these developments to those going on contemporaneously in León–Castilla must be set against the quite different geographical context in which they were taking place.

On the one hand, Barcelona was a port, if not yet great one. In 1052 when Ramón Berenguer I wished to organize the kidnapping of a bride from Narbonne, he had to depend upon the ships of Muslim Tortosa. Yet if Muslim seafarers controlled the Gulf of Lions, they called regularly at Barcelona, and a sea trade with Tortosa, Majorca, Valencia, Denia, Alicante, and Almería resulted. Barcelona seems to have contributed largely an agricultural surplus and perhaps some ore and metal products. Nevertheless, it had its merchants and a money economy based upon both gold and silver. The counts of Barcelona are known to have issued a gold coinage as early as 1018. But Barcelona was also at least a transit point on another artery of trade. Two old Roman roads, still major highways for both merchants and armies, passed close by Barcelona on their way to the south of France. One ran up the eastern coast from Alicante through Valencia and Tortosa, and one which took the alternative route from Andalucía through Toledo and Zaragoza. The county of Barcelona was, then, a mercantile center almost from the beginning, in a way that would have no parallel in León–Castilla until Sevilla and Cádiz were captured in the 13th Century and the opening of the Basque ports created an alternate trade route. Moreover, the diminutive size of Cataluña would magnify the effect of the Barcelona phenomenon within it.

In rather another fashion, the peculiar geography dictated a distinctive development for Cataluña's political life. At the eastern end of the Pyrenees any border drawn between France and Spain is arbitrary. Cataluña stretched more naturally northward than in any other direction. Its bishoprics were suffragans of Narbonne until the restoration of the archbishopric of Tarragona in the 12th Century. Its dynasties were most closely related to those of the Midi. In 1067 Ramón Berenguer I (1035–1076) purchased the rights of his rivals to the counties of Razes and Carcassonne whose incumbents had died without direct heir. William IV of Montpellier was already his vassal. In Toulouse the sons of the deceased Count Pons were the children of Ramón's wife, Almodis, who had been previously married to Pons. Count Peter of Melgueil was married to her daughter, Almodis, in 1067. About the same time, Raymond Bernard, viscount of Béziers and Agde, became a vassal of Ramón Berenguer. In concert with these moves, the latter began the creation of a merchant marine whose natural ambit would be the south French littoral and the west coast of Italy as well as the east coast of Iberia.

The natural corollary of this active northern policy was a relatively passive one in the peninsula proper. That was not a new development, for the reign of his father, Berenguer Ramón I (1018–1035), had been largely pacific, and the expansion westward into the Sierra de Castelltallat had paused at the edge of the plain of Lérida. To the south, Tarragona was still the center of a deserted district between Barcelona and Tortosa. In the face of a vigorous al-Muqtadir in Zaragoza, Ramón Berenguer sought defensive alliances with the former's brother, al-Muzaffar, of Huesca and with the taifas of Tortosa and Denia. The price of these treaties was the usual payment of *parias* by the Muslim powers. The flow of gold allowed the Barcelona count to subdue a stubborn revolt of his own nobility and generally to bring the other Catalan counts into greater dependence upon himself. In one instance, he was even able permanently to absorb the county of Ausona, or Vich, into the possession of Barcelona after the death of its last alternative heir, Guillermo, in 1054. Ramón Berenguer did undertake some aggressive operations in the lower Ribagorza after 1060, and even al-Muqtadir may have purchased peace at the price of *parias*.

Nevertheless, none of this activity prevented the Zaragozan from overrunning the taifa of Tortosa in 1060–1061 and incorporating it finally in his own domains. Eventually he was able to reclaim Lérida as well and reunite the realm of his father. Ramón Berenguer was thus to lose his chance at peninsular expansion and his *parias* to boot. In addition, in 1071 the son of Ramón by a previous marriage, Pedro, was to have his stepmother and Ramón's wife, the Countess Almodis, assassinated, and the Barcelona hegemony in the Languedoc began to unravel. For these and a number of other reasons the role of Barcelona in the peninsula over the next quarter-century was destined to be very small indeed.

3

The Emerging Society of the Christian North

The world of Christian Iberia in the first three-quarters of the 11th Century was somewhat more rustic than contemporary taifa Islam, but in many respects it resembled its southern counterpart more than we ordinarily are accustomed to think. The new political organization slowly taking shape in the former had little more historical legitimacy than did the taifas themselves. To all of these fledgling structures one may apply what Thomas Bisson has so finely said of the northeast, "Aragon and Catalonia are thus, strictly speaking, products of the Middle Ages; products of the confrontation between Islam and Christianity in the eastern peninsula. Neither had any basis in tribal culture, both were inherently geopolitical constructions."[1] What was taking shape everywhere was the product of the configuration of the land, the dynasty which strove to master some discrete portion of it, and the strength or weakness of the particular Islamic power which adjoined it.

For the most part, the lands these dynasties came to dominate were new. Accustomed to thinking in terms of an abstract state, we routinely extend the names created for those realms back to their chronological and geographical predecessors. We refer, for instance, to Vermudo III (1028–1037) as king of León. He himself appears never to have done so but rather identified himself as king by virtue of his genealogy, "son of," rather than territorially.[2] Only gradually and tentatively would his successors, indeed supplanters, come to style themselves kings of León and Castilla. Except in very small

---

[1] *The Medieval Crown of Aragon* (Oxford, 1986), p. 28.
[2] Luis Núñez Contreras, "Colección diplomática de Vermudo III, rey de León," *Historia, Instituciones, Documentos* 4 (1977):381–504, edits the twenty known charters of Vermudo. Neither in the institutulations, the subscriptions, or the dating formulae is León or any other territorial designation mentioned.

circumscriptions, a Pamplona or a Barcelona, the former practice seems to have been customary among rulers prior to the last half of the 11th Century, although we do lack critical editions of the charters of most of them, to be sure. Kingship was conceived, apparently, as consisting of the possessions of a dynasty in their then-present extent, rather than of a fixed, territorial content.[3] The dynasty was the nexus about which the kingdom took shape. It was a personal and family creation and thus strictly analogous to the taifa of Muslim Iberia. Unlike the latter, however, it was destined to create its own proper, institutional form.

That process was a by-product of strong personal rule extended over a considerable period of time. By way of example, Fernando *el Magno* came in 1037 to rule an area more than the size of the kingdom of England by virtue of the battle of Tamarón. If documents are any guide, from that time forward Fernando and his successors came to rule it ever more strongly. That is, for Fernando, we are aware of some 124 extant, genuine documents, or an average of 4.5 per year over his reign.[4] The reign of his son, Alfonso VI, provides us with some 268, for an average of 6 per year. During the reign of the latter's daughter, Urraca, we have 142 documents for 8 per year. Finally, for the reign of her son, Alfonso VII, we know of some 924, or 30 per year. The kingdom takes shape as king, dynasty, and chancery.

The person of the king nevertheless remained primary. He was the administration of the realm, and that fact ordinarily entailed his physical presence. In any but the most diminutive kingdoms, great demands in time and energy were levied by this necessarily peripatetic existence, one of the least-appreciated realities of medieval political life. For one period in which we can trace his movements most precisely, the first five months of 1075, Alfonso VI of León–Castilla covered some 1,363 kilometers.[5] And this was peacetime. Some help

---

[3] It is within this context, I believe, that the so-called traditions of equal inheritance in the peninsula should be considered. For instance, see José María Lacarra, *Historia del reino de Navarra en la Edad Media* (Pamplona, 1975), pp. 113, 115, 119–20, and 170. For León, see Claudio Sánchez-Albornoz, "La sucesión al trono en los reinos de León y Castilla," in *Viejos y nuevos estudios sobre las instituciones medievales espanolas*, Vol. 2 (Madrid, 2nd ed., 1976), pp. 1107–72. The latter was originally published in *Boletín de la Academia Argentina de Letras* 14 (1945):35–124.

[4] This is a very rough figure since I have not yet investigated the products of his chancery in any great depth. Pilar Blanco Lozano, ed., "Colección diplomática de Fernando I (1037–1065)," *AL* 40 (1986):7–212, has given us a listing of ninety-seven genuine acts in a very valuable doctoral thesis.

[5] Bernard F. Reilly, *The Kingdom of León–Castilla under King Alfonso VI, 1065–1109* (Princeton, N.J., 1988), pp. 148–160, for the explication and implications.

could be had by pressing into service the other members of the dynasty. Indeed, that device was advisable on other grounds, for the reigning family functioned as a whole and no member of it could be neglected with impunity. Sancho II of León–Castilla lost his life and his kingdom in 1072 because he alienated his sister Urraca. Sancho García IV of Navarra was assassinated in 1076 by his brother and sister. The Countess Almodis de la Marca was a major collaborator of Count Ramón Berenguer I of Barcelona, and his grandmother, Ermesinda, was to become one of his most dangerous opponents.

The acts of royal government solemnized and recorded by the chancery had overwhelmingly to do with alienations of land from the royal fisc. In an agricultural society these lands were the fundamental resource of government. They literally fed it, housed it, supplied the transport that moved it from estate to estate, and purchased its allies. The officer through whom the fisc functioned was essentially an estate manager, called *merinus* in most of the peninsula but *bajulus* or *bailli* in Cataluña. Ordinarily drawn from the ranks of the peasantry, he supervised the work and the collection of rents and dues on the royal lands of his particular jurisdiction. But he was more than simply a steward. He also administered justice on those estates, and in the surrounding district when there was no private jurisdiction to compete with royal justice, and was responsible for seeing that its men answered the call to the royal host when summoned. Such officers must have been responsible to the majordomo of the royal household when the court was in their vicinity, but, in the 11th Century, there is no evidence for the existence of a central staff at court which would have coordinated or regulated their activities. For the better part of the year he was literally king in his own locale.

But, fisc lands aside, the vast majority of the realm was composed of lands owned by the nobility, the monastery, and the episcopacy, and of those lands dominated by them if not legally subject to them. The first of these, certainly, and sometimes the latter two, were private warriors. They controlled a private army, maintained private fortresses of some dimension, and reinforced their economic preponderance in the local community not only by the menace of their own person but also by the right to administer justice in the name of the crown over lands far beyond their familial patrimony. Frequently they were *señors* of the smaller, nonepiscopal villages as well. The extent to which the crown had control over such magnates, and thus over the lands they dominated, was crucial to the order and the tranquility of the realm. It is not too much to say that the territories subject to them were the most important constituent parts of the kingdom during the 11th Century. Provinces, districts, counties: these were names. Family possessions were the realities.

There is no doubt that princely control over the nobility during the age was growing weaker. It was also altering its form. The process has been closely catalogued for Cataluña during the reign of Ramón Berenguer I (1035–1076).[6] The period saw an enduring crisis associated with the rebellion of the castellan, or viscount, class led by Mir Geriberto. When it was finally resolved, those offices had become hereditary and their holders bound to the count of Barcelona not by public and official ties but by oath and influence. The changing structures of the countryside, the new technology of war, the fluidity of the political structure, the constant enmity with Islam – all enhanced the practical power of the rural nobility. In 1054 on the field at Atapuerca the disaffection of his nobility cost García Sánchez III of Navarra his life at the hand of Fernando I of León. In 1072 a similar denial of support cost Alfonso VI, at least briefly, his kingdom of León, which his brother, Sancho II, won on the field of Golpejera. Sancho García IV of Navarra lost his life to similar unrest in 1076, and this time the kingdom itself disappeared for more than a half century, partitioned between León–Castilla and Aragón.

Although the countryside predominated, some small leaven was provided by the somewhat different life and social structure of the towns, tiny to begin with in comparison with the cities of the Muslim south. Medievalists speak of the rise of the medieval cities, but in Christian Iberia at this time it is more accurate to regard them simply as episcopal centers. Doubtless they served as markets where the agricultural surpluses of the surrounding district could be sold. That such markets attracted artisans, carpenters, shoemakers, weavers, tailors, butchers, and so on, some of whom were regular residents of the town, is not to be doubted either, but there is no evidence of any marked, urban specialization in such crafts or an organization to support them. Still the most distinctive feature of the town was its religious character. We might briefly consider the physiognomy of three of the greatest of these episcopal centers early in the 11th Century.

Santiago de Compostela is famous, of course, for its cathedral, which was also the shrine church of Saint James the Great whose relics were believed to repose there. As the only apostolic church in Western Europe save Rome, it was then already the object of a major pilgrimage. The cathedral itself was the second such structure on the

---

[6] Pierre Bonnassie, *Cataluña mil años atrás, siglos X–XI* (Barcelona, 1988), pp. 259–300.

site, but a splendid new Romanesque cathedral was being planned by 1075. Compostela itself had no episcopal tradition in antiquity, but the local bishop of the nearby old Roman port of Iria Flavia had long since become resident there. Yet that episcopal household was far from the only religious establishment of the town. Closely associated with the service of the apostle's shrine was the monastery of San Pelayo de Antealtares and its household. Almost as intimately related with that shrine was the monastery of San Martín Pinario hard by the cathedral complex. Also within the circuit of the town walls were the churches of San Felix de Lovio, San Benito del Campo, and San Miguel de Cisterna.[7] A town, then, of a population of roughly 1,000, it boasted six religious households, which were its most visible and certainly its most important occupations.

The structure of León was quite similar. It was a cathedral city, of course, and housed the most important of all the bishops of León–Castilla at the time. In addition, the city's most recent historian counts no less than twenty churches and monasteries within the walls for the first half of the 11th Century.[8] Even if one allows for some confusion of terminology and the disappearance of some smaller monasteries as well as the appearance of new ones, a total of twelve to fifteen such institutions seems probable, and that is in addition to the cathedral itself. León was also the site of a royal castle–palace which was always occupied by a castellan and a royal garrison. In this respect it differed from Santiago de Compostela which seems never to have had one. Nevertheless, the king was rarely in residence there, and it would be foolish to see León as anything but an overwhelmingly clerical town.

For Barcelona, which was to become the commercial center par excellence by the 13th Century, we are less precisely informed, but we know that in addition to the cathedral there were at least three other churches and monasteries.[9] However, what is more significant is the presence of a comital palace in a realm of such diminutive size. That is, the count was able to spend more time in residence, and the city would come to have rather more of the flavor of an administrative center than any other Christian town in the peninsula. Barcelona was also remarkable for its thriving Jewish community. When we recall that it was a port frequented by ships from a variety of

[7] Fernando López Alsina, *La ciudad de Santiago de Compostela en la Alta Edad Media* (Santiago de Compostela, 1988), is a most useful guide if one discounts a certain credulity about the period prior to A.D. 900.

[8] Carlos Estepa Díez, *Estructura social de la ciudad de León, siglos XI–XIII* (León, 1977), pp. 116–19.

[9] Bonnassie, *Cataluña*, pp. 221–25.

Mediterranean lands, it becomes obvious that there were here materials out of which something other than an exclusively clerical high culture might be formed. Yet even in Barcelona at this period the formal life of the intellect found its major expression in and through its churches.

The government of these towns was ordinarily an episcopal function as well. It was royal only in the sense that the bishop, like the *merinus* but on a far higher level, was usually still a royal appointee, with only the briefest of nods to what a later age would regard as the canonical decencies. In addition to his religious authority per se, the bishop saw to the defense of the town, administered its justice in his court, and oversaw its market. Where there was a royal castle within the walls, the bishop perforce shared his authority with the castellan who had his own court with its own proper jurisdiction and a body of men-at-arms to enforce it. Nevertheless, even such a royal appointee seldom competed on a level of equality with the bishop, for he was rarely of such origins to have the ear of the king to the degree that prelate enjoyed. As everywhere, of course, when the peripatetic royal court was actually present in the town, its authority superseded every local jurisdiction.

This royal court, this *curia regis*, which was the supreme government of the realm, might be just as simply and accurately described as the king and his entourage. The king, at the center of it, is of the ordinary type of Western European monarch. That is, he is a war chief, the greatest of the fighting men in an age when every man of any account was a warrior. But in addition to the military nature of the office is its religious nature: a charisma of the divine which surrounds the king. It may be a pagan remnant and a superstition in which a special authority is transmitted through the bloodline, hence the importance of dynasty. For churchmen and at least some others it may be the grace that derives from anointing by the church. In any event, the king is by the very fact of his kingship a religious figure. Bishoprics and monasteries are in his gift. He directs the life of the church of the realm by effectively selecting its officers, and his *curia* legislates church law and morals rather more than it does secular law and morals, when the two are distinguished. Indeed, it would be difficult to say by precisely what right, human or divine, the king enforces the customary law and administers justice.

But if the king is the quintessential figure of government it is never in isolation. The other adult members of the royal dynasty are members of the court and regularly present in it. The court is the family of the monarch. Beyond the family itself, the greatest member of it is the *mayordomus*. His duties seem simply to be to look to the material welfare of the royal family. He is always a member of the nobility and so has a variety of lesser folk at his command to do those humble things requisite to the providing of food, drink, and shelter, but there is no sign of a regular hierarchy of functions and offices. He does not head a department in any modern sense of the word. Also visible is the *alférez*. This is a military office and its holder is always a noble. He is essentially the commander of those men-at-arms who are the ever-present bodyguard of the royal person. Since they are also the core of any royal army, he is commander-in-chief as well, in the absence of the king himself. Both offices seem to be held at the good pleasure of the king and hence are part of the political life of the court.

Other members of the *curia* are less visible ordinarily. There is the notary; always a cleric, frequently changed, and sometimes accompanied by a scribe or two. Again, there is no sure sign of subordination of one to the other or of regular distinction of one from the other. The chancery, so to speak, is not yet a department, either. Since the court sins and gives birth like any other collection of human beings, there is also a royal chaplain or chaplains sometimes in evidence, probably on their way to becoming bishops, one suspects.

All of these household figures were members, in some degree, of that active portion of the court which assisted the king in the government of the realm, when he was engaged in anything so grand. But he would also call on the assistance of those casual members of the court, bishops, abbots, and nobles who happened to be present either because they were in search of something only the king could give or because the court happened simply to have come into their district. There would seem to be no court nobility or court bishops as yet at least.

Such was the *curia regis*. It was surrounded by a motley collection of servants, grooms, stable boys, cooks, trainers of dogs, horses, and hawks, procurers of this and that, merchants, favor seekers, fools, prostitutes, and thieves. Since it was also a court in motion, it numbered as well carters, carpenters, blacksmiths, doctors, veterinarians, tentmakers, shoemakers, and so on, along with pilgrims and ordinary travelers who joined the caravan for the safety it afforded. One estimates the court in motion to have consisted of no fewer than 250 to 450 persons, depending on whether we are talking about the court of the count of Barcelona or that of the king of León–Castilla.[10]

---

[10] Reilly, *Alfonso VI*, pp. 150–60. Here I have attempted to analyze the composition and character of such a court in 1075.

Ordinarily, the cost of supporting this ménage cum government fell upon the fisc lands. The king was expected to live "of his own." As regards war in particular, that expectation was always tempered. War was perhaps the one great joint endeavor of this very decentralized society. The major point and purpose of medieval western monarchy was to lead the realm into battle. Not to do so was to incur the most serious unrest among a nobility whose image of self was even more exclusively "warrior." To underwrite the cost of such undertakings the crown had everywhere in Iberia the right to levy the *fossatum*, the free military service expected of adult males for a certain period of time each year. In addition there was *fossateria*, or scutage, that is, a payment made in lieu of actual service, which might be rendered in coin, pack animals, or supplies. *Fossateria* was the most useful of taxes in underwriting campaigns. It required the unwilling to help bear the expenses of the willing, it was collectible in connection with the general muster of the host and hence required no permanent machinery, and it obviated the necessity of coercing the unwilling, who were unlikely to be of much help on the field of battle in any event.

In addition to host service, the more mundane and generally defensive military needs of the realm were met by a variety of other owed duties, which included a general rally of neighbors to defend a particular position, militia service in its vicinity, castle guard itself, and participation in the victualing and repair of fortifications. These obligations, like host service itself, were ordinarily specified in charters, or *fueros* granted to local populations on a variety of occasions. For the very greatest nobles they might be spelled out in specific pacts and, for the lesser, were likely dictated by custom. But again, under ordinary circumstances, it is clear that certain portions of the fisc were specifically designated as *castellariam*, that is, their produce was dedicated to the upkeep of a particular castle or castellan.[11]

In similar fashion, like the rents of the fisc, much of the other local revenues due the crown must have been consumed at that level, obviating the need of a central collecting agency. This would have been true, one suspects, of the *portaticum*, the most pervasive of the nonmilitary imposts. This tax on trade appears to have been levied at a wide variety of passes, ports, bridges, and towns, and along main roads. In all probability the right to collect it was sold or rented, the only way it could provide an income directly to the crown. The same was true of the various market and sales taxes that existed in the larger towns.

[11] A great mass of material on the subject has recently been organized and clarified in James F. Powers, *A Society Organized for War: The Iberian Municipal Militias in the Central Middle Ages, 1000–1284* (Los Angeles, 1988).

The identical practice can confidently be asserted to have obtained in respect to the coining of money. The beginnings of the coinage of money in the Christian north is the surest indication of the rise of prosperity there. It was a regalian right everywhere, of course, but it was also a business. Mints were supposed to turn a profit by producing a coinage which was more valuable than the raw metal purchased to make it. But such a business was sold or leased to private moneyers and in that fashion furnished revenue to the crown. Neither in this nor in any other regard is there evidence of a central machinery which could have controlled or directed the everyday operation of such an enterprise.[12] Silver coins begin to be minted in Navarra during the reign of Sancho *el Mayor* (1000–1035). In Barcelona during that of Ramón Borell I (992–1018) there was even some minting of gold coins, although the issues were sporadic and subsequently discontinued. Aragón began to mint a silver coinage at Jaca in the time of Sancho Ramírez I (1063–1094). León-Castilla seems to have lagged in this respect. Although there have been scattered assertions that coins of Fernando I (1037–1065) exist, no one has been able to satisfactorily demonstrate that fact.

Another revenue peculiar to the crown was the tribute due it from the Jewish population of the realm, possibly annually, although more likely on occasions felt appropriate by the king. Jews, like free Muslims later, were special subjects and wards of the Christian rulers. Subject to royal law alone, they paid heavily for that privilege and protection. Occasionally it, too, was farmed, but ordinarily money went directly to the crown, for the Jewish communities possessed their own officers who could be relied upon to assess and to collect it.

Finally, no survey of princely resources in 11th-century Iberia could be complete without taking into account the peculiar institution of the *parias*. This tribute levied on the wealthier but more pacific Muslim taifa kingdoms had no counterpart elsewhere in Western Europe. For a very considerable time in that century it allowed the unsophisticated monarchies of the north to field armies sufficient for the gradual reduction of those same Muslim societies which paid it. In 1074 Alfonso VI, who became a major player in this game, must have realized an income of something on the order of 70,000 gold dinars annually from the *parias* of the taifas of Granada, Sevilla, Badajoz, Toledo, Zaragoza, and Valencia, and possibly half as much again from the lesser taifas. Such a sum made

[12] For another point of view, see Claudio Sánchez-Albornoz, "La primitiva organización monetaria de León y Castilla," *AHDE* 5 (1928):301–05.

armies easy to maintain in the field and, distributed as largesse to nobles, bishops, and abbots, the realm simpler to pacify. Such sums were the object of lively competition among the Christian realms of the north, especially in the case of Zaragoza, Lérida, Tortosa, and Valencia. Navarra, Aragón, and Barcelona disputed for them as well as León–Castilla. However, the *parias* were a resource likely to diminish as a result of the very dynamic they set up. The availability of such funds might help finance the conquest of a taifa, but then that new territory must be defended and so was transformed into an item of expense.

When available, such revenues went to the support of the royal court. Local administration, if it may be called that during such a simple age, was supported out of local revenues. As already explained, in most places it was simply the administration of the fisc lands and any other surrounding populations that were not subject to private jurisdiction. Where territories were subject to a noble or a bishop, royal government hardly existed, except for the most notorious crimes. Therefore, estate officers such as the *merinus* or *bailli* sufficed for local royal administration in most instances. These minor figures must have been fairly regularly responsible to the crown and could have possessed no independence against it except that afforded by royal neglect. Doubtless they were removable at will and without redress.

On the other hand, castellans were members of the nobility and possessed an independent power and jurisdiction of their own, usually in the same district as the castle they held from the crown. They were entitled to the enjoyment of the revenues of some of the fisc lands of the vicinity and to the oversight of those *merinos* necessary to guarantee it. Under those circumstances it was increasingly difficult to keep separate royal estates from private ones, for the same *merino* must often have overseen both. It was equally difficult to distinguish that royal justice meted out by the castellan from the private justice enjoyed and administered by the same individual. Ultimately, therefore, it became more and more difficult to separate the land, the castle, or the justice from the holder thereof or to prevent them from passing to his heirs. A castellan may be dispossessed for some egregious fault, but his son or brother is most likely to turn up holding all those perquisites which were previously the offender's. That would seem to be the universal tendency of the age in Christian Iberia.

That development is even more true of the counts, in a great kingdom like León–Castilla, and of abbots and bishops everywhere. It has been asserted, and it may even be true, that in the old kingdom of Asturias the countship was an office and its incumbent removable at the royal pleasure. However that may be, countship in León–Castilla was becoming a dignity rather than an office in the 11th Century. It long since had in Cataluña. In theory, it might still be revocable in the west and was inseparable from the county as a unit of government. In observable practice, countship had become an honor customarily held by one of the male members of a certain number of great magnate families. Increasingly it was becoming detachable from any specific territory and firmly associated with a particular family, if not necessarily the son of a given father in strict hereditary succession. Yet the lands of the fisc assigned to it and the rights of justice inherent in it tended to go with the honor.

In that fashion large portions of the countryside escaped any formal royal control at all. This was equally true, of course, of lands held by monasteries in the rural districts and of episcopal towns. There the problem of royal control was differently structured nevertheless. Even in this rough society bishops and abbots were clearly differentiated as officers of the church. That was a blessing for kings, and sometimes great noble families in the case of monasteries, for these offices could not become the objects of simple family inheritance. He who had them in his gift therefore would continue to have the opportunity to manipulate them at least occasionally. The frequency of that opportunity was, of course, limited by the fact that both offices were held for life once bestowed. Short of the death of the incumbent, the attempt to manipulate by deposition and transferral of either dignity was a scandal and a major undertaking, not infrequently productive of more trouble than it was worth. In that sense, monastic and abbatial properties and jurisdictions also escaped royal control, although less completely. Yet it should be borne in mind that, although a less than sovereign authority outrages our modern sense of political proprieties, the practical problem of order and peace in the countryside was likely to be more closely addressed by these lesser authorities than it could possibly have been by any contemporary royal authority. In that age, political consolidation could only have been realized through the mediation of such lesser hierarchs.

High Culture in 11th-Century Christian Iberia

Christian Iberia in the first three-quarters of the 11th Century was a simple, agricultural society with a minimum of central direction of any kind. It was a provincial, even parochial world in the strictest sense of those terms. Still, an agricultural society is never quite as simple as city folk would make it, and we have already seen some of its gradations, the old ones and the newer ones, coming into being. But all this having been said, it was still a rural society, and the ordinary definitions of human beings in it were farmer, warrior, and priest, or wife or child of the first two. In the formal sense only the religious would possess a high culture. The farmers and the warriors had their own culture, in the anthropological sense, but it was not a literate one. There was, at that time, no cultivated urban laity, either noble or non-noble, which could have been the vehicle of a high culture.

The high culture that existed was a clerical, professional one. The major institutions which preserved and transmitted it were the episcopal *familia* and the monastic community. However well or badly realized, the ideal of literacy was integral to the clerical estate. As it long had, in the 11th Century it continued to express itself in a clerical education, consisting, in the first instance, of literacy in Latin which was the language of Scripture for practical purposes. A Latin grammarian, or access to one, was then the first necessity of every episcopal establishment and monastery. The second necessity was a master of song, or *primicerius*, for the liturgy of the Latin mass and the sacraments had long since come to be imbedded in a larger liturgical ordo which was sung daily by these communities. The necessity of training neophytes for the full life of the community thus institutionalized education in the Latin language and in music at the episcopal and monastic levels. It is difficult to say more about the structures of this education in the early 11th Century, for we must depend almost entirely on chance references in the documents to a *grammaticus* or a *magister scolarum*.

The content of this education may be fairly described as traditional and classical. That is, teaching Latin involved not only the Latin grammarians but also those Roman authors who served as texts and models for the students. Therefore, at least a smattering of classical Latin literature, history, and philosophy was absorbed by indirection. The northern Iberian world seems generally to have been as well supplied with the antique Latin authors as the Early Middle Ages had been elsewhere in western Europe. The recopying of such manuscripts when they began to show wear was a typical employment of better monastic scriptoria. However, the point of this education was professional in the clerical sense. The major objects of study, beyond the preparation in language, were the Bible itself, the great commentaries upon it, and the theological treatises elaborated out of both by the Latin fathers of the church. The major products of the scriptoria were the mass books needed for the regular and ordered celebration of Christian worship. Again, this direction and purpose of education in Iberia did not differ markedly from developments elsewhere in the Medieval West at the time.

The study of manuscripts preserved and recopied, which is the chief resort of the historian in this instance, does establish two particular notes of the Iberian Christian world, however.[13] As would be expected, in addition to the standard patristic authors, Augustine, Jerome, and Saint Gregory the Great, there is substantial attention given to Iberian authors proper. Among these Saint Isidore of Sevilla was by far the most important, but constant reference was also made to the great 7th-century archbishops of Toledo, Eugenius, Alfonso, and Julián, and also to the authors of monastic rules, such as Saint Fructuoso of Braga. In this respect, the northern Christian world remained a cultural extension of the more advanced Mozarabic Christian communities of the Muslim south. Many manuscripts traveled to northern scriptoria in the hands of Mozarab refugees from Islam. This phenomenon was especially marked in the great migrations of the late 9th Century, but it continued to be a feature of Iberian Christian life well into the 13th Century.

The same characteristic is to be noted in the transmission of important manuscripts such as that of the *Collectio Hispana*, a compendium principally of the legislative canons of the great Visigothic church councils, and of the *Liber Judiciorum*, the Visigothic legal code. These collections seem to be well distributed throughout the north, which argues their continuing use in some degree, although this latter is a controverted subject.

Original work performed in the north itself is scant, at least that portion of it which has survived. The best-known manuscripts of this sort are those of the 8th-century *Beatus de Liébana*, a commentary on the Apocalypse whose vivid illustrations preserved them and inspired imitation of and elaboration upon their illuminations. The chronicles of the cycle of Alfonso III of Asturias (866–910) were widely recopied and additions made to them, but the weight of antiquity was heavy. Orosius's *Seven Books of History against the Pagans* was well known also, and the tendency simply to continue this 5th-century work was often overpowering. In the first half of the 11th Century Bishop Sampiro of Astorga (1035–1041) put

---

[13] The outstanding scholar in this field is Manuel C. Díaz y Díaz. See his *Index Scriptorum Latinorum Medii Aevi Hispanorum*, 2 vols. (Salamanca, 1958), for example, and a variety of special studies since. Those collected in his *Libros y librerias en La Rioja altomedieval* (Logroño, 1979) are particularly relevant to our purposes here.

Plate 2   Mozarabic church of San Miguel de Escalada, province of
León

together a chronicle which brought these disparate materials down to
his own times, and his work seems to have been fairly widely
distributed. Otherwise the period is largely innocent of new intellectual contributions.

Some further qualifications must be made. Unique also to the
Iberian scene are some traceable borrowings from the world of
Spanish Islam. Manuscripts of Muslim works on astronomy and
mathematics, some using the so-called Arabic numbers, were to be
found for as early as the 10th Century in the libraries of the monastery of Ripoll in Cataluña and in those of the Navarrese monasteries
of San Martín de Abelda and San Millán de La Cogolla in the Rioja.
These works may also have traveled north with Mozarab refugees
who came to these regions, although in lesser number than to León.
On the other hand, they may have been borrowed from flourishing
centers such as Islamic Tudela or Zaragoza through the medium of
the cultivated Jewish communities there. Both Navarra and Cataluña
had documented Jewish communities that would have been in touch
with their fellows in the neighboring Islamic taifas, but there is no
evidence of specific, independent intellectual activity on the part of

the former during this period. In any event, these materials were at hand when a very real sport indeed for the age, Gerbert of Aurillac, later Pope Sylvester II (999–1003), visited the monastery of Ripoll and spent some time in their study.

Gerbert's visit may be taken as symbolic of two changes which, although scarcely begun in the early 11th Century, were fated to alter the scene we have been describing in fundamental fashion. One of these was the travel to the peninsula of generations of Western scholars in order to appropriate not only the intellectual achievements of Islam but also the surprisingly full corpus of classical scientific and philosophical works which the Muslim had preserved. Conversely, this movement will also be a portion of a much wider phenomenon, the spread of Western European influence in Christian Iberia.

Iberia between Africa and Europe

One of the most important agencies of both changes was to be the pilgrimage to Santiago de Compostela. The discovery of the relics of Saint James the Great at Compostela took place at the beginning of the 9th Century, and the popularity of the pilgrimage had been slowly gaining ground ever since. Already, for example, in 951 Bishop Godescalius of Le Puy in France stopped at the monastery of San Martín de Abelda during a pilgrimage to Santiago de Compostela and had copied there a manuscript which still exists in the Bibliotheque Nationale. Somewhat later, in 997, the shrine became sufficiently notable for al-Mansūr himself to think it worthwhile to march north, sack and burn it, and carry off its bells to grace the great mosque of Córdoba. Still, it was the 11th Century that would see the beginnings of an almost explosive growth in the popularity of that pilgrimage, both in Iberia and in Western Europe generally. The road from the passes of Somport in Aragón and Roncesvalles in Navarra across the northern *meseta* to Galicia and Santiago de Compostela would become the major artery of Christian Spain. Along it flowed not just the pilgrims themselves but with them the currents of developments as diverse as Romanesque architecture, ecclesiastical reform, and the Caroline script.[14] If most of the dateable and tang-

---

[14] Luis Vázquez de Parga, José María Lacarra, and Juan uría Ríu, *Las peregrinaciones a Santiago de Compostela*, 3 vols. (Madrid, 1948–49), synthesized the knowledge of the subject up to that date, but the pilgrimage has a great and lively historiography as well as history. Richard A. Fletcher, *St. James's Catapult: The Life and Times of Diego Gelmírez of Santiago de Compostela* (Oxford, 1984), is recent, delightful, and scholarly.

ible landmarks of this growth belong to the latter three decades of the century, still it is clear that they grew out of the earlier increase.

Yet the question of the preponderance of influence was still obscure before the final quarter-century. However vibrant their internal dynamic, the Christian kingdoms of the Pyrenaen east were still tiny enclaves around the perimeter of Muslim Zaragoza. In León–Castilla, Fernando *el Magno* paid precious little attention to Santiago before the final years of his reign. Even then it must be recalled that the cult of Saint James the Great at Compostela was a specifically Iberian phenomenon related primarily to the dialectic of Muslim and Christian in the peninsula long before it became a European institution.[15] The great pious initiative which Fernando I undertook in 1063 had to do rather with a search for the relics of Santa Justa, virgin and martyr of Sevilla of Roman times, to grace the church of León. Despite the help of the taifa king, al-Mutadid, the body of the virgin was nowhere to be found. Instead, the great Saint Isidore of Sevilla himself chose to reveal his whereabouts, and the Leonese mission departed just as happily with those relics. In León, Fernando responded by installing the body in a shrine–church, to which a splendid new royal pantheon would be conjoined and about which an official cult would grow.[16]

Nevertheless, along the way of Saint James a stream of European traffic was growing. We can document it ordinarily only in the case of the great. In 1063 a Bishop Peter of Puy in Velay made the trip. A bit later the widow of the German count of Sponheim chose that particular form of devotion. In 1065 what was described as a "multitude" of little folk from Liège set off for Galicia. Paradoxical or not, the uniquely Iberian devotion to Santiago was to become a powerful force for the Europeanization of Christian Iberia, and that in the not-too-distant future. Numbers elude us, of course, but the fact that Iberian society was beginning to make provision for them is a sure guarantee that their aggregate was considerable. The widow of García Sánchez of Navarra, Estefania, donated a hostel–hospital to the church of Santa María el Real of Nájera not long after mid-century, and even earlier, Count Gomez Diaz of Carrión de los Condes had a hospital for pilgrims erected at Arconada in León.

[15] Fortunately, it is possible to ignore the great, interesting, but fundamentally wrong-headed debate over its significance which so entertained Americo Castro, *The Spaniards: An Introduction to Their History*, trans. W. F. King and S. Margaretten (Berkeley, 1971), and Claudio Sánchez-Albornoz, *Espana, un enigma histórico*, 2 vols. (Buenos Aires, 1957). Mercifully, the rage for the personification of nationalities has abated.

[16] The story is told in Justo Pérez de Urbel and Atilano González Ruiz-Zorilla, eds., *Historia Silense* (Madrid, 1959), pp. 198–204, which is an early 12th-century source.

At some point this flux and reflux of pilgrims from beyond the Pyrenees caused even the humblest members of Iberian society to turn their attention toward that distant Europe which each year provided a new horde of purchasers of their bread, drinkers of their wine, pilferers of their chickens, and molesters of their daughters. No one who lived along the *via francigenea* could ignore this phenomenon which passed before their doorways almost daily. In addition, although most of this peculiar crew were transients, some of them came to stay. Doubtless some, faced with legal or illegal prosecution, never intended to return home, some had accumulated a little capital along the way and found more opportunity in this new land than they knew at home, and others found propertied widows to console or landlords eager for new hands and backs. Whatever their motivation, they added a Western European leaven to the new Iberian world taking shape.

The scholarship of not too long ago customarily associated the growth of the Compostela pilgrimage with the influence exercised by the famous French Burgundian monastery of Cluny. That notion has since been properly discredited, but the instinct that detected French monastic influence in northern Iberia was quite sound. Christian Iberia was never entirely closed to European contacts, even when its major orientation was toward the Mozarab and Muslim south. Cluny was a latecomer. Benedictine monasticism, in the form of the Rule of Benedict, preceded it in the 10th and early 11th Centuries. The penetration was modest, and the indigenous rules of Saint Isidore and Saint Fructuosus retained their sway almost everywhere, but the French monasteries were proof that wider European norms had some attraction.[17]

The gradual infiltration of Cluniac influence began with Sancho *el Mayor* of Navarra (1000–1035). He reacted to the spreading fame of that house in Europe by seeking its liturgical intercession for himself and his own purposes in the time of Abbot Odilo (994–1049).[18] At the same time, Abbot Oliva of the Catalan house of Ripoll and bishop of Vich (1018–1046) was an admirer, imitator, and propaga-

---

[17] Antonio Linage Conde, *Los orígenes del monacato benedictino en la península Ibérica*, 3 vols. (León, 1973), is the essential work. Justo Pérez de Urbel, *Los monjes españolas en la Edad Media*, 2 vols. (Madrid, 2nd ed., 1945), is an older survey still useful in some respects.

[18] Charles Julian Bishko, "Fernando I and the Origins of the Leonese-Castilian Alliance with Cluny," in *Studies in Medieval Spanish Frontier History* (London, 1980), pp. 1–136. First published in Spanish in *CHE* 47–48 (1968):31–135, and 49–50 (1969):50–116, it is the fundamental study. For miscellaneous earlier developments along this line, see the same author's "The Abbey of Dueñas and the Cult of Saint Isidore of Chios in the County of Castile (10th–11th Centuries)," in *Homenaje a Fray Justo Pérez de Urbel, OSB*, Vol. 2 (Silos, 1977), pp. 345–64.

tor of Cluniac practices farther to the east. Something of this sort would be taken up in León–Castilla in the time of Fernando I. At this time the Burgundian house had reached the apogee of its prestige under the great Abbot Hugh of Saint-Maur (1049–1109). Sometime between 1049 and 1053 that Leonese monarch initiated the annual payment of 1,000 gold dinars to Cluny out of the *parias* which he was beginning to collect from the taifas. In return, the king and the dynasty were to benefit from the formal liturgical intercession of that house. After the death of Fernando it is possible that the assistance of Cluny took a more mundane turn: Hugh may have appealed successfully to the victorious Sancho II in 1072 to release the latter's brother, Alfonso, and to allow him to go into exile in Toledo.

I am speaking now only of influence. Cluny had not yet begun to accumulate possessions and authority in the peninsula. Nor was its influence exclusive or even preponderant. Notably, in Cataluña Saint-Victor of Marseilles and Saint-Pons de Thomières each would develop a system of daughter houses that would parallel the local Cluniac network. Moreover, during this period the favorite monastery of Fernando I was Sahagún, the house of the very indigenous Iberian saints Facundus and Primitivus, and the place of his interment would be hard by at San Isidoro in León.

Roughly contemporary with the first known contacts with Cluny was the initiation of more regular ties between the Christian societies and the Roman church. In this regard, the response in Iberia was no different from the response of local churches everywhere in Western Europe. In fact, it was rather typical. If, almost as one, they were experiencing a new vigor and restlessness, what could be less surprising than that they should seek some direction from the patriarchate of Western Europe? It is sobering to realize, for example, that between A.D. 950 and 1050 there were known to be more pilgrims from Cataluña to Rome than from Cataluña to Santiago de Compostela. Again, as early as 993 Pope John XV was involved in the formation of a monastic federation which was to include Cuixa, Ripoll, and eventually Montserrat. Pope Clement II in 1047 was consulted about some of the affairs of the monastery of Oña in the Rioja. And 1054 the opponents of the marriage of Ramón Berenguer I of Barcelona and Almodis de la Marca considered it useful to approach Pope Victor II to secure the excommunication of the pair on the grounds of adultery.

This reaching out to a Rome never entirely unfamiliar would be conditioned by the special local concerns of each European Christian church, and the relationship finally achieved would be realised in each one of them in a somewhat different fashion. At the same time the response of Rome to their overtures would be a function of local developments in Rome itself. The 11th Century saw the rise in the Christian West of a party of reformers who were concerned with the regeneration of the morals, education, and practice of its members, clerical and lay. By 1046 the most significant of those reformers had managed to secure control of the bishopric of Rome and originated there what has subsequently come to be known as the Gregorian Reform.

That program took an organizational form. The reformers quickly came to the conclusion that the regeneration of the church depended upon its emancipation from lay control in the crucial matter of the selection of its own chief officers, that is, the bishops and abbots. To achieve that programmatic end, they systematically undertook to extend the authority of the Roman bishops from its already generally recognized magisterial preeminence into the more controversial arenas of judicial and executive supremacy. This enterprise resulted in a titanic struggle which fundamentally conditioned the directions of European history in many ways. For one, it resulted in the creation of the papacy as we now know it. This ideal had wide appeal throughout Western Europe, and local forces were often as eager to support it as they were at other times to oppose it. Nevertheless, Rome had its own agenda which often dictated the manner in which it responded to those local initiatives increasingly directed to it.

In Iberia that intellectual and organizational revolution came into contact with four major peninsular realities. In brief, these were the emergence of a new and most unstable political order which reacted at every moment upon the religious order there; a church in the Christian north which was an autochthonous growth largely subsequent to the Muslim conquest of the 8th Century, which had its own internal balances and its own distinctive Mozarabic liturgy; an incipient *Reconquista* of lands lost since the 8th Century to Islam whose recovery would pose the question of the nature of religious restoration there; and finally, the presence in those Muslim territories of a hitherto largely autonomous Mozarabic church which must then be integrated into both the political and religious order of the north. Nor were any of these realities susceptible of adjustment and rationalization without reference to the others.

Between 1065 and 1068 the first known papal legate visited Iberia. He was Hugh the White, a prominent member of the reform party at Rome.[19] Hugh seems to have traveled as far west as León and to

---

[19] Gerhard Säbekow, *Die päpstlichen Legationen nach Spanien und Portugal bis zum Ausgang des XII Jahrhunderts* (Berlin, 1931), is the surest guide. Purported earlier legations of 1039 and 1055 never took place.

have raised the question of the Mozarabic Rite with Fernando I. As a result, a commission of bishops was dispatched to Rome whose explanations apparently satisfied Pope Alexander II (1061–1073). Just why the legation should have been sent in 1065 is far from clear, but it may have been a natural complement to that ill-fated attack by a French expedition on Barbastro in 1064–1065 which had something of the aspect of a crusade. Alexander had been instrumental in organizing it. In fact, Roman interest in Iberia had been closely associated with the *Reconquista* from the very beginning. About ten years later the most outstanding of the papal reformers, Gregory VII (1073–1085), would also attempt, without success, to organize a French crusade into Iberia, led by Count Ebles of Roucy in Normandy.[20] Neither effort had a permanent effect upon the course of the *Reconquista*, but subsequent papal exhortations sometimes prompted substantial contributions.

The most concrete result of the legation of Hugh the White and the Barbastro expedition may have been the decision of Sancho Ramírez I of Aragón to visit Rome in 1068. While there Sancho surrendered his kingdom to the pope and received it back as a papal vassal.[21] At this point, Sancho was the least powerful of all of the Christian monarchs of northern Iberia, so one may assume that he thought the pope could be of some real help. It was, perhaps, not a coincidence that Count Ebles of Roucy was in 1073 Sancho's brother-in-law. But the recurring interest of Rome in the question of the Mozarabic Rite was illustrated again when Sancho Ramírez authorized the introduction of the Roman Rite in Aragón in 1070. This was not long after his return and probably represented a concession he had made while in Italy. The question of ritual would not arise in Cataluña, for practice there had long conformed rather to south French influences dating as far back as Carolingian times.

But even given these few departures, the Iberian church in the north about 1075 was still a traditional and local church in most respects, accustomed to recognize princely leadership in ecclesiastical matters and to suffer such aberrations and distortions as that influence might visit upon its religious life.[22] Yet the impulse to

---

[20] The fundamental work is José Goñi Gaztambide, *Historia de la Bula de la Cruzada en España* (Vitoria, 1958), but a useful consideration of the Spanish events against a wider background is Hans Eberhard Mayer, *The Crusades*, trans. John Gillingham (Oxford, 1972).

[21] Paul Kehr, "El papado y los reinos de Navarra y Aragón hasta mediados del siglo XII," *EEMCA* 2 (1946):74–186, is the best short study. It should be supplemented by Odilo Engels, "Papsttum, Reconquista, und spanisches Landeskonzil im Hochmittelalter," *AHC* 1 (1969):37–49 and 241–87.

[22] Andrés E. de Mañaricua, "Provisión de obispados en la Alta Edad Media española," *Estudios de Deusto* 14 (1966):61–92, is the most general illustration of the extent

reform, more staidly defined, was present in both king and episcopate. In 1055 Fernando I of León–Castilla held a great council of the realm and of its church at Coyanza, now Valencia de Don Juan, about 40 kilometers south of León. There king, queen, and prelates agreed upon and promulgated no less than thirteen canons directed toward the amelioration of conditions in the church of the realm. However, a consideration of their text reveals immediately that they took for granted the stucture and practices of the traditional Iberian church. There is no hint of the new conceptions and norms that would be the stuff of Roman reform thinking.[23]

The new ferment flowed, at least modestly, through the largely ecclesiastical channels of legates and canons, crusades and rites. Nonetheless, there were some secular avenues along which the novel and the non-Iberian found entrance. One of these was the readiness of its rulers to find brides from beyond the Pyrenees. As usual, we are uninformed as to the motives in particular cases, but two influences were predictably at work. Where all politics were dynastic politics, the search for a foreign bride had distinct advantages. A foreign bride increased the prestige of the dynasty in the eyes of its subjects. Also, the practice avoided giving too great influence to any one of its competing domestic families, thereby disappointing the expectations of the others. To this sort of internal consideration we should add that such unions could be a part of a larger scheme for securing foreign aid for Iberian projects. Both motivations were doubtless present in virtually all such unions. We are inclined to overemphasize the latter. But in an age when political leadership lacked almost all of the instrumentalities for projecting its power over any great distance, the former was probably more often the predominant factor. Irrespective of motive, for present purposes, these marriages would carry with them tastes, persons, and permanent links to the European world north of the mountains.

The practice was particularly congenial in Cataluña, perhaps because of its particularly close relationship with the French society of the Languedoc. So, for example, we see very early the marriage

and the routine character of such royal power. Some few examples exist in a more accessible form in Reilly, *Alfonso VI*, p. 98.

[23] There is no really adequate church history for this period. Francisco Javier Conde, ed., *Historia de la iglesia en España*, Vol. 2 (Madrid, 1982), is, in disappointing degree, a résumé of old scholarship and old conceptualizations. For the Council of Coyanza, see Alfonso García Gallo, "Las redacciónes de los decretos del concilio de Coyanza," *El concilio de Coyanza, miscelanea* (León, 1951), pp. 25–39, and the other articles in the same volume. Gonzalo Martínez Díez, "El concilio compostelano del reinado de Fernando I," *AEM* 1 (1964):121–38, is an important addition to the earlier findings.

of Count Ramón Borrell II (992–1017) to Ermesinda, daughter of Count Roger I of Carcassonne. Then, skipping a generation, is his grandson, Count Ramón Berenguer I (1035–1076), he of the famous marriage to Almodis de la Marca, former wife of the count of Toulouse. Ramón's first of three marriages was possibly to Isabel, daughter of Count Sancho of Gascony.

In Aragón, the line of Sancho el Mayor followed the same practice. Ramiro I (1035–1063), founder of the kingdom, married Giselberga who was a daughter of Count Roger Bernard of Couserans-Foix and of Countess Garsenda of Bigorre. In a second marriage he wed one Inés, whose parentage is unknown but whose name suggests a non-Iberian origin. Ramiro's son, Sancho Ramírez I (1063–1094), in a second marriage took to wife the sister of Count Ebles of Roucy in Normandy. The Navarrese line of Sancho el Mayor behaved much the same. His son, García Sánchez III (1035–1054), married Estefania, another daughter of Count Roger Bernard of Couserans-Foix and Garsenda of Bigorre. Sancho's grandson, Sancho García IV (1054–1076), wed another Frenchwoman, Placencia, whose full procedence is unknown.

In the westernmost kingdom of León-Castilla, the practice began late. It was only with a grandson of Sancho el Mayor, Sancho II of Castilla (1065–1072), that a foreign bride appears, and even then the record is singularly confused. His wife, Alberta by name, may have been a daughter of William the Conqueror of England. The name is certainly not Iberian. Moreover, it is entirely possible that his two brothers, García I of Galicia (1065–1071) and Alfonso VI of León, were rivals for her hand.[24] However that may be, after 1073 when he reunited his father's realm, Alfonso VI was to embark on a series of no fewer than six marriages. Five of his brides were drawn from beyond the peninsula. Here, as in so many other matters, Alfonso VI's reign marks the apogee of characteristics already observable in the earlier part of the century.

The other secular machinery to promise an eventual reorientation of Christian Iberia was that of trade. The growth of what was to be, by the end of the century, something like a French majority in the little Aragonese town of Jaca was due to its position at the foot of the Somport Pass. Over that path flowed not only the pilgrim traffic but also the merchant community in search of the marts of Muslim Zaragoza almost directly to the south. At some point it became more convenient to have a permanent establishment in Jaca for the exchange and trans-shipment of goods than to make the complete journey each time.

[24] See Reilly, *Alfonso VI*, pp. 45–48, for this most tangled affair.

The best example of this is Barcelona. From Narbonne in the north almost to Valencia in the south the valley of the Penedés formed a natural highway along which flowed the trade of Muslim and Frank. On that route, Barcelona was a natural resting place or point of exchange which would prompt the growth of some foreign settlement to facilitate those processes. And, of course, what was true of Barcelona was true as well, in lesser degree, of places like Vich, Urgel, Gerona, and Perpignan even later.

Yet Barcelona had the inestimable advantage of being a port. The Mediterranean would give it easier access than the land route to the south of France and to Italy. Before the end of the 11th Century this relationship with Italy was doubtless a passive one. While the city would have had its own fishing fleet, which could furnish some trade goods for consumption and trade with its hinterland, the mercantile fleets of the Muslim Balearics, Tortosa, and Valencia, along with those of Genoa and Pisa, dominated the eastern coast of Iberia. Ramón Berenguer I (1035–1076) is reported to have ordered the construction of a fleet. He must have implemented that resolve in some degree, for, we are told, his sons decided to maintain it. Nevertheless, that fleet is invisible in the history of the period and must have been diminutive indeed.

The 11th Century was precisely that period in which the spectacular emergence of the Italian city fleets of Genoa, Pisa, and Venice would throw both Muslim and Byzantine Mediterranean seafarers back on the defensive. In the western sea, Genoa and Pisa had already liberated Corsica and Sardinia from the Muslim by 1015. Within another decade they seemed able to make almost unhindered descents upon the African coast around Algeria. At the same time they were making themselves familiar at Barcelona, as at other ports of the northern shore of the Mediterranean. In the process, not only would they have facilitated the already-established custom of pilgrimage from Cataluña to Rome, they would also have developed trading contacts to draw Barcelona toward those eastern possibilities, which it was later to develop to such an extraordinary degree.

At the inception of the last quarter of the 11th Century, then, Christian Iberia was a strangely volatile society. Its trade, like its coinage, was marked by its dependence upon the world of the Muslim south. Its agriculture was quite progressive, but the instruments of its advance were also derived from that quarter. The very Christianity to which it adhered had been accustomed to defer to the south where its classical past and intellectual capital were to be found. Nevertheless, it possessed a political life both rawly new and in rapid ferment, conscious of its own strength and of the weaknesses of the traditionally dominant Muslim world which it everywhere abutted. At the same time Europe north of the Pyrenees was being stirred by much of the same excitement and experimentation. But the barrier of that mountain chain was always sufficiently porous to allow the strongest currents on either side to impinge on the other. Under these circumstances the question already had become, not whether or not northern Iberia would become more closely assimilated to Western European society, but the extent to which it would retain its more traditional character.

4

The Hegemony of León–Castilla under Alfonso VI (1065–1109)

After the assassination of his brother Sancho II under the walls of Zamora in October of 1072 and the imprisonment of his brother García in February of 1073, Alfonso VI swiftly moved to restore the hegemonic position León–Castilla had enjoyed in the peninsula at the death of his father, Fernando I, in 1065. The new king seems to have experienced no difficulty in securing the full allegiance of both the episcopate and the nobility of the provinces so recently independent under his brothers. Nevertheless, in the next two years he visited each one of them personally mending those fences that required it.

That done he could bring pressure upon the neighboring realms. In the spring of 1074 he seems to have already asserted his authority in the borderlands of Castilla, wooing the potent monastery of San Millán de La Cogolla and bringing a reluctant Sancho García IV of Navarra again to recognize the preeminence of León–Castilla.[1] Then, just to the south, lay the great taifa of Zaragoza under the energetic al-Muqtadir. In the spring of 1076 the latter took control of the taifa of Denia and then attempted, we are told, to purchase the permission of Alfonso VI for the conquest of Valencia.[2] Doubtless the reference is to *parias*, which may have been regarded as a simple bribe by al-Muqtadir who probably was making similar payments at this time to his ally, Sancho García IV of Navarra, and his opponent, Ramón Berenguer I of Barcelona. The wealth of the taifa was such that money could be a preferred instrument of diplomacy if necessary.

[1] Ramón Menéndez Pidal, *La España del Cid*, 2 vols. (Madrid, 4th ed., 1947), 1:206–09, believed that the two fought a brief border war, but the evidence is not persuasive.
[2] Afif Turk, *El reino de Zaragoza en el siglo XI de Cristo, V de la Hégira* (Madrid, 1978), pp. 109–17.

Still, the incident testifies to the recovery by León–Castilla of the *parias* of Zaragoza.

The *parias* of Toledo, customary since the time of Fernando I, had probably already been reclaimed by Alfonso by 1074. In the summer of that year the Leonese had mounted a great offensive in al-Andalus whose particular target was the taifa of Granada under its new king, Abd Allāh.[3] The campaign was extremely successful, and Granada now began the payment of *parias* to León–Castilla. In this effort Alfonso had been assisted by the troops of al-Mamūn, king of Toledo, and opposed by those of al-Mutamid, king of the taifa of Sevilla who had his own designs on Granada. The Toledan also had plans to seize the city of Córdoba, then in the possession of Sevilla. In January of 1075 Córdoba did indeed fall to al-Mamūn. The cooperation of Alfonso and the Toledan indicate the close rapport established between them at this time. This latter could only have been consequent upon the renewal of the Toledan *parias*.

One other initiative of Alfonso VI in this period should be reported. As early as June of 1074 a charter of Alfonso is confirmed by his wife and queen, Inés. The new queen was the daughter of Duke William VIII of Aquitaine; thus the Leonese claimed the first of his long succession of brides from beyond the Pyrenees. Duke William had had firsthand experience with Iberia when in 1064 he participated in the initially successful capture of Muslim Barbastro. Doubtless the major purpose of the marriage was, in addition to the always pressing necessity under the monarchy of providing male heirs to the throne, to enhance the prestige of the king by demonstrating the high regard in which he was held in foreign parts. Nevertheless, Alfonso may also have been mindful that the duke was the opponent, ordinarily, of the count of Armagnac and of the viscount of Bearn. These latter enjoyed cordial relations with Sancho Ramírez I of Aragón, but the marriage of Alfonso VI with their duke's daughter may have suggested to them the merit of limiting their possible cooperation with the Aragonese. The great monastery of Cluny may have been midwife to the marriage. The spring before Alfonso had made his first donation of a Leonese monastery to what was to become a long list of such holdings of the Cluniacs in the peninsula.[4]

[3] The campaign and its outcome are described in the autobiography of that king. Abd Allāh, *El siglo XI en 1ᵃ persona; Las "Memorias" de Abd Allāh, ultimo rey Zirī de Granada destronado por los Almorávides (1090)*, trans. Évariste Lévi-Provençal and Emilio García Gomez (Madrid, 1980), pp. 153–62.

[4] For particulars and additional possible dimensions in this regard, see Bernard F. Reilly, *The Kingdom of León–Castilla under King Alfonso VI, 1065–1109* (Princeton, N.J., 1988), pp. 79–82.

The Annexation of La Rioja

In the spring of 1076 the position of Alfonso VI, king of León–Castilla, may already be fairly described as imperial. His realm, about the size of England, comprised some 128,000 square kilometers. In extent alone it dwarfed every other monarchy in the peninsula, Muslim or Christian. For what it was worth, León also exercised suzerainty over the kingdom of Navarra, the next most puissant of the tiny remaining Christian realms of the north. More important by far, the king of the Leonese held in tribute the Muslim taifas of Zaragoza, Toledo, and Granada. The annual *parias* of the latter alone amounted to 10,000 gold dinars on the testimony of its king himself. In 1069 al-Muqtadir of Zaragoza had agreed to pay 12,000 annually to Navarra for its friendship. It is unlikely that Alfonso VI exacted less. The sum required of Toledo would have been comparable. Although the taifas of Badajoz and Sevilla thus far eluded his attentions, the approximately 30,000 dinars collected annually by Alfonso allowed him to field the most formidable army in the peninsula, as subsequent events would demonstrate. Yet he was, unknowing, on the eve of still another major addition to his kingdom.

That spring the king was in the vicinity of Burgos actually preparing a military expedition to Andalucía. Al-Mamūn, the taifa king of Toledo, had been assassinated the previous June in the city of Córdoba which he had so recently gained. The death of Alfonso's ally had been immediately utilized by al-Mutamid of Sevilla to reclaim Córdoba and some of the adjoining southerly reaches of the taifa of Toledo. In Valencia, Abū Bakr had seized that occasion to declare himself independent of Toledo. Of necessity these developments must concern Alfonso almost as much as the young al-Qādir, son and successor of al-Mamūn. It is possible that during his exile in Toledo in 1072 the Leonese had, already, formed an opinion of that hapless heir, who would prove totally unable to master the problems which would now confront him. But even if Alfonso had not, he could scarcely expect to do less than aid his ally in the combined crises of succession, revolt, and invasion. The indications are that he was preparing to do just that when diverted by an unparalleled opportunity closer to home.

On June 4, 1076, in one of the more spectacular assassinations of the 11th Century, King Sáncho García IV of Navarra was pushed from a cliff at Peñalén. The deed seems to have been perpetrated by his own older brother and sister and may have resulted from some obscure family dispute. Although it has been asserted that they intended to replace him on the throne, it is difficult to imagine that a conspiracy so executed could have had any reasonable chance of success. In any event, the brother, Ramón, fled to Zaragoza, there to become a pensioner of al-Muqtadir. The sister, Ermesinda, passed into the custody of Alfonso VI, who arranged her marriage to a noble Navarrese. Two other siblings, a younger sister, Urraca, and a younger brother, Ramíro, also became wards of Alfonso. The first he eventually married off to the Castilian noble García Ordóñez.

Given the distance and terrain involved, the Leonese monarch probably received the news of the tragedy about mid-June. The murdered king was, of course, not merely his subject in some sense but his cousin as well. If he set out for the Rioja as soon as that new course of action could be agreed upon, he could have reached the favorite royal residence of the Navarrese kings at Nájera by about June 25. That would have been the obvious place to begin to arrange the recognition of his annexation of most of the former possessions of Sancho. He did confirm the *fuero* of Nájera, probably at this time, but the document is dated only to the year 1076.

This and other contemporary documents reveal the impressive entourage which surrounded the king. The new queen Inés was there along with the bishop of Santiago de Compostela. León was represented by Count Pedro Ansúrez and Castilla by the brothers of the Lara family, Gonzalvo and Salvador, by Vermudo Gutiérrez, and by the royal *merino* Martín Sánchez. Finally there were the Castilian magnate Diego Alvarez of Oca and his brother-in-law Lop Jiménez of the comital house of Alava and Vizcaya. Jimeno López, the latter's father, held the tenancy of Nájera itself as well as that of Vizcaya and Alava. The Leonese party was thus so strong as to be practically irresistible. Nevertheless, the king tarried at Nájera for the inevitable negotiations preliminary to the general submission of the bishops and nobles of the realm.

The Aragonese king, Sancho Ramírez I, reacted to the murder of the Navarrese monarch by seizing Pamplona and the countryside around it. Therefore, when the two monarchs, or at least their agents, met in late July, a treaty of partition of the kingdom of Navarra was arranged. Sancho Ramírez was to receive only the old heartland around Pamplona, reaching southwest as far as Estella. Even then, he was to agree to do homage for it to the king of León. To Alfonso went the entire middle Ebro down to Calahorra, that is, La Rioja and the lands to the east of that great river up to their mountainous borders. To him as well went the old Navarrese hegemony over the still wild Basque provinces Alava, Vizcaya, and

Guipúzcoa.[5] There seems to have been no serious resistance to any of this, and, even though the two cousins profited greatly from the demise of the third, neither contemporaries nor subsequent historians seem to suggest the possibility of their implication in the latter's assassination. By August the matter was so far closed that Alfonso VI should already have returned to Castilla.

The annexation of the Rioja by León–Castilla added about another 4,000 square kilometers of some of the most fertile farmland in the peninsula to that kingdom. Most of it would be retained permanently. More important in the long run were the unforeseeable results associated with it. For the next fifty-eight years the kingdom of Navarra would disappear from the politics of Iberia. In 1134 it would reemerge as the kingdom of Pamplona, whose role would be indeed modest in the future. The Rioja had become Castilian, and the path of Navarra south toward the plain of Zaragoza was blocked forever. In addition, that tutelege over the Basque territories which Navarra had exercised would now be assumed by León–Castilla. Thereby, even the more modest role that the former kingdom might have played as the leader of a Basque federation, for which it was fitted by both linguistic and geographic affinity, was denied to it by the new hegemony of Alfonso VI and his successors there.

Yet even the near future was to demonstrate the limitations of the triumph of León–Castilla in 1076. If the first dispositions awarded the entire east bank of the Ebro to it, those territories soon proved impossible to defend against Aragón which controlled the mountains to the east and northeast of them. Even though he had had to do homage for it, the possession of Pamplona made Sancho Ramírez I and his heirs players in the frontier politics of the Ebro. Bit by bit Alfonso VI would become as unhappily aware as al-Muqtadir of Zaragoza himself of the difficulties of holding a stable position when a mobile opponent commands the heights about it. But the gradual appropriation of those lands along the Ebro by Aragón would position it for a much greater triumph. In 1118 those territories would furnish part of the springboard for the attack which would deliver the great city and taifa of Zaragoza itself into Aragonese hands. That audacious conquest would double the size of the kingdom of Aragón and vault it almost overnight into a position of the second Christian realm of Iberia, the only real counterweight to León–Castilla in the Christian north. Such it was to remain until the marriage of Fernando and Isabel in 1469.

[5] A more detailed account may be had in Reilly, *Alfonso VI*, pp. 87–92. The terms of the final settlement are defined by Antonio Ubieto Arteta, "Homenaje de Aragón a Castilla por el condado de Navarra," *EEMCA* 3 (1947–48):1–22.

The Repopulation of the Trans-Duero: The Reconquest of Toledo

Alfonso VI was nevertheless, like most of us, blissfully unaware of what were to be the final results of that train of events. In the late summer and fall of 1076 he was already near Sepúlveda, south of the Duero, where two charters give evidence of his initiation of the repopulation there. The king was now to begin reaping the benefits of the work of his father, Fernando I. That monarch had created the political conditions necessary for the annexation of the 50,000-square-kilometer trans-Duero. His son was to incorporate that vast territory into the realm.

The beginning at Sepúlveda is easy to understand. It perhaps had some semipermanent population already. The village, perched above the junction of the Castilla and Duratón rivers, was easy to defend. It could be readily reinforced, if necessary, for the Duratón ran down to the royal fortress of Peñafiel on the Duero only 45 kilometers to the northwest. Just 25 kilometers to its southeast lay the 1,440-meter pass of Somosierra which led over the Guadarrama Mountains to the lands of the taifa of Toledo. The strategic position of Sepúlveda at the eastern edge of the trans-Duero is therefore clear.

Bishop Pelayo of Oviedo, a figure in Alfonso's court and eventually his historian, credits the king with the repopulation of Avila, Salamanca, Segovia, Cuéllar, Coca, Arévalo, Olmedo, Medina del Campo, and Iscar.[6] The first three of these lay too far to the south for their settlement to be feasible in 1076 or even soon thereafter. For none of these foundations does the good bishop give a date. However, I believe that Alfonso was busy about some of them again in 1078. Cuéllar, Fuente el Olmo de Iscar, Coca, Olmedo, and Medina del Campo form a rough wedge from 20 to 40 kilometers deep to the south of the Duero at about the midpoint of that river as it flows toward the mountains of Portugal in the west. Not only could such foundations reinforce one another if necessary but one or all could also be succored without too much difficulty from a number of established fortresses along the Duero to the north. From west to east, these are Tordesillas, Valladolid, and Peñafiel. If Arévalo, which is some 50 kilometers south of the Duero, was also resettled at this time, then the repopulation of Salamanca, Avila, and Segovia would have been moved a long step toward feasibility. That would be a natural progression once these earlier settlements reached some degree of maturity.

But such a gradual peopling of the lands south of the Duero with

[6] Benito Sánchez Alonso, ed., *Crónica del Obispo Don Pelayo* (Madrid, 1924), p. 81.

the burgeoning population of León–Castilla, under the aegis of the crown and all the while sheltered by a buffer of Muslim tributaries still farther south, was not destined to be. Instead, the always unstable world of the taifas of al-Andalus was to erupt in 1078. One of the major actors was al-Mutamid of Sevilla who in that year extended his control over the taifa of Denia on the Mediterranean south of Valencia. For the moment he was master of territories which stretched from the Atlantic up the valley of the Guadalquivir and across the gap at Albacete and down to the coast. They also reached some considerable distance northward into La Mancha and lands traditionally subject to Toledo. Then, late in 1078 or early in 1079, a revolt took place in Toledo against al-Qādir, a king who had let first Córdoba and then Valencia slip away while he paid court to the detested Christians of the north. Al-Qādir fled east, first to Huete and later to Cuenca, and appealed to Alfonso VI for assistance in regaining his throne. In the meanwhile the conspirators had recognized al-Mutawakkil, taifa king of Badajoz, as their sovereign and had introduced his forces into the city of Toledo.

By April of 1079 the Leonese monarch was already in the field shoring up his beleaguered ally. While the king led a force which blocked reinforcements for Toledo by taking up a position on the Río Guadarrama some 12 kilometers west of Toledo, other forces were also besieging Coria far to the west. That town's strategic importance lay in the fact that it closed the gap between the western end of the Guadarrama Mountains and the mountains of Portugal that gave access from the trans-Duero to the lands of Badajoz, or the reverse. By September Coria had fallen to Alfonso's forces, and he could mount a credible threat to the territories of Badajoz in the lower Tajo basin.

Simultaneously, al-Mutawakkil found himself threatened by an alliance between al-Mutamid of Sevilla and Alfonso VI. The latter had sent the Cid south to negotiate, for the Sevillan was clearly the best makeweight against the king of Badajoz. In a thoroughly confused melee, even the kingdom of Granada became involved, and, at one point, an ambassador of Alfonso to the latter was in the field against the Cid and Sevilla. The combination of threats was sufficient, however, to convince al-Mutawakkil that the game was hardly worth the candle. He withdrew from Toledo, the revolt there collapsed, and al-Qādir was able to return.[7]

---

[7] The sources for these events are quite difficult and have been interpreted differently. For the account given here, see Reilly, *Alfonso VI*, pp. 124–26. Ambrosio Huici Miranda, *Historia musulmana de Valencia y su región*, 3 vols. (Valencia, 1969–70), 1:200, is largely in agreement with it. José Miranda Calvo, *La reconquista de Toledo*

For all of this assistance al-Qādir must pay a price. According to the Pact of Cuenca, he was compelled to admit the permanent stationing of two Leonese garrisons within his territories and to assume the costs of their maintenance. These forces were placed at Zorita some 110 kilometers northeast of Toledo and at Cantuarias roughly 70 kilometers west of that city. The possession of the two strongholds gave Alfonso VI the ability to block access to the lands of his ally either by the armies of the latter's enemies in Valencia and Zaragoza to the northeast and east or by the army of Badajoz from the west. In brief, by 1080 the Leonese monarch had assumed the responsibility for maintaining the territorial integrity of the taifa of Toledo against external attack. A stable, friendly Toledo was essential to the progressive opening and settlement of the transDuero, and the events of 1079 had demonstrated to Alfonso the inability of al-Qādir to master the combination of internal and external enemies out of his own resources.

Yet, however much such a policy of limited intervention in the affairs of his tributary might have to recommend it, that action would itself have consequences which ultimately would require still further involvement on the part of the Leonese monarch. If al-Qādir's subjects were already restless because of the payment of tribute to, and cooperation with, León, how much more would they resent the new Christian garrisons and the expense of supporting them. Indeed, a new revolt did break out in May of 1082, but it failed in the capital and the rebels were pursued and besieged in Madrid and finally defeated there by al-Qādir. This episode may have finally convinced Alfonso that nothing less than outright annexation of Toledo was feasible. Even though al-Qādir not require his assistance on this occasion, he was still demonstrably less than fully in command of his own people. In the long run, Alfonso's own direct and strong rule might prove more effective and even more economical.

Anything less than outright annexation was incomprehensible to his own subjects as well. In 1080 when the king was active in the west in support of his Toledan ally a band of Muslim from the vicinity of Medinaceli had staged a raid on the fortress and settlement of San Esteban de Gormaz in the upper valley of the Duero. One of Alfonso's nobles, Rodrigo Díaz de Vivar, *el Cid*, had seized the opportunity to conduct a counter-raid deep into the lands of al-Qādir. As a result, the king found it necessary to discipline one of

por Alfonso VI (Toledo, 1980), relates all these and other events to a fixed design of Alfonso to conquer Toledo itself. I believe that it is simply too early for that project to have appeared either practical or necessary to the king.

his own nobles. To do otherwise would raise the question among the taifas of the ability of their overlord to protect them and hence the very utility of paying *parias*. At the same time, to ignore the raid of *el Cid* would be to encourage the same sort of recklessness on the part of the rest of his fractious petty nobility. The king did the only thing he could. Sometime in late 1080 or early in 1081 Rodrigo Díaz de Vivar was sent into a fateful exile in eastern Iberia.

To say that the possession of Toledo became the central contest between Muslim and Christian in the peninsula for the next fifty years is to underscore the obvious. In view of the conquest of the city in 1085 by Alfonso VI, later Christian historians would make that the objective of his policy from as early as 1078. That opinion is hard to correlate with his observable activities during those years, but it possessed the charm of the number seven in years and early found its way into the accepted histories. Although absent from Bishop Pelayo's chronicle in the first half of the 12th Century, it did appear in the *Cronica Nájerense* in the latter part of the same century. By then it may have been based upon the interpolated charter of Alfonso VI to the cathedral of Toledo of 1086. By the 13th Century one finds it in Muslim histories as well.[8] When it was made, however, this decision, and even more its accomplishment, was to make the Leonese monarch the great enemy, the great villain, of subsequent Muslim historians. That must be kept in mind constantly when evaluating their testimony.

Sometime in late 1082 or early 1083, according to the 17th-century Muslim historian, al-Maqqarī, drawing on a now lost source, Alfonso sent an embassy to al-Mutamid of Sevilla. Reputedly, Ibn Shalib, the Jewish counsellor who led the embassy, demanded the entire wealth of the taifa for his master, rather than just the usual *parias*. Instead of acquiescing, the Sevillan executed Alfonso's ambassador and imprisoned the escort, later releasing the latter at the demand of the Leonese. The Muslim leader then crossed into North Africa to seek the assistance of the new Murābit power there for the struggle in Spain. The Murābit leader, Yūsuf ibn Tāshufīn, was at the time besieging the port of Ceuta and would not make a commitment until it had fallen.[9]

Some elements of the story are inherently unlikely. The demand for the entire wealth of the taifa is clear hyperbole designed to point up the overweening arrogance of the Christian leader. Still, a failed

---

[8] Antonio Ubieto Arteta, ed., *Crónica Nájerense* (Valencia, 1966), p. 116.
[9] Al-Maqqarī, *The History of the Mohammedan Dynasties in Spain*, trans. Pascual de Gayangos, 2 vols., 1840–43, Reprint (New York, 1964), 2:252–53.

Plate 3   The *Aljafería* of Zaragoza

embassy to Sevilla during the winter of 1082–1083 is quite probable if Alfonso had then decided upon the annexation of Toledo. An agreement to assure the neutrality, of the powerful Sevillan king, perhaps in return for the cession of some of the more southern portions of the Toledan territories, would have been a reasonable gambit. However, it seems more likely that al-Mutamid understandably preferred not to become the immediate neighbor of Alfonso and refused.

The next step of the Leonese monarch was permitted by events in the great northeastern taifa of Zaragoza. When, in 1082, the able al-Muqtadir sickened and died, a wild scramble ensued between his heirs and his neighbors in Aragón and Barcelona for all possible advantages. In the midst of this melee the Muslim castellan of Rota on the Leonese–Castilian border in the west decided to raise the standard of al-Muzaffar, the brother of the deceased al-Muqtadir, whose warder he had previously been. Alfonso VI was offered the castle of Rota, Rueda de Jalón, in return for his support. Before the Leonese could reach that fortress, however, al-Muzaffar had in turn died himself. The castellan decided to repair his fortunes with al-Mutamin of Zaragoza and hence planned an ambush instead for the

Christians. Alfonso himself was not involved, but his cousin, the *infante* Ramiro of Navarra, and the Lara count, Gonzalo Salvadorez, were set upon and killed when they entered that castle to receive its surrender on January 6, 1083.[10] The king had to retire, bilked of his object, but the new weakness of Zaragoza in the east left him entirely free to act in the south.

In the summer of 1083 Alfonso VI led a major invasion of the territories of al-Mutamid. In the course of it, the Christian army lay for three days before the city of Sevilla itself before going on to the Mediterranean at Tarifa, where the king rode his horse into the surf as a symbol of his mastery of Iberia. This great raid was intended to overawe al-Andalus and Muslim Spain generally and to prevent any interference with the subsequent campaign against Toledo. It was probably after this raid that the Sevillan, al-Mutamid, decided to ask the Murābit to intervene. Certainly the former sent naval forces to aid in the siege of Ceuta, which fell to Yūsuf in August or September of 1083. The road was now open to an invasion from Africa. Alfonso VI must have been aware of the danger from this quarter, but he may well have underestimated the abilities of the Africans to operate effectively so far from their base, or their intention to do so given the chronic instability of those territories in North Africa which they had so recently overrun.

In the fall of the following year the Leonese king set up a camp to the south of Toledo ot begin a formal siege. It was maintained throughout the winter and served to both iterdict the movement of supplies into that city and make impossible the planting of crops in those territories except on the occupiers' terms. There is no record of any impassioned resistance or pitched battles. The king himself spent the winter in his regular haunts around León and Sahagún in the north. Only in late February of 1085 did he begin to move south, traversing the Guadarramas by the long and low pass of Arrebatacapas southeast of Avila. The army could hardly have reached Toledo before the middle of March. On May 25, 1085, Alfonso would make a triumphal entry into the city.

In none of this is there evidence of significant engagements or protracted siegework. The garrison was extended the usual courtesy of appeal to possible sources of assistance among the other taifas, but none was forthcoming. Doubtless Alfonso had brought with him a large enough army and retinue to overawe any possible opposition and to provide sufficient reason for a plausible decision to surrender

---

[10] The date occurs in a document dated January 18, 1083, AHN, Codices, 989B, fol. 94v. The literary account is given in "Historia Roderici," in Ramón Menéndez Pidal, ed., *La España del Cid*, 2 vols. (Madrid, 4th ed., 1947), 2:927–28.

on the part of al-Qādir. One suspects that most of it was concerted in advance.

Now master of the city and the taifa, the Leonese monarch was prepared to be generous. A new kingdom was to be found for al-Qādir in the form of the kingdom of Valencia, formerly part of the Toledan lands, and that worthy moved some 160 kilometers east to Cuenca to await the fulfillment of that promise. The Muslims were assured of the continued possession of their lives, and property, and the free exercise of their religion under their own leaders on the condition that they annually pay a special tax to the king whose wards they now became. These conditions mirrored those usual for Christians under Muslim sway and for Muslim subject populations in all the Iberian Christian kingdoms at the time. Those Muslim who wished to leave were free to do so and could take their moveable property with them. The central mosque of Toledo continued in Muslim hands, but the implication is that the other mosques of the taifa and their endowments passed into the hands of Alfonso, as did the personal property of al-Qādir.

The city itself was terribly important to the Leonese king. At the time of its conquest it had a thriving economy, and its population of about 28,000 exceeded the combined populations of all of the major towns of his own realm. Therefore, although we have no contemporary evidence for the conclusion of agreements with the Mozarabs, who probably constituted 15 to 25 percent of its inhabitants, or with the Jews, who made up something like another 15 percent, similar terms were surely worked out.[11] Jews elsewhere in the realm had a position strictly equivalent to that now guaranteed the Muslim of Toledo. Subsequent testimony indicates no distinction of circumstances for the Jews of Toledo. The Mozarabs were Christians, of course, but since León–Castilla had recently adopted the Roman Rite for liturgical purposes, they had to be guaranteed the continued use of the old Mozarabic Rite. Again, subsequent evidence indicates that they were, and indeed they long maintained some six churches in the city dedicated to such usages.[12]

These conditions were intended, in all likelihood, to be applicable

[11] I rely upon Josiah Cox Russell, *Medieval Regions and Their Cities* (Bloomington, Ind., 1972), pp. 187–88. The standard work on the Jews is still Yitzhak Baer, *Historia de los judios en la España cristiana*, trans. José Luis Lacave (Madrid, 1981). The above estimate is based upon the more recent Eliyahu Ashtor, *The Jews of Moslem Spain*, trans. Aaron Klein and Jenny Machlowitz Klein, 2 vols., 1966, Reprint (Philadelphia, 1973–79), 1:223.

[12] On the subject of the Mozarabic Rite, see Ramón Gonzálvez, "The Persistence of the Mozarabic Liturgy in Toledo after 1080 A.D.," in Bernard F. Reilly, ed., *Santiago, St.-Denis, and Saint Peter* (New York, 1985), pp. 157–85.

to the entire territory of the taifa, but the ability of the king to enforce them was inversely proportional to the distance from the city itself. Traditionally, the victors expect at least some of the spoils, and there was an army and its inevitable adventurers who must be appeased. The lands and houses of those Muslim who chose to depart, despite the royal guarantees, would have provided for some of these. Departure must have been not too subtly encouraged. And forced sales were probably also imposed on Jews and Mozarabs although in lesser proportion, particularly those at some remove from the city where appeal to the crown was more difficult. In any event, there would shortly come to be a sizeable number of Castilians, Leonese, Asturians, Galicians, and even French in the city.

Of the extended territories of the taifa stretching east to the Sierra de Albarracín, north to the Guadarramas, west down the valley of the Tajo, and southwest to the Sierra Morena, some would continue to be held over the next twenty-five years and some would not. It was, after all, another kingdom whose extent approximated some 90,000 square kilometers no matter how it is estimated. The king spent the summer of 1085 visiting and pacifying it as best he could, and his efforts, if not his control, came to reach as far to the southwest as Albacete, 200 kilometers southeast of Toledo. It did not include the *campo* of Calatrava, however, whose castle remained in the hands of al-Mutamid of Sevilla.

The Murābit Invasion

The following winter Alfonso spent in and around León, planning the reorganization of the new territories. Of necessity these plans involved the taifa of Zaragoza. In January of 1085 al-Mutamin had married his son and heir, al-Mustain, to the daughter of the taifa king, Abū Bakr, of Valencia, in an elaborate and public ceremony. Invitations were widely distributed in all of al-Andalus. Clearly, what was being coordinated, beyond the marriage itself, was a drawing together of all of Muslim Spain against Alfonso VI in the face of the latter's plain intention to annex Toledo. More might have come of this alliance had it not been followed almost immediately by the death of Abū Bakr of Valencia and then al-Mutamin in 1085.

What did result was a siege of Zaragoza in the spring of 1086 by the Leonese king. The Muslim sources allege the motive to be the conquest of that taifa, and use it to demonstrate the necessity of calling in the Murābits from North Africa, given the insatiable appetite of Alfonso for conquest. The 13th-century *Primera crónica general* has followed these Muslim accounts, and, in the 20th Century, so has Menéndez Pidal.[13] Still, the motive itself is incredible. The siege can be understood in terms that are much more credible, if less satisfying for literary purposes: Alfonso VI undertook it to compel the renewal of the *parias*, whose payment had been suspended at the beginning of the previous year, and to tie down Zaragoza while the simultaneous reduction of the Valencian taifa and the installation in it of his ally, al-Qādir, was in process. Nevertheless, precisely because it gave his enemies the perfect opportunity to misrepresent and caricature him, the wisdom of the operation can be questioned.

Sometime in early March of 1086, al-Qādir did indeed become king of Valencia. His appearance before the city, together with the troops of Alfonso's commander, Alvar Fáñez, led to its quick surrender. However, the important city of Játiva 60 kilometers to the south refused to recognize him and appealed to the taifa king, Mundir, of Lérida and Tortosa for assistance. Mundir responded with an invasion of Valencia and a brief siege in 1086. He was finally forced to withdraw by Alvar Fáñez's troops and Játiva in turn surrendered. Nonetheless, the episode reveals the difficulties that faced Alfonso VI's even limited objectives in the east of the peninsula. At this same time he was attempting to find a substantial boundary to his new Toledan territories in the south. The fortress of Aledo, 45 kilometers southwest of Murcia and 55 kilometers northeast of Cartagena, drove a wedge between Murcia and its sister kingdoms in Andalucía proper.

Now all of this activity is understandable in light of the circumstances in which Alfonso VI found himself at the beginning of 1086. However, his neighbors and rivals in Andalucía viewed them in the context of the abrupt disappearance of one of the greatest Muslim taifas in Iberia. No Christian success of these dimensions had occurred in the entire history of Islam in Iberia since the Carolingian liberation of Cataluña at the beginning of the 9th Century. Moreover, unlike even the Carolingian success, Alfonso VI's annexation of Toledo had created a León–Castilla whose bulk of 270,000 square kilometers made it more than twice the size of the kingdom of England and whose central position would make it a participant in the political calculations of every realm in the peninsula. Even though the cultured Muslim ruling classes of Andalucía had no particular liking for the rough, reformist Murābit of North Africa,

---

[13] Menéndez Pidal, ed., *La España del Cid*, 1:300–01. Turk, *El reino de Zaragoza*, pp. 149–52, has corrected his chronology.

they would prefer them to the continuance of the position of hegemony which León–Castilla had now clearly established.

At any rate, the Murābit landed at Algeciras on July 30, 1086,
while the army of Alfonso VI still lay before Zaragoza. After secur-
ing Algeciras as a base, Yūsuf advanced to Sevilla where he issued a
call to all of Spanish Islam to join him in a war against the king of
León–Castilla. The response was not reassuring. In the northeast of
Iberia al-Mustain of Zaragoza and his uncle, Mundir, of Lérida and
Tortosa, could or would not join him. Al-Qādir of Valencia remained loyal to his Christian ally. Almería sent no help, nor does
Murcia seem to have done so. When the Murābit commander left
Sevilla, he was accompanied only by the troops of al-Mutamid of
Sevilla. At Jerez de los Caballeros they were joined by the contingent
from Granada under the command of its king, Abd Allāh, who will
write the only eyewitness account of the ensuing battle. Something
like two and a half months after landing in Iberia Yūsuf ibn Tāshufin
reached Badajoz. There that taifa's king, al-Mutawakkil, joined the
alliance, and indeed the choice of that route north may have been
made precisely to compel him to do so. In any event, Yūsuf
advanced no further.

Alfonso learned of the landing at the beginning of September. He
must then have struck camp in the face of an undefeated foe, shipped
his wounded home, and sent messengers to all points to rally troops.
Most of those who joined him now would have come by way of
Coria so as to effect a juncture with the king before he entered
enemy territory. The king and the remainder of his field army
proceeded directly from Zaragoza to Toledo, arriving there about the
end of the third week in September.[14] Here the king was joined by
Alvar Fáñez and his troops, recalled from Valencia. An Aragonese
force, perhaps led by the *Infante* Pedro, son of his vassal Sancho
Ramírez I, also appeared. Other reinforcements concentrated at
Coria and met the king as he marched east down the valley of the
Tajo. Approximately south of Coria, Alfonso struck south from the
river and past Cáceres descending into the valley of the Guadiana
not far from Badajoz. He must have been there by October 20.

To the battle which took place on October 23, 1086, at Zalaca just
north of Badajoz, Alfonso brought an army that numbered about
2,500 men if he had managed to muster and was willing to commit

[14] For a more detailed account of the campaign and of the calculations used to
determine travel times and numbers involved, see Reilly, *Alfonso VI*, pp. 180–90. In
both that account and the one presented here I also draw heavily upon Ambrosio
Huici Miranda, *Las grandes batallas de la Reconquista durante las invasiones africanas* (Madrid, 1956), pp. 19–82.

about half of the military force of his entire kingdom. Of these, only about 750 would have been heavy cavalry, with another 750 lighter, less experienced cavalry in reserve, and about 1,000 foot soldiers of all description. It was a small enough force, and Yūsuf's army likely outnumbered it about three to one, although our ability to calculate numbers on the Muslim side is even more limited. Despite that fact, and the fact that the battle was to take place in enemy territory, the Leonese monarch attacked, counting on the ability of his heavy cavalry to break up the enemy formations and give him a quick victory. After some initial success against the Andalucian contingents, however, Alfonso found himself being pressed back. By this time his camp had been overrun and his main force was in danger of being enveloped by the numerically superior enemy. He therefore tried to break off the engagement, and a running fight developed as the Christian force retired, which seems to have lasted until nightfall. Sometime during the battle the king himself was wounded in the calf, giving him a bone scar which would still be discoverable 900 years later.[15] The survivors managed to retreat to Coria some 125 kilometers to the northeast. Alfonso retired to Toledo and prepared it for possible attack and siege. He had lost half his field army, but his position was still strong and so he would make the most of it, as always. Yūsuf estimated things in the same light, and so retired first to Sevilla and then to North Africa.

Nevertheless, the victory of the Murābit at Zalaca set the conditions which were to dominate the politics of the peninsula for the next thirty years. Theirs was to be the initiative, and the role of León–Castilla, as the most powerful Christian kingdom and the primary target of a series of Muslim offensives, was to conduct a stubborn defense which should yield as little as possible to the new foe. The prime objective of the Murābit was the recovery of the taifa of Toledo, whose fall had so profoundly altered the balance between Christian and Muslim in the peninsula. That they failed in that ambition was fateful. Still, the territories of Toledo were sometimes reduced almost to the beleaguered city itself. Even when the Murābit Empire crumbled in the next century, Toledo long remained the forward bastion and military staging ground of León–Castilla rather than its center or capital.

Alfonso VI appealed to Western Europe for help when he learned of the Murābit invasion, and a major French expedition arrived in Iberia during the winter of 1087. It settled down to an unsuccessful

---

[15] Elías Gago and Juan Eloy Díaz-Jiménez, "Los restos mortales de Alfonso VI y de sus cuatro mujeres," *BRAH* 58 (1911):43–47.

siege of Tudela, the forward position of Zaragoza, in the spring before breaking up and going home. The event is memorable chiefly for the diplomacy that accompanied it. One must understand that at this time Alfonso VI was fifty years old and had no male heir after fourteen years of marriage. A first marriage in 1074 to Inés, daughter of Duke William VIII of Aquitaine, had been dissolved in 1077, probably for that reason. In 1079 he married Constance, sister of Duke Eudes I of Burgundy, who by 1080 had given birth to a daughter, Urraca, who was to prove the only issue of that union to survive. Even the birth of Urraca may have been accompanied by complications, which made further live births problematic. In any event, in 1081 the king had taken a concubine, Jimena Múñoz. This daughter of a magnate of the Bierzo was to give him two more daughters, Elvira and Teresa, but no sons.

Now when Duke Eudes of Burgundy visited León and his cousin, Queen Constance, after the siege, he was accompanied by two of her nephews, Raymond and Henry of Burgundy. Raymond was to be betrothed to Urraca in 1087 and probably designated as future heir of the realm. Henry was somewhat later married to Teresa. It may also be that Elvira was betrothed to Count Raymond IV of Toulouse at this time, although it is not clear that he was actually at Tudela. By 1094 he was already married to her.[16] Also at Tudela, Sancho Ramírez I of Aragón had done homage to Alfonso VI, promised to aid in the future defense of Toledo, and secured a new definition of his border with León–Castilla along the middle Ebro. If he did not realize much in the way of military assistance – Counts Raymond and Henry seem to have had no substantial following – he at least bolstered his damaged prestige and perhaps secured promises for the future.

Fortunately, the Murābit did not return to Iberia that year. Instead, the king had to deal with revolt in Galicia. Sometime that spring Santiago de Compostela and Lugo were briefly in the hands of rebels, led by the bishop of the former city and Count Rodrigo Ovéquez, whose family dominated around the latter. The only possible object of the revolt was to free Alfonso's brother, García, imprisoned in the castle of Luna in northwestern León since 1073. Otherwise the cause of the rebels was hopeless from the first, for they were not formidable in themselves. García, it seems, had been once betrothed to a daughter of William the Conqueror of England, and the plotters may have alleged that aid would be forthcoming

---

[16] John H. Hill and Laurita L. Hill, *Raymond IV de Saint-Gilles* (Toulouse, 1959), p. 19.

from that quarter. At least subsequently, Bishop Diego Peláez of Compostela, who had been made bishop by García when the latter had ruled Galicia, was to be deposed on grounds of having planned to betray the realm to William I.[17]

The revolt was quickly put down by the king. Count Rodrigo fled into exile. Bishop Diego Peláez was deposed at the Council of Husillos in 1088. Alfonso visited Galicia, installing Count Raymond of Galicia as his viceroy in that province and a new bishop in Santiago de Compostela, drawn from the distant Castilian monastery of Cardeña.

A Most Stubborn Defense

That same year Yūsuf ibn Tāshufīn came again to al-Andalus and attempted to reduce the fortress of Aledo, without success. The following year he was occupied in North Africa, and Alfonso wooed the taifas, offering to defend their independence in return for their *parias*. But in 1090 the Murābit emir returned and led an army north to Toledo itself in the depth of summer. The Leonese monarch summoned Sancho Ramírez I of Aragón to his side and advanced slowly, counting on the heat and the exhaustion of the enemy to do his work. Yūsuf did withdraw and marched south, taking the taifa of Granada instead in September. Shortly thereafter he overran the taifa of Málaga as well and both kings were exiled to Morocco. In no one of his three expeditions to Iberia had he enjoyed the full cooperation of the Andalucians. Now he would command their obedience. This year, when he returned to Morocco, Yūsuf left behind a formidable army under his cousin, Sir ibn Abū Bakr, who was instructed to carry out the reduction of the remaining taifas.

The Murābit commander siezed Tarifa in 1090, and overran the taifa of Sevilla the following spring and summer, taking Córdoba, Carmona, and Sevilla itself in September. The lesser taifas of Jaén, Murcia, and Denia then rapidly submitted. In the south only the great taifa of Badajoz remained independent. Alfonso had tried to aid Sevilla against the Murābit but without success. In 1092 he attempted, with the aid of Sancho Ramírez of Aragón and the count of Barcelona, to strengthen the Christian position in the east by an assault on Valencia and Tortosa, which was to be aided by a Genoese fleet. That fleet was late in arriving and the attempt came to nothing.

[17] Emma Falque Rey, ed., *Historia Compostellana* (Turnholt, 1988), pp. 15–16 and 221.

Rather, it sparked a reaction against the hapless al-Qādir in Valencia, who was overthrown and beheaded in a local revolt. Meanwhile, farther south, another son of Yūsuf, Muhammad ibn Āisa, had forced the Christian evacuation of Aledo, and then advanced up the east coast, occupying Denia, Játiva, and finally Alcira, only 35 kilometers south of Valencia.

The route of diplomacy, employed in the west of the peninsula, yielded only slightly better results. In late 1091 or early 1092 the Leonese monarch had taken a Muslim concubine, the Princess Zaida, who had been the former daughter-in-law of al-Mutamid of Sevilla. The move was intended to enhance his credibility as a defender of Andalucian Islam. Ultimately, it proved of no use in the struggle to save Sevilla, but it had its uses in arranging an alliance with Badajoz once the realm of al-Mutawakkil became the sole surviving Andalucian taifa. During the winter of 1092–1093 that wily monarch purchased the aid of Alfonso by ceding to him the towns of Lisbon, Santarém, and Sintra. The Leonese monarch took posession of them that spring and turned them over to Count Raymond, now married to Princess Urraca. Alfonso's magnate son-in-law briefly became the governor of an area that stretched from Cape Finisterre in the north to the Tajo River in the south.

The Leonese king had gone through the usual pretense of overrunning these cities, but Muslim opinion turned against the ruler of Badajoz just the same. During the winter of 1093–1094 Sir ibn Abū Bakr marched on al-Mutawakkil, and Badajoz fell to a combination of conspiracy and assault. Its king and his sons were captured and then murdered on the road to Sevilla. In November of the same year Sir ibn Abū Bakr surprised Count Raymond near Lisbon and inflicted a major defeat upon him. In a single stroke Lisbon and its companion cities were retaken and the frontier again pushed back to the Mondego from the Tajo. The only permanent consolation of this period occurred when Valencia surrendered in June of 1094 to an independent siege carried out by the Castilian adventurer *el Cid*. When a major Murābit force advanced to reverse that loss it was routed by Rodrigo Díaz de Vivar at Cuart de Poblet in October. The advance of the Murābit was finally halted at what was to be the effective frontier for approximately the next ten years.

Happily, the Murābit were to be occupied with the consolidation of their gains in Andalucía over the past four years and would not take the field in 1095–1096. Alfonso VI was to be busy with internal strains and would have been in poor condition to repel further attack. The Muslim Zaida had given birth to a son, Sancho, in 1093, which gave the king cause to rejoice.[18] Then, at the end of that year, his queen, Constance of Burgundy, died. Both events were serious setbacks for Count Raymond of Burgundy, whose chances of succeeding Alfonso were materially reduced by them. Worse, in 1094, the Leonese took still another wife, the north Italian Berta, which further impaired Raymond's position at court.

Under these circumstances, Count Raymond came to an openly treasonous agreement with his cousin, Count Henry. He also enlisted the support of Abbot Hugh of Cluny. The understanding provided that, on the death of Alfonso, Henry would assist Raymond in seizing control of the kingdom. In return, Henry would be given the kingdom of Toledo or, if that were impossible, the kingdom of Galicia, presently ruled by Raymond. The pact could not have been a very well kept secret, and Alfonso was faced with a flagrant challenge to his authority. Nonetheless, the Leonese could hardly run the risk of civil war under the circumstances then obtaining. Instead, he chose to face down Raymond while detaching Henry from him. The former was accomplished by staging a formal procession through the realm in the summer and fall of 1095, ostensibly to honor his new wife. The tour included the territories held by Raymond, who did not dare act openly against his king. Having seized the initiative, Alfonso now allowed the marriage of Henry to his illegitimate daughter, Teresa, and bestowed on them the county of Portugal in 1096. That stroke, a major loss of territory, materially weakened Count Raymond, detached the now Count Henry from his party, and made of the latter an additional possible rival for the succession.[19]

The conclusion of this internal crisis came but months before the return of Yūsuf ibn Tāshufīn to the peninsula in 1097. The Muslim army now advanced against Toledo once more. Alfonso appealed for aid to Pedro I of Aragón and also to *el Cid* in Valencia. Neither appeared. The Christian set up a front stretching 80 kilometers from Consuegra at the eastern end of the mountains of Toledo to Bel-

---

[18] The question of the exact identity of Zaida, the date of her death, and of Sancho's birth, have been the subject of considerable debate. For the most recent and thorough treatment, see Reilly, *Alfonso VI*, pp. 234–35.

[19] The so-called Pacto Sucessorio, *DMP* 1, pt. 1:1–2 and pt. 2:547–53, is an undated document which exists only in a late copy of Cluniac provenance. Gonzaga de Azevedo, its most recent editor in the above, assigned it merely to the period 1095–1107. Charles Julian Bishko, "Count Henrique of Portugal, Cluny, and the Antecedents of the Pacto Sucessorio," *RPH* 13 (1970):155–88, argued for the date of 1105. However, see the analysis in Reilly, *Alfonso VI*, pp. 248–55.

monte on the western edge of the Sierra de Albarracín. In August of 1097 it seems that both flanks of the Christian position were punished severely, but the line held and the Murābit withdrew to the south. In 1098 there was no Muslim offensive, and Alfonso was busy strengthening the northeastern flank of the territories of Toledo beyond Guadalajarra where local Muslim governors held strong-points at Atienza, Sigüenza, and Medinaceli.

The necessity of such constant activity was pointed up in 1099 when Andalucian forces, under the command of a grandson of Yūsuf, Yahyā ibn Tāshufīn, marched north again and rolled up most of the Christian possessions south of the Tajo, including the castle of Consuegra. That campaign allowed Yahya to lay direct siege to Toledo itself in the summer of 1100, but the city held out as it was to do time and time again. Alfonso VI seems to have left that defense to his new son-in-law, Count Henry. He himself was busy in the east. In July of 1099 Rodrigo Díaz de Vivar, *el Cid*, had died and left the practical rule of the city of Valencia to his wife, Jimena Díaz. In 1100 the Leonese monarch visited Valencia to see to its defenses. Two years later he would decide that it could not be held. In late March of 1102 Alfonso supervised the evacuation of the city and its Christian population and set what remained to the torch. Before the end of May, the Murābit emir, Mazdali, had marched north from Denia to occupy it.

Nor was the growing Murābit threat to the eastern flank of León–Castilla to end there. The new governor of Valencia pressed his advantage with a major raid on the territories of Barcelona, and the counterattack led by Count Armengol V of Urgel was defeated with great slaughter at Mollerusa, 20 kilometers east of Lérida, on September 14, 1102. At Zaragoza, al-Mustain had despatched his son to Morocco in the same spring, and an alliance was arranged between Yūsuf and the last of the great Iberian taifas. It must have appeared that the bad old days of al-Mansūr were about to return.

Alfonso VI had begun to prepare for the worst, which is to say, the possible loss of Toledo. In an effort to avert that eventuality, he settled some of the Christian refugees from Valencia north of the Tajo and northeast of Toledo in 1102. Nevertheless, it was about this time that he directed Count Raymond to undertake the repopulation of Avila and Salamanca. The former protected the easiest pass over the Guadarrama into the trans-Duero, and the latter backed up Coria to prevent movement from the south, around the western end of the same chain into that precious territory. Some of the Valencian refugees were also resettled in Salamanca, and the former bishop of Valencia, Jerome, now became the first bishop of Salamanca.

Together with Segovia, which Alfonso had already repopulated in 1088 and which dominated the pass of Navacerrada, these fortress towns bade fair to become the next line of defense if Toledo should finally fall to the Murābit.[20]

The old king did not accept that possibility as inevitable. In 1103 he moved to avert it by initiating the siege of Muslim Medinaceli. Now that Valencia was Murābit and Zaragoza allied with them, that town stood guard over the passage into the lands of Toledo from the east by way of the valley of the Río Jalón. The enemy understood very well what he was about, and the governors of Valencia and Granada took the field to prevent it. Nonetheless, Valencian troops were prevented from reinforcing Medinaceli, and the Granadan governor was defeated and killed near Talavera while attempting to create a diversion. The siege continued and by July of 1104 the crucial fortress was in Leonese hands.

During the next three years Alfonso VI was even able to carry the war to the enemy. In 1104 he conducted a successful raid into Sevillan territory. The following summer Leonese forces operated in the lands around Calatrava la Vieja, just north of Andalucía. They were defeated there, but the initiative remained with the Christians. The king himself led a great raid which penetrated all the way to Málaga on the Mediterranean in 1106 and so far dominated the enemy that he was able to escort large numbers of Mozarabs north to be resettled in his own lands. Although Alfonso was able to maintain the offensive to such good advantage, he could not alter the new strategic balance in the peninsula, which had shifted against him over the last twenty years since the battle of Zalaca.

The End of an Era

One factor that contributed to the late successes of the Leonese was the growing debility of Yūsuf ibn Tāshufīn, which culminated in his death on September 2, 1106. Fortunately, he had designated his son, Alī, as his heir and secured his recognition some years before, but there was, nonetheless, some hesitation in the pattern of Murābit activity until the new emir could consolidate his position. At the same time, Alfonso VI, now some sixty-nine years of age, was attempting to deal with a prospective succession crisis of his own.

[20] Angel Barrios García, *Estructuras agrarias y poder en Castilla: El ejemplo de Avila, 1085–1320* (Salamanca, 1983), pp. 128–71, makes a useful attempt to describe the course and nature of the early settlement of the trans-Duero. His beginning chronology is a bit optimistic, however.

The trouble had been brewing for years as a result of the lack of a male heir despite marriage after marriage. The king's only son, Sancho Alfónsez, now about thirteen, was a product of his liaison with the Muslim Zaida and had that disability as a prospective heir. After the death of Constance of Burgundy in 1093, Alfonso married Berta of Italy, but she died in January of 1100 without having borne him any children at all. In May of the same year the king would appear again married, this time to a French bride of uncertain derivation, Elisabeth. In due time she would present him with two more daughters but no son.

Simultaneously, the royal household came more and more under the influence of his daughters, Urraca married to Count Raymond and Teresa married to Count Henry, after the death of the king's two sisters, Elvira in 1099 and Urraca in 1101. The two Burgundians themselves resided at court in the winter months, visiting their respective counties of Galicia and Portugal in spring and summer. The circumstances promoted the growth of intrigue, which would have been increased even more by the birth of a son to Raymond and Urraca in March of 1105. The king now had a legitimate grandson, Alfonso Raimúndez, to inherit his throne, with a mature mother and father to protect his claim.

For one year Alfonso VII temporized with this delicate situation. He himself had signaled clearly his preference of Sancho Alfónsez to inherit. Since 1103, when the boy was about ten, he had begun to confirm his father's charters with great regularity, but no further step had been taken. Then, in March of 1106, the king had moved with great firmness. He had his marriage to the French Elisabeth annulled and married Zaida, thus legitimizing the position of his son.[21] The action could not have been welcome to his daughters or their husbands, but the old king would carry through with his design, and in May of the following year Sancho Alfónsez was officially recognized as heir to the realm at a great council held in León. Obviously no one was prepared to withstand the will of the old king publicly, but private opposition to his acts must have been fierce and their reconsideration upon Alfonso's death contemplated.

The monarch must have been relieved, then, when Count Raymond himself died after a short illness in September of 1107. That event opened the way for a hopeful resolution of the entire question. In December of 1107, in a council held in León, Alfonso arranged that his daughter, the widow Urraca, should hold Galicia as

---

[21] To the confusion of all subsequent historians, Zaida was baptized with the Christian name of Elisabeth as well. For the explication of the affair, see Reilly, *Alfonso VI*, pp. 338–40.

a virtual *appanage* during her lifetime, although not the other posses-sions that had accrued to Raymond in the trans-Duero. If she should remarry, however, the province was to pass immediately to her son, and the nobles of the province and the bishop of Santiago de Com-postela were sworn to uphold that arrangement. These dispositions were accepted also by the boy's uncle, Archbishop Guy of Vienne, who had traveled to the peninsula to protect his interests. This brother of the deceased count was to become Pope Calixtus II in 1119. Alfonso must now have been confident that the peaceful acces-sion of his son was at last assured. In fact, the settlement endured but six months.

For the first time in six years a major Murābit army marched against Toledo in 1108. Commanded by Tamīn ibn Yūsuf, brother of the emir Alī ibn Yūsuf, it was comprised of forces drawn from Granada, Córdoba, Murcia, and Valencia. This formidable army struck first against the town of Uclés, 100 kilometers east of Toledo, in a bid to flank that redoubtable fortress. Uclés fell on May 27 but its citadel held out. The approach and intentions of the Murābit force had been detected well in advance by the Leonese, and a relief force was already en route. On May 29 just outside Uclés this Christian army of about 2,300 to 2,500 was surrounded and then destroyed. No less than seven counts of the realm perished in the disaster. Worst of all, so did its heir, Sancho Alfónsez, who had been allowed to accompany the expedition. As a result of the battle, Uclés and the entire south bank of the Tajo from Aranjuez east to Zorita passed at once into Muslim hands, and there was grave danger to the whole of the remaining territories of Toledo as local Muslim populations rose in revolt. Only a general mobilization of the realm seems to have held the line of the Tajo in the summer of 1108.

The disaster at Uclés meant that Alfonso VI must confront the question of succession once again. This time the choice must fall upon the oldest legitimate heir, his daughter Urraca. But under the circumstances the king apparently did not even consider the possibil-ity of her ruling in her own right, and sometime in the fall of 1108 chose the king of Aragón, Alfonso I *el Batallador*, to become her husband and future king of Léon–Castilla. In so doing, he had selected a member of the same dynasty, a formidable warrior whose reputation was already made, and someone who bore the charisma of kingship as well. At the same time that choice removed a potentially dangerous foe on the eastern border where Aragón and León–Castilla had jostled of late over the potential spoils of the taifa of Zaragoza. It seemed an eminently sensible choice.

Nevertheless, he had, in fact, made the worst decision of his long reign. His daughter would initially abide by her father's decision and the marriage would be duly solemnized in late 1109, but the result was to be civil war and the prolongation of the succession crisis for another eight years. The marriage of Urraca and Alfonso, which would prove to be sterile, was shortly condemned by the papacy because the spouses shared a common great-grandfather in Sancho *el Mayor* of Navarra. Without an heir of their own blood, the couple could not hope to maintain themselves. Moreover, the old king's choice had immediately alienated those who saw their own prospects tied to the eventual succession of Alfonso Raimúndez, Urraca's son by Count Raymond – including Count Henry of Portugal and the *Infanta* Teresa herself. There was, in addition, a Castilian party which had urged Urraca's marriage to Count Gomez González of Lara, and which felt a special hostility to the Aragonese because of its members' own ambitions in the Rioja and the east generally.[22]

Doubtless the old king had considered all of these possibilities, but he felt that Urraca could not rule without a husband, and that her own son's claims could be manipulated against her and a regency forced upon her. To choose the Lara count, or any other magnate of the realm, for her husband instead would have aroused the same enmities as did Alfonso of Aragón, but without the strengths associated with the latter. Notoriously, the most important factor, which the old king ignored, was the intransigent determination of his own daughter. His solution was contrived because he feared her weakness, a woman's weakness we may suppose, in those critical times. Ironically, because she possessed the same dogged persistence that marked Alfonso himself, Urraca would abandon his design after a short trial to rule León–Castilla in her own name. She would do so for seventeen years until her death finally delivered the kingdom to her son by Count Raymond.

The succession crisis would ultimately be overcome in quite different fashion than Alfonso VI had disposed. In 1109, however, the seventy-two-year-old king had himself borne south in a litter to Toledo, once again to direct its defense against the expected attack of the Murābit. He was not to see that assault, for he died there on July 1. At his death, the question remained whether or not León–Castilla could maintain mastery of Toledo, and of the trans-Duero which it protected, which he had achieved. With that question was bound up the predominance of Christian or Muslim in the Iberian Peninsula.

---

[22] Rodrigo Jiménez de Rada, *De Rebus Hispaniae* (Turnholt, 1987), pp. 217–18, relates that its leaders convinced Alfonso's Jewish physician, Joseph Ferrizuel, also known as Cidellus, to advance the cause of the count, but the king angrily rejected the idea.

5

The Murābit Empire and the Other Spains

The African power which had intervened so abruptly in Iberian affairs in 1086 and had overrun Andalucía by 1094, Valencia in 1102, and by 1109 was threatening Zaragoza and Toledo simultaneously, was itself a product of forces which always had had the potential for disruption and change in Iberia. The Straits of Gibraltar are, after all, only seven miles wide. The combination of the inspiration of Islam and the power of the Berber peoples had conquered Iberia in the 8th Century and now appeared ready to at least dominate it in the 12th. That the result was quite different in the latter bespeaks the reality of an altered Africa and an altered Iberia.[1]

The Murābit were first and foremost a nomadic Berber tribe which had its origins in the western Sahara desert in the region which we should now call Mauretania. These were the Lamtūna, a branch of the Sanhāja Berber group. Their ordinary range lay across at least two of the major caravan routes from equatorial Africa to the northern coast in modern-day Morocco and Algeria. Stock raisers themselves, they both participated in and preyed upon the caravan trade as part of their way of life. In the 9th Century they had been converted to Islam and subsequently considered it part of their faith to war upon the pagan Negro kingdoms of the upper Niger and upper Senegal regions. They were a permanent threat to these latter

[1] Charles-André Julien, *History of North Africa*, trans. John Petrie (London, 1970), has been recognized as a classic almost from the time of the appearance of the first French edition in 1931, but it now needs to be supplemented. For the period that concerns us, the *UNESCO General History of Africa*, Vol. 3 (Paris, 1988), is the most authoritative. *The Cambridge History of Islam*, Vol. 2 (Cambridge, 1970), is useful. Jean Brignon, Abdelaziz Amine, Brahim Boutaleb, Guy Martinet, and Bernard Rosenberger, *Histoire du Maroc* (Paris, 1967), expends the coverage of all three to some extent.

and an occasional nuisance to their more settled northern neighbors. The Lamtūna themselves moved from rough unity to equally rough disunity, depending upon the vigor of one or another sheik as is usual with nomadic peoples. In the middle of the 11th Century they were united not only among themselves but also with two neighboring Sanhāja peoples, the Guddala to their west and the Massūfa to their northeast.

About that time their chief, Yahyā ibn Ibrāhīm, fixed on that staple of Islamic piety, a pilgrimage to Mecca, which he undertook in company with a number of the prominent men of the tribe. Returning by way of Kairouan, he met a famous legal scholar of the Malikite school, Abū Imrān al-Fāsī, who had been a native of Morocco. No doubt moved to a new piety by the experience of pilgrimage and the sight of the holy places, Yahyā requested the scholar to depute one of his disciples to bring the correct knowledge of the *Koran* to his desert tribesmen. The disciple eventually chosen for that mission was one Abd Allāh ibn Yāsīn, also a Moroccan from the region of Sus near present-day Agadir.

Now it is fair to say that the Malikite school was both literalist and fundamentalist.[2] It held for the eternal and uncreated nature of the *Koran* itself, which was, as it were, eternally present to Allāh. It insisted upon the literal truth of the language of the Book and opposed as heretical any attempt to understand it in a symbolic or allegorical sense. Malikitism regarded as impudent and unnecessary the other great traditions of Koranic interpretation based upon the tracing of the descent of various passages in the *Koran* itself or in the traditions of Muhammad, the *hadīth*. Paradoxically, since its faith lay in the book itself literally interpreted, it had little use for either theoretical scholarship or for a divinely appointed individual who would prevent the community from apostasizing. The school had viewed with horror the deviation of 7th-century Islam from rule by the blood-descendants of the Prophet and the subsequent development of the caliphate. It regarded both the Sunnite Caliphate at Baghdad and the Shiite Caliphate at Cairo with equal indifference. Such leadership as was needed for the dar al-Islam, or for the local community, could be perfectly well supplied by ad hoc election as the occasion demanded.

Abd Allāh, described to us by a near-contemporary, appears to have been more notable for his vigor than for his learning. His leadership seems to have consisted rather in the uncompromising

---

[2] For the uninitiate, the best introduction into the serious study of Islam today is Gustave E. von Grunebaum, *Medieval Islam* (Chicago, 2nd ed., 1953).

assertion of the Koranic ethical prescriptions against drinking, womanizing, and lying than in doctrinal positions per se. Certainly, these were the notes most likely to appeal to the rude understanding of nomads. His central contribution to the movement as it subsequently developed may have lain in the foundation of a very popular military monastery on an island off the Mauretanian coast in the Atlantic. This was a *ribāt*, from which the movement was formerly held to have taken its name, *murābitum*, or "men of the *ribāt*." More recent scholarship prefers to trace the word to a root meaning of *jihād*, or holy war. In any event, the *ribāt* as an institution was not new in the Islamic world, but, under Abd Allāh's stern direction, the *ribāt* in Mauretania became famous for the austerity and purity of its observance of Islam, and men flocked to it. These military monks then returned to the Sanhāja world which had furnished them and saw to its conversion by conquest.

In 1054 and 1055 the arrival of a new force in northwest Africa was first made evident by the Murābit conquest of one city in the north of the Negro kingdom of Ghana and another in the desert, the oasis city of Sijilmāsa. The latter city had been ruled by the great enemy of the Sanhāja, the Zanāta Berbers, who had dominated two of the trans-Saharan caravan routes from it. The Zanāta were defeated and massacred, and the city thoroughly plundered. These early conquests were directed not by Abd Allāh himself but by a Lamtūna chief, Yahyā ibn Umar. On this latter's death in 1056, command passed to his brother, Abū Bakr ibn Umar.

Under this leader, the capture of the district of Sūs, in the valley of central Morocco between the Anti-Atlas and the High Atlas Mountains, was carried through in 1058. Abū Bakr now signaled his ambitions clearly by taking in marriage the Princess Zainab of a people dwelling in the High Atlas range. Such a marriage cleared the path north onto the great plain of Morocco, and the eradication of heretical forms of Islam and of political opposition there was energetically pursued. Still, the Berbers of that area put up a fierce resistance, a Murābit army was defeated, and Abd Allāh ibn Yāsīn himself was slain in battle. Civil war had also broken out between various of the Sanhāja nomads in the desert, which demanded Abū Bakr's personal attention. He therefore was to leave the control of the Murābit army in Morocco, to his cousin, Yūsuf ibn Tāshufīn, in 1070 and to arrange the latter's marriage to his own former wife, Zainab. The power that he surrendered then he was never to reclaim. The two avoided an outright clash, but relations between them were strained and awkward until the death of Abū Bakr in 1087.

The man who thus came to power among the Murābit was already of mature years. He was reputed to be almost one hundred years old at his death. An experienced warrior by this time, he also possessed the personal characteristics necessary to the leadership of a movement in which religious reform was inextricably mixed with the lust after empire and glory which would constitute its realization. He was courageous and determined but also something of an ascetic. He wore, we are told, naught but wool clothing, and his diet was limited to barley, camel's meat, and the milk of the same beast. The new camp and base of operations, which was established about 1070 on the edge of the High Atlas, was to become the great city of Marrakesh. Contemporary sources assure us that Yūsuf worked in the loincloth of a common laborer in the raising of its first structures. The most recent studies would, however, attribute the foundation of Marrakesh to Abū Bakr. At the very least, Yūsuf obviously knew how to catch the religious imagination of his rude followers.

He now took in hand the reduction of the remainder of the great plain of Morocco. Fez fell in 1075, followed by the lesser towns. But the capture of Fez also opened the route to the Mediterranean coast north of the Atlas, and both Tlemcen and Oran were captured in 1082. Nevertheless, Algiers and the coast beyond it were to remain closed to the Murābit. The Zīrīd Kingdom centered in Tunisia had recently fallen on hard times indeed. Its kings had shaken off their nominal subjection to the Fatimid caliph in Cairo, and the latter persuaded numerous groups of Arab bedouins then harassing Egypt to move west. In 1052 these Banū Hilāl nomads had defeated the Zīrīds and were gradually to spread their control through Tunisia and eastern Algeria. Their influence would thus effectively set a term to that of the Murābit. The attention of the latter now turned to the north.

The Iberian Peninsula was far from being a mystery to either the Sanhāja Berbers or the peoples whom they had just conquered. From the time of the Muslim Conquest of the 8th Century, Berbers had moved back and forth across the Straits as warriors and merchants. The Cordoban Caliphate had recruited its mercenaries there and had balanced Sanhāja against Zanāta as it strove to keep the trade routes open and power fragmented in North Africa. The extreme north of Morocco around Ceuta had been a formal part of the territory of the caliphate of Córdoba and, on the latter's collapse, a taifa dynasty had established itself there as well as at Algeciras on the opposite coast. In mid-century Sevilla had annexed Algeciras, but the successors to the Hammūdid dynasty still ruled Ceuta.

Such an enclave in the now-Murābit Morocco would, one thinks, naturally have attracted the attentions of Yūsuf. In any event, he was to lay siege to its chief city and capture it in in the fall of 1083. Seen from Iberia, that action would appear to be a prelude to invasion. So, in fact, it was subsequently to become, but was it the original intent of Yūsuf ibn Tāshufīn? The Murābit leader would prove, over the years, to be quite reluctant to become permanently involved in the Spains. The chronology of these relationships is tangled, in any case. The first appeal from Muslim Andalucía is said to have been made by al-Mutawakkil of Badajoz after the capture of Coria by Alfonso VI in 1079. In 1083 al-Mutamid of Sevilla traveled to Morocco to appeal to Yūsuf. Still, the leader of the faithful did not come.

Further representations from al-Mutamid in 1086 after Toledo had fallen to the Leonese did finally procure the arrival of Yūsuf in Algeciras. This city he took under his own control to guard his line of retreat. It was his first permanent acquisition in Iberia, and it came at the expense of Sevilla. The atmosphere and the context of the events that followed are convincingly portrayed for us by Abd Allāh, king of Granada and party to most of them, in his memoirs, written later as a pensioner–prisoner of the Murābit in Morocco.[3] He makes it clear, for example, that the costs of the emir's expeditions were financed by the taifa kings, and that the latter were expected to furnish substantial gifts over and above that financial aid in addition to participating directly in the military actions.

That Yūsuf was treated almost as the natural sovereign of the Iberian taifas was obvious from the very first. The first sinners in this regard were the rulers of those principalities themselves. In Sevilla in 1086, after the return from the victory at Zalaca, Tamīn of Málaga asked the Murābit to render judgment against his brother, Abd Allāh of Granada, but the emir refused to become involved. On the other hand, in 1088 during the siege of Aledo, the rebel and king of Murcia, ibn Rashīq, sought Yūsuf's support against al-Mutamid of Sevilla, whose former governor in Murcia the rebel had been. On this occasion the Murābit did intervene and ordered the submission of ibn Rashīq.

But not only did the taifa kings themselves behave in such a manner as to positively invite Yūsuf ibn Tāshufīn to assume supreme power, their subjects of all ranks did the same, from the very moment of his arrival in the peninsula in 1086. They appealed against their own kings to him. Rebels and conspirators sought his support. The qādīs and faqīhs issued condemnations of the conduct of their own rulers and judgments, or fatwāhs, to justify on religious

---

[3] Abd Allāh, El siglo XI en 1ª persona, trans. Évariste Lévi-Provençal and Emilio García Gomez (Madrid, 1980), pp. 199–276. All memoirs are self-justifying by their very nature, of course, but the Granadan is remarkably evenhanded in his treatment of the other principals, with the obvious exception of his own brother and rival, Tamīn of Málaga.

grounds Yūsuf's actions, from his seizure of Algeciras in 1086 to his very deposition of those kings, beginning with Abd Allāh of Granada in 1090. Furthermore, if the emir himself began circumspectly, it appears from the first moments of his arrival in Iberia that his subordinates interfered in the relationships of the various taifas and even in their internal affairs. They demanded bribes from all parties, citing their alleged influence with the great Murābit and threatening to bring it to bear against those who resisted them.

All of these circumstances, as well as what must have been his hopes for an easy redemption of Toledo after the victory of Zalaca in 1086, gradually convinced the ally of 1086 to become the master of 1094. The Iberian Muslim supported his campaigns of 1086 and 1088 only partially, and his campaign of 1090 not at all, so far as we can determine. They continued to show more disposition to fight with one another than with the Christian Alfonso. Worse, they showed some increasing interest in allying with the Leonese against their Muslim rivals or even against himself. These latter are the charges which Yūsuf will bring against Abd Allāh of Granada in 1090. As the author of the memoirs himself admits, they were partially true. He can adduce in his own defense only that he agreed to resume the tribute to Alfonso because he was not sure of the ability of Yūsuf to protect him, and that he had resisted the blandishments of the Leonese to join in an attack against al-Mutamid of Sevilla.

Of course, the taifa kings had distrusted Yūsuf from the beginning and had viewed with dismay the preference that their own subjects showed for the latter's rule. They chafed under his financial exactions. When the Murābit began the process of direct annexation in 1090, their reactions were twofold. The smaller taifas generally accepted the inevitable. The greatest ones, Sevilla in 1092 and Badajoz in 1094, elected to fight for their independence. Of course they lost, but in the process of resistance they in desperation allied themselves with León–Castilla and so came to justify, at least after the fact, the Murābit charges. After his defeat, Al-Mutamid of Sevilla, despite his determined resistance and his appeal to Alfonso, was allowed to retire to private life in Morocco, as had been Abd Allāh of Granada before him. On the other hand, al-Mutawakkil of Badajoz and his sons were murdered after their surrender. One thinks that the Aftasid monarch had never been a willing supporter of the Murābit presence in the peninsula.

If we accept, then, the essential accuracy of the picture drawn by Abd Allāh, Yūsuf ibn-Tāshufīn emerges as something less than a religious fanatic. He was willingly drawn into the fight against Alfonso VI and for the recovery of Toledo, but for a price, and apparently a substantial one. As his very participation progressively revealed the weakness and irresolution of the taifa kings, he chose a course that would both enlarge his own empire and create the optimum conditions for the continuing struggle against Alfonso VI. No doubt he disapproved strongly of the lax religion of his Andalucian compatriots, their use of wine, their addiction to music and poetry, their dabbling in theology and philosophy, and their resort to taxes, not sanctioned by the *Koran*, to support themselves. Subsequently he would support the Malikite judges of Andalucía in their assault on these failings. But the reasons which according to Abd Allāh, he himself alleged for his destruction of the taifas we should regard as political.

In the reorganization of Andalucía subsequent to the elimination of the taifas, Yūsuf resorted to familial rule. The governorships went largely into the hands of his sons and grandsons. The jurisdictions of those governorships roughly followed the boundaries of the former taifas, for both were determined in large measure by geography. As for the treatment of the taifas of the east coast and the far northeast, the necessities of the continuing war against Alfonso VI and the opportunities presented by circumstance were the determinants. Between 1099 and 1102, the death of *el Cid* and the weakness of his widow, Jimena, created the possibility of the annexation of the Valencian taifa, realized at the latter date.

If Zaragoza had held aloof from the campaign of Zalaca and all subsequent Murābit initiatives and had paid *parias* to Yūsuf's enemy when necessary, its kings could adduce with justice the difficulty of their position in the peninsula. Moreover, al-Mustain of Zaragoza seems to have been careful to maintain good relations with Yūsuf. About 1093 or 1094 he despatched his son to Morocco with presents. In 1103, when Yūsuf was touring Andalucía to secure acceptance of his son, Alī, as heir, al-Mustain again sent his own son to Córdoba to participate in the festivities and to pledge his good will. After the surrender of Valencia in 1102 at the latest, and perhaps as early as the death of *el Cid* in 1099, the Zaragozan monarch ceased the payment of *parias* to Alfonso, and Yūsuf was to rest satisfied at that. The independence of Zaragoza would be respected by the Murābit during Yūsuf's lifetime and that of al-Mustain.

Aragón and the Shadow of León–Castilla

The county of Aragón emerged from the splintering of the greater kingdom of Navarra consequent on the death of Sancho *el Mayor* in 1035 to become the kingdom of Aragón at the time Ramiro I (1035–1063) effectively managed the annexation of the eastern counties of Sobrarbe and Ribagorza. Yet the new realm did little more than survive behind its mountain ramparts. When Sancho Ramírez I (1063–1094) succeeded at the death of his father during the unsuccessful siege of Graus, it still constituted but a modest Pyrenaen kingdom faced by the more substantial kingdom of Navarra to the west and the expanding taifa of Zaragoza under al-Muqtadir to the south. Aragón had the typical motives for expansion of a growing population, a changing agriculture, and the resultant clamor for land, but its resources were scarcely equal to its necessities.

During the initial years of his reign, Sancho Ramírez could do little more than survive in a political world dominated first by his uncle, Fernando el Magno of León–Castilla and then by his cousin, Sancho II of Castilla. These two were often in concert with al-Muqtadir of Zaragoza, his most dangerous immediate neighbor. The Aragonese found himself sometimes allied with his cousin, Sancho García IV of Navarra, against the two and sometimes alone as Navarra and Zaragoza allied against him. In 1068 he had felt sufficiently threatened to donate his tiny kingdom to the papacy and to receive it back as a papal fief.

That the fortunes of Aragón would begin gradually to improve after that date was due more to circumstances and his ability to respond to and to manipulate them. The first great stroke of luck, for he was not implicated as far as we can tell, was the assassination of his cousin, Sancho García IV of Navarra in 1076. Aragón participated with León–Castilla in the consequent dismembering of that realm, receiving the central core of Pamplona and its territories. The price of that advance was homage to León–Castilla, but the preoccupation of the former with the opening up of the trans-Duero to the south soon diverted it from exploiting its advantage in the east. The benefit, on the other hand, was that Aragón's share in the spoils roughly tripled the size of that kingdom. To mark the new, enhanced status of his realm, Sancho Ramírez would found the city of Jaca in Aragonese territory rather than take up residence in the old royal city of Pamplona in Navarra. He would insist as well that the Mozarabic Christian bishopric in Muslim Huesca be transferred to his new city.[4]

With the accession of the new lands of Navarra to the west, Aragón now dominated the heights which overlooked the sprawling

---

[4] Domingo J. Buesa Conde, El rey Sancho Ramírez (Zaragoza, 1978), pp. 48, 51, and 54, dates these events to 1077 rather than earlier. I believe he is correct.

plains of the Ebro basin all the way from the Rioja in that west to the *contado* of Lérida in the east. From those commanding positions Sancho Ramírez could survey the holdings of Alfonso VI, the territories of Tudela, Zaragoza, and Huesca of al-Muqtadir, and the lands of al-Muzaffar's Lérida in the extreme east. The assault against the possessions of al-Muqtadir was indicated, for to attack Alfonso would have been madness, and al-Muzaffar could often be counted upon to join in an attack upon his brother and rival.

However, while the control of the heights was most useful for raids upon and the harassment of the Zaragozan lands, it was difficult or impossible to assemble in them a force and supplies sufficient to mount a major offensive that would result in the permanent acquisition of territory. Therefore, the efforts of Sancho Ramírez would be concentrated upon those positions that controlled access to the southern plains from the valleys of Aragón, Sobrarbe, or Ribagoza. He had already made a beginning in this enterprise with the capture of Alquézar in 1067. As its name indicates, Alquézar was a castle–settlement at the mouth of the valley of the Vero River which runs down from Sobrarbe onto the eastern part of the plain of Huesca. Small successes of this sort were possible, but the manpower of Aragón, even after 1076, was hardly comparable to that of the great taifa of Zaragoza.

The solution for Aragón, in the long run, would be to draw upon the manpower of the south of France. The first marriage of Sancho Ramírez had been to Isabel, daughter of Count Armengol III of Urgel, which magnate's lands in the valley of the Segre River also oriented him south along its flow toward the territories of Lérida. But Isabel had died about 1068, and Sancho's second marriage was to Felicia, sister of Count Ebles of Roucy on the border of Normandy. This took place sometime about 1069, and in 1073 Count Ebles was designated leader of an abortive crusade into Iberia that Pope Gregory VII had attempted to organize. Sancho Ramírez was probably one of its promoters, but its failure to materialize left him still in a position of marked inferiority to Zaragoza.

There was little he could do about that situation for the next decade. In some respects things got worse, for in the spring of 1081 Alfonso VI made a series of adjustments in his eastern policy which were threatening, at least partially, to the Aragonese. For one, the Basque territories of Alava, Vizcaya, and Guipuzcoa were consolidated under Lop Jiménez.[5] This Basque noble had cooperated with the Leonese in the partition of Navarra in 1076. He also earlier had served the Navarrese monarchy, or at least was recognized by it as nominal leader of the Basques. The Navarrese territories which Sancho Ramírez ruled were in good measure Basque themselves. The three counties which Lop Jiménez now headed in the name of Alfonso had never been effectively incorporated into the political life of northern Iberia, but the possibility that they now would be could hardly have been reassuring to the Aragonese king.

In fact, at the same time that he allowed the organization of this Basque principality, Alfonso himself had taken other steps to ensure that its repercussions on his own interests were controlled. That is, the Leonese monarch had created at the same time what amounted to a county of La Rioja under the powerful and well-connected Castilian magnate, García Ordóñez. García had been the royal *alférez*. His brother, Rodrigo Ordóñez, currently held that sensitive post. García will now begin to appear in the documents not only as a count but also as the husband of Urraca, sister of the former king of Navarra. But if the new county were designed in some measure to contain the Basque and in another to strengthen the frontier to the south with Zaragoza, it also provided maximum strength along the frontier that León–Castilla shared with Aragón in the upper Ebro basin.

What was to be even more important over the next two decades was another decision that Alfonso VI made about the same time. Sometime in early 1081 he exiled Rodrigo Díaz de Vivar, *el Cid*, to the eastern lands of the peninsula. The subsequent operations of the Castilian in that theater were to prove that he was indeed one of the tactical geniuses of the time. From his advent in the east in the spring of 1081, and for the next eighteen years, there was to be a wholly new unpredictable factor in the politics of the east of the peninsula.

Meanwhile, Sancho Ramírez sought to further reinforce his position by securing the betrothal of his son, Pedro, to Inés of Aquitaine, the daughter of Duke William VIII about 1079.[6] However useful the alliance may have been in terms of prestige, it seems to have had no practical effect. When al-Muqtadir died in 1083, after a long and successful reign which had most recently included the overthrow of

---

[6] Antonio Ubieto Arteta, ed., *Colección diplomática de Pedro I de Aragón y Navarra* (Zaragoza, 1951), p. 31. Buesa Conde, *Sancho Ramírez*, p. 56, had the duke campaigning, or attempting to, in Iberia the following year and being expelled by the Aragonese. The document upon which he relied was probably misdated at the very least. Antonio Ubieto Arteta, *Historia de Aragón: La formación territorial* (Zaragoza, 1981), p. 97, would redate the document to 1088, but we have no other source which would put the count in the peninsula at that date.

al-Muzaffar at Lérida, Sancho Ramírez was unable to profit from the new division of the lands of that taifa among the former's sons. The Aragonese monarch allied himself with the count of Barcelona and with Mundir, who had secured Lérida and Tortosa as his portions of the patrimony, for an attack upon the possessions of al-Mutamin, the other heir. The three focused their attention in 1083 upon the castle of Almenar, some 20 kilometers north of the city of Huesca. There they were routed by the combined forces of al-Mutamin and the Cid.

If that kind of major assault upon the holdings of al-Mutamin was to prove unsuccessful in 1083, more humble measures taken at the same time did result in permanent gains. That year the castle of Graus, in whose unsuccessful siege his father had lost his life some twenty years before, fell to Sancho Ramírez. This position, at the juncture of the Esera amd Isábena rivers flowing down from Ribagorza, was the key to debouching onto the plain of Huesca in the northeast. During the same period, the Aragonese also took Ayerbe, which similarly controlled access to that plain in the northwest, by way of the Gállego River which flows down from Aragón proper.

This selective assault on strategic strongholds, which avoided battle in the open field against forces that almost always must have been superior in numbers, was the course of action that worked best. The capture in 1084 of Secastilla which reinforced Sancho's hold on Graus is a case in point. On the other hand, his capture of Arguedas only 15 kilometers north of Tudela on the east side of the Ebro, and a possible raid in force against Zaragoza itself, were exploits that invited reprisal by powers stronger than himself. This boldness can probably only be explained by the contemporary absorption of Alfonso VI in his impending annexation of Toledo. Al-Mutamin himself would have been reassured in the face of these petty losses by another defeat of Sancho at the hands of the Cid at Morella in 1084.

About a year later, after the fall of Toledo, the Leonese monarch would be ready to undertake his own demonstration against Zaragoza. He was busy at the same time installing al-Qādir in Valencia. The Zaragozan king, al-Mutamin, had died in the fall of 1085, and his son, al-Mustain, was married to a Valencian princess. Moreover, Zaragoza had plotted against Alfonso, even if the conspiracy had come to naught, and had ceased the payment of *parias*. A punitive expedition was definitely in order.

Serious historians have suggested that Sancho Ramírez of Aragón either was engaged in his own siege of the city and retreated before Alfonso VI's approach or collaborated in the Leonese siege of the city. There is one document that would place the Aragonese at Zaragoza on July 6, 1086, but it is badly dated. Another document grew out of a 12th-century ecclesiastical dispute and so is suspect. It related that the brother of Sancho, Bishop García of Jaca, was promised the archbishopric of Toledo by Alfonso VI while he was besieging Zaragoza in return for the surrender to the latter of the castle of Alquézar. The facts are that Alfonso seems already to have had an archbishop-elect of Toledo at least and would hardly have been in a position to renege on that commitment, and that the said fortress would have been too far east to interest him.[7] The likelihood seems to be that Sancho was campaigning in the lands around Tortosa during the summer of 1086.

The Leonese monarch had to lift the siege of Zaragoza in September when news arrived of the Murābit landing in Algeciras. Under these circumstances he did appeal for Aragonese help, and a contingent, perhaps led by the *Infante* Pedro, marched with him to defeat at Zalaca in October. The year 1086 had gone rather better for Sancho Ramírez. In January his son, Pedro, had been married to Inés, daughter of the duke of Aquitaine. Probably to add fitting solemnity to the match, the *Infante* had been raised to the dignity of king in Sobrarbe and Ribagorza and allowed to associate in the government of the realm with his father. In addition, Sancho took advantage of al-Mustain's preoccupation with the Leonese siege and began to erect the castle of Montearagón only 5 kilometers from Huesca, the third city of the Zaragozan realm and long an object of Aragonese ambition.

Certainly Sancho Ramírez was in the tents of the crusaders before the city of Tudela the following year. The force from the south of France and the Leonese king were operating in lands very much a concern of the Aragonese, and he could not afford to be absent. That the joint forces failed to take Tudela could not have been much of a disappointment to him, for, if they had, the passage of that key town under the control of Alfonso or his ally, Duke Eudes of Burgundy, would have been impossible to prevent. But while in camp, he did do homage to Alfonso VI for the lands of Navarra, and a more or less autonomous principality was agreed upon, a county of Navarra,

---

[7] Ramón Menéndez Pidal, ed., *La España del Cid*, 2 vols. (Madrid, 4th ed., 1947), 1:300–01 and 2:746–47. Ubieto Arteta, *Historia de Aragón*, pp. 98–99, would redate the first document to 1089 when an Aragonese raid on the city may have taken place. On the general question of Sancho's presence at Zaragoza, see Ambrosio Huici Miranda, *Las grandes batallas de la Reconquista durante las invasiones africanas* (Madrid, 1956), p. 37, and Antonio Ubieto Arteta, "Homenaje de Aragón a Castilla por el condado de Navarra," *EEMCA* 3 (1947–48):17.

Plate 4   The pilgrim bridge at Punte la Reina, Aragón

which would become a buffer between the two monarchs in the hands of a count, Sancho Sanz, mutually acceptable to them. That meant that the town of Pamplona passed out of Sancho's control, an indication of his poor bargaining position at the time. He also had to agree to participate in the defense of Toledo whenever that should be necessary.[8]

Nevertheless, the king of Aragón was free to continue his patient nibbling at the perimeters of the Zaragozan taifa and to consolidate them, when possible, with diplomatic initiatives. Thus in 1088 he made new approaches to the pope, Urban II, promising to renew the feudal relationship of twenty years before and, this time, to honor the provision for an annual tribute in gold. On another front, a year or two earlier, Sancho had married a granddaughter or grandniece to a scion of the viscomital house of Bearn on the northern end of the pass of Somport. Of all of his ventures into foreign relations this was to be the most fruitful. It would prove to be the conduit through

---

[8] The sketchmap in Buesa Conde, *Sancho Ramírez*, p. 72, is useful to guage the full implications of the agreement.

which the manpower of the south of France flowed into Aragón and provided the resources for its conquest of Zaragoza. But, in 1088, the Bearnese alliance suffered a temporary setback when Viscount Centulle IV was murdered in the territories of Aragón in what seems to have been a rivalry of noble houses. The Aragonese king was not directly involved, but it was a serious embarrassment for him nonetheless.

Still, Sancho carried forward his stubborn offensive against the great enemy. In the early summer of 1089 he captured the fortress of Monzón. That position was roughly midway between the Muslim centers of Lérida and Huesca and controlled the direct line of communications between them. It also flanked the important Muslim fortress of Barbastro. Yet his relations with Alfonso VI continued to be good. Sancho Ramírez accompanied the Leonese south to quell the Murābit siege of Toledo in the summer of 1090.

During these and the next dozen years two major factors helped to account for the increasing success of Aragón against the great taifa on the Ebro. One is the already amply chronicled preoccupation of León–Castilla with the Murābit threat in the center of the peninsula. The other is the decision by Rodrigo Díaz de Vivar to leave the service of al-Mustain and begin the construction of a principality of his own centered upon Valencia. Sancho Ramírez was thus able to seize Estadilla in 1091, further strengthening his hold on Monzón and menacing Barbastro. The same year saw the Aragonese undertake a bold new initiative in the west by constructing a fortress at El Castellar on the Ebro a mere 20 kilometers northwest of Zaragoza and directly across its communications with Tudela. The major intervention of Alfonso VI in the Levant in 1092 effected a temporary hiatus in these activities as both the king of Aragón and the count of Barcelona collaborated with the Alfonsine attempt to rein in the ambitions of Rodrigo Díaz at Valencia and Tortosa. When the Castilian expedition withdrew in frustration, the young *Infante* Pedro was to seize Almenar on the northern approaches to Lérida while his father began the building of a fortress at Luna on the northern edge of the plain of Zaragoza.

In 1094, after thirty years of patient but persistent advance, the king of Aragón would now attempt to bring his long-cherished plans to fruition with the formal initiation of the siege of the major city of Huesca. Sancho Ramírez would not live to see the fall of that bastion, however. On June 4, 1094, while directing operations there, he was struck fatally by an arrow. He was succeeded immediately by his eldest son, Pedro, but the siege had to be lifted for a time.

Pedro I (1094–1104) ordinarily stands in the shadow of his more-famous brother and successor, Alfonso I, but he himself was a major architect of the emerging greatness of Aragón.[9] He played a not inconsiderable role, even during the lifetime of his father. On the death of Sancho Ramírez, Pedro gathered up the momentarily disjoined segments of his father's plans, augmented them in major fashion so that they became more feasible than they originally had been, and then carried them to a resoundingly successful conclusion with the definitive reconquest of Huesca in 1096.

From the first moment of his accession, the new king of Aragón understood, better than his father it seems, the major implications of an assault on the city of Huesca, so important to al-Mustain and Zaragoza. The city was not only key to the defenses of Zaragoza in the northeast, but itself the center of a large, fertile plain which merged without break into the plains surrounding Lérida and Zaragoza. There are no detailed studies of Muslim Huesca in the late 11th Century, but we know it was not simply a city wealthy by virtue of agricultural hinterland. It seems to have boasted some active intellectual life on the part of its Muslim community. It also had a Jewish community, and, until most recently, possessed a Christian bishopric and was therefore doubtless the center of a substantial Mozarabic Christian community. Contemporary Muslim accounts relate that it had nine gates in its walls and ninety towers bolstering them. The ninety towers may be hyperbole, but a consideration of its extant ground plan suggests that it may well have had nine gates. The same plan also indicates that a population of 2,000, perhaps as many as 3,000, was likely. If so, Huesca would have been larger than any contemporary Christian city of Iberia, except for Barcelona and the recently captured Toledo. It was three times the population of either Pamplona or Jaca at the time, and, once captured, Pedro would have promptly made it the chief city of his realm. Moreover, depending upon exactly how much of the city's hinterland could be appropriated at its fall, the geographical extent of the then kingdom of Aragón would be almost doubled and the area of its workable farmland quadrupled.

The threat to such a prize was not one that al-Mustain could ignore. Nor, more distantly, would Alfonso VI be inclined to take lightly the menace that such a loss would constitute to that Zaragoza which had long been marked as the eventual prey of León–Castilla. If an Aragonese siege of Huesca were to begin to demonstrate any prospect of imminent success, the intervention of the Leonese

[9] He is, however, one of the few figures of the period whose documents have been satisfactorily edited. See Ubieto Arteta, ed., *Colección de Pedro I.*

monarch could be anticipated, along with the strongest sort of reaction from al-Mustain. Those probabilities had to be offset to the degree possible. Therefore, the new king, busy reducing scattered strongholds on the plain of Huesca in 1095, was even more busy on what may loosely be termed the diplomatic front.

A series of papal documents from Urban II attest to the approaches made by Pedro I at this juncture and to his sweeping renewal of the Aragonese feudal subordination to the papacy. The undertaking was successful and ensured that Huesca would fall to a papal vassal and it would do so in the presence of a papal legate.[10] Such a maneuver might hope to temper the reaction of León–Castilla and indeed may have. A more mundane necessity was for sufficient manpower to make the siege a success. Aragón could not hope to supply it alone. We are told that in the climactic battle some 20,000 men were engaged on each side. Even if we were to reduce that estimate to a tenth of the number, which is cautious but realistic in terms of what we know about the ordinary conditions of medieval warfare, such a force on the Aragonese side had to be recruited from beyond the realm. All of the evidence indicates that it was to be found in the south of France. We do not, in this case, have the names of the actual combatants However, after the fall of the city, the archbishop of Bordeaux and the bishops of Oloron and Lescar in Bearn were prominent in the rededication of the principal mosque as a Christian cathedral, and the abbey of Saint-Pons de Thomières was the recipient of the royal largesse.[11] It very much appears that the Bearnese alliance had proven its worth.

His preparations made, Pedro began the siege of Huesca in May of 1096. The results were what one would expect in this sort of warfare. The garrison held out well over the summer but by fall was beginning to feel the pinch. The governor of the city informed al-Mustain, who raised a large army himself but also appealed to the Leonese for the sort of assistance to which the payment of *parias* had entitled him. Alfonso VI did not respond in person, deterred perhaps by the papal interest, or by the delicate internal negotiations then in process with the Burgundian counts Raymond and Henry. Al-Mustain's army, however, was joined by contingents led by Count

---

[10] Paul Kehr, ed., "Papsturkunden in Spanien, II: Navarra und Aragon," in *AGWG*, Philologisch-historische Klasse, N. F. Vol. 22 (Berlin, 1928), pp. 129–34, for the ecclesiastical aspects. Ubieto Arteta, *Historia de Aragón* pp. 118–28, and Afif Turk, *El reino de Zaragoza en el siglo XI de Cristo, V de la Hégira* (Madrid, 1978), pp. 175–79, both treat the campaign in some detail.

[11] Marcelin Defourneaux, *Les français en Espagne aux XIe et XIIe siècles* (Paris, 1949), p. 150.

García Ordóñez of the Rioja and by the Castilian count Gonzalo Núñez de Lara, neither of whom would have participated without Alfonso's permission. The crucial battle was fought at Alcoraz on November 18, 1096. The garrison does not seem to have attempted a sally against the besiegers on the approach of the relief army from Zaragoza. What followed was a battle of cavalry, with the Aragonese and French winning by a charge which split the opponent's center, probably where the Muslim and Christian segments of it joined. Al-Mustain fled back to Zaragoza having sustained serious losses. García Ordóñez was said to have been captured. If so, his captivity must have been brief, for he appears with regularity in Castilian documents of 1097. The dispirited defenders of Huesca surrendered the city to Pedro on November 27.

A triumph of such dimensions was important to Aragón but no less so to her neighboring kingdoms in the north of the peninsula. Zaragoza might lack the resources to respond, especially if Pedro continued to enjoy substantial French assistance, but León–Castilla might not. To provide against foreseeable eventualities would have been merely prudent. It is just at this time that Diego Peláez, the former bishop of Santiago de Compostela, deposed in 1088 for participating in a revolt against Alfonso VI, first appears at the court of Pedro I. The Galician prelate will continue to enjoy the hospitality of Pedro down to the latter's death in 1094. Certainly this sheltering of a former rebel and continuing opponent in the ecclesiastical affairs of the Leonese king would have given further offense to him. At the same time, however, it would give the Aragonese reliable intelligence of the latter's realm, and perhaps an ability to make some small trouble there if necessary.

In the year immediately following, Pedro I would take a second wife. His first wife, Inés of Aquitaine, is last mentioned in a charter of May 9, and on August 16, 1097, Pedro took a bride named Berta in the cathedral of Huesca. The new queen was of Italian origin. Certainly the marriage would have added to the luster of the crown, but further motives for it are difficult to adduce since military reinforcement from Italy was most unlikely. That same year Alfonso VI had in fact projected a major attack against Pedro of Aragón, and had actually begun to lead an army toward the east when his progress was halted by news of a Murābit landing. Unavoidably, that force had to be diverted to the south where it was roughly handled in the campaign of that summer. Instead, the Leonese monarch had to appeal to Pedro for assistance, which, in this instance, did not materialize.

The spring and summer, at least, of 1098 were devoted to the capture of the fortress of Calasanz to the east of Barbastro. The place was one of the last of the interlocking system of strongholds that guarded the high frontier of the Zaragozan taifa. Its reduction made somewhat simpler the siege of Barbastro which Pedro I now undertook, beginning in February or March of 1099. This town was important in itself, but it also was a major station on the road to Lérida to the southeast. Earlier it had been the defensive center against attacks emanating from the Ribagorza region, but the fall of other positions such as Graus and Estadilla had left it isolated. Even so, the capture of the town required another major effort, and it did not surrender until October 18, 1100. Apparently the army of Aragón had again been complemented by substantial French forces. After its fall Barbastro was assigned a new bishop, a former French monk, Pons of Saint-Pons de Thomières. Also, Saint-Foy de Conques and Saint-Gilles de Provence were both rewarded with large grants of property.

The following year Pedro of Aragón seems to have attempted an assault upon Zaragoza, but his forces were unequal to the task. Again, he had recruited widely. The papal legate, Abbot Richard of Saint-Victor of Marseilles, was in Barbastro in January, and Bishop Berenguer of Barcelona was there in May. By June the Aragonese was campaigning in the environs of Zaragoza and in August had struck south some 100 kilometers to Alpenes. These were actions that went well beyond the likely capabilities of the Aragonese themselves. It has been suggested that Pedro I took the cross after the fall of Barbastro, but was dissuaded by Pope Paschal II from a crusade to the Holy Land in concert with some French barons in favor of one against Zaragoza. The chronology of such a theory is impossible.

During the next two years, the king would be fully occupied by the threat now posed by the flood of Murābit power up into the northeast of the peninsula consequent on the disappearance of the principality of Valencia. At the death of *El Cid* in 1099, Pedro was busy with the siege of Barbastro. At that point he would have lacked the resources to absorb or prop up that realm. Alfonso VI of León–Castilla, who did intervene twice in Valencia, finally abandoned the city to the Murābit in 1102.

Valencia was effectively occupied by Emir Mazdali before the end of May. Not stopping there, he swept north into the county of Barcelona, sacking what he could in a largely uncontested raid through the countryside. In September the forces of Barcelona and Urgel attempted a counterattack, but were defeated at Mollerusa some 20 kilometers east of Lérida. Count Armengol V of Urgel was killed in the same battle that destroyed his army. For the moment at least, King Pedro I of Aragón was the only undefeated Christian ruler in northeast Iberia.

Pedro of Aragón died without further laurels in September of 1104. His son had predeceased him. Therefore, the throne of Aragón passed to his brother, Alfonso I *el Batallador* (1104–1134). Fortunately, there was no disturbance at his accession, but the situation of the Christian northeast remained dangerous. Still, despite the conflict of its interests with those of Aragón over the eventual disposition of Zaragoza, León–Castilla was compelled by imbalance in the peninsula between Christian and Muslim forces to help redress the preponderance of Islam there.

In 1104 the Leonese count Pedro Ansúrez had been despatched to the county of Urgel where he would serve as regent for the next five years for the young Armengol VI.[12] The boy count was his grandson. Count Pedro then drew Count Ramón Berenguer III of Barcelona into a joint expedition, which would result in the capture of the major Muslim fortress of Balaguer on the Segre River 25 kilometers north of Lérida by November 3, 1105. This victory, the campaign of Alfonso VI in Andalucía the following year, and the death of Yūsuf ibn Tāshufīn that September, all had the effect of freeing the hands of the king of Aragón. Sometime during the summer of 1106 his forces overran Ejea de los Caballeros, thus inching yet farther toward Zaragoza on the plain only 55 kilometers to the southwest from that point.

Far more important, however, was the *Batallador's* capture of Tamarite de Litera and San Esteban de Litera to the north and northeast of Lérida, respectively. These were the last of the advance frontier fortresses along the foothills of the central and eastern Pyrenees still in Muslim hands, and their fall opened up the prospect of far easier communication and travel between Barcelona and Urgel in the east and Aragón in the west. That is, from Urgel to Sobrarbe there are a series of valleys and mountain ridges running south from the Pyrenees that make travel east and west almost impossible to anyone but the most mobile and lightly equipped. In this way, geography assured the practical independence of those river valleys ever since the first Muslim conquest. A series of strongholds along the edges of the plain of the Ebro – Balaguer, Alfarras, Tamarite de Litera, San Esteban de Litera, Monzón, and Barbastro – denied to the Christians of those areas any effective way to travel between

---

[12] In fact, the count was also likely in the position of an exile. The play of faction at the Leonese court had forced Alfonso VI to remove him from that scene to Urgel. See Bernard F. Reilly, *The Kingdom of León–Castilla under King Alfonso VI, 1065–1109* (Princeton, N.J., 1988), pp. 319–20 and 331–33.

them, except by permission of the Muslim of the south. For almost four centuries they remained isolated from the Aragonese and the west of Christian Iberia and from Barcelona and the extreme east of Christian Iberia.

Now the increasing debility of the taifa of Zaragoza was to result in the dissolution of that age-old condition. The counts of Barcelona had already reached the eastern edge of the plain of Lérida in 1026 with the capture of Cervera. But their expansion farther west was blocked by the strength of Lérida itself and the meager nature of their own resources. Furthermore, cooperation and coordination with the Christians of the west was virtually impossible because communication with them was so difficult. It was probably simplest by way of France. Now that problem was gone, forever, as it proved. Sancho Ramírez I had taken Monzón; Pedro I, Alfarras and Barbastro; and Alfonso I Tamarite de Litera and San Esteban de Litera. Count Pedro Ansúrez and Ramón Berenguer III had taken Balaguer. As long as Lérida remained in Muslim hands, travel could be interdicted. Now, however, travelers could seek shelter in that same string of fortresses. The isolation of Barcelona from the remainder of Christian Iberia was effectively over. Less than a quarter-century would see even the union of the crowns of Aragón and Barcelona. For the moment it should be noted that, probably in 1106 or early 1107, Count Pedro Ansúrez ceded one-third of the city of Balaguer to Alfonso I of Aragón and one of its churches to the bishop of Huesca.[13] Count Pedro himself swore fidelity to the Aragonese monarch, and the document makes clear that the young count of Urgel was also to do so at some future date.

The Tardy Emergence of the County of Barcelona

During the last third of the 11th Century the county of Barcelona had almost no importance in the development of the political life of the peninsula. The reasons for that fact are manifold. In the first place, what we should today regard as Cataluña was at that date still divided into a series of counties of which Barcelona was the most important merely by virtue of its port and its relatively larger area of arable land. Even so, that county comprised scarcely more than about 8,000 square kilometers and was hemmed in both physically

---

[13] Francisco M. Rosell, *Liber Feudorum Maior* (Barcelona, 1945), pp. 166–67. This document is undated. For the second, Antonio Durán Gudiol, ed., *Colección diplomática de la catedral de Huesca*, Vol. 1 (Zaragoza, 1965), p. 123.

and politically. To its northeast were the Pyrenees; to the east, a series of ranges, less formidable than the Pyrenees, but beyond which lay the great plain of the Ebro dominated by Muslim Lérida, Muslim Huesca, and Muslim Zaragoza. Sometimes these powers were united in the hands of a single leader like al-Muqtadir, sometimes not, but singly or in unison they were beyond the powers of the count of Barcelona to reduce. To the south, the plain of Barcelona narrowed down sharply, and the hills overlooking it were dominated by Muslim shepherds, small farmers, and fortresses all the way down to Tarragona, then deserted, and beyond to the holdings of the taifa of Tortosa.

Faced by such a prospect, Count Ramón Berenguer (1035–1076) turned toward the less-forbidding north. Seizing a French wife, he constructed a loose dominion over places as various as Toulouse, Carcassonne, Béziers, Agde, and Montpellier. This was the origin of the familial Catalan Empire in the Midi, which, like most other structures of the period, made little ethnic, linguistic, or political sense. However, in the long run, Barcelona proved poorly sited to control such an area, and its attempt to do so directed its resources north and away from the peninsula.

Finally, the personal history of the counts of Barcelona during the period guaranteed that any policy they would pursue would be severely handicapped. In 1071 Pedro, the son of Ramón Berenguer by a former marriage, assassinated his mother-in-law, Almodis de la Marca, because he suspected her of plotting against him and because of the aggrandizement of her sons, his stepbrothers. His father could hardly do less than exile him, and so Pedro went off on a pilgrimage to the Holy Land from which he was never to return. In any event, the assassination of Almodis furnished the cause, or pretext, for her sons by a former marriage who now governed the county of Toulouse, to throw off their allegiance to Barcelona and to encourage the rest of the Midi to do likewise. The claims of Barcelona in that area were thus to become a major preoccupation rather than a source of strength for the next forty years.

At his death, Ramón Berenguer I was succeeded by the twin sons of the late Countess Almodis, Ramón Berenguer II and Berenguer Ramón II, whose joint rule (1076–1082) began in great ambition and ended in disaster. During those periods when the dynastic necessities of the Beni Hūd of Zaragoza required the division of the domains of that taifa, the counts of Barcelona had sometimes been able to exact *parias* from the resulting, weaker taifas of Lérida and Tortosa as the price of their alliance against Zaragoza. Sometime between 1076 and 1078, the document is undated, the twin rulers of Barcelona negotiated an agreement with Count Armengol IV of Urgel. By its terms that upland ruler was to become their ally-mercenary captain in a plan to extract *parias* not only from Lérida and Tortosa but also from Valencia, Denia, Murcia, and Granada. They intended to lay the entire Muslim world of the Mediterranean coast subject to their suzerainty. The reward for the count of Urgel would be a portion of the *parias* annually.[14]

Even with the strength of Barcelona joined to that of Urgel, whose counts had more than once led the armies of Barcelona and would again, these ambitions outran their real prospects. A campaign against Murcia undertaken in 1077, even in alliance with al-Mutamid of Sevilla who had his own ambitions in the region, fell afoul of the superior resources of al-Mamūn of Toledo who held the city of Murcia for his own. The Barcelonan expedition had to withdraw. A campaign against Denia was planned for 1081 when the approaching death of al-Muqtadir of Zaragoza made it clear that Denia was to become a part of the inheritance of al-Mundir along with Lérida and Tortosa. Since that worthy would in all likelihood become their ally against his brother, al-Mutamin of Zaragoza, and could thereby be expected to pay them *parias*, the project had become pointless.

The ongoing frustration of their plans may have contributed to the growing alienation of the twins from one another. Be that as it may, one day in 1082 Count Ramón Berenguer II's body was found in a ravine in Barcelona, the obvious victim of foul play. Despite his denials of responsibility, his brother was at once the prime object of suspicion. From this point on, the rule of Berenguer Ramón would be hampered by the continuous opposition of a portion of the nobility of the county who rallied around the widow of the slain twin. However, a new factor just introduced into the kaleidoscopic affairs of the Mediterranean coast was the advent of the Cid, now an exile from León–Castilla and a new and major ally for al-Mutamin of Zaragoza. This combination of events would continue to hinder the best plans of Barcelona.

In 1083 Berenguer Ramón joined with Sancho Ramírez of Aragón in support of al-Mundir of Lérida against the attack of al-Mutamin and the Cid only to be defeated and captured at the engagement of Almenar. He was released on condition of withdrawing from that alliance. In early 1086 he supported al-Mundir's attempt to prevent Alfonso VI from introducing the former king of Toledo, al-Qādir, into Valencia, but the Leonese troops under Alvar Fáñez secured

---

[14] Pierre Bonnassie, *Cataluña mil años atrás, siglos X–XI* (Barcelona, 1988), pp. 428–29.

their aim regardless. After 1086, the Cid was to leave the service of Zaragoza and begin to build a principality for himself, based on the *parias* of Valencia which would allow him to support the army he needed. This contest seemed rather more equal, and Berenguer Ramón attempted in 1089 a siege of Valencia to claim that objective for himself. A counterblockade by Rodrigo Díaz forced him to abandon it, however. At the death of al-Mundir of Lérida in 1090, the Cid seemed on the point of establishing his suzerainty in that taifa. But Berenguer Ramón again intervened, this time in league with al-Mustain of Zaragoza, only to be defeated and captured once more at the battle of Tevar. The Cid then established his indirect control over that city and over Valencia outright in 1094.

Perhaps because of these continuing failures in his plans for expansion – we do not know the particulars – his domestic enemies at last began to make headway against Berenguer Ramón. Sometime in 1096 or 1097 he was apparently forced to submit to a judicial duel to prove his innocence of the murder of his twin brother. Very late sources assert that the ordeal was staged before the court of Alfonso VI, but Leonese chroniclers make no mention of such an event. At any rate, the count, vanquished in the ordeal, had to abdicate and go into exile in the Holy Land where he died some time later. The comital crown now passed to Ramón Berenguer III (1097–1131), the son of the fratricide's late brother. The new count fifteen years of age at his accession, was destined for a long reign, and would subsequently be given the sobriquet of *el Grande*. The early stages of his rule, however, were anything but promising. He had scarcely married the daughter of *El Cid* in 1098 when the death of that adventurer made the arrangement fruitless.

Indeed, Barcelona was to live in the shadow of imminent Murābit attack for the next twenty years, and there appeared to be little that its young count could do, of himself, to alter that situation in any fundamental way. Barcelona would have to draw on the strength of the other Christian principalities of Iberia, a long process to be sure. But a very significant beginning was made in 1104 when Ramón Berenguer III participated in the capture of Balaguer. The fall of that fortress on the Segre River opened the way to communication, coordination, and cooperation with Aragón against the common enemy, as we have already seen. Almost as important, in the long run, was that this initiative helped to keep the Catalan-speaking county of Urgel out of the orbit of Castilian-speaking Aragón.

The counts of Urgel were, of course, related to the comital house of Barcelona and had often served as the commanders of its armies This was due to the fact that the upland valley that was Urgel already produced a simpler, more aristocratic type of society than lowland, increasingly commercial Barcelona. But these characteristics gave Urgel rather more affinity with the rising crown of Aragón, and intermarriage with the house of Ramiro I had been frequent.

In fact, the late king of Aragón, Pedro I, had been named heir to the county by Armengol IV, somewhere prior to 1086, if the latter had died without direct descent. Armengol's mother had been a daughter of Ramiro I of Aragón.[15] Perhaps fortunately for Barcelona, Armengol V had married a daughter of the Leonese magnate, Pedro Ansúrez, and, when the Urgelese count was killed at Mollerusa in 1102, the regency of the county had gone to Ansúrez. The assistance to Barcelona would prove to be the same, but the threat of aggrandizement in Urgel was less in the case of the Leonese than it would have been if that office had fallen to Alfonso I of Aragón. As it was, Pedro Ansúrez found it necessary to swear fidelity to the Aragonese and to promise that the young Armengol VI would also do so when he assumed personal control of the county. Still, all in all, it appears that at the beginning of the 12th Century an incorporation of the Catalan counties into a rising kingdom of Aragón seemed more likely than that the peculiar count–kingship of Barcelona and Aragón should emerge.

El Cid Campeador *and the Taifa of Valencia*

Rodrigo Díaz de Vivar is perhaps the most widely known Spaniard of the 11th Century and at the same time the most misperceived. Put another way, he is an historical figure viewed ordinarily through a literary lens, that is, through his portrait in the early 13th-century epic, *Cantar de mio Cid*. The historical mischief that such a practice ordinarily wreaks has been compounded, in this case, by the insistence of the great Spanish linguistic and literary scholar Ramón Menéndez Pidal that the Spanish epic is peculiarly faithful to historical fact and may be relied upon for an almost literal account of the past. Because Menéndez Pidal is considered to be the most important modern editor of not only that epic, but also the 13th-century *Primera crónica general* which drew upon it for its portrait of 11th-century Iberia, and finally the author of a history of the Cid which has gone through five editions in the first half of this century, his views have had what may fairly be called particular authority.[16]

---

[15] Ferran Soldevila, ed., *Historia de España*, Vol. 1 (Barcelona, 1952), pp. 122–23.
[16] Menéndez Pidal, ed., *La España del Cid*, is the best of them. Also see his *Primera crónica general de España*, 2 vols. (Madrid, 1955), and *Cantar de mio Cid*, 3 vols. (Madrid, 1954).

Current work has revised them considerably, and what follows here is fruit of that reworking.[17]

Rodrigo Díaz was born in the tiny village of Vivar which is about 9 kilometers north of Burgos on the eastern edge of the great *meseta* of northern Spain. He was born into the León–Castilla of Fernando *el Magno* (1037–1065), probably about the same time as was Alfonso VI, and his first public appearances were in the court of Sancho II of Castilla (1065–1072). That fact seems to have done him no particular harm, for he played an honorable if modest part in the subsequent court of Alfonso VI until he led a raid into the territories of Toledo, then allied with León–Castilla. For that impertinence he was to be exiled to the east of the peninsula. In the long run, it turned out to be the most fortunate of misfortunes, for that arena furnished a scope for the operation of his great military and political talents which the center of the peninsula must always have denied.

The Cid went into exile at the head of a small band of trained warriors, and, as we have already seen, from 1081 to 1087 he served the interests of the taifa of Zaragoza, which were most often those of León–Castilla as well. But the appearance of the Murābits in the peninsula began then to disrupt all of the old political verities, and the Cid chose, from the spring of 1088, to operate independently and in his own best interests. To do so it was above all necessary to procure an income that would allow him to support a force of about 700 horse, with auxiliaries of about 2,500 men in all. This then, was to be the size of his force, and it was a tribute to his reputation, even then, as a successful military leader. At the same time, the support needed for a force of that size was Rodrigo's first and most enduring problem.

Over the next six years he solved that problem by extraction of *parias* from all of the still-independent taifas of the east, except Zaragoza, which was too powerful to coerce with the forces at his disposal. First came the petty principality of Albarracín, which paid 10,000 dinars annually, and then the proud city of Valencia, which ransomed its lands for 12,000 a year. These were followed by Sagunto and Alpuente, then Murviedro, Segorbe, Almenara, Jérica, and Liria, and finally Játiva and Denia, as the power of the Castilian cut across all bonds of coercion among Muslim to impose his preferred set of relationships. After the death of al-Mundir in 1090, the Cid was even able to establish a protectorate over Lérida and Tortosa in the name of the former's sons.

This situation, so long as he could maintain it, gave him a truly

[17] Reilly, *Alfonso VI*, pp. 37–39, for instance. The most recent synthesis is found in Richard A. Fletcher, *The Quest for El Cid* (New York, 1990).

princely income in excess of 100,000 dinars annually. Yet during this period his rule was never more than a single defeat from dissolution, although his military genius did prove sufficient against Barcelona, Lérida, and Aragón, in turn or in combination, as we have already seen. It also raised the most serious misgivings on the part of his former king, Alfonso VI, especially after Rodrigo failed to respond to the royal plea for assistance to raise the Murābit siege of Aledo in 1088. In 1092 Alfonso even intervened in the east personally, and in cooperation with the rulers of Barcelona and Aragón, but Rodrigo evaded the thrust he could not parry and reestablished his position when the various royal concerns drew the three elsewhere.

Indeed, over the next seven years *El Cid* became truly a territorial prince in the east. Ironically, that metamorphosis was stimulated by the advance there of the Murābit. After 1090, the new policy of Yūsuf ibn Tāshufīn would lead to the absorption of the taifas of Almería and Murcia in 1091. In 1092, his son and governor, ibn Āisa, forced the abandonment of Aledo by the Christians and then advanced to overrun Denia, Játiva, and finally Alcira. That carried them to within 35 kilometers of Valencia itself and sparked a revolt in that city which cost al-Qādir both his throne and his life. Still, local Muslim forces preferred to avoid the direct embrace of their African coreligionists. Rodrigo intervened both to recognize the new regime there and to force the payment of *parias* by it.

An arrangement so unstable could not endure, and the following summer saw the new advance of the Murābit toward Valencia. What followed seems to have been a complex war of maneuver in which the Cid balked any chance of his opponent to engage on favorable terms, and, in late fall, the Africans retired south. But during that period the Muslim of Valencia had broken with the Christians, even if they had given no effective help to the Murābit. Rodrigo now embarked on that course which was to make him, until his death in 1099, truly one of the princes of the east. Through the winter and spring of 1093–1094 he laid siege to Valencia, wasting its hinterland and denying provisions to the city. His forces were not adequate to the direct assault of such a place, but terror, intrigue, and hunger wrought their effect and the city surrendered to him on June 15, 1094.

Following the surrender, the Cid expelled part of the Muslim population of Valencia and replaced it with such Mozarabs as could be found in the suburbs, in the interests of the greater security that such a measure would provide. The property of the expellees was apparently handed over to his troops. However, at least a minority of the Muslim population was allowed to remain, guaranteed the possession of its property and the exercise of its religion. Ibn Yahhaf, former ruler, was to continue as its *qāḍī*.

But the fall of the taifa of Valencia into the hands of the infidel horrified Islam in Andalucía and Africa only slightly less than did that of Toledo nine years earlier. Yūsuf ibn Tāshufīn despatched his nephew with an army from Africa. Several Andalucian contingents could be spared to reinforce it, especially since the last of the major independent taifas, Badajoz, had fallen to the Murābit earlier in the year. This army did not reach Valencia until September of 1094, however. Apprised of its approach and size, Rodrigo had appealed to Alfonso VI for assistence, who prepared to aid Rodrigo, even though, as it was to develop, that aid was unnecessary. What followed was variously reported by the sources. Apparently, however, observing lax discipline and even desertion in the Muslim camp, *El Cid* launched an audacious attack on the enemy at Cuart de Poblet in October, routed them, and seized their camp and its treasure.

The city was now safe, and Rodrigo Diaz's hold on it was now secure while he should live. He, and his family summoned from the Castilian monastery of Cardeña, installed themselves in the royal palace there. Well they might, for they had become a ruling dynasty. For the next four years, until his death in 1099, Rodrigo Díaz de Vivar would be prince of Valencia. His wife, Jimena Díaz, would rule after him for another three years, until April or May of 1102 when the city with the help of Alfonso VI had to be evacuated and left, finally, to the Murābit. The progeny of the Castilian would disappear as an independent dynasty, and Valencia would continue as a Muslim city for more than a century and a quarter. The result of all this would be a brilliance that would incite a legend in which Rodrigo would become incomparably more significant than he had been in life. Nonetheless, for a dozen years he had defied, bluffed, and beaten kings, counts, and emirs, in a military and political *tour de force* that still provokes one's wonder and admiration. *El Cid* might well have been content with that.

6

The Dynastic Crisis in León–Castilla
(1109–1126)

On July 1, 1109, in the seventy-second year of his life and the forty-fourth year of his reign, the most powerful Christian ruler the peninsula had seen since the Muslim Conquest died in Toledo. Queen Urraca, his daughter and just-proclaimed heir, escorted the body of Alfonso VI north and saw to its interment on July 21st in the monastery church of Sahagún, where the king would rest beside the remains of those five wives who had predeceased him. The ordinary, prosaic rituals of mourning were to be the prelude to almost two decades of desperate crisis in the kingdom which Alfonso had constructed.

Little than a year before his death, a Murābit army had defeated an army of the realm led by his son and heir, Sancho Alfónsez, on May 29, 1108, at Uclés, a small town but 30 kilometers south of the Tajo and 105 kilometers east of Toledo. By that victory the empire of Alī ibn Yusuf recovered the last vestiges of the southern half of the former taifa of Toledo, and the frontier between León–Castilla and the Murābit stood at the line of the Tajo with that great city perched vulnerable on the north bank. Alfonso VI himself, although infirm with age, had come south twice, in 1108 and again in 1109, to see to the defenses of the city whose capture in 1085 had confirmed the hegemony of León–Castilla in all of Iberia, Muslim as well as Christian. At his death, the situation of Toledo could only be described as untenable. The city must fall to Alī, who that summer was debouching another army from Africa. Should it fall, the collapse of what remained of the old taifa of Toledo north of the river was foreordained, and the frontier between the two faiths in the center of the peninsula would be restored to the line of the Guadarramas.

Incredibly, under those circumstances, Christian Toledo was to be left to survive or to perish largely upon its own local resources, for in the disaster at Uclés Alfonso had lost the only son that six marriages over forty-two years had provided him. In Toledo in June of 1109 he had proclaimed his eldest daughter, Urraca, as his heir in the presence of a great assemblage of the prelates and magnates of his kingdom. The dying king had also compelled their assent to the marriage of his new heir to her cousin, Alfonso I of Aragón, *el Batallador*. Thereby he hoped to provide his realm with a male capable of leading and defending it in those most dangerous circumstances. Nevertheless, the final dispositions of the old king were unpopular in many quarters of the realm, and he had to compel assent by sheer force of will and the prestige of age and honors.[1]

The most threatening aspect of the domestic situation in 1109 was that the dynasty itself was in disarray. Since the dynasty was the fundamental element of all monarchical political life, its disagreement now was ominous.

In Coimbra in their county of Portugal, Teresa, the half sister of the new queen, and her Burgundian husband, Count Henry, viewed the whole proceeding sourly. They either were already, or were shortly to become parents of the second grandson of the dead king. Alfonso Enríquez, destined to be the first king of Portugal, was born sometime in 1109.[2] Teresa and Henry had objected to the old king's decision and so signaled that fact to the entire realm by absenting themselves from the proclamation of Urraca in Toledo. Although they probably had no real opportunity to attend Alfonso's obsequies at Sahagún because of the distance involved, they conspicuously failed to rejoin the court of Urraca in the months after.

To the northwest, in Galicia, a party was also in the process of forming around the claims of the five-year-old Alfonso Raimúndez, son of Urraca and the deceased Count Raymond and the grandson of Alfonso VI. This party would have several advantages over that of Portugal. Urraca had been born in lawful wedlock but Teresa was daughter by a mistress. Alfonso Raimúndez had already survived to almost five years in an age when infant mortality was the commonest

[1] More than a century later the dissent is reported in Rodrigo Jiménez de Rada, *De Rebus Hispaniae*, ed. Juan Fernández Valverde (Turnholt, 1987), pp. 217–18. The most detailed and accessible modern accounts of these events are to be found in Bernard F. Reilly, *The Kingdom of León–Castilla under King Alfonso VI, 1065–1109* (Princeton, N. J., 1988), pp. 345–63, and *The Kingdom of León–Castilla under Queen Urraca, 1109–1126* (Princeton, N. J., 1982), pp. 45–86.

[2] Luiz Gonzaga de Azevedo, *História de Portugal*, Vol. 3 (Lisbon, 1940), pp. 240–43, reviewed the various sources available for determining the date of his birth and came to the conclusion that 1106 was most probable. I believe that he must discard too much of the evidence to do so and that 1109–1110 is the more likely date.

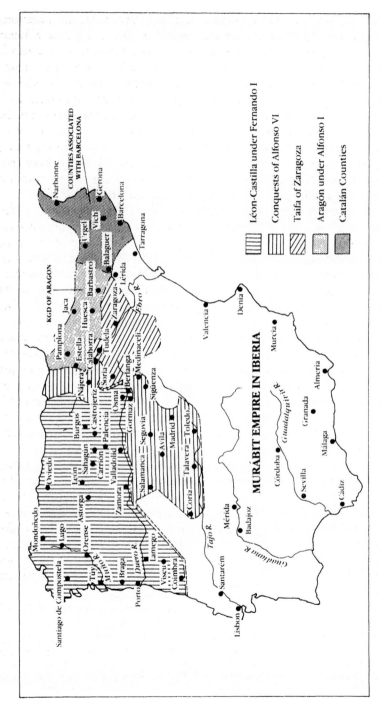

Figure 3 Murābit and Christian Iberia at the death of Alfonso VI in 1109

of experiences.[3] The pretensions of the boy already had the sanction, in some degree, of the deceased monarch. In 1107, after Sancho Alfónsez had been recognized as heir, and subsequent to the death of Count Raymond, the then *infanta* Urraca had also been recognized as the ruler of Galicia up until such time as she should remarry. On her remarriage, it was stipulated, her son would succeed her in the possession of Galicia. Now the queen was preparing to marry, and her son had powerful and ambitious guardians in Count Pedro Froílaz of Traba, the head of the Trastamara family of Galicia, and Bishop Diego Gelmírez of Santiago de Compostela. These two would be perfectly capable of asserting their ward's rights to either Galicia or the entire kingdom as the occasion offered.

The youngest half sisters of Urraca, Sancha and Elvira, born of the French Queen Elizabeth, would have been too young to be important politically. Another Elvira, half sister of Urraca and sister of Teresa of Portugal, born of the concubine Jimena Múñoz, was abroad. She had been married off to the crusading Count Raymond IV of Toulouse at a date unknown and had borne him a son to whom the name Alfonso Jordán was given, after the river of his baptism. Only Sancha Raimúndez, older sister of Alfonso Raimúndez, born before 1095 and therefore probably at least fifteen years old, was a dynastic figure capable of being manipulated, but we know nothing of her so early.[4] Among the regular members of the queen's court, the most serious dissenter was Archbishop Bernard of Toledo. A long-time collaborator of the deceased king, he was still troubled by the fact that the projected marriage transgressed the canon law of consanguinity and thus could not fail to be an additional handicap to the stability of the realm.

Queen Urraca herself was a mature woman of twenty-nine years, no stranger to either marriage or politics. She had borne the late Count Raymond two children who survived childbirth and likely a few who did not. She had been the count's consort for the seventeen years before his death and had actively ruled in Galicia for the twenty-two months following it. Now she would rule León–Castilla alone and in her own name until her marriage in October some two months later. Urraca was neither a blushing bride nor a political neophyte as events were to demonstrate.

In October at the castle of Monzón just 10 kilometers north of

---

[3] Enríque Flórez, *Memorias de las reinas católicas de España*, 2 vols., 1761, Reprint (Madrid, 1964); 1:234–35, reviewed the materials then available and settled the date as March 5, 1105. No new data has appeared since.

[4] Luisa García Calles, *Doña Sancha* (León, 1972), is an attempt at a biography of an admittedly difficult subject.

Palencia, Urraca and Alfonso of Aragón were married. When the formal *carta de arras*, or marriage contract, was worked out in December, it was surprisingly favorable to León–Castilla. The *Batallador* was willing to pay a considerable price for such a prize. Both agreed that if either partner deserted the other, the offender would forfeit the loyalty of their supporters. Alfonso agreed, in particular, that neither the argument of blood relationship nor the excommunication which might follow from it would deter him. If he should have a son by Urraca, she and the child would jointly inherit his territories after his death. Urraca alone would inherit if there were no offspring. On the other hand, if Urraca died first, although Alfonso would inherit jointly with a child, in the absence of issue he would have only the usufruct of her lands for his lifetime At his death, León–Castilla would pass to Alfonso Raimúndez.[5] Despite all such provisions the marriage would quickly prove be doomed.

Personal incompatibility has often been urged as the reason for its failure. Contemporaries tended to regard a strong-willed queen as something not quite in accord with nature, and most subsequent historians have followed that lead. It has also been suggested that the Aragonese monarch was perhaps homosexual or simply a misogynist. Certainly the thirty-six-year-old Alfonso had never been married before, and would not be again. Moreover, surprising in the age, or perhaps in any age, he had not used his power to take a mistress or to produce any known bastards. Later on, Urraca was to accuse him of physical abuse. All of this may or may not have been true. In any event, none of it mattered in any degree except as it bore on the inability of the pair to conceive a child. It has been suggested that he was sterile and I am inclined to believe it.[6]

The inability to conceive a child, and to do as quickly, was the crucial failure of the union. Neither Urraca nor Alfonso were children nor were they romantics. The business of the marriage could only have been to produce an heir in whose name one or the other or both could then rule both their realms. As such, it had powerful enemies in León–Castilla from the beginning. Since the marriage was clearly uncanonical, that its enemies would appeal to the Roman pope to condemn it was a foregone conclusion. That they would follow up such a condemnation by rebellion was likely. Only a child

[5] José María Ramos y Loscertales, "La sucesión del rey Alfonso VI," *AHDE* 13 (1936–41):36–99, published the text from surviving 18th-century copies and makes an ingenious but unconvincing argument that the two were married before Alfonso VI's death.

[6] Elena Lourie, "The Will of Alfonso I 'El Batallador,' King of Aragon and Navarre: A Reassessment," *Speculum* 50 (1975):639–41

and heir could forestall both. Even if Urraca and Alfonso were forced subsequently to separate, the child would still have a claim, by virtue of which they could rule until his maturity. But no such child was to appear.

While the new royal couple was arranging the terms of the marriage, the frontier with Islam was erupting. Alí ibn Yūsuf had invaded the lands of Toledo, taken Talavera de la Reina to its west, and rolled up the Christian flank north of the Tajo in the east, overrunning and pillaging the lands about Guadalajara and Madrid. That seems to have occupied him until the end of the campaigning season, although the sequence of these early years is far from clear.[7] In the far west, Count Henry was fully occupied in defending his territories. In 1110 he was badly defeated, and in May of 1111 Santarém was taken by the Murābit. The one bright note was that al-Mustain of Zaragoza, who joined the general onslaught in the winter of 1109–1110, was defeated and killed in January by Alfonso of Aragón at Valtierra north of Tudela.

During that winter Urraca and Alfonso made processions through some parts of Aragón to show off the new queen. In their absence León–Castilla remained quiet, but in far Galicia Count Pedro Froílaz of Traba raised the standard of young Alfonso Raimúndez. Deciding to squelch the revolt, in May Alfonso and Urraca invaded the north of that province, but there had been a falling out of some nature and the queen returned to León. The *Batallador's* successes in that mountainous country were slight, and that encouraged his enemies. On his return journey he was refused entrance to the city of Astorga. Even worse, the expected papal condemnation of the marriage had arrived during his absence, and Urraca, after conferring with the archbishop of Toledo and the bishops of León and Oviedo, agreed to separate from him. One suspects that the queen's compliance had its real cause in the fact that she had not conceived and hence lacked what would have been the best grounds for resistance. Still, once back in León, the Aragónese seems to have overridden all objections, perhaps on the basis of a further appeal to Rome.

Alfonso then had to hasten east to Aragón. In his absence, the partisans of the Murābit in Zaragoza had rejected the heir of al-Mustain, Abd al-Malik who took refuge in the fortress of Rota, and surrendered the city to the governor of Valencia. Thus, the last of the taifas had perished. The empire of the Africans now stretched from the Straits of Gibraltar to within sight of the Pyrenees. In addition,

[7] Julio González, *Repoblación de Castilla La Nueva*, 2 vols. (Madrid, 1975), 1:100–01.

during that summer the Murābit besieged Toledo for nine days, although they failed to take it.

At the same time, in Galicia, Count Pedro Froílaz had consulted with Count Henry of Portugal and then had gone on the offensive against the supporters of the queen, who were concentrated in the south of the province. After initial successes he was discomfited, however, and the queen's position in that region became somewhat stronger. By winter Count Henry felt it politic to attend her Christmas court at Sahagún. Alfonso of Aragón was also there briefly. It is also probable that the queen was negotiating with Count Pedro Froílaz for the association of her son in the government of the realm. The events of the year had convinced her that some accommodation was necessary and perhaps also that the marriage had been an error.

None of this had gone unreported to Alfonso of Aragón, and in April of 1111 he reacted by marching south and taking possession of Toledo. Count Henry of Portugal also decided that the time had come for strong measures. The Burgundian departed for France to raise troops for the impending civil war. In his absence two important events took place. One was the anointing and coronation as king of Alfonso Raimúndez in Santiago de Compostela on September 19, 1111.[8] Although that act was carried out by his guardians, it obviously had the consent of Urraca, as events were to show. Meanwhile, the queen had apparently taken a lover, Count Gomez González, of the rising noble house of Lara, in a bid to strengthen her support in Castilla.

Outright war began in the fall. At Candespina in the *Campo Gotico* Urraca's army was defeated, and Count Gomez was killed on the field on October 26, 1111, by the joint forces of Henry of Portugal and Alfonso of Aragón, who had made common cause for the moment. Apparently the two had agreed to divide the realm between them, but the victory had hardly been won when Count Henry deserted. Approached then by emissaries of Urraca with an offer to divide the kingdom with him, Henry accepted and the forces of the two now joined to attack Alfonso of Aragón, his erstwhile ally, who retreated into the fortress of Peñafiel and safety.

The new allies marched to Palencia. There they worked out the details of a division which would have given Henry not only Zamora but also other strategic positions in the very heart of the realm. They were joined there by Teresa who had begun to style herself queen, much to the disenchantment of Urraca. The count now set off to take possession of Zamora, but Urraca opened secret communication

[8] Emma Falque Rey, ed., *Historia Compostellana* (Turnholt, 1988), pp. 105–06.

with Alfonso of Aragón before herself departing for Sahagún with Teresa. Now it was the Aragónese who would respond to her overtures, and the *Batallador* marched on Sahagún, only just missing there the capture of Teresa herself. Even Urraca now found her husband's success perhaps a little too complete and withdrew into Galicia.

The year's end would find Urraca ruler of little more than that province. Late in the fall an army of Galicia, marching to assert her claims and that of her son, blundered into an ambush a few kilometers west of the city of León at Viadangos and roundly defeated there by Alfonso of Aragón. Count Pedro Froílaz was captured, but Bishop Diego Gelmírez escaped back to Galicia, taking the boy king with him to join his mother. The Aragónese monarch now patched up his agreement with Henry of Portugal and appears to have recognized the latter as ruler not only of Portugal but also of Leonese Zamora and Astorga. The remainder of León–Castilla Alfonso kept for himself.[9]

The success of the allies had been complete, but to win a kingdom was one thing and to rule it another. The arms of the Aragónese had provided Count Henry with his spoils in fact, but what he desired was legitimate title, and that was only to be provided by the dynasty itself. During the winter, then, he reconciled with Urraca. The queen in turn began to associate her son with herself in her public acts in an effort to heal some of the wounds of the past two-and-a-half years. Alfonso of Aragón, on the other hand, seems to have found an appeal to the authority of the late Alfonso VI insufficient to rally his new subjects. Accordingly, he began to introduce Aragonese garrisons into the major towns of the pilgrimage road, expelled the bishops of León and Burgos from their episcopal cities, and took prisoner those of Toledo, Osma, Palencia, and Orense. Those expedients may have done him more harm than good, but doubtless they seemed necessary in a land where every man's hand seemed increasingly to be raised against him. The humiliating knowledge must have begun to dawn on him that his wife was as much his superior in diplomacy as he was hers in battle.

When Urraca advanced to Astorga to join Count Henry in the spring of 1112, many of the nobility of León–Castilla rallied to her there. Alfonso of Aragón had no choice but to attempt a siege of the

[9] These and other events of the years are recounted in Reilly, *Urraca*, pp. 71–78. There the bits and pieces of documentary evidence are assembled. A contemporary narrative source for some of this also exists in Julio Puyol y Alonso, ed., "Las crónicas anónimas de Sahagún," *BRAH* 76 (1920):7–26, 111–22, 242–57, 339–56, 512–19; and 77 (1921):51–59 and 151–61.

pair, but Astorga, strong behind its old Roman walls, prevailed. What the siege did achieve was more to his former wife's advantage than his own. By May 12, 1112, Count Henry of Portugal died as a result of wounds received in the defense. Urraca now decided to rejoin her former husband, and for a short time they were reconciled. They even contrived to wage a joint siege against the Countess Teresa of Portugal in Astorga, which was no more successful than the first siege had been. The Aragonese king then began to suspect that his wife was about to betray him once again. A series of conferences to establish the terms of their new reconciliation came to nothing, and Alfonso withdrew to the east. The war would continue, but bereft of Count Henry, Teresa for the time being had to abandon her active role of the last three years. As the daughter of Alfonso VI and the mother of one of his grandsons, she could afford to wait for events to provide her with a new avenue toward the throne of León–Castilla. The death of either Urraca or Alfonso Raimúndez, all too possible even in the most tranquil of times, would effect that instantly. For five years the countess of Portugal waited in vain.

Aragón and León–Castilla at War (1113–1117)

Strictly speaking, the succession crisis that attended upon the death of Alfonso VI was now over. Teresa had retreated to the sidelines. Alfonso Raimúndez had been at least nominally associated in the government of the realm with his mother. The attempted marriage with the king of Aragón had been condemned, discredited, and broken off. Through all of the turmoil Urraca had remained mistress of her own fate and the fate of the kingdom of her father, now hers. She had clearly come to prefer that state of affairs and was to maintain it against all odds down to her death in March of 1126. Urraca continued to be what she had styled herself from the beginning in her diplomas, "totius ispaniae regina." By right of inheritance she claimed not simply the rule of León–Castilla but that hegemony in all of Iberia which had been her father's also as "totius ispaniae imperator."

To expect that Alfonso of Aragón would have accepted either the loss of his prize or subordination to his erstwhile wife as implied in her documents would be to totally misconstrue the normal ambitions of the time. He was, after all, a cousin of the queen and the husband designated by her father. He was also the most renowned warrior of the Christian north in a time of great peril. He was king of a greater Aragón than had ever been. In addition, practically speaking, he was master of all that was left of the old taifa of Toledo, of the Rioja, and of a long salient along the pilgrim road which stretched from Burgos, through Castrojeriz, Carrión de los Condes, to Sahagún itself, the pantheon of the dynasty and the burial place of Alfonso VI. Alfonso of Aragón had adopted the title of "imperator" as a documentary style first when he was associated with Urraca in some of the early products of her chancery. He would now use it in his own for as long as there was any hope of realizing its claim.[10]

For the next three years the struggle between the two was to monopolize the attention of both. That in turn meant that the frontier with Islam was left to the care of mostly local forces. The occupation of Toledo by Alfonso of Aragón in the spring of 1111 must have brought at least some evanescent aid. In that July Alvar Fáñez had been able to reclaim Cuenca briefly from Muslim occupation, but that flanking position to the east of Toledo could not be held. The summer of 1112 had seen extensive raids against the city, and in 1113 a very substantial Murābit force raised by the governors Mazdali and Alí Bakr, including contingents from Granada, Córdoba, Sevilla, and even Africa, would return to the valley of the Tajo. Alvar Fáñez was defeated and penned up, the land was ravaged, and the castle of Oreja to the north of that river was taken and permanently garrisoned. Sorties against the territories of Toledo and Madrid could now be carried out all year round. During these times, Alvar Fáñez seems to have been virtually an independent ruler of the unhappy territory although the king of Aragón never ceased to claim it.

Urraca, meanwhile, in a lightning offensive, had rolled up many of the positions of Alfonso along the pilgrimage road in June of 1113. She took Carrión de los Condes and then even Burgos, while Alfonso's attempt to relieve his garrison in the latter city failed. Urraca spent the summer there and had enough strength to send a relief force to Berlanga, near Soria in the upper valley of the Duero, which was under Muslim attack. While the queen was in Burgos the *Batallador* made overtures to renew their marriage, which is some indication of his relative weakness at the time. The burghers of the city favored the idea, but the nobility of the realm opposed it. The queen had to promise to call a general council of the realm for Palencia in the fall to consider the state of the realm generally and the question

---

[10] A critical edition of the charters of Alfonso of Aragón continues to be a prime necessity. Pascual Galindo Romeo is reputed to have done one as a doctoral thesis, but no one has succeded in establishing its actual existence to date. Many of them have been printed in the "documentos" section of the various volumes of the *EEMCA*.

of the marriage in particular. When it met in October, however, the council dealt with matters, of justice, trade, and administration, and with strengthening the royal position in the west of Iberia. The question of the queen's marriage does not appear to have been considered. In the west, the bishop of Lugo, who had supported the Aragónese king in 1110, was deposed and replaced by the queen's chaplain; and the archbishop of Braga was suspended for resisting the primatial authority of the archbishop of Toledo, that is to say, of Urraca's chief adviser and confidant. Additionally, the queen was to ally herself firmly with the Galician supporters of her son, and that meant supporting the plans of the bishop of Santiago de Compostela to replace Braga as the metropolitan of the northwest. Despite her overtures, the west continued to give her only lukewarm support, and her sister, Teresa, continued to boycott her court.

The spring of 1114 saw the Leonese monarch planning to regain her control in the trans-Duero and Toledo, but everything misfired and the year was one long reverse. Alvar Fáñez was killed in a revolt against her authority in Segovia in April, and the beleaguered outpost of Toledo was left, more than ever, without a strong leader. In July and August it was again under attack, but again the Murābit forces failed. On the northern *meseta* Bishop García of Burgos died, and Urraca's attempt to impose one Paschal as the new bishop was met by the revolt of the burghers and their return to the party of Alfonso of Aragón. The brother of Alfonso, Ramiro, was now elected bishop of Burgos. He had previously been installed by that king as abbot at Sahagún but fled the town before the advance of Urraca the year before. At Sahagún, by the queen's support for the return of the unpopular abbot who had preceded Ramiro led the burghers of that town too to declare for the Aragonese. In short order, all of the gains of the preceding summer had been lost.

Negotiation continued with the Aragonese during the following year, which had no real issue but may have had the merit, from Urraca's standpoint, of preventing her former husband from capitalizing on the advantages secured in 1114. Alfonso had installed his French cousin, Bertrán de Risnel, over the garrison of Sahagún at the beginning of 1115 but then seems to have taken no further actions. In the summer of that year Urraca decided to grasp the nettle and proceeded to have her candidate, Paschal, consecrated as bishop of Burgos. In October she held a council of the realm, attended by Diego Gelmírez, bishop of Compostela, and graced by the public presence of her two half sisters, the *infantas* Sancha and Elvira, now about eleven years old. With some measure of support from Galicia so assured, the queen now secured the agreement of the assemblage to seek the aid of the papacy. The abbot of Sahagún was despatched to present her case to Pope Paschal II, and even Alfonso of Aragón had to agree to grant the latter safe conduct through his realm. Events would soon prove that the queen had again outmaneuvered her former spouse.

While all of this was going on north of the Guadarramas chain, events to the south had taken a new and unexpected turn. In stark contrast to the years preceding, the forces of Toledo had assumed the offensive, raiding deep into the Muslim province of Córdoba. In March, Emir Mazdali, its governor, was defeated and killed in battle; his son and successor, Muhammad ibn Mazdali, met the same fate in June, and in mid-November the newest governor of the province was defeated in turn, although he did escape with his life. The leadership of these Toledan expeditions was provided by one Oriel, whose name suggests an Aragonese origin. In all probability, the authority of *El Batallador* had been reasserted in the city on the Tajo.

The active struggle between León–Castilla and Aragón had now been in process for some three years and neither had been able to gain a decisive advantage. In 1116 the positions of each stood just about where they had stood in 1113. Nevertheless, the world was changing around the two contestants, and conditions that were unacceptable when the issue had first been joined would shortly begin to appear rather more tolerable. Alfonso of Aragón had been neglecting the *Reconquista* against Zaragoza, which had been the preoccupation of his predecessors for at least forty years, in his futile quest for the Leonese throne. The achievements of his lieutenant in Toledo must have suggested to him that the Murābit were substantially weaker than imagined, and that a bold stroke against the great city on the Ebro might succeed.

For her part, Urraca scored substantial advances during that year. In Rome, Pope Paschal II had decided in favor of the abbot of Sahagún. Faced with a combination of papal condemnation and possible attack by the queen, the burghers of Sahagún capitulated. After a surprise attack by an Aragonese force had failed, late in the year, the town returned permanently to Leonese control. Probably as a result of negotiations with its burghers, Burgos also came again under her authority at this time, threatening the other Aragonese positions in Castilla. At the same time, her son, now eleven, was accompanying Count Pedro Froílaz on a campaign in the trans–Duero against Aragónese supporters there.

If the king of Aragón were to find an extended truce most attractive under these circumstances, so ultimately would Urraca. She had begun the year well with a great *curia* in León, attended by her son, daughter, and two minor half sisters. Except for Teresa, the dynasty was reunited. In the early spring the Leonese monarch had campaigned on the borders of the county of Portugal in the south of Galicia. She then contemplated a *coup* against the too-independent Bishop Gelmírez of Compostela but abandoned the idea when it was prematurely revealed. Instead, she reached a temporary understanding with the bishop and returned to León. But when Count Pedro Froílaz learned of the attempt, he abandoned the campaign in the south and returned to Galicia with her son, raising the standard of rebellion there once more. Urraca now marched back to Galicia and forced Count Pedro, her son, and their troops to abandon Compostela and entered into another patched-up agreement with Bishop Gelmírez, who had major problems with a conspiracy of the burghers of his episcopal town. Trouble remained, however, for in a subsequent campaign along the Portuguese border, Urraca was surprised and briefly besieged in her castle of Sobroso by the combined forces of Count Pedro and her sister, Teresa. When she returned to León in the late fall of that year, the queen was convinced that a major new effort would be required to consolidate her position in the west.

The year 1117 was to see a fundamental recasting of the ambitions of both Urraca of León–Castilla and Alfonso I of Aragón. It began with a truce which was to last for three years. Although neither of them would have anticipated it at the time, that truce was to be renewed periodically at intervals of three years down to the death of the queen in 1126. The relative positions of the two in 1117 would thus become those inherited by her son, Alfonso VII, on his accession in 1126. But neither party could see that far ahead in 1117. To achieve this *détente* with Aragón Urraca had first to put her own house in some sort of order. This was done in a great *curia* held at Sahagún in October of 1116. In order to put an end, hopefully, once and for all to the use of her own son against her, the queen agreed to the establishment of a condominium by which each of them would rule a portion of the realm. To Alfonso Raimúndez she ceded the control of the trans–Duero and Toledo. She may have agreed to his control of Galicia as well, but if she did she had no intention of abiding by this particular stipulation.[11]

---

[11] Falque Rey, ed., *Historia Compostellana*, pp. 197–98, contains the description of these events. The *Historia* is a highly partial source, of course, and magnifies the part in negotiations of Bishop Gelmírez. It also implies that Galicia was to be one of the portions of the young king without describing clearly the allocations which took place.

By and large the division of authority was a triumph for Urraca, and its acceptance by the opposition is a measure of their weakness at the time and of the real success of the past year's campaign in Galicia. In reality, the eleven-year-old king was himself to rule nothing for the foreseeable future. The real question, therefore, was to turn on the identity of his advisors, actually guardians, and of course regents. By associating her son with the rule of Toledo – the greatest conquest of his grandfather, Alfonso VI, and the primatial see of Spain ancient capital of the Visigoths – Urraca flattered his vanity and that of all those who were moved to support him out of loyalty to the dynasty and concern for the proprieties of succession. At the same time, she propelled the young king into a theater of operations in which he was to be effectively separated from Galicia and those guardians of his youth who had formed the backbone of his party. Neither Bishop Gelmírez nor Count Pedro Froílaz would have been unaware of this aspect of things, but the queen's use of both diplomacy and force had rendered them incapable to resist those seeming concessions at the end of 1116.

The grant of this *appanage* was nonetheless real and therefore could have had dangers of its own if not properly controlled. Over the next nine years the young king's government would begin to grant charters in his name; some twenty-seven of them are presently known.[12] Fewer than a third deal with Galicia, illustrating the preoccupation of the young king's court with matters in the south. Moreover, the lists of those who confirm the charters do not show those of his old party of Galicia as ordinarily present. Indeed, the major advisor of the young king was that ancient and loyal servitor of the realm, Archbishop Bernard of Toledo. For twenty-nine years the one-time Cluniac had served the old king unstintingly, for another eight that king's daughter. Now, for another eight years, until his death in 1125, Bernard would guide the grandson. The queen could count upon his prudence and restraint. Better, in all matters ecclesiastical he was the opponent of the vaulting ambitions of Bishop Gelmírez of Santiago de Compostela.

Finally, such authority as Alfonso Raimúndez could establish over the troubled territories of the trans–Duero and over the threatened

---

[12] The charters of Alfonso VII have been inadequately studied. At present, the basic work is Peter Rassow, "Die Urkunden Kaiser Alfons VII von Spanien," *AU* 10 (1928):327–468; and 11 (1930):66–137. It should be supplemented, however, by Bernard F. Reilly, "The Chancery of Alfonso VII of León–Castilla: The Period 1116–1135 Reconsidered," *Speculum* 51 (1976):243–61. Much still remains to be done, and I hope to complete the study in a book now underway on the reign of Alfonso VII.

outpost of Toledo would only come at the expense of Alfonso of Aragón rather than the queen. Since 1111 the control of Urraca there had been intermittent at best, most often supplanted by that of her former husband when it was not vested, by default, in some purely local figure. The Leonese monarch was ceding an opportunity rather than a possession in 1116. But the province would respond in some measure to the appeal of a young, legitimate king, especially since the years 1116 and 1117 had seen the struggle with the Murābit again take a turn for the worse. In November of 1117 Alfonso Raimúndez would be formally received into the city.

With the affairs of her own realm in order, then, Urraca could approach the negotiations with Alfonso of Aragón with some confidence. In fact, it was not simply the inclinations of the two contestants themselves that were moving the negotiations. From the first moments of his accession, Pope Paschal II (1099–1118) had been perturbed by appeals and counterappeals from Iberia. He had also been concerned by the progress made by Islam there as the Christian princes quarreled among themselves. At a council in the Lateran in 1116, Paschal was to appoint a new legate to visit the peninsula, Cardinal Boso of Saint Anastasia. Before that prelate had presided over a council at Burgos in February of 1117 he would visit Barcelona, Palencia, León, Compostela, and Braga to acquaint himself with the problems and opportunities of the peninsula.

The ecclesiastical canons of that council do not concern us here, except to note that they did contain a ban on consanguineous marriage.[13] The reconciliation of the former spouses was no part of any papal plan. But from related documents we can discern the general outline of the truce agreement reached on the basis of the existing status quo. The council dealt with the problem of those burghers of Sahagún who had been exiled from that town by Urraca in the fall of 1116. They were to be allowed to return to their homes upon the rendering of suitable satisfaction to the abbot of that monastery who held secular jurisdiction over the town. These arrangements were to be overseen by Bishop Hugh of Oporto, by Bishop Paschal of Burgos, and by Count Bertrán of Risnel. The first was already personally known to the pope and the legate and was a confidant of Bishop Gelmírez of Compostela. The second was, of course, Urraca's candidate for the see of Burgos since 1114. His role here points to his recognition by the papacy and also to the withdrawal by Alfonso of Aragón of his own brother, Ramiro, as candi-

---

[13] Pub. Fidel Fita, "Concilio nacional de Burgos (18 Febrero 1117)," *BRAH* 48 (1906):394–99.

date for that crucial see. The last of the arbiters was Count Bertrán. We may see his role here as typical of that which he was to play over the next nine years as the guardian of Aragonese interests in the kingdom of León–Castilla. His counterpart within the territories of Alfonso I was Diego López of Haro, who was acceptable to the former as a representative of the interests of Urraca in Vizcaya and the Rioja.

On such foundations was a truce constructed. By it, Queen Urraca had freed her hands for more vigorous action in the west of the peninsula; her former husband was left in control of much of the former territories of León–Castilla. Alfonso I continued to hold the Leonese Rioja. He would also retain some claim to the eastern lands of the former taifa of Toledo, and would possess much of Castilla north and east of Burgos and a salient of it stretching west along the *via francigena* through Castrojeriz to Carrión de los Condes within some 80 kilometers of the city of León itself. This Aragónese strip was bounded both to the north to the south by the territories overseen by the counts of the Castilian house of Lara. Rodrigo González was count in Asturias de Santillana and his brother, Pedro González, count in Lara and custodian of the Duero fortress of Peñafiel, guarded from the south. By this point Urraca had probably taken Count Pedro as her lover. She would have two children, Fernando Pérez and Elvira Pérez, by him, but the major necessity behind the irregular union was the alliance with a Castilian house capable of withstanding the Aragonese influence there.

Of course, in 1117 the queen could hardly have foreseen the great triumph that Alfonso I was to score less than two years later when he would wrest the former taifa of Zaragoza from its Murābit masters. The possession of the *parias* of that realm and the eventual acquisition of it had long been an object of Leónese policy. Its passage instead into the hands of Aragón in late 1118 would profoundly alter the balance of power in the Christian portion of the peninsula. For the first time, Aragón would become even comparable to León–Castilla itself. But surely it must have seemed that such an achievement was safely beyond the capabilities of Aragón as it existed in 1117, even under the direction of a warrior such as *El Batallador.*

The Emergence of Portugal

The new dispositions of the Leonese queen would have been most profoundly disturbing to her half sister, Teresa of Portugal. We moderns tend to assume that the appearance of a separate and autonomous Portugal was natural and inevitable. We take for granted, too, the existence of a distinct Portuguese people. Countess Teresa would have made no such assumptions. The county she ruled had long been part of León–Castilla. Her subjects spoke a language common to Galicia as well. There was a Portuguese particularism, as there was also a Castilian one or a Galician one, but the queen did not share it. She herself was a princess of León–Castilla and expected that her rights and those of her son would find recognition within that framework.[14] But Portugal, like all of the other political constructions we are concerned here, with was to be the product of particular persons, times, and circumstances. Teresa has a better claim than most to be its inventor, but her initiatives were, in reality, reactions of desperation.

It may be that Teresa had already experimented tentatively by late 1116 with the notion of taking the title of queen rather than countess. Her clear use of that title begins the following May, and by November she is styling herself queen of Portugal. Teresa had done with watching passively the course of developments in León–Castilla. Somehow her sister, Urraca, had avoided disaster and now appeared stronger than ever. Alfonso Raimúndez not only survived the dangerous years of childhood but now held the unchallenged position of successor and was governing the old lands of Toledo. She, on the other hand, was but five years older, the possessor of no greater dignity than before. Her own son still lived and had attained the age of eight but was further from his grandfather's throne than ever. Something had to be done to emphasize their mutual dignities, even if with the unheard-of title of queen of Portugal.

But if the dream of the throne of León–Castilla was becoming ever more evanescent and the throne of Portugal was to take shape as a substitute for it, the question then arose as to the proper identity of this Portugal. How large or small was it, and along what divides should its frontiers run? Since the county of Portugal had never been more than an administrative convenience of the kingdom of León–Castilla, the "land around the town of Oporto," there was no ready

---

[14] In general, Gonzaga de Azevedo, *História de Portugal*, remains serviceable. It should be supplemented with Fortunato de Almeida, *História da Igreja em Portugal* (Porto, new ed., 1967), up to the 14th Century. Torquato de Sousa Soares, "O governo de Portugal pelo Condo Henrique de Borgonha: Sus relações com as monarquias Leonesa–Castelhana e Aragonesa," *RPH* 14 (1974):365–97, and also his "O governo de Portugal pela Infante–Rainha D. Teresa," *Colectanea de Estudios im honra do Prof–Doutor Damião Peres* (Lisbon, 1974), pp. 99–199, are the best detailed studies.

answer to that question at hand. A mere eight years of de facto independence since 1109 furnished no real guide to anything. The essential key to the politics of the west over the next eight years is that Portugal would be as large as Teresa could make it and no larger than Urraca could prevent.

For the moment, however, the conflict between the two sisters would be delayed, for each had problems that would concern them more directly. The emerging realm of Portugal had frontier problems to the south. At the beginning of the 12th Century the settled land was still essentially a collection of shallow river valleys between the ocean and the mountain escarpment rising steeply to the east, from the valley of the Mino River in the north to that of the Duero around Oporto, and finally the valley of the Mondego dominated by Coimbra on its mount. The great basin of the Tajo to the south had been held only momentarily toward the end of the reign of Alfonso VI as the taifa of Badajoz struggled to survive. Then Lisbon had been lost to the rising power of the Murābit in 1094, and Santarém in 1111. The control of the latter city was the key to mounting a campaign in central Portugal from the south.

In the spring of 1117 Alī ibn Yūsuf came again to the peninsula from Morocco, and this time his ambitions were focused upon the west. A Murābit army marched north to lay siege to Coimbra for some three weeks in late June and early July, but, in the end, failed to take it. Although the control of the country between the Mondego and the Tajo was to continue to be contested for yet another thirty years, Coimbra was never again to be directly threatened. No one perceived it so at the time, of course, but the siege of Coimbra in 1117 was to mark the apogee of Murābit power in Iberia. Now it would wane as rapidly as it had waxed. For the time being, however, the Murābit threat preoccupied Teresa.

After the truce established with Aragón at Burgos, Urraca moved to establish her authority in the west. In the late spring she was in Galicia and apparently did some minor campaigning in the south against local supporters of Teresa. Her major concern, however, was to reach some sort of settlement with the troubled church of Santiago de Compostela and its ambitious prelate, Bishop Diego Gelmírez. For the past two years the bishop himself had been having grave problems of his own, and a conspiracy among the burghers of the town had substituted their government for his in the episcopal town itself. Urraca had enjoyed the bishop's embarrassment and had cooperated with the burghers to strengthen her own control in the south of Galicia, but now the moment was at hand to reach a more stable settlement. Since, taken together, the town and the holdings of its church in the countryside constituted the greatest power in the south of the province, the question was vital to the queen's own power there. Gelmírez, acting in concert with the great power of the north of the province, the counts of Trastamara, had often frustrated Urraca's purposes.

Early in June, then, Urraca came to Santiago de Compostela to confer with Bishop Gelmírez about these matters. What followed must have been one of the most terrifying experiences of her life. In one fashion or another the townspeople became convinced that their bishop and the queen were conferring together to deprive them of the liberties which they had so recently won, and surely some limitation of those must have been envisioned precisely as part of any permanent, mutual reconciliation. Suddenly, the more violent spirits among the populace rose and launched an attack against the episcopal palace where Urraca and Gelmírez were meeting. The pair fled into a new bell tower, part of the grand, Romanesque cathedral then under construction. The rebels, in turn, set fire to the wooden scaffolding within it, and the occupants were forced to emerge. In the confusion, Gelmírez escaped, although his brother and his *majordomo* were seized and killed. The queen also was captured, and stripped of her clothing and pelted with refuse and stones. Fortunately for her, some cooler heads among the rioters managed to rescue her and, after extracting promises that she would take no reprisals, ultimately allowed her to leave the town safely.

Outside the town, Urraca rejoined her forces and those troops under the command of her son and Count Pedro Froílaz which had come up. In fairly short measure they were also joined by Gelmírez. The joint forces now settled down to a siege of the town. The burghers soon realized the hopelessness of their cause; the town was surrendered, and the rebels threw themselves on the mercy of the queen. The government of the burghers was now dissolved, of course, and full power over it returned to its bishop. Aside from that, roughly a hundred of their party were deprived of their property and exiled from the town, and a general indemnity was levied on the townspeople.[15] But the queen, too, suffered a loss even beyond her humiliation. The full restoration of Gelmírez in Santiago de Compostela was not in her interest, but the popular regime there had made itself insupportable.

During the spring of the following year Urraca concentrated first on the trans–Duero region, leading a large force south to the

---

[15] The entire episode is retold at great length in Falque Rey, ed., *Historia Compostellana*, pp. 199–217.

troubled area around Segovia. While there she held a *curia* in the city and to it came the newly elected archbishop of Braga, Paio Mendes, to be consecrated by Archbishop Bernard. That was a remarkable step, for it implied the recognition of the authority of the Leonese queen as well as that of her archbishop. It was even more significant since Paio Mendes was the scion of the important north Portuguese noble family of Mendo Goncalves of Maia. Teresa of Portugal had thus suffered a significant loss of control and support in the north.

Other major events took place in the south. Archbishop Bernard led part of the forces Urraca had raised over the Guadarramas and retook Alcalá de Henares east of Madrid from the Murābit. Later, in November of 1118 a *fuero* of some sort was issued to the inhabitants of Toledo in order to encourage further settlement in that be-leaguered stronghold.[16] The improvement of affairs in the valley of the Tajo was a reflection of the increasing preoccupation of the Murābit with the maintenance of their hold on Zaragoza. Alfonso of Aragón had unleashed a furious attack upon the city. In the fall of 1118 the governor of Córdoba, Abd Allāh ibn Mazdali, went to the relief of the city but found only his death there in November. Zaragoza fell to Alfonso in December, and the second city of that former taifa, Tudela, would pass into his hands in February of 1119.

The sudden collapse of the northeast frontier of the Murābit must have been received with mixed emotions by Urraca. On the one hand, she could not but rejoice at the defeat of the Muslim enemy and the prospect that it brought for the relaxation of their pressures on the line of the Tajo. On the other hand, the major aggrandize-ment of Aragón and her former spouse cast the political relationships of the entire north of the peninsula in a new light. In the short run, it raised the problem of the willingness of Alfonso I to continue to observe the truce to which he had agreed in 1117, since he had already achieved its major conditions.

At the end of 1118, that question was provoked by the death in October of Bishop Paschal of Burgos. At a great *curia* held in León in November of that year, Urraca approved the choice of one Jimeno as the new bishop there, but the burghers of that city had other ideas and so did the Aragonese king. After the fall of Zaragoza and Tudela, the forces of Alfonso I began to push along the old Roman road that leads west from the Ebro opposite Tudela toward the headwaters of the Duero around Soria. They took Tarazona where the road starts up into the Sierra de Moncayo about May of 1119 and

---

[16] González, *Repoblación*, 1:133–34. The *fuero* of 1118 is not reliable in its present form but is based on some such grant of the time. On the subject generally, see Alfonso García Gallo, "Los fueros de Toledo," *AHDE* 45 (1975):5–171.

pushed over the mountains past Agreda and down into the valley of the Duero at Soria. This last lay within 55 kilometers of Urraca's chief supporter in the area at Burgo de Osma, Bishop Raymond. Now, technically, none of these events may have transgressed the terms of the truce of 1117, but inevitably they did raise tensions along that frontier.

In the meantime, news arrived in Iberia of the death of Pope Gelasius II (1118–1119), and in March of 1119 a pilgrim to Santiago de Compostela brought a letter from the new pontiff, Calixtus II (1119–1124), to Bishop Gelmírez. Since the new pope was Guy of Burgundy, former archbishop of Vienne, uncle of Alfonso VII, and friend of Gelmírez, the bishop of Santiago de Compostela decided immediately to send an envoy to the pope who was then in the south of France. That the relationship between Alfonso of Aragón and Urraca was at least correct if not cordial at this time can be gleaned from the fact that this envoy sought and obtained a safe conduct through his lands.

But the queen was to have trouble at home in the summer of 1119. Sometime during the spring of the year her lover, Count Pedro González, of Lara, was seized by Urraca's former *majordomo*, Guter Fernández, and briefly imprisoned in the castle of Mansilla 20 kilometers southeast of the city of León. The reason given by the source was the count's excessive familiarity with the queen and the enormous growth of his power in Castilla thereby. The difficulties continued, and Urraca was herself besieged in the royal palace in the city of León in July.[17] The queen was able to overcome her opponents, but the incident had been serious. In the spring Archbishop Bernard of Toledo had written to the new pope suggesting that irresponsible initiatives undertaken by supporters of the immediate accession of Alfonso Raimúndez to the throne of León–Castilla might indeed end by costing the papal nephew his due succession to it.

The hand of Bishop Gelmírez was clearly suspect in this regard, and doubtless that was one of the reasons for which the queen had denied him permission to himself visit the new pope earlier that spring. At the same time the conspiracy had had the cooperation of Guter Fernández, who not only had been *majordomo* of the queen earlier but was himself a great Castilian noble, whose house had holdings now in the hands of Alfonso of Aragón, and was rival to

---

[17] Huici Miranda, *Las crónicas latinas deo la reconquista*, 2 vols. (Valencia, 1913), 1:50. A later siege of the royal stronghold in León occurs in 1126 at the beginning of the reign of Alfonso VII. The two incidents have been confused but should be distinguished. See Luis Sánchez Belda, ed., *Chronica Adefonsi Imperatoris* (Madrid, 1950), pp. 6–7.

the house of Lara. Urraca's truce with the Aragonese thus ran counter to his interests, as did her liaison with Count Pedro. Moreover, by this time she probably had two children by the latter whose future claims conceivably could threaten the right of succession of her firstborn son. Fortunately for the queen, the conspirators could not trust one another, and Archbishop Bernard held true and made his young charge count for her rather than against her in the emergency. The assistance of Bernard of Toledo should probably also be seen in the restoration by the queen of the episcopate of Segovia at the beginning of 1120. That action reduced the direct authority of Toledo in most of the eastern half of the trans–Duero, but it was probably necessary to assuage the feelings and interests of the settlers around that new city. The new bishop, Pedro, was another of those French clerics and protégés drawn to Spain by Bernard.[18]

Nevertheless, the support of the primate could not solve all of the queen's difficulties, least of all with the new pope, Calixtus II. That Bishop Gelmírez had the ear of the pontiff is evident from the fact that in February of this year Calixtus threw the entire church of Iberia into confusion by transferring the metropolitan dignity of the Muslim-held see of Mérida to Santiago de Compostela. That action was to create ecclesiastical and political problems which were not finally resolved until a century later. In another action Calixtus wrote a letter to the bishops, princes, and counts of Iberia in which he bitterly attacked Urraca's behavior toward her son and insisted that the oath taken by the nobles of Galicia in 1107 still validated the right of Alfonso Raimúndez to rule that province. Unfortunately, before that letter had reached the peninsula, Urraca would have taken another measure which would validate the pope's misgivings and draw the most drastic response. By the following year Urraca would be in danger of losing her command of.León–Castilla.

Yet the year augured well for her at its outset. The politics of the west were as complex as always, but the queen had secured support among some of the major noble families of northern Portugal. That opportunity may have come about as a result of Teresa of Portugal having taken as a lover the son of Count Pedro Froílaz, Fernando

---

[18] Antonio Ubieto Arteta, "Los primeros años de la diocesis de Sigüenza," *Homenaje a Johannes Vincke*, Vol. 1 (Madrid, 1962), p. 140, argues that the restoration of Segovia was the work of Alfonso of Aragón. The evidence and probability for such an initiative are not convincing. Alfonso I's charter, which has been dated to December 13, 1119, which would put him near Segovia, is obviously misdated and corrupt. Pub. Tomás Múñoz y Romero, ed., *Colección de fueros y cartas pueblas* (Marrid, 1847), pp. 413–14.

Pérez, of the Galician Trastamara family. It was a political arrangement primarily, of course, but it would lead to the alienation of some of Teresa's own nobility and of her son as well. In 1128 she would lose her realm to precisely that combination. At the same time, Teresa's actions confirm that the alliance with the Trastamara family was also accompanied by one with the other great power in Galicia, the now archbishop of Santiago de Compostela.

That was the situation when Urraca marched west into Galicia in the company of her son in the spring of 1120. After a brief but successful campaign against some of the local partisans of Count Pedro Froílaz, the monarch went to Compostela in June where she confirmed some major possessions and powers of that church. Having done that, Urraca then insisted that Archbishop Diego and his vassals and the militia of Compostela accompany her on a campaign against Teresa of Portugal. This was a request the prelate could not refuse.

The campaign in the north of Portugal went very well from the beginning. The crossing of the Miño River was met with force. Teresa, driven back upon her castle at Lanhoso, ten kilometers northwest of Braga, was there besieged while Urraca's troops raided throughout the countryside as far south as the Duero itself. The siege was not finally successful, for the surrender of Teresa could not be forced, but the Leonese monarch was able to rally her half sister's enemies. On June 17, 1120, Urraca granted an important charter to the church of Braga which treated that see as essentially a part of her realm. It was confirmed not only by Alfonso Raimúndez and Archbishop Gelmírez but also by the border magnates Counts Rodrigo Vélaz and Alfonso Núñez.[19] The suggestion has also been made, and is likely true, that the young *infans* of Portugal, Alfonso Enríquez, recognized the suzerainty of Urraca at this time.

If the queen had not accomplished everything she hoped, at least enough had been done to keep Teresa occupied for a time. On the journey back to Compostela, Urraca decided to solve her problems in the south of Galicia as well by making Archbishop Gelmírez her prisoner. The queen then entered the city on the eve of the feast of Saint James and the following day informed the cathedral chapter that she was revoking the secular authority of the archbishopric and taking control of its castles. She was prepared to release the archbishop if they would accept what she had done, but, even so,

[19] Arquivo Distrital de Braga, Livro de Cadeias, fol. 54v. Unknown to previous historians of the question, this charter is one of the pieces of evidence that aids in untangling the chronological confusion created by the literary devices of *Historia Compostellana*.

there must be an investigation of the uses to which Gelmírez had put his authority.

There were some among the canons who would have been pleased to accept the humbling of their prelate, but the chapter could hardly accede to the royal demands. The assault on the rights of the see had been too direct, and the demands were too sweeping. When the chapter refused, the queen's son himself left the city to join the forces of Count Pedro Fróilaz camped nearby. Riot broke out in the city, and the queen found herself unable to control it. Without having achieved a political settlement she would deem it politic to release Gelmírez, only eight days after taking him prisoner.

The entire episode had been most ill-advised, and there were signs already that the queen was beginning to realize how serious the repercussions to her act might become. Doubtless the counsel of Archbishop Bernard of Toledo, who rejoined her court in León, was a factor in convincing her that Pope Calixtus II was likely to take her seizure of the man whom the pontiff had just raised to the archepiscopal dignity five months before as a personal affront. Meanwhile, in Galicia, Archbishop Gelmírez was furiously negotiating with Alfonso Raimúndez, with Count Pedro, and with Teresa of Portugal to devise a way to recoup his diminished fortunes. But Urraca had dealt with the machinations of that group more than once. The essential consideration this time was to detach her son from the conspirators in order to limit the expected papal reaction. A variety of private documents dating from the late fall of that year indicate that the queen had taken the step of surrendering control of a large bloc of fisc lands in central León to her son. Although the action left the direction of political affairs still in the hands of Urraca herself, it would give her son much increased resources with which to built his party in the realm while he awaited his own accession to royal power.

At the same time, royal policy had to pay some attention to events to the east. On June 17, 1120, the defeat at Cutanda by Alfonso of Aragón of a major Murābit army had opened the way to the consolidation of his control over the whole of the territories of the old taifa of Zaragoza. In its aftermath Caltayud and Daroca had surrendered, and a great task of reorganization lay before him. Also, in Castilla, Burgos had again returned to his allegiance. That seems to have satisfied the ambitions of the *Batallador* there for the time, and he agreed to extend the three-year truce made in 1117. Urraca needed no additional problems just then. Apparently, she was willing, to accept the loss of Burgos, and that agreement was duly made.

That the Leonese monarch would thus be free to concentrate on the affairs of her own kingdom was fortunate. On October 7, 1120, at Melfi, Pope Calixtus had authorized a series of letters to the bishops of Spain, to Urraca, to Archbishop Bernard, to Alfonso Raimúndez, and to the new papal legate, Cardinal Boso, whom he was despatching to the peninsula. In them he demanded the release of Archbishop Gelmírez and the return of his castles and honors. If the queen should refuse to comply, the legate, the primate, and the bishops were to hold a council in which the queen and her supporters were to be excommunicated and the kingdom placed under interdict.[20] The letters indicate the difficulty distance posed for papal policy. By the time the pontiff had been apprised of the situation and could respond, conditions had changed significantly. Nevertheless, once it became known in the realm, papal action could be dangerous because of the opportunities it offered for manipulation.

In the spring of 1121 Urraca again visited Galicia. A council was now held in Compostela at which the papal legate, Cardinal Boso, was also present. The queen now agreed to restore Archbishop Gelmírez's secular authority and to arrange the return of the confiscated castles by Christmastime. It was further agreed to hold a general council of the realm at Sahagún the following August to address the general problems of the church and the kingdom. That council was to be small and dominated by the party of Gelmírez. We know of the attendance of only ten bishops, and three of these could be called supporters of Urraca. Remarkably, even the archbishop of Toledo was absent, as were the bishops of Palencia, Burgos, Osma, Astorga, and Lugo. The actions of the council are known to us only from Portuguese sources and deal mainly with ecclesiastical affairs, with one most significant exception. Because of "all these evils," beginning on November 11th, an interdict was to be leveled on all of Spain.[21] Queen Urraca although not directly mentioned in the documentation, was clearly the object of the threat. The papal authorization of October had to be reworked since the conditions it had stipulated had, in fact, been met. Different reasons had to be adduced, but the net effect of the interdict would still have been to advertise the queen as an incompetent at least, and to invite her overthrow. But well before the council Urraca had sent an embassy to appeal directly to the pope. In the summer of 1121 the fate of the kingdom of León–Castilla was to be decided at the papal court.

---

[20] These papal letters have commonly been dated to 1121, but see Reilly, *Urraca*, p. 151.

[21] Carl Erdmann, ed., "Papsturkunden in Portuqal," in *AGWG*, Philologisch-historische Klasse, N. S., Vol. 20 (Berlin, 1927), pp. 177–81.

In any event, Calixtus II decided to take the matter into his own hands. He effectively nullified the actions of his own legate in the peninsula and on November 3, 1121, made a sweeping renewal of the authority of Bernard of Toledo as legate and as primate. Calixtus II stated that this action was being taken at the request of the papal nephew, Alfonso Raimúndez, and he made no mention of Urraca at all. The letters can only be understood as a repudiation of both Gelmírez and his personal legate, and as an endorsement of Archbishop Bernard of Toledo as the pontiffs favored instrument in León–Castilla. The aged former monk of Cluny is to be the arbiter of affairs between the sixteen-year-old Alfónsez Raimúndez and his mother. It was a brilliant diplomatic *coup*. It completely undercut her enemies and assured that Urraca's reign would continue essentially unchanged.

Still, not all of the problems of the Leonese queen were solved thereby. During Urraca's harrowing involvement with Cardinal Boso and Gelmírez, her sister, Teresa of Portugal, had invaded the south of Galicia with considerable success. We cannot be sure of its exact timing, but in February of 1122 the Portuguese queen granted a charter to Bishop Diego of Orense and the inhabitants of that city. The acceptance of a charter from Teresa signaled the defection of Bishop Diego of Orense from Urraca's cause, but the situation was more serious than that. The charter was also confirmed by Counts Fernando Yáñez and Gomez Núñez. The former was lord of Puente Sampayo on the border between the provinces of Túy and Santiago de Compostela. As its name implies, this lordship controlled a strategic bridge on the road south from Compostela to Túy and the Portuguese border. The second count held the territory of Toroño which was roughly coterminous with the diocese of Túy. Gomez Núñez was also the son-in-law of Fernando Yáñez. If these two magnates had decided that the future belonged to Teresa of Portugal, the bishop of Túy, Alfonso, would hardly have been able to resist joining her party as well.

That situation was intolerable for Urraca. Further successes by her half sister would risk the recreation of the kingdom of Galicia–Portugal of her uncle, García I, which lay but fifty years in the past and for which there was far better dynastic warrant than for an upstart kingdom of Portugal. On March 7, 1122, the Leonese monarch was in Lugo, only a few days' march from either Santiago de Compostela or Orense. With her were her son and the bishops of León, Oviedo, and Segovia, in addition to the archbishop of Santiago, Diego Gelmírez. She had come early in the year and as soon as she could prepared either for war or for peace. In fact, an understanding was already being worked out. It was more satisfactory to Teresa than to Urraca, for it provided a sort of condominium by the sisters over the valley of the Minõ from Orense down to Túy. About this time Bishop Diego of Orense granted a charter to the men of Orense with the consent of Urraca, Alfonso Raimúndez, and Teresa.[22] Such an arrangement was far more favorable to Teresa than to the others. She had the advantage of proximity. That edge was illustrated in November of the year when she issued a charter to the see of Coimbra, which was confirmed by the bishops of Orense and Túy and by the abbot of Celanova. They were now following her court. Moreover, in mid-summer of 1122, the Portuguese monarch further strengthened her ties with the north Galician house of the Trastamara. She married off her daughter, Urraca, to Vermudo Pérez, another of the sons of Count Pedro Froílaz and the brother of her own consort, Fernando Pérez. Furthermore, there seems to have been some reconciliation with her son at this period. They issued a charter jointly in May which rewarded the services of her paramour, Fernando Pérez.

We cannot be sure just why Urraca should have accepted such a diminution of her powers in Galicia that year. Certainly it must have had something to do with the balance of forces in that region. But then it may have had almost as much to do with concern over her eastern frontier with Alfonso of Aragón. She may have had warning of what was to transpire in the summer of 1122 on that front. Her former husband, in fact, struck deep into the trans-Duero sometime late that summer. In November he was at Olmedo, just 20 kilometers east of Medina del Campo. In December, at Fresno de la Fuente, 70 kilometers northeast of Segovia, the Aragonese granted a charter to Bishop Pedro of Segovia. Clearly Alfonso was making a show of force, for he could hardly hope to hold territories so far west without major hostilities at least. By the same action that demonstrated the extent to which he could be a danger to the Leonese hold on the trans–Duero, he was also signaling that conciliation was possible. The charter to Segovia was a grant to a supporter of Urraca, after all, and in it he also recognized explicitly the authority of Archbishop Bernard at Toledo, of Bishop Pedro at Palencia, and of Bishop Bernard at Sigüenza, the latter see not yet reconquered from the Murābit. Urraca responded to the combination of threat and overture of good will. In 1123 the truce between the two

[22] AC Orense, Privados 1, no. 1. Emilio Durop Peña, ed., *Catálogo de los documentos privados en pergamino del archivo de la catedral de Orense, 888–1554* (Orense, 1973), pp. 17–18, calls it an original and assigns it to 1122. The document is undated, but I believe that is the most likely date.

monarchs was extended for another three years. It would last to the death of Urraca herself in 1126, and during that period the *Batallador* would not again appear in the trans-Duero.

The more pressing concerns of Urraca quickly became evident. In March of 1123, in Galicia, she took an important step, one that she must have long desired but until now lacked strength to effect. She imprisoned Count Pedro Froìlaz and some of his sons and reclaimed the lands they held as "honors" from the crown. Such an action meant that she must have reached an understanding with her own son as well as with Archbishop Gelmírez. Two months later she was still in Galicia mending fences, and the bishops of Orense and Túy were to be found at her court. Clearly she was then a power to be reckoned with in the lower valley of the Miño.

The agreement of her son to these measures may have been contingent upon the promise of a major, joint effort in the eastern trans–Duero. In any event, that is where the queen would be later in the year. In December a Leónese army began the conquest of the hill fortress of Sigüenza northwest of Madrid. We know nothing of the campaign except that the town surrendered sometime before the last week in January of 1124. On the first day of February Urraca bestowed a charter on its newly installed bishop, which indicated that the fortress towns of Atienza and Medinaceli were also in her hands.[23] That meant that the critical stretch of the old Roman road from Córdoba, which ran through the rolling hills of this gap between the Guadarrama Mountains and the Sierra de Albarracín, had passed into the control of León–Castilla, and that the shortest route for the Murābit to the northeast of the peninsula was closed to them for the first time since the death of Alfonso VI.

The conquest of the area was important to Urraca and to Alfonso Raimúndez because it improved their position on the eastern flanks of Toledo and the trans–Duero, but more so in that it barred the road of Alfonso of Aragón south at the same time that it barred the road of the Murābit north. If it protected his newly conquered territories of Zaragoza, it also sealed off his path to Toledo, and, by implication, the imperial title which was dependent upon his grasp of the old Visigothic capital. That monarch himself was more than busy with the repopulation and the rounding out of the additional kingdom won in 1118 and now acquiesced in a *fait accompli* that would come to define the borders between the two major Iberian kingdoms

---

[23] Antonio Ubieto Arteta argued that Sigüenza had already been recaptured by Alfonso of Aragón and that this charter of Urraca is false and another of Alfonso Raimúndez is badly dated. The evidence is inferential at best. See Reilly, *Urraca*, p. 179, n. 79.

until the emergence of a unified Spain at the end of the medieval period.

By the time that Sigüenza had fallen there was a new papal legate in the peninsula. Cardinal Deusdedit was in Valladolid where he convoked a council of the Iberian churches attended by eleven of the twenty-four bishops, including two of the three Portuguese bishops. Two steps were taken there that had clear political bearing. For one, the decision was made to proceed to the consecration of Bishop-elect Jimeno to the see of Burgos. Jimeno had been Urraca's candidate from the first, and papal support for him made it difficult for Alfonso of Aragón to refuse to recognize him any longer. Thus, his hold on Burgos was weakened. Second, a general assent to the knighting of the now nineteen-year-old Alfonso Raimúndez was secured. To be carried out by Archbishop Diego Gelmírez at Santiago de Compostela on Pentecost, May 25, 1124. The implications were great, of course. That same prelate was authorized to consecrate the bishop of Burgos in the place of the pope himself, for that see was directly dependent on Rome. Finally, in the spring, Calixtus would award the disputed suffragan sees of Coimbra and Salamanca to Compostela as metropolitan, and would make permanent the transfer of the archepiscopal dignity of Mérida to Santiago de Compostela. Archbishop Gelmírez's cup runneth over, indeed. Gelmírez even had designs on the primacy of Spain itself, but the death of Calixtus II on December 24, 1124, and the accession of Honorius II (1124–1130) were to radically undercut Gelmírez's influence in Rome.

Nevertheless, the major concern of Urraca continued to be her restless half sister in Portugal. Teresa was determined to contest the lordship of southern Galicia, and in September of 1125 two of her charters made the bishopric of Túy the center of administration for Portugal between the Miño and Limia rivers. Again the important Galician counts Fernando Yáñez and Gomez Núñez confirmed the grant. More important, so did her son, Alfonso Enríquez. Earlier the same year the diplomacy of Urraca had detached the young *infans* of Portugal from his mother, and the sixteen-year-old boy had actually been knighted in Zamora on Pentecost, May 17, 1125.[24] That ceremony would have been performed by Bishop Bernard of Zamora, protégé of Archbishop Bernard of Toledo, Urraca's unfailing supporter. Such an event would have been highly dangerous to Teresa, and she must have made great exertions to coax him back into her camp by September.

---

[24] Gonzaga de Azevedo, *História*, pp. 141–42. Sánchez Belda, ed., *Chronica*, pp. 8–9, n. 5., saw this as evidence that rather Zamora had fallen into the hands of Teresa. No other testimony of the time would support such a contention.

Urraca's response to these initiatives is not known. She and her son were in Galicia in June of 1125. In fact, it is the last time the two are known to have been together. But they were in the north. Whether they knew it or not, their attempt to wean the Portuguese *infans* from his mother was to fail. Teresa's position in Portugal and southern Galicia was to outlast Urraca's lifetime and her own to become a legacy boding ill for both of their sons.

In truth, the troubled reign of Urraca was drawing to a close. Archbishop Bernard, advisor of her father and unfailing prop of her own government, died on April 2, 1125.[25] The young Alfonso Raimúndez would now of necessity begin his personal rule, subject only to such restraints as his mother's authority might impose. There could be no thought of another tutor such as Bernard had been. Moreover, a decent eye to the future was already suggesting to the magnates of the realm the utility of becoming known at the young king's court. But still, his mother was queen. The known output of charters, those indispensable instruments of medieval government, of Alfonso in 1125 is actually quite modest.

The activities of Urraca herself following the spring of 1125 are largely unknown. In late summer it is likely that she was in Castilla with her lover and consort, Count Pedro González of Lara, when she confirmed an exchange of property between the count and the monastery of Silos. She may never have returned to León, for it was in Castilla that she died. Fittingly, one thinks, the last business with which she is known to have been concerned dealt with Galicia and Archbishop Gelmírez. An embassy from that prelate was waiting upon the queen to complain about her failure to return one of his castles while she was making her last dispositions. On March 8, 1126, in Saldaña in the Tierra de Campos, the queen died after seventeen years of rule.[26] One source, albeit an unfriendly one, asserts that she died in childbirth. She would have been about forty-six years old at the time, so the possibility cannot be ruled out, and would have been in accord with the general vigor of her reign.

However that may be, Urraca had ruled against all odds and generally successfully from 1109. In general outline her reign followed the policies already adopted by her father. She retained his advisors and alliances so long as the former lived and the latter were at all workable. The biggest mistake she made, in fact, was to carry

[25] Angel González Palencia, *El arzobispo D. Raimundo de Toledo* (Barcelona, 1942), p. 52. The date has been and is contested, but close consideration of the relevent charters makes it evident that González Palencia has been right all along.

[26] The sources vary as to the exact date, giving either the 8th or 9th. See Sánchez Belda, ed., *Chronica*, pp. 4–5, n. 1.

out the marriage that her father had ordained for her. But when the union with the Aragonese king proved destructive, she had forthrightly decided to rule in her own name, and in her choice she was quite right. The alternatives to that choice were displayed by the anarchical and kaleidoscopic events of 1111–1112. However, once made, that choice necessarily involved a war with Alfonso of Aragón which neither of them could win. The resulting weakness of her dynastic and political position also made inevitable the challenge of her sister, Teresa.

Urraca had quickly learned the unavoidable logic of her choice and properly reached an interim arrangement with her former husband, which, if it did not solve the problem of Aragón, at least freed her hands to restore relative order in her own realm and to limit its partition to the west. But, in Teresa, she found an opponent as determined as herself, and, in the end, Urraca lacked the political resources to bring her sister to heel permanently. The inescapable, brute fact was that Teresa's claim to rule was virtually as good as her own, and Alfonso Enríquez was as much the grandson of her father as was Alfonso Raimúndez. As both of the cousins were shortly to discover for themselves, the realities of noble self-interest and provincial particularism became an almost impenetrable puzzle when their subjects were able legitimately to pick and choose between monarchs.

At the end of Urraca's reign, then, even her best choices had resulted in an Aragón more than doubled in size by the acquisition of Zaragoza and by occupation of the Rioja and a substantial salient of land in Castilla. The circumstances of 1109 had also eventuated in a Portugal which had now enjoyed de facto independence under an alternative branch of the dynasty for seventeen years. As events were to demonstrate, most of these new arrangements were so reinforced by time and the logic of geography that they would prove impossible to reverse for any monarchy of the period, no matter how vigorous. The Iberia of the Late Middle Ages already existed in germ. What would follow, put briefly, would be the parallel extension southward of the divisions already consolidated in the Christian north. What each of these kingdoms was too feeble to accomplish against their Christian neighbors in the north could be realized against a Murābit, Muslim south in the throes of a new dissolution.

7

A New Aragón and a New Cataluña
(1104–1134)

In 1104, at the death of Pedro I (1094–1104), the dynasty of Aragón was poised for a great assault upon the taifa of Zaragoza. Since the time of Pedro's father, Sancho Ramírez I (1063–1094), the aggression of that mountain kingdom around the northern perimeter of the Muslim Kingdom had been steady and successful in the main. Resounding victories, such as the capture of the major city of Huesca in 1096, had been few, but for over forty years the frontier fortresses of the ibn Hūd had been reduced one by one and the way was now clear for the descent onto the great plain of the Ebro. Nevertheless, the new king of Aragón faced a problem insuperable in ordinary terms.

Even though the lands controlled by the dynasty of Aragón had grown with the occupation of the eastern territories of Navarra in 1076 and the subsequent appropriation of Zaragozan borderlands, especially around Huesca after 1096, the kingdom still comprised only a rough 9,000 square kilometers in extent. The potential prey sprawled over 30,000 or more. The largest town of Aragón was Huesca with perhaps 3,000 inhabitants. The capital of the foe, Zaragoza, "the White City" of the Muslim chroniclers, boasted on the order of 25,000 citizens between those dwelling in the area enclosed by its still-standing Roman walls and its suburbs.[1] Then, beyond the capital itself, were the cities of Tudela, Tarazona, Calatayud, and Daroca, all of them formidable in turn to an attacker who disposed of such lean resources.

The greatest advantage of the Aragonese monarchs had always lain in the weakness of the rival dynasty of the ibn Hūd. By 1104 Lérida

---

[1] María J. Viguera, *Aragón musulmán* (Zaragoza, 1988), pp. 231–32. This little work is a recent and scholarly survey.

and Tortosa in the eastern reaches of its territories had been lost as a result of a series of divisions and rivalries between brothers and uncles of the dynasty, always assiduously nurtured by the counts of Barcelona and the then *El Cid* of Valencia. The ultimate result of those plots and aggressions, by this time, had been the occupation of those lands by the Murābit. Relations between the Africans and al-Mustain of Zaragoza (1085–1110) were generally cordial; but, notwithstanding, the resources of those eastern lands were no longer available to the latter. Other territories in the east – Calasanz, Barbastro, Balaguer – had fallen one by one to Pedro of Aragón or the count of Urgel in the years after the surrender of Huesca. Still, the attempt of Pedro against Zaragoza in 1101 was fruitless.

Another weakness of al-Mustain was his inability, after 1086, to play off the interests of León–Castilla against those of Aragón. The regular intervention of the former to prevent too resounding a success of Aragón against Zaragoza proved impossible to continue after the appearance of the Murābit in the peninsula. The designs of León–Castilla itself upon the taifa on the Ebro were no less treasured, but defense of the Toledo frontier had made it increasingly difficult to sustain them. Accordingly, Alfonso of Aragón had been able to thrust forward onto the plain of the middle Ebro in 1106, seizing the commanding position of Ejea de los Caballeros only 40 kilometers east of Tudela and 55 northwest of Zaragoza. Busy there and further east, the *Batallador* had made no further progress when the dynastic crisis in León–Castilla opened the vista of a more spectacular opportunity.

Negotiations for his marriage with Urraca would have demanded most of his attention from late 1108 until its actual consummation in the fall of 1109. From then until he discarded the dream of the crown of León–Castilla in 1116, that quest engrossed his energies almost entirely. At the same time it demonstrated the limitations of his power if indeed he still needed to be taught them. Far from his base in Aragón, Alfonso might win battles but he could not hold the land in the absence of a strong party among the nobility of the western kingdom to support him. Aragonese garrisons abetted by discontented, or self-seeking, burghers allowed him to hold the eastern towns at Burgos, Castrojeriz, Carrión de los Condes, and even one as far west as Sahagún for a time, but he had not the troops or wealth for a general occupation. When he finally accepted that fact he must, at the same time, have realized that the conquest of the taifa of Zaragoza would present a similar problem, if on a somewhat smaller scale. He must, then, find resources over and above those furnished by his own modest kingdom.

In the meantime, the problems of the ibn Hūd had become even more serious. In January of 1110 the *Batallador* had rushed back from León to meet a Zaragozan offensive, and defeated and killed al-Mustain at the battle of Valtierra. The Zaragozan king was then replaced by his son, Abd al-Malik, and Alfonso was unable to make further headway, nor, at that time, could he tarry long to attempt it. By May he was engaged, far to the west in the mountains of Galicia, in an unsuccessful effort to put down a revolt there. At the same time a rebellion of Murābit partisans within the city had forced out Abd al-Malik, and on the 31st of that month the African governor of Valencia took possession of Zaragoza and placed a garrison within it. The dethroned Hūddid king retired to the castle of Rueda de Jalón some 35 kilometers west of the city, dominated that river valley, and maintained his claim to the taifa. Alfonso was presented thereby with a situation at once of great opportunity and equally great peril. The Murābit could not be permitted to consolidate their hold on Zaragoza.

Alfonso had rushed back from Galicia, and, over the ensuing year, allied with Abd al-Malik to carry the attack to the city. All attempts these to dislodge the Murābit failed. Instead, the rupture of his marriage with Urraca of León made incumbent the attempt to impose his authority in her territories, his chief preoccupation in the years 1112–1116. The offensive passed instead to the Murābit governor, who struck north of even Huesca during that time and in 1114, and had strength left to make a general attack on Barcelona. Then, in the summer of 1115, the African governor was called south to Córdoba to help deal with a Leonese attack there and lost his life in the process. A new scion of the Murābit dynasty was despatched to Zaragoza but died in that city during the winter of 1117 without having accomplished anything of note. Before another leader of this rank should have arrived, Alfonso I would already have begun his siege.[2]

As we have already seen, in February 1117 at Burgos and with the aid of the Roman legate Cardinal Boso, Urraca of León and Alfonso of Aragón agreed to a truce which left each free to pursue other concerns. For the *Batallador*, that meant Zaragoza, and his search for adequate resources probably began immediately. The directions of that quest were already indicated by the traditions of his house. The papacy would be enlisted. The truce at Burgos had been effected in part because Pope Paschal II was interested enough in peace among

---

[2] José María Lacarra, "La conquista de Zaragoza por Alfonso I, 18 diciembre, 1118," *Al-Andalus* 12 (1947):65–96, remains the indispensable guide.

Christians in the peninsula to have sent Cardinal Boso as legate to Iberia to negotiate it. In 1118, in response to an appeal from Alfonso, his successor would raise the effort against Zaragoza to the level of a crusade. Gelasius II would rally what help the spiritual arm could furnish at a council held in Toulouse in the fall of 1118, but by that time the issue had already been decided.

The familial linkages of the Aragonese dynasty with France were more effectively exploited. Alfonso's cousin, Count Rotrou of Perche, led a Norman contingent which included Robert Burdet, Rainaud of Bailleul, and Gautier of Gerville. More important still was the aid from just beyond the pass of Somport. Viscount Gastón of Bearn and his brother, Viscount Centulle of Bigorre, both of them veterans of the First Crusade and thoroughly experienced at siege-work, Count Bernard of Comminges, Viscount Pierre of Gabaret, married to a daughter of Gastón of Bearn, Viscount Augier of Miramont, Arnaud of Lavedan, Viscount Bernard Atto of Carcassonne and Béziers, and Bishop Guy of Lescar, all participated and brought with them followers, mercenaries, and adventurers recruited in their districts. It is likely that the French knights outnumbered Aragonese ones, but that the foot soldiers so essential in siegework were largely Aragonese. Help was also forthcoming from the Count of Urgel.

By May 1118 the siege was in progress. Early sallies by the defenders were beaten back and the fortress–palace of the *Aljafería*, then outside the city proper, fell in mid-June. Its loss galvanized the Murābit of the south, and the governor of Granada, Abd Allāh ibn Mazdali, led an army north. He avoided the Christian forces initially and established himself at Tarazona, 80 kilometers northwest of Zaragoza. There he defeated a Christian force sent against him and then marched east to Tudela, reinforcing the garrison of that second city of the Ebro. With what remained of the army he had brought with him he once again managed to elude the besiegers and to enter Zaragoza in September. His arrival enormously heartened the defenders of the city and discouraged the Christians in the same measure.

Still, Alfonso of Aragón held the attacking army together and two months later the audacious Murābit governor died within the city. No one could effectively take his place, and a little more than two weeks after his demise the Zaragozans would ask for terms. Their provisions were exhausted and their population divided. The *Batallador* was prepared to be generous and the surrender took place on December 18, 1118. Without losing the momentum thus gained, the Aragonese hastily invested Tudela, and the dejected garrison of that city yielded it up by February 22, 1119. Resistance was more determined in Tarazona which did not fall until the following May. Borja just to the southeast of the latter probably was taken just before or after it, and the entire upper and middle basin of the Ebro was now in the hands of Alfonso.

The same season saw Alfonso push his new frontier west, over the Sierra de Moncayo to Soria, until it bordered Leonese territory in the region of the upper Duero. More important, however, was his progress toward the southwest and up the valley of the Jalón River, the passageway from Sevilla and Córdoba, against the inevitable reaction from Murābit Andalucía. After all, the loss of Zaragoza was a defeat to Islam in the peninsula, which could only be compared with the fall of the taifa of Toledo some thirty-three years earlier and the fall of Valencia in 1094, which latter had been reversed successfully in 1102.

In the spring of 1120 the *Batallador* had already advanced to the siege of Calatayud on the Jalón and had pushed some of his forces south along its tributary, the Jiloca, to the city of Daroca. As it turned out, the latter was the direction from which the attack would come. The Murābit governor of Sevilla and brother of Emir Alī ibn Yūsuf, Ibrāhīm ibn Yūsuf, passed through the gap by Albacete and was joined by contingents from Murcia with which the governor's forces advanced to Valencia. There additional reinforcements came in from Lérida to the north. The entire force then moved up through the valley of Teruel and so down the valley of the Jiloca toward Daroca. Muslim sources allege that the army numbered 5,000 cavalry and 10,000 foot soldiers. Given the general size of peninsular armies, half that number is more likely.

Alfonso I knew of their approach well in advance and made his preparations accordingly. The same Muslim sources credit him with 15,000 horse and countless infantry. There is clearly some self-serving here, but the battle that took place may have been one of the few instances when a Christian numerical advantage was likely. After Zaragoza, some French allies had doubtless gone home. Others, however, notably Count William of Poitiers, had arrived. In addition, the former ibn Hūd ruler of Zaragoza, Abd al-Malik of Rueda de Jalón, fought with the Aragonese. Other Muslim may have followed his lead. The two forces met at Cutanda in the valley of the Jiloca on June 17th. One suspects that the Aragonese took the Murābit by surprise for what followed was a complete rout. The latter were so far destroyed that even on the Christian side there was a saying that the unlucky might "come to a fate like Cutanda." That same year both Calatayud and Daroca fell, and by 1124 Christian control had been pushed up the valley of the Jiloca to Monreal del

Campo and even to Singra beyond. To hold Monreal, Alfonso established the military order of the same name in 1124, as he had done with Cofradía de Belchite the year before.[3] Also, in 1123, the *Batallador* had turned his attention toward the old lands of Zaragoza in the east, making preliminary thrusts toward Lérida and Fraga. But with all of the other territories of the taifa of Zaragoza already in his grasp, the immediate concerns of the Aragonese monarch must be with their consolidation.

The New Aragón and Its Neighbors

The king of Aragón now ruled a realm of about 40,000 square kilometers with an estimated population of close to 500,000. A quarter of these may have comprised the population of old Aragonese territories, virtually all Christian except around Huesca. Of the new population surely something on the order of three-fourths were Muslim. Mozarabs and Jews would have made up the remainder. The loyalty of these latter could ordinarily be assumed. Still, the fact remained that something better than half of the population of the kingdom was Muslim and therefore potentially hostile. Immigration of Christians from the north and emigration of Muslims to the south could be expected to gradually redress this militarily dangerous imbalance, but only gradually. In the meantime the security of the new conquests required immediate attention.

We have seen that security was provided above all by the victory at Cutanda in 1120, and subsequently by the establishment of the two military orders of Monreal, to patrol the southern approach to the kingdom through Teruel, and Belchite, to block an enemy approach up the basin of the Ebro from the east. By 1124 the conquest of Urraca of León in the area around Sigüenza had the effect of choking off any further Muslim advance along the old road through Medinaceli and down the valley of the Jalón. Additional precautions could be taken by installing Aragonese nobles in various portions of the conquered territories. But it was absolutely critical that the major cities of the new lands, Zaragoza, Tudela, Tarazona, Calatayud, and Daroca, be safeguarded since they were also the major fortresses of the realm. It appears by the terms of surrender, which are fairly well known to us, that that necessity was taken into account.

[3] See Antonio Ubieto Arteta, "La creación de la cofradía militar de Belchite," *EEMCA* 5 (1952):427–34. See also Bernard F. Reilly, *The Kingdom of León–Castilla under Queen Urraca, 1109–1126* (Princeton, N.J., 1982), pp. 171–73.

These terms uniformly allowed a one-year transition period, during which time the Muslim population could continue to reside within the walled city and even retain the major mosque there. After that, they were to move to the suburbs or even to their lands in the countryside. The walled precinct was itself to become a Christian stronghold. The Muslim were guaranteed the right to sell their real property and to emigrate if they so desired. Muslim sources assert that 50,000 did so from Zaragoza alone, but we may well question whether so many left from the entire kingdom in the period 1118–1134. However, only the relatively well to do would have the luxury of emigration. Those who remained would represent so large a portion of the total population that their interests would have to be looked after if any sort of tranquility was to prevail, and the terms reflect the recognition of that brute fact.

The Muslim community would continue in the enjoyment of its property and the ability to come and go in the realm which its use demanded. They might go to work their fields outside the cities, and their flocks were free to circulate, subject only to the traditional charges. They were safeguarded in the practice of their religion. Their religious law was to continue to prevail, and their own officials from before the conquest were to be retained in their former positions. They could continue to bear arms, but no military service would be demanded of them against either Muslim or Christian. No claims against person or goods anterior to the surrender was to be admitted, no Jew was to be placed in authority over them, and only Christian officials of good repute were to be allowed to supervise them. No reprisals were to be taken against them in the eventuality of future Murābit attacks. The number of Christian merchants in the city would be regulated. Of course, Muslims would be subject to the annual tax of a tenth, which was the price of their royal protection.[4]

All in all, it was a generous settlement for a conquered population, even a familiar one since it followed the general pattern of relationships between the various religious populations of Iberia at that time. Nevertheless, more had to be done to provide for the safety of the new realm vis-à-vis its neighbors. The *Batallador* was to address this problem in a spectacular fashion in 1125.

In September of that year the Aragonese monarch had assembled an army that would spend the next nine months engaged in a great raid through the Muslim territories of southeastern Iberia. The only detailed account of its progress comes from three Muslim sources,

[4] Antonio Ubieto Arteta, *Historia de Aragón: La formación territorial*, Vol. 1 (Zaragoza, 1981), pp. 154–55.

and these have the usual problems of distortion for partisan purposes. Nevertheless they are indispensable and form the basis of most modern accounts.[5] Alfonso is said to have led out an army from Zaragoza which numbered between 4,000 and 5,000 on horse and 15,000 on foot. This is the army that will cover some 3,000 kilometers, by the most conservative reckoning possible, over the next nine months and achieve an average daily speed of 10 kilometers per day through some of the most rugged country in the peninsula. It is absolutely safe to say that a force so composed could not have transported its own supplies through that terrain nor fed itself from the land being traversed. The only sensible presumption is that Alfonso's army was sizeable, 1,000 to 1,500 horse perhaps, for he was accompanied by Gastón de Bearn, Rotru of Perche, and the bishops of Huesca and Zaragoza, which argues for a major effort. But the presence of infantry would have made impossible the speed or mobility which the army was to display and was not relevant to its purposes.

On September 2nd the king left Zaragoza and by October 10th had reached Valencia some 350 kilometers distant at a minimum, where some fighting took place. Then, by October 31st, the Aragonese moved 100 kilometers farther down the coast to Denia and again there was fighting in that vicinity. Leaving Denia in turn the army struck through Murcia and into the rugged southern sierras, arriving at Guadix on November 11th, a distance of more than 500 kilometers, at an average speed en route of about 28 kilometers per day. That kind of movement through country of that nature could only have been achieved by a mounted force. The fighting around Guadix apparently lasted close to a month.

During January Alfonso marched and countermarched about the foothills of the Sierra Nevada, trying to get closer to the city of Granada which lies in its folds. However, by this time all of Murābit Andalucía and North Africa was thoroughly alarmed, and Granada had been heavily reinforced. Eventually the Aragonese monarch moved off west to Lucena where he was to arrive by January 23rd. In that vicinity he seems to have made winter camp for a time, but he was on the move again by March 10th when he routed a Murābit force under Abū Bakr, son of Emir Alī, at Arnisol a few kilometers south of Lucena. That victory left him free to strike through the

[5] See Ubieto Arteta, *Historia de Aragón*, pp. 172–78. Ambrosio Huici Miranda, *Historia musulmana de Valencia y su región*, 3 vols. (Valencia, 1969–70), 3:53–57, also describes it in detail. Unfortunately, the former had little experience of the country which it had to traverse and equally small experience of military necessities. For those reasons, Huici Miranda is to be preferred when they differ.

mountains of Málaga to the Mediterranean coast. After passing some restful days there Alfonso then moved east along that narrow and tortuous strand to Motril and from there up the valley of the Isbor River into the Sierra Nevadas, approaching the city of Granada again but this time from the south. He spent some five days in its immediate vicinity and there was more hard fighting.

Finally leaving the Granada territories, the *Batallador* withdrew in the direction of Guadix on the first leg of the return journey. The Muslim cavalry shadowed him and attacked near Guadix, inflicting considerable losses. From there he continued back through Murcia and into Valencia, finally arriving in Aragón itself by June 23rd, 1126. The return journey saw almost continuous skirmishing as well as some larger engagements, but the Aragonese force apparently maintained good order and was never in danger of breaking up. The assertion of the Muslim sources that Alfonso's army suffered heavy losses can readily be accepted. Aside from the casualties in battle, the loss of both men and horses from general exhaustion and exposure to the mid-winter rains and snow must have been considerable. The claim of victory made by those same authors, based as it was on his failure to take any fortified city, must be scrutinized more closely.

Any serious reflection on the campaign of 1125–1126 in Andalucía must conclude that its purpose was in good measure preventive. That is, its objective was not to seize cities, which could not have been held in any event, but to savage their hinterlands. The destruction of crops, vines, trees, and livestock had effects that went beyond any one year. New grapevines take five years before they begin to produce, the olive tree must be fifteen to twenty years old before it reaches full production, and herds have to be painstakingly replaced by cumulative, annual breeding. Such widespread destruction along the future invasion route impaired for a long time the ability of armies to move across it, and all of the sources admit that precisely such destruction took place.

But to carry out such destruction took many more hands than the army had with it, and here we reach another rationale of the campaign. Muslim authors account for Alfonso's invasion by alleging a plot on the part of portions of their own Mozarab population, whose leaders appealed to the Aragonese monarch for help and promised a general rising upon his entry into Andalucía. Certainly during that campaign there were revolts of the Mozarab population, which furnished precisely the sort of engineering and infantry dimensions which the invaders did not bring with them. We cannot measure its extent, although it has been asserted by some sources that Alfonso's army thereby momentarily achieved the size of

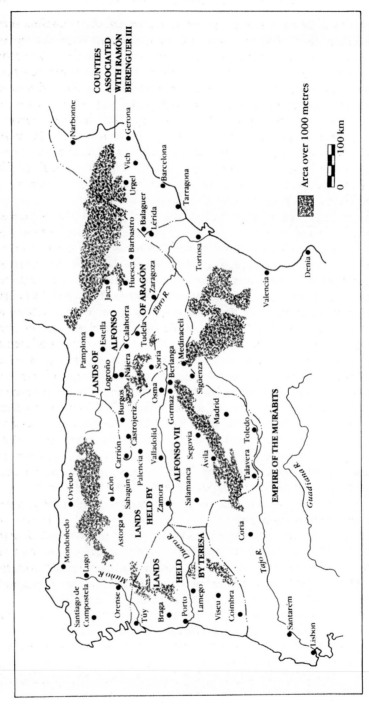

Figure 4   Christian Iberia at the accession of Alfonso VII in 1126

50,000. While that number is simply unbelievable, it is possible that the Murābit losses at Zaragoza and Cutanda had had serious repercussions on their control in the south, and that the subject Mozarabs saw finally some chance of liberation from their ancient conquerors. Certainly large numbers of Mozarabs accompanied the Aragonese army back to the new territories of Aragón and were granted a general *fuero* there by Alfonso I in June of 1126. They can scarcely be the 10,000 sometimes given in texts, but any influx of Christian settlers into the new Aragón was more than welcome. Not only was Alfonso's army able to retreat in good order from Andalucía, it obviously also successfully served as a covering force for sizeable, civil migration of Mozarabs.

A commentary on this whole aspect of the events of 1125–1126 is furnished by the fact that the Murābit carried out a sizeable deportation of Mozarabs to Morocco in the fall of 1126.[6] Doubtless this was not a general deportation, for that would have further depressed agricultural recovery, but it seems to have been large enough to affect the remaining leaders of that subject community, their families, and followers. Finally, all of this interior turmoil reflected the increasing difficulties of the Murābit in Andalucía. The Africans had never been really popular there, and there had been noticeable disturbances among the Muslim population in some cities as early as 1120.[7] In addition, an element of religious protest was beginning to be felt as some of the Andalucían *faqīhs* were attracted to the upstart African fundamentalist Muwāhhid movement. The dissent reached even the ruling dynasty itself, and that spectacularly. In 1128 the governor of Sevilla and son of Emir Alī, Abū Bakr, had refused to accept his father's designation of his younger half brother, Sir, as eventual successor to the Murābit Empire and had to be arrested and returned to Morocco to disappear from subsequent history.[8]

Set against such a background the otherwise vainglorious though arresting campaign of Alfonso of Aragón through Andalucía in 1125–1126 becomes an understandable strategic gamble rather than a piece of military bravado. It would have been foolish of him to ignore the pot that was beginning to boil in Andalucía. However, he had been preoccupied there for some nine months and much had

---

[6] Rafael Gerardo Peinado Santaella and José Enríque López de Coca Castañer, *Historia de Granada: La época medieval*, 2 vols. (Granada, 1987), pp. 223–28.

[7] Jacinto Bosch Vilá, *Historia de Sevilla: La Sevilla islámica, 712–1248* (Sevilla, 1984), pp. 143–44.

[8] Ambrosio Huici Miranda, "Contribución al estudio de la dinastía almorávides: El Gobierno de Tasfin ben Alī ben Yūsuf en el-Andalus," in *Études d'orientalisme dédiees a la memoire de Lévi-Provençal*, Vol. 2 (Paris, 1962), p. 106.

transpired elsewhere during that time. Now he must address the problems occasioned by his Christian neighbors.

Foremost among these was the changing relationship with León–Castilla. For some nine years he had enjoyed the luxury of a truce renewed every third year with Urraca of León. During his absence she had died, and by the time he had returned to Aragón her son, Alfonso VII, was firmly planted on the throne of that kingdom. From the first, the new Leonese king was to reverse his mother's policy of peace with Aragón in order to consolidate her control in Galicia and Portugal. Since the excuse of rebellion in Galicia had always reposed in the appeal to the rights of the young heir against his mother, on her death and his accession the province ceased to be a problem. Its leading nobles sought out the young king in Zamora in April of 1126, and their numbers included the powerful Trasta-mara clan of the north. Archbishop Gelmírez hastened to that city as well to court the new monarch. In addition, from Zamora the king had ridden west to meet with his aunt, Teresa of Portugal, and to conclude a peace with her of whose terms we are ignorant. Clearly Alfonso of León was initially to pursue an eastern policy.

If the adversary of choice was to be the king of Aragón, the logical course was to seek an alliance with the counts of Barcelona who also usually opposed the *Batallador*. Negotiations were certainly under-way by 1127 at least, for some time in October or November of that year Alfonso of León had married Berengaria, daughter of Count Ramón Berenguer III (1097–1131). The young king had also coupled with this diplomacy a vigorous offensive in Castilla, which by April 30, 1127 had delivered the key city of Burgos into his hands In addition, Count Bertrán de Risnel, the Aragonese monarch's cousin and guardian of his interests in Castilla since 1117, appears to have gone over to the side of the Leonese. That defection cost Alfonso I the control of Carrión de los Condes and pushed his advance post back upon Castrojeriz. The whole of the Aragonese position in Castilla appeared on the verge of collapse.

Reacting to this threat, the *Batallador* fielded an army in the summer of 1127 and advanced into eastern Castilla. It met with the force directed by his cousin, Alfonso VII, at the Vale of Tamara not far from Castrojeriz. There, on July 31st, a battle was averted and a peace mediated by Gastón of Bearn and Centulle of Bigorre.[9] By its terms, known only indirectly, Alfonso of Aragón agreed to surrender those towns and strongholds which belonged to Alfonso

---

[9] José María Lacarra, "Alfonso el Batallador y las paces de Tamara. Cuestiones cronologicas (1124–1127)," *EEMCA* 3 (1949): 461–73, is authoritative.

VII by hereditary right and to desist from employing the imperial title. The young Leonese monarch had adopted the imperial title immediately upon the death of his mother, and there could be but one emperor in Iberia. In the dating formula of his documents, nevertheless, the now merely king of Aragón continued to claim Castilla, probably Castilla la Vieja, northeast of Burgos, until 1130. He also sometimes explicitly claimed the Basque county of Alava to its northeast, and the Rioja which adjoined it to the east. As we shall see, he did not return Castrojeriz.

All in all, the Bearnese had done a signal service by avoiding the recurrence of war between Aragón and León–Castilla, which in 1127 would have been characterized by the same futility that had marked it fifteen years earlier. The *Batallador* was much better exercised in guarding his southern frontier, where he was fortifying the town of Cella, 20 kilometers northwest of Muslim Teruel, in August. He also had to guard against losses in the east, such as that at Monzón, just south of Barbastro, which had been seized by Ramón Berenguer of Barcelona in that same year.

Still, the peace with León–Castilla could never be final as long as the *Batallador* retained so much of the old territories of Alfonso VI. The Aragonese monarch was preoccupied with his western frontier for all of 1128. That spring he conducted a siege of the Muslim town of Molina de Aragón, which controlled a secondary approach, just north of the Sierra de Albarracín, to his southern lands from the old territories of the taifa of Toledo. He did take the town in the course of the year, but in so doing apparently menaced the Leonese position at Medinaceli some 60 kilometers to the northwest. At least the people there believed so and appealed to Alfonso VII, who moved into the district with a small force. In the meantime the Aragonese had marched north to the fortified town of Almazán on the upper Duero, midway between Medinaceli and Soria, in August. There ensued a confrontation and negotiations at Almazán, but not a battle. The negotiations came to nothing and Alfonso VII withdrew into Castilla after reinforcing Medinaceli.[10]

Clearly, in this round the Leonese king had been outmaneuvered and humiliated. The loss seems to have been due to the failure of most of his Castilian subjects to respond to his summons. The culprits are identified as the powerful brothers Counts Pedro and Rodrigo González of the Lara family. In fact, Alfonso of Aragón

[10] Luis Sánchez Belda, ed., *Chronica Adefonsi Imperatoris* (Madrid, 1950), pp. 15–19. This chronicle narrates the episode with the implication that it was a clear moral victory for Alfonso VII. It also dates it to the start of 1129, but it is likely that some activity in the vicinity continued into that year.

had taken advantage of the changed political balance in León–Castilla himself. As long as Urraca had been queen, Count Pedro González her lover, and the *Batallador* in control of most of Castilla, the Laras and the Aragonese had been determined enemies. Now that Urraca was dead, Alfonso VII in control of most of Castilla, and the Lara counts facing declining fortunes, the latter and the Aragonese were natural allies. The new Leonese king would have to deal with the domestic problem before returning to that of his eastern frontier.

The internal troubles of Alfonso VII in 1129 and 1130 were fortunate indeed for the Aragonese king. During the spring of 1129 the Murābit emir Alī ibn Yūsuf prepared another major offensive for the east of Iberia. Forces sent from Africa joined those of Murcia, Córdoba, and Sevilla, under the governor of the latter, in Murcia and moved north into Valencian territory. Apprised of their approach, Alfonso I declined to wait, but struck south into the lands around Valencia. Although even the Muslim sources admit that their forces were more numerous, the Aragonese again scored an impressive victory, at Cullera, near the mouth of the Jucar River south of Valencia, in May of 1129. Virtually that entire Murābit army appears to have been destroyed and their baggage train captured, and some Muslim fortresses in the area seem to have been occupied.

The latter advantage was to be short lived. A new and energetic Murābit governor took control of Valencia in 1130 and began a campaign against Christian forces in the area. At the beginning of May he had at least one remarkable success. He defeated an Aragonese force of some considerable size which had been operating in the vicinity. Among the fallen were Bishop Esteban of Huesca and Viscount Gastón of Bearn. The head of the viscount was sent to Granada where it was paraded through the streets on the point of a lance. Nevertheless, the success was local enough in character that the Muslim were unable to follow up their advantage in that year, and during the succeeding year their attentions were for the most part directed to the central, Toledan frontier.[11]

That conjuncture of events was also fortunate for Alfonso I. By the time that Gastón of Bearn had perished the Aragonese king was marching into southern France at the head of an army. He was to spend something like the next year and a half laying siege to the port of Bayonne in Gascony. Why he should have done that at this juncture is something of a mystery. The best conjecture is based upon the known fact that the dukes of Aquitaine were usually allied,

---

[11] Huici Miranda, "Gobierno de Tasfīn," pp. 608–10, is the best guide generally to things military during this period.

in this period, with the counts of Barcelona against the counts of Toulouse and the viscounts of Carcassonne, who in turn were ordinarily the allies of the kings of Aragón. In 1130 Count Alfonso Jordán of Toulouse was at war with Duke William of Aquitaine, and so perhaps the ordinary alliance with Aragón explains the *Batallador's* actions. In that year he was certainly at war with Ramón Berenguer of Barcelona, and in February had reclaimed the stronghold of Monzón from the latter. Or it may be that he was simply repaying the assistance of Gaston of Bearn by defending that viscount's interests in the south of France. Whatever the reason, there he was, at a time when he might better have been employed in Aragón itself, or at least on its western approaches.[12]

To be sure, everything had not been going perfectly for his adversary, Alfonso VII of León–Castilla. The western frontier of this latter was unsettled in 1128 by the overthrow of Teresa of Portugal by her son, Alfonso Enríquez. Teresa and her consort, Fernando Pérez of Traba, were defeated in battle and driven into exile in Galicia. Before long the new Portuguese monarch would abandon the quiescent policy his mother had adopted in 1126. Also, in late 1129 or early 1130, the Lara counts had risen against the new king of León and thrown themselves and their followers into the city of Palencia. However, they then found themselves unable to withstand the popularity of the young monarch. The citizens of Palencia made their peace and so did Rodrigo González of Lara, although at the price of his countship of Asturias de Santillana. Pedro González, deprived of his countship of Castilla, chose to flee to the court of his supporter, Alfonso of Aragón, then before Bayonne. There his turbulent career ended when he was killed in a duel with Alfonso Jordán of Toulouse. Alfonso Jordán was himself a grandson of Alfonso VI of León–Castilla and doubtless had some strong feelings about the former lover of Urraca, his maternal aunt.

With his own house in order for the time being, Alfonso VII was able to turn his attention once again to the Aragonese problem precisely when his rival was tied down in the south of France. The prime target was the fortress of Castrojeriz, which was both the westernmost position held by the Aragonese in Castilla and the

[12] French historians have regarded the entire idea of such a campaign as fanciful. See J. Vaissete and Claude Devic, *Histoire de Languedoc*, Vol. 3 (Toulouse, 1872), pp. 680–81. Nevertheless, the expedition is too well documented on the Spanish end to be dismissed, despite the difficulty in understanding its rationale. Marcelin Defourneaux, *Les Français en Espagne aux XIe et XIIe siècles* (Paris, 1949), pp. 161-63, accepts it as true and points out that Centulle of Bigorre had done homage to the Aragonese.

center of their activity in that province. The Leonese king surrounded and besieged it from May until it surrendered in October of
1131. The *Batallador* had been unable even to despatch relief to its
commander, and its fall was accompanied by the surrender as well
of lesser Aragonese fortresses, which effectively ended their two-
decades-long occupation of Castilla west of the Sierra de la Demanda
East of that watershed they continued to hold Castilla la Vieja and
the Rioja, but Alfonso VII was now in a position to attempt their
recovery when the time was propitious.

It is also possible that diplomacy, combined with his developing
successes, gave Alfonso VII a slight foothold within the territories of
his rival at this time. The major literary source for his reign narrates
the exchange by the ibn Hūd prince, Saif al-Dawla, or the "Zafadola" of the Christian authors, of his territories in the valley of the
Jalón and the fortress of Rueda for other lands within the territories
of Alfonso VII as he became the vassal of the latter. Both the Muslim
prince and his father had generally cooperated with Alfonso of
Aragón since the Murābit had expelled them from their capital of
Zaragoza. They had probably done homage to the *Batallador* in that
relationship, and now the son was transferring his allegiance to
León–Castilla. Since the valley of the Jalón was the major route from
the central *meseta* down to the valley of the Ebro just above Zaragoza, the territories which now passed into the control of León–
Castilla were important indeed.[13]

In any event, during the following year the Aragonese king was
busy strengthening his frontiers both in the Rioja and in and around
Soria at the headwaters of the Duero. He could not have been too
concerned, however, for he was already planning to retrieve the
remaining portions of the historic taifa of Zaragoza for his rule.
These lay in the east and comprised the lands of the cities of Lérida
and Tortosa, which had also been a part of the Hūddid patrimony.
In the three decades since the Murābit conquest of Valencia to the
south, these cities had sometimes recognized the sovereignty of the
Africans when the latter were strong and had sometimes paid *parias*
to Barcelona when they were not. The object had always been to
maintain their independence of whoever ruled Zaragoza.

Lérida was the most proximate goal, but apparently the Aragonese
intended that his siege forces there be supplied in good measure by
stores floated down the Ebro from Zaragoza. From that direction,

---

[13] The story of the change of lords of Saif al-Dawla is told in Sánchez Belda, ed.,
Chronica, pp. 23–28, just after the Castrojeriz campaign, and begins with "In those
times." It is arguable that the surrender may have taken place at almost any time
during the next two years. The dating of the *Chronica* is not always accurate.

the approach was guarded by the strongholds of Mequinenza, where that river is joined by the Segre River which flows past Lérida, and Fraga some 18 kilometers farther north. From January of 1133 until July of 1134 the last campaign of Alfonso of Aragón swirled around those two points. Mequinenza was taken almost immediately, but Fraga was steadfast in its resistance. The citizens of Lérida, meanwhile directed their appeals to the Murābit of Valencia exclusively, since the death of the old count of Barcelona in 1131 had left his son of but seventeen years, Ramón Berenguer IV, in control there.

At Valencia the active governor who had defeated Gastón of Bearn in 1130 had been since rewarded with the governorship of Sevilla. He had been replaced by ibn Gāniya who now held the governorship of both Murcia and Valencia and was to prove a more than worthy adversary. He will figure prominently in Christian accounts as "Abengania." On at least two occasions he advanced to the relief of Fraga. The first time, at the beginning of 1134, he was repulsed. On the second occasion the outcome was very different. The climax came on July 17, 1134, when the Murābit attack coincided with a sally on the part of the Fragans. Taken by surprise for some reason by Muslim military tactics of encirclement, which should have been familiar, the Aragonese and their allies were routed and decimated. Viscount Centulle of Bigorre, Bishop Pedro of Rota, and Bishop Arnold of Huesca all perished on the field. Bishop Guy of Lescar was taken prisoner and carted off to Valencia. Alfonso I was wounded but managed to escape from the field and also from a determined pursuit. But even that respite was temporary. On September 7, 1134, the king of Aragón died of wounds contracted at Fraga.[14]

The disappearance of El Batallador after thirty active years immediately called into question the survival of that new Aragón whose construction had been his life's work. The acuteness of the crisis was due in part to the fact that he had no children. After the failure of his marriage to Urraca in 1109 he never remarried. Nor, peculiar in the powerful, had he any known mistresses or children by them. To be sure, there were other living members of the dynasty, but in 1131 Alfonso I had taken the most peculiar step of willing his kingdom to a collection of religious orders. That will had been reaffirmed on September 4, 1134, just before his death. The demise of the king of Aragón under these circumstances initiated a crisis of the entire realm which was not to be resolved for three years, nor would there be a return to the state of affairs at the beginning of his reign, but rather in the most unimaginable and unlikely sort of novelty.

[14] Ubieto Arteta, Historia de Aragón, Vol. 1, pp. 189–99, narrates the campaign in much detail from the fairly copious original sources.

Barcelona into Cataluña (1097–1131)

The final heirs to the legacy of Alfonso I *El Batallador* of Aragón were to be the counts of Barcelona and a totally new and somewhat strange construction that was to appear on the Iberian stage where it would endure against all odds for the next three hundred years. This was the realm of the count–kings of Aragón. The dynasty of Barcelona continued adding to this duality throughout the Late Middle Ages until it included the Balearics, Valencia, Sicily, and the south of Italy. Before any of this could happen, however, the county of Cataluña itself had to be created, and it can be argued that the crucial steps in that process were taken by Count Ramón Berenguer III.

When that fifteen-year-old became the leader of the dynasty in 1097 prospects were anything but bright. His uncle had been forced to abdicate for complicity in the death of the young man's father. Rodrigo Díaz de Vivar dominated the affairs of northeast Iberia from Valencia and blocked any advance toward the south. After the collapse of *El Cid*'s power the Murābit took control of Valencia in 1102 and that year defeated the combined forces of Barcelona and Urgel at Mollerusa. In 1107–1108 and again in 1114 Muslim armies surged up to the gates of Barcelona itself for the first time in a century. Nonetheless, Ramón Berenguer *El Grande* would not only survive but prosper and enhance the strength of his small possessions in three distinct arenas.[15]

His most fundamental achievement may be said to be the creation of Cataluña. That is, since the late 9th Century a congeries of related families had been ruling the former Carolingian county of Barcelona, roughly corresponding to the later Cataluña. Although they more often cooperated with one another than fought, there was no central political direction. The counts of Barcelona had come to control not just the hinterland of that city itself but also that of Gerona and the more western district of Osona. They also enjoyed some political preeminence among the families. Still, strictly speaking, no realm of Cataluña existed. In this most basic sense, Ramón Berenguer III moved quickly to consolidate the realm to be. In October of 1107 he secured the marriage of his daughter, María, then seven, to the widowed Count Bernat III of Besalú, who was more than fifty and not in good health. A condition of the marriage was that, in the absence of children to this peculiar union, the count's domains

---

[15] Thomas N. Bisson, *The Medieval Crown of Aragon* (Oxford, 1986), is the best brief but general treatment in English.

would pass to the county of Barcelona at his death. Not surprisingly, Bernat died in 1111 before there was any possibility of a child, and his county of Besalu and the associated territory of Vallespir passed to the county of Barcelona.[16]

Six years later the importance of that accession of territory was magnified further when Count Bernat Guillem of Cerdanya died. A close friend and collaborator of the Barcelonan, who was also his nearest kin, the count died without children, and the county of Cerdanya and its associated districts of Conflent, Capcir, and Berga all passed to the direct control of Ramón Berenguer. Altogether these acquisitions increased the lands under the direct political control of Barcelona by more than a half. Roussillon and Empúries to the north and Urgel and Pallars to the west were still related politically only by the ties of vassalage for long years to come, but among the lands of the Catalan language the preponderance of the counts of Barcelona had become unchallengeable.

Inevitably we see these activities in terms of state buildings, for that is one of the fundamental categories of our own political and historical thought. Ramón Berenguer III would not have understood, since he thought in terms of dynasty. So it is that we find the second great area of his activity to be jarring and even frivolous, but to him his actions made sense. That is, the count not only became the preeminent leader of the Catalan lands of Iberia, he also came to control most of the southern coast of France as well. As with the consolidation of Catalan lands, that process was predominantly legal and peaceful; the function of diplomacy and marriage. He sought in it the glory of his dynasty and the pursuit of their legitimate claims.

During the latter half of the 11th Century his family had come into possession of, and then lost, the counties of Carcassonne and Razès to the doughty Viscount Bernard Atto of Béziers. The viscount had subsequently ceded possession of Razès to Alfonso I of Aragón. Giving up the attempt to conquer them, the Barcelona count in 1112 recognized Bernard's and Alfonso's possession of them if they would hold them as fiefs with the eventual right of reversion to Barcelona.[17] A few months after the resolution of that question, Ramón Berenguer went on to marry the heiress Dolce of Provence. That union made him count in Provence as well, with the control of the entire south French littoral from the French Alps to

---

[16] Santiago Sobreques i Vidal, *Els grans comtes de Barcelona* (Barcelona, 1961), pp. 170–71. This handy and scholarly little book carries the story up through the end of the succeeding reign.

[17] Ferran Soldevila, *Historia dels Catalans*, 3 vols. (Barcelona, 2nd ed., 1962–64), 1:127, rightly defends the moderation of this settlement.

the Rhone. That innocent *démarche* was to involve him yet further in the whole web of politics in the Languedoc and would demand that his policies somehow speak to the interests of its peoples. It also arrayed against him the interests of the German emperor Henry V, the Provençal magnate house of the Baux, and the counts of Toulouse.

Inseparable from this development was the emergence of Barcelona as a power in the maritime and naval affairs of the western Mediterranean. The presence of Muslim merchants and pirates operating from the Balearics had been a concern of the seafaring element of that littoral for long centuries, and the count of Barcelona would now join with the Pisans and the papacy to attempt to reorder the naval balance off the south French coast. Our source for the episode is a contemporary Pisan account which establishes it as their initiative. In 1113 Pope Paschal II responded to their requests by authorizing the archbishop of Pisa to preach a crusade against the Muslim at sea; and in that year an expedition, which included ships from the whole of the western Italian coast from Lombardy south to Rome, departed but somehow failed to reach its objective. Perhaps they found their strength insufficient.

In any event, some of this fleet wintered over on the coast of Cataluña, conducting negotiations there with Ramón Berenguer who agreed to accept leadership in the enterprise and to organize its further reinforcement. In the early summer of 1114 a fleet and army, made up of contingents from Barcelona, Narbonne, Montpellier, Nimes, and Provence, as well as Pisa, sailed and effected the conquest of Ibiza by early August. It then proceeded to Majorca, and by April of the following year had taken the capital. In the long run it would prove impossible to hold the motley force together, and in 1116 the island would be regained by a Murābit fleet despatched by Emir Alī ibn Yūsuf. We are told that the Christian fleet numbered some 500 vessels, but the recorded numbers of 80 Italian ships and 47 French make a total force of about 200 more likely. Nevertheless, the expedition both demonstrated and strengthened the new position of the counts of Barcelona at sea in the Christian western Mediterranean.[18] Ten years later, in 1127, even haughty Genoa sought out and obtained the same protection and rights in Catalan ports as the vessels of Montpellier already enjoyed, and agreed to pay ten *morabetinos* per vessel to obtain them.

---

[18] Sobreques i Vidal, *Els grans comtes*, pp. 175–79, is a good short account of the compaign. Defourneaux, *Les Français*, pp. 155–56, stresses the French participation, of course. Pierre Bonnassie, *Cataluña mil años atrás, siglos X–XI* (Barcelona, 1988), p. 415, suggests, probably with reason, the major contribution of Barcelona.

But the position of Barcelona needed to be bolstered by a reasonable diplomacy as well. The count would find himself embroiled in major military action in Provence with the magnate house of Baux during a visit in 1116, and the possibility that the new possessions would be an occasion of weakness more than of strength was clearly demonstrated. Ramón Berenguer moved to meet that eventuality when, in September of 1125, he signed a partition treaty with Count Alfonso Jordán of Toulouse. By it, Barcelona surrendered to Toulouse all of Provence from the Durance River north to the Isere River. In return, Toulouse recognized the rights of Barcelona to the entire Provençal coast north to the Durance and from the Alps to the Rhone. Finally, by his will, Ramón Berenguer was to leave the Provençal possessions to his second son in 1131, separating them from the inheritance of his firstborn.

Even on our terms, the value of these territories beyond the Pyrenees can be recognized. They contributed their weight to establishing a position that could command respect, and therefore aid for enterprises nearer home. That meant useful assistance to the renewal of the expansion of Barcelona southward along the coast.

The eastern coast of Iberia is difficult terrain, often narrow to the point of vanishing between the inland mountains and the sea. Barcelona itself is so pressed against its waterfront. To the south the next large coastal plain valuable for exploitation was that dominated by the old Roman city of Tarragona sitting on its hill. Nonetheless, that potentially rich domain had been largely deserted for centuries due to its position on the frontier. The Barcelonans had been perched on the northern edge of it, at what is now Villafranca de Penedès, until the Murābit raids of 1107 wiped out the Christian settlement there. Now the repulse of the Murābit before Barcelona itself in 1107–1108, and, more recently, the stunning defeat again of the combined Murābit forces of Zaragoza and Valencia just outside of Barcelona in 1114, while Ramón Berenguer was occupied in the Balearics, opened the way for a new attempt to expand toward the south.

The Roman popes had long been interested in just such an effort, particularly as it would involve the restoration of the old metropolitan see of Tarragona. As early as 1089 Pope Urban II had moved to restore that archepiscopal province, but its prelates had no more been able to establish themselves on its throne than the counts of Barcelona had been to appropriate its territory. Now, in 1116, Ramón Berenguer would coast along the south of France to Provence and past to Genoa and then to Pisa, where he was received with pomp and ceremony. But the supreme objective was Rome, and there, in May of 1116, Pope Paschal II issued a bull of crusade whose object was the liberation of Tarragona from the Muslim. It was the

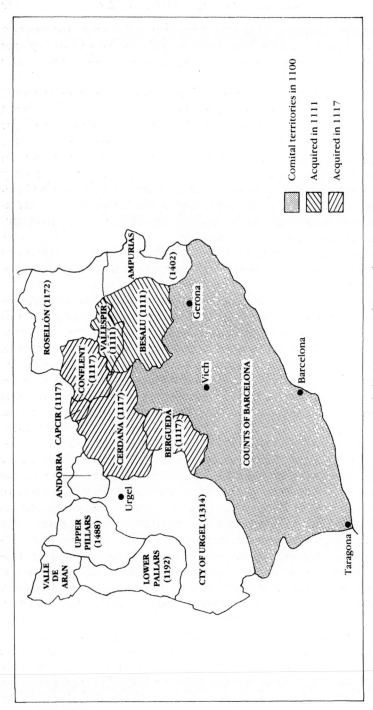

Figure 5 Growth of the county of Barcelona to 1137

least the pontiff could do for the victor of the Balearics who had also agreed to make an annual payment of gold to the papacy for that territory and whose person and possessions now were taken under the protection of the Holy See.[19]

Yet the plans of 1116 were of little import. Everyone, it seems, was hypnotized by the far greater drama being played out around Zaragoza in 1117 and 1118 by a king of Aragón newly freed for decisive action in the east of Iberia. Ramón Berenguer entrusted military and civil authority over the entire Tarragona district to Bishop Olegario of Barcelona in January of 1117, but that worthy could make no headway there on his own. Pope Paschal having died, the new pontiff, Gelasius II, made Olegario archbishop of Tarragona in 1118, and stipulated that Muslim Tortosa, the great city dominating the delta of the Ebro, would also become subject to his jurisdiction when it was conquered. It was the power of Tortosa, of course, that stood behind the resistance of the local Muslim of the Tarragona area.

Yet, in the final analysis, it was the resounding victories of Alfonso I of Aragón – at Zaragoza in 1118 and at Cutanda in 1120 – which were to make the progress of Barcelona south along the Mediterranean coast possible. Those two battles broke forever the power of the Murābit in the plain of the Ebro and threw the former subject cities of Lérida and Tortosa essentially back upon their own resources at a time when the enormously magnified power of the king of Aragón was a real threat to their very existence. The two cities of the lower Ebro reverted, under these circumstances, to the behavior which had marked their earlier period as independent taifas. That is, they sought the protection of one of the Christian powers against the other. In 1119 Tortosa accepted the suzerainty of Barcelona and Lérida did so in the following year. Both renewed the payment of *parias*. Neither was then able to block the progress of Ramón Berenguer on the plain of Tarragona any longer.

Nevertheless, local resistance in the hinterlands of Tarragona remained strong even if its more powerful protectors had been nullified. The successor of Pope Gelasius, Calixtus II (1119–1124), was to attempt to put Olegario at the head of a crusade but without producing any tangible results.[20] The former, despairing of a better

---

[19] Catalan historians have been very concerned with whether or not their count actually did homage to the pope and so became a vassal of the Holy See. See *Soldevila*, 1:133, and Sobreques i Vidal, *Els grans comtes*, pp. 182–83. It seems that the evidence would be clearer had such a definitive step been taken.

[20] See the bull in Ulysse Robert, ed., *Bullaire du Pape Calixti II*, 2 vols. (Paris, 1891), 2:266–67, which is undated. The editor placed it between April 1121 and April 1124. I believe the latter year to be the most probable.

way to secure the territories of his metropolitan see, granted them in fief in 1128 to the Norman adventurer Robert Burdet, who had come to Spain in 1118 to participate in the siege of Zaragoza and who was now, apparently, seeking a lord who would be more generous than the *Batallador*. From this time on, the Christian strength in the surroundings of Tarragona began to grow steadily, but when Olegario died in 1137 that archbishop had still not found it practicable to take up residence in his own provincial capital.

Toward the end of his reign Ramón Berenguer III was himself more preoccupied by the problems of his western frontier. Alfonso I of Aragón had clear designs upon both Lérida and Fraga, and capabilities of those Muslim cities to resist were not such as to inspire confidence. If they should come into the possession of the new Aragón, Barcelona would be permanently locked into a tiny pocket of northern Iberia. Its destiny could only then have been to become a southern extension of the Languedoc or, alternatively, a satellite of a greater Aragón if not a part of it. When he returned from his raid through Andalucía in 1126 the *Batallador* held some talks with the count of Barcelona which must have had just such concerns as their content. The Aragónese monarch was obviously unable to allay the suspicions of Ramón Berenguer, for the latter returned to Barcelona to negotiate a marriage of his eldest daughter and an alliance with Alfonso VII of León–Castilla.

In all three respects, then, by the time of his death Ramón Berenguer III had converted his county into the beginnings of something quite different. Thirty-five years had seen the county of Barcelona metamorphose into the "Kingdom of Cataluña," or almost that. It had also become, one may fairly say, an imperial realm, whose influence and power extended along the southern coast of France and which had significant friends among the sea powers of the western Italian coast. Finally, Barcelona had taken up once more the effort to construct a yet greater realm by establishing itself in the environs of Tarragona to the south and by reasserting its own intention to absorb the Muslim territories of Lérida and Tortosa to the southeast. Most of this legacy he willed on July 19, 1131, to his first son and successor, Ramón Berenguer IV, then seventeen years of age. Provence he separated from the rest and left to his secondborn, Berenguer Ramón.

8

The Emerging Status Quo in Christian Iberia (1135–1143)

The death of Alfonso I of Aragón shortly after the battle of Fraga in 1134 left a situation that could not be other than unstable in the extreme. His new Aragón was just that, a largely personal creation whose ability to stand the test of transition was simply unknown. The results of his eight-year adventure in León–Castilla were not yet liquidated, but that kingdom had been reorganized and strengthened by the young Alfonso VII who was obviously not inclined to accept the continuance of what had never been more than a temporary expedient, at least from the Leonese point of view. The young Ramón Berenguer IV of Barcelona enjoyed a position unique in its advantages for one of his dynasty, and he was sure to make use of the collapse of Aragonese pressure upon Lérida and Tortosa for his own ends. The ability of the Murābit to follow up their crushing victory at Fraga was an open question, as was the continued peaceful acceptance by the Muslim majority of Aragón of their relatively new subjection to Christian rule. Compounding all of this potential for conflict were the twin facts of the absence of children of Alfonso's own and the most peculiar of wills.

In October of 1131, before the walls of Bayonne, The *Batallador* had made a solemn testament in which he left his entire kingdom to the three religious orders of the Holy Sepulcher, the Hospitallers, and the Templars. This will was reaffirmed by him at Sariñena in Aragón after the battle of Fraga and just three days before his death on September 7, 1134.[1] Despite all attempts to account for it, the reasons for such a decision remain a mystery. Alfonso did have an

---

[1] The text of the will, which is not entirely trustworthy in its present form, has been most recently published in Santos A. García Larragueta, *El gran priorado de Navarra de la Orden de San Juan de Jerusalén*, 2 vols. (Pamplona, 1975), 2:15–18.

unusual personal life by the ordinary norms of his day. He was born somewhat prior to 1080 and was probably in his late fifties by the time of his death. At his marriage to Urraca, then, he was already thirty or more. That was late for a first marriage, and no prior ones, are known. The reasons for that marriage were blatantly political, and it was politics that destroyed it, although a personal antipathy may have had some minor part in its unhappy history. No children resulted from the marriage, although Urraca later had at least two children by Count Pedro González. Subsequently, Alfonso never attempted another marriage, although marriage alliances were the most ordinary feature of the diplomacy of the age. Nor is there any hint that he engaged in sexual liaisons.

The suggestion, then, is overwhelming that he was surely infertile and probably impotent. Homosexuality seems ruled out by the lack of any such suggestion in the quite hostile Leonese sources which would have been happy to have had such an additional stick with which to beat him. If his condition had not fastened him into a sort of permanent misogyny before the Urraca marriage it probably did so afterward. With such a background, the experience of war and politics may have turned him into something of a misanthrope by 1131. He may, by that time, have been able to see no happier future than the one he devised for the realm which he would leave orphaned at his death. If such an explanation does not entirely suit us, surely no explanation was adequate to meet the outrage of his contemporaries.[2]

After all, these orders were new creations of the crusaders in the Levant. The military order of the Knights Templars was a completely novel phenomenon whose rule had only just been approved by the Council of Troyes in 1128. The Hospitallers had been formed earlier to perform an essentially nursing function, and it is not clear at all that they had already been transformed into an order of military monks at this date. The Order of the Holy Sepulcher was an association of secular canons which served that shrine in Jerusalem in a liturgical and administrative function. Such property as each of them was just beginning to accumulate back in Europe was intended to provide revenue and recruits for their Levantine establishment. No one could have known what to expect from the joint rule of such

[2] Elena Lourie, "The Will of Alfonso I 'El Batallador,' King of Aragon and Navarre: A Reassessment," *Speculum* 50 (1975):635–51, has wrestled with the problem and has produced a solution based upon political considerations so intricate as to lack conviction. Her argument is that the will was meant not only to fail but also to block the accession of Alfonso VII by advancing the rights of the religious orders until Ramiro II was strong enough to subvert them in his own behalf.

curious entities. If these orders were just beginning to be known in France and Italy they were even less familiar in Iberia.[3] There must be a more comfortable, traditional solution.

In fact, the line of Sancho *el Mayor* (1000–1035) did have some remaining branches. Alfonso VII of Castilla was a great-great-grandson if it came to that. Closer to home in Aragón itself, two living magnates, García Ramírez and Pedro Talesa, were also great-great-grandsons, if through bastard lineages. Closest of all was the younger brother of Alfonso, Ramiro (b. 1087?), not yet fifty years of age.[4]

Now Ramiro Sánchez had some curious disabilities of his own, but the circumstances offered good cause to wink at them. Called the monk, he had been enrolled in the monastery of Saint-Pons de Thomières at about six or seven years of age. At the height of his brother's power in León–Castilla, Ramiro was briefly installed as abbot of Sahagún in 1112. Ejected from Sahagún, he was then elected bishop of Burgos in 1114 by a faction of that city, doubtless again due to his brother's influence. It is not clear whether he was ever regularly consecrated to that see, but he still maintained his claim as late as 1116. When the Leonese claimant to Burgos was accepted by Alfonso of Aragón in the settlement which accompanied the truce of 1117, García dropped from sight. It has been alleged that he was subsequently bishop-elect of Pamplona, but the probabilities seem long against it. He was for a time a monk in the Huescan monastery of San Pedro el Viejo, which house was affiliated with Saint-Pons. Just after the battle of Fraga it may be that he was nominated by his brother for the see of Barbastro, whose bishop had perished on that field. Such a record at least suggests that Ramiro was sensitive to the demands of dynastic necessities.

Was he was designated by his brother, this time as his heir, after a series of monumental arguments in the three days that lay between the reaffirmation of the will of 1131 and the actual death of the *Batallador*? If he was with Alfonso I at Fraga and again when the

---

[3] On the early history of these orders in Iberia, see A. J. Forey, *The Templars in the Corona de Aragón* (London, 1973), and Gracía Larragueta, *El gran priorado*.

[4] Antonio Ubieto Arteta, *Historia de Aragón: Creación y desarrollo de la corona de Aragón* (Zaragoza, 1987), is the fullest treatment of the whole subject of the union with Barcelona. The approach is perhaps a bit too legalistic in some particulars. For the genealogy relevant here, see p. 80. The entire life of Ramiro II has been traced by Szabolcs de Vajay, "Ramire II le Moine, roi d'Aragon, et Agnés de Poitou dans l'histoire et dans la legende," *Mélanges offerts a René Crozet*, 2 vols. (Poitiers, 1966), 2:727–50. For the career of Ramiro Sánchez in Castilla, see Bernard F. Reilly, *The Kingdom of León–Castilla under Queen Urraca, 1109–1126* (Princeton, N.J., 1982), pp. 80, 101, 112, and 233–34.

latter died on September 7th at Sariñena, 45 kilometers southwest of Huesca, he must have set off immediately for Jaca, the traditional royal city of the Aragonese kings roughly the same distance north-west of Huesca. There he was hailed as king by the assembled bishops and notables of the realm, and we find him already con-firming the customs of that city on September 11, 1134.[5] While his itinerary from there is not as clear as we would like, Ramiro II had reached the all-important Zaragoza by November 2nd. For the mo-ment that was the critical area in which he had to rally support.[6]

Another member of the dynasty was also with the *Batallador* at Fraga and probably subsequently at his deathbed. This was García Ramírez. Of necessity he had a longer journey if he planned to contest the accession of Ramiro. He was the current tenant of the honor of Tudela, and the strength of his immediate family lay in Navarra. Rather than Jaca, then, his goal was to reach Pamplona and be recognized there as king. He did achieve that, although the date is unknown to us. There are two documents in which the now García Ramírez IV *el Restaurador* (1134–1150) styles himself "rex Pampi-lonensium" which date simply to 1134.[7] While subsequent events will result in García becoming merely the king of a restored Navarra, there is no immediate indication that his aims were so limited at this early juncture. To the east along the valley leading to Jaca and to the south along the valley of the Ebro, the logical issue between him and Ramiro II would be the succession to the realm of Alfonso I.

Of course, it was not to be as simple as that. As soon as he heard of the disaster at Fraga, and surely when he heard of the death of his rival, Alfonso VII of León–Castilla must have set about collecting a suitable force and marched for the Rioja. In early November he was already at Nájera, for we know he granted a charter to the Riojan monastery of San Millán de La Cogolla then. Nájera had apparently already declared for García Ramírez, but the appearance of the Leónese monarch made that allegiance untenable and most of the nobility of the district went over to Alfonso. In short order Alfonso VII was to regain the entire west bank of the Ebro, which had first become a Castilian possession during the partition of Navarra in 1076. Now the question was how much farther to the south, or east, would he push. Ramiro II of Aragón accepted what he could not

---

[5] Luis Sánchez Belda, ed., *Chronica Adefonsi Imperatoris* (Madrid, 1950), pp. 42–53. This chronicle has a long treatment of the succession for reasons which will become obvious. It speaks of Ramiro's "election," but the term is used with great freedom.

[6] Antonio Ubieto Arteta, ed., *Documentos de Ramiro II de Aragón* (Zaragoza, 1988), appears to have collected and edited most of the surviving charters of this king.

[7] García Ramírez is another Iberian monarch whose documents lack a critical edition.

prevent and surrendered the territory of Zaragoza to him. In return, Alfonso VII did homage to the Aragonese monarch. By Christmas-time the Leonese had moved south and entered Zaragoza. A charter he then granted to the cathedral of Zaragoza was confirmed not just by the bishop of Zaragoza but also by Guy, bishop of Lescar, and Oleguer Bonestruga, archbishop of Tarragona, as well as by Count Armengol of Urgel, Count Alfonso Jordán of Toulouse, and Count Bernard of Comminges. Clearly, all of the powers of northeast Iberia as well as south France intended to have a hand in the settlement.

Ramiro II reacted strongly against this situation in the only fashion immediately open to him. In January of 1135 he made common cause with García Ramirez IV of Pamplona who agreed to do homage to the Aragonese in return for recognition of his own regal status. At this time García Ramirez claimed to rule not only Pamplona but also the Basque provinces of Alava, Vizcaya, and Guipúzcoa. Alfonso VII seems to have been absent in León during these maneuvers. By May, however, he was back in Nájera in the Rioja where he displayed his superior bargaining powers. García Ramirez of Pamplona met him there and did homage. Alfonso then recognized him as rightful king in Pamplona as well as in all of the east bank of the Rioja and down to Tudela and Zaragoza, which were both turned over to the latter. García Ramírez IV and Bishop Garcia of Zaragoza then accompanied Alfonso VII back to León for his imperial coronation late in that month. Less than eight months after his coronation in Jaca, then, the situation of Ramiro II appeared to be desperate. Nonetheless, if he could not win by force of arms, surely he must succeed, in some measure, by diplomacy.

One of his first actions had been to negotiate a two-year truce with ibn Ganiya, the victor of Fraga and the Murābit governor of Valencia and Murcia. One thinks that the advantage in the truce was all on the side of the Aragonese, and it is difficult to imagine why the Muslim should have given up the initiative just then. Yet they did, and the credit for the respite, among the terrified Christians of the Ebro basin, would go to Ramiro.

The new Aragonese monarch must have entered almost im-mediately into marriage negotiations – to provide that essential guarantee to his supporters that their loyalty would have permanent rewards. By November of 1135 Ramiro appeared with a bride, Agnes, the daughter of Duke William IX of Aquitaine and widow since 1127 of Viscount Aimery of Thouars. Within six weeks it would be known that the queen was pregnant and that a permanent continuation of the direct dynastic line was possible. That reassur-ance was the most fundamental event in securing Ramiro's position.

He had already faced one conspiracy, if not revolt, among his supporters during the preceding summer.

Clearly, in all of this jockeying for position, the one thing that was roundly ignored was the last testament of the late Alfonso I. No one, to our knowledge, was negotiating with or for the three military orders. However, some accommodation was ultimately going to have to be made with them. That was clear when Pope Innocent II (1130–1143) wrote to Alfonso VII directing him to see that the provisions of the will were observed. This letter was written in either 1135 or 1136; we cannot be more sure of the date.[8] Just at that time the papacy could not act with great firmness, for there had been a disputed election in 1130, and there was another contestant for the office, Anacletus II (1130–1138), but that situation would not endure forever.

Meanwhile, change continued to rule in northeast Iberia during 1136. The marriage of Ramiro II had profoundly affected the policy of Alfonso VII, since the birth of an heir to the former would make the ability of García Ramírez of Pamplona to hold Zaragoza for any length of time extremely doubtful. Sometime in the spring, before June 10th, the Leonese monarch had made an arrangement to hold the city on the Ebro – and its western territories including Calatayud and Daroca – from Ramiro II instead, and perhaps again did homage to him for them. Since Bishop García of Zaragoza had apparently died during the winter, the two monarchs seem to have collaborated in moving the election of a new bishop, Guillermo. The name suggests a French cleric who would not have been too closely allied with either of them. All of this did not sit well with García Ramírez IV, and the remainder of the summer was spent in fighting. Alfonso VII managed to penetrate as far into the territories of the Navarrese as Estella.

The fighting thus went well against the king of Pamplona, but otherwise the summer of 1136 was more unpleasant for Ramiro of Aragón. His heir Petronila, was born in August, but the birth of a girl could not solve the question of inheritance as could the birth of a son. No one would have expected her to inherit in her own right. The immediate question posed by her birth was to whom she would be married by her father, presuming that she survived to adulthood, which was always problematic is this period. The game thus would continue. A further problem for the king of Aragón was that the truce with the Murābit was broken. In the late summer of 1136,

---

[8] The papal bull is a fragment; only the date, June 10th, and the place, Pisa, survive from the dating formula. On that day Innocent was in Pisa in both years. See Ubieto Arteta, *Historia de Aragón Creación y desarrollo*, p. 132, n. 112.

ibn Gāniya of Valencia, with the aid of troops from Lérida, Tortosa, and Fraga, attacked the town of Mequinenza on the lower Ebro and retook it. That of course closed off the Aragonese approach to Fraga from the south. It also posed the question of a continuance of the Murābit counteroffensive against the holdings of Aragón generally which had begun so well at Fraga two years before. As it developed, Alfonso of León would have his difficulties too, for Alfonso Enríquez of Portugal used the former's preoccupation that summer to attack Galicia.

The Leonese monarch spent the late fall and winter of 1136–1137 in the Burgos area monitoring developments in Aragón. It may be that he was attempting to arrange a betrothal of his son Sancho, born about 1133, to the *infanta* Petronila of Aragón. Duke William X of Aquitaine, brother of Queen Agnes of Aragón, may also have been involved in the negotiations. Later in the spring, on April 9th, the duke died at Santiago de Compostela while completing a pilgrimage. By that time Alfonso VII had moved south, first to Cuenca and then to Toledo, presumably to see to the condition of the frontier at the beginning of another campaigning season. Then, however, he had to proceed to the northwest to meet the challenge posed by Alfonso Enríquez of Portugal. Alfonso would be occupied there during June and July at the very least. Not until October can we place him back in the east in the Rioja.

In the meantime, certain important events had occurred. The year-old *infanta* Petronila of Aragón had been betrothed to Count Ramón Berenguer IV of Barcelona. On August 11, 1137, Ramiro II of Aragón surrendered the whole of his realm to his future son-in-law, saving only the obedience which it owed to himself and his daughter. The realm was to pass forever and without condition to the count of Barcelona on the death of Ramiro II, even if Petronila had predeceased the latter and no children had been born of the pair.[9] In fact, the formal marriage of Petronila and Ramón Berenguer did not take place until 1150 when the former came of canonical age; Ramiro himself survived until 1158. Following the betrothal and the formal investiture with the reign, the king and his new son-in-law apparently made a progression through the realm, with the latter receiving the homage of his new subjects and confirming their rights.

Alfonso VII may have consented to these developments before departing the Burgos area in early 1137, or it may simply have been a *fait accompli* by the time when he reached the Rioja at the beginning

---

[9] For the text, see ubieto Arteta, *Historia de Aragón: Creación desarrollo*, pp. 141–42.

of October. We cannot be sure. What is clear is that he accepted the accession of Ramón Berenguer, who was his brother-in-law after all, on the condition that the count do homage to him as emperor for the territory of Zaragoza. He also made peace with García Ramírez of Pamplona that fall, probably after carrying out still another punitive campaign against him which resulted in the capture of Count Latro, the leader of the Basque lands. Alava, Vizcaya, and Guipúzcoa seem now to have been permanently lost to the Navarrese monarch and enter definitively into the Leonese orbit. The peace with García Ramírez lasted no longer than most of the others on which the two had agreed, but it does look as though the Leonese monarch was attempting to minimize his further involvement in the east.

Ramón Berenguer now assumed the rule of the kingdom of Aragón, taking the title not of king but of "princeps." Ramiro II returned to the monastic life, this time permanently, until his death twenty years later. His wife, the queen mother Agnes, returned to the south of France, and we see her subsequently attending to the affairs of her sons by her previous marriage to the viscount of Thouars. In his government of the new realm, the count of Barcelona appears to have utilized the magnates of Aragón as instruments, and they gave him their loyalty in return. Despite the most unusual character of his accession, there is no evidence of resistance to his rule in Aragón itself. The relationship with the new king in Pamplona was quite different. There the boundaries between the two realms had been established by force during the brief reign of Ramiro II and had only the roughest traditional justification. They would therefore be the object of continuous dispute over the next four years.

The king of Pamplona gave a good account of himself, even contriving to threaten Jaca itself at one point, but the coalition against him was too powerful. It is clear that in these struggles Alfonso VII of León–Castilla and Ramón Berenguer IV of Aragón–Barcelona cooperated in the field. In February of 1140 they were confident enough to draw up a formal treaty at Carrión for the partition of the Navarrese territories.[10] Nevertheless their joint offensive against García Ramírez miscarried and in October of 1140 Alfonso VII and he concluded a separate peace whereby the latter continued to hold most of the eastern bank of the Ebro down to and including the city of Tudela. At that same time the betrothal of the

[10] The treaty is published in Francisco M. Rosell, ed., *Liber Feudorum Maior* (Barcelona, 1945), pp. 37–38, with the date of February 21, 1140. However, the editor has incorrectly redated it to February 21, 1141. On that date the emperor and some of the principals named in the treaty were at Segovia, not Carrión. Peter Rassow, ed., "Die Urkunden Kaiser Alfonso VII von Spanien," *AU* 10 (1928):436.

son of Alfonso VII to the daughter of García Ramírez took place. In 1141 an uneasy truce would be made between Navarra and Aragón–Barcelona as well, although border warfare continued intermittently until 1146. The ultimate result would be the reconstitution of that Navarra which had been partitioned in 1076. The reborn realm lacked the Rioja district west of the Ebro which had passed permanently to Castilla, but it had gained the east bank as far as Tudela. This modest kingdom would continue to survive all vicissitudes down until its incorporation into early modern Spain in 1512. Yet it would, by virtue of its size, seldom play a major role in the Christian Iberia which was now in the process of rapid formation.

Before the new political hybrid which had now emerged could begin its career in full respectability, a settlement had to be reached with the three religious orders which were the legal heirs of Alfonso I according to his final testament. Doubtless negotiations alternating with contrived delay and obstruction had been going on from much earlier than 1140, but we are not informed of it nor of much of what followed. Some pieces of a very lengthy process are all that remain to us. In September of 1140 the orders of the Holy Sepulcher and the Hospitallers made a joint offer to Ramón Berenguer which became the basis for a counteroffer on that prince's part. Almost a year later the patriarch William of Jerusalem and the prior of the order of the Holy Sepulcher yielded their title under the will of Alfonso I to Ramón Berenguer IV and his children in perpetuity. If his line were to die out, however, title would revert to them. Two years subsequent to that, in November of 1143, the master of the Knights Templars did the same. When the agreement with the Hospitallers was reached we do not know, nor do we know its particulars, although it would have run along the same lines.

What the three religious orders received in return for their cessions was the same sort of property which they were already accumulating in a thousand places all over Western Christendom. They received castles and fields, fiefs and villages, parts of villages and towns, the income from offices or parts of it, parts of the incomes from judicial proceedings, rents, and even a fifth portion of the booty from future raids into Muslim territory. In short, they became, in Aragón and Cataluña, the possessors of a variety of property and revenues which they administered in the support of an establishment in the Levant. It was something which administrators of the orders were learning to do more or less well everywhere. No more than elsewhere, despite the will of Alfonso, did they become rulers independent of the dynasty.

Even so, the agreements reached in these years must have been challenged on various grounds by a variety of parties. Surely those who lost income or possessions would have done so. The crown must find the wherewithal somewhere, and not always from its own coffers, of course. Some of those within the religious orders themselves doubtless appealed to religious courts. We do know that the full rights of the count of Barcelona over his new acquisition, Aragón, were not finally recognized by the papacy until the time of Pope Adrian IV in June of 1158. Nevertheless, by 1143 the problem of the will was well on its way to resolution.

What finally resulted from the defeat of Fraga and ten years of struggle, diplomacy, and war was the new kingdom of Aragón – an unlikely combination, under the dynasty of Barcelona of the old realms of Aragón and Barcelona. Ramón Berenguer continued to be count of Barcelona, but he now also would become prince of Aragón. The government of each part of this new structure continued to be distinctive in form and persons if not always in fact. Its languages, written or not, were severally Catalan, Provençal, Castilian, Aragonese, Arabic, Hebrew, and Latin. It was destined to continue to become even more diverse, polyglot, and improbable. Notwithstanding, it held together. For the first time it had in 1137 a population with a likely Christian majority. The numbers of that population overall might have reached to as many as 700,000. With a total area now of roughly 45,000 square kilometers, that would have given it a population density of about 15 people per square kilometer.

Put another way, for the first time in the north there was now another Christian realm at least roughly comparable in resources to León–Castilla. The latter did have something on the order of twice the population and somewhat more than twice the land area, but a population density of no more than 12 people per square kilometer. León–Castilla would continue to dominate the peninsula but not so comfortably or easily in the future.

First among Equals

The accession of Alfonso Raimúndez to the throne of León–Castilla upon the death of his mother, Urraca, on March 8, 1126, was inevitable. As the grandson of Alfonso VI he had been associated with her in the leadership of the realm and dynasty for some nine years. He was already of mature age, as the times counted it, being twenty-one, and had been knighted almost two years before. In theory, then, the realm of Toledo had been in his government since 1117, and surely in fact for the most recent year following the death

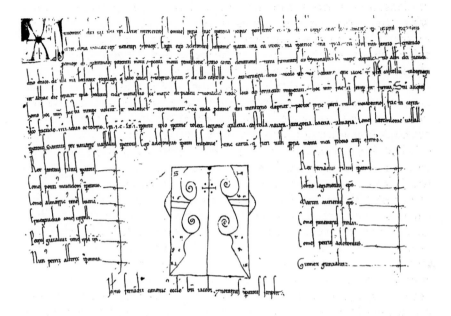

Plate 5 Original charter of Alfonso VII of October 12, 1153

of Archbishop Bernard of Toledo in April of 1125. However, that his succession was inevitable did not mean that it was agreeable to all factions of the realm.

At the time his mother died Alfonso was at the royal residence adjoining the monastery of Sahagún, an easy ride from León. He entered the royal city the following day and probably himself brought the news of the queen's demise. His young first cousin, Count Alfonso Jordán of Toulouse, was with him at the time. Doubtless that made his acceptance by the bishop, the clergy, and the general populace of the city even more irresistible. His coronation seems to have taken place immediately in the cathedral of the city, but that may represent a foreshortening of the actual order of events by our source.[11] One would expect that it must have waited on the interment of his mother who was buried in the royal city. Also, Alfonso would probably have preferred to await the arrival of

---

[11] Sánchez Belda, *Chronica Adefonsi Imperatoris*, pp. 4–10, gives the best account of the first months of the new reign. It is supplemented by Emma Falque Rey, ed., *Historia Compostellana* (Turnholt), pp. 382–90.

as many of his supporters as was feasible in order to solemnize and grace the occasion.

In this latter regard, the new king received the immediate support of several of the great nobles of the territories of León, Astorga, the Bierzo, and parts of Asturias. But there was also a problem in that the castellan of the royal citadel in León, who is unidentified, refused to surrender that stronghold. After some negotiation and on the advice of his supporters, Alfonso ordered the assault of the fortress, which seems to have capitulated after merely token resistance. When the news of the fall of the citadel spread into the countryside, many of the remaining leaders of the provinces of León and Asturias hastened to make their submission to the new king.

Alfonso VII appears to have set the major lines of his early policy quickly, for scarcely a month later we find him in Zamora, holding court but also meeting with his aunt, Teresa of Portugal, at Ricobayo some 20 kilometers west of that city. Given the difficulties of communication in the age, the young king must have requested such a meeting almost immediately on hearing of his mother's death. The Portuguese queen was accompanied by her consort and lover, Count Fernando Pérez, of the Galician house of the Trastamara, but not by her son, Alfonso Enríquez. A peace was concluded for an unstated period so as to free the Leonese monarch's hands to deal with the problem of Aragón in the east. However, we must understand that the peace also implied the choice by Alfonso VII of an alliance with Teresa and her faction in preference to an understanding with her son. That option must have seemed obvious in 1126, but it was to occasion difficulties almost from the beginning in the pacification of the far west.

To the *curia* at Zamora came the nobles and bishops of Galicia. Theirs was the longest journey, and indeed they had gone first to León expecting to find Alfonso still there. The bishops of Mondeñedo and Lugo and the archbishop of Compostela waited on the king in Zamora, but significantly the bishops of Orense and Túy in the southernmost reaches were absent. Caught between the ambitions of Teresa and León–Castilla, they preferred an uncomfortable neutrality. The other sons of the house of Trastamara, brothers of Fernando Pérez, came to make their obedience, but the head of that house, their father, Count Pedro Froílaz, was conspicuously absent. Pedro had been imprisoned by Urraca since 1123, so we must assume that he had either died in prison or was too ill to make the journey. As a former guardian of the king in the latter's youth, he would surely have been present otherwise.

The other of the king's guardians, Archbishop Gelmírez, had

hastened to the royal presence bringing with him the usual tangle of problems. At the time of the queen's death, the ambitious archbishop had been engaged in a local war with the most powerful noble in the south of Galicia, Fernando Yáñez, over the possession of a castle. The young king would find a compromise solution for the moment, but the incident was symptomatic of the situation in the province. Fernando Yáñez was allied with the Trastamara of the north against the growing power of the archbishop of Santiago de Compostela. He was also caught between his usual loyalty to the house of Urraca and the claims and ambitions of Teresa of Portugal whose territories bordered his own. If Alfonso intended to make the recovery of the Castilian and Riojan lands from the king of Aragón his first priority, he was well advised to avoid immediate involvement in the affairs of the west.

While the king was at Zamora, our source tells us, he also received overtures for an understanding with the Castilian house of Lara. Count Pedro González held most of the lands in Castilla not actually in the hands of Alfonso I of Aragón. His brother, Count Rodrigo, held the province of Asturias de Santillana north of Castilla. Together they had been among the most effective supporters of Urraca in her struggle against the Aragónese. More to the point now, Count Pedro also had been the lover and consort of Urraca. As a result of that liaison, two children were born, Fernando and Elvira, who were thus themselves grandchildren of Alfonso VI and half brother and sister to Alfonso VII. Since the count thus had children of royal blood, he also had royal aspirations for them. In addition, he was related to the house of Trastamara in Galicia through his wife, the daughter of Count Pedro Froílaz. The Castilian brothers had been behind the brief resistance of the castellan in León and were said to be in contact with Alfonso of Aragón as well.

In the midst of this dynastic tangle, one of the first initiatives of Alfonso VII had to be his own marriage. One suspects that his mother had effectively prevented any marriage before her death, for the two had often been rivals and a child born to her son would have strengthened his position against hers prematurely. Now he was free to wed and to beget a son who would be a stabilizing factor in this welter of dynastic relationships. Until he had thus assured his own descent and so guaranteed his supporters against another change within the dynasty, the claims of his first cousins, Alfonso Enríquez of Portugal and Alfonso Jordán of Toulouse, to the throne of León–Castilla were almost as good as his own and sure to be asserted in the event of his early death. At only slightly more remove, were those of his bastard half brother and sister of the house of Lara and then a variety of more distant cousins. The marriage negotiations must have begun at once, but it was to take more than a year for them to bear fruit.

In the meantime, the actions of the new monarch were nothing if not vigorous. By the spring of 1127 he was already in a position to begin military operations against Alfonso *el Batallador*, then the most respected field commander in the peninsula. The campaign was to be preceded by an intensive wooing of the Castilian noble houses, which would produce large-scale adhesion to his cause, and was subsequently to be rewarded by the judicious distribution of countships. The Lara counts were conspicuously absent from this rally to Alfonso VII, but, on the other hand, it seems to have been joined by Bertran de Risnél, the protector since 1117 of the Aragonese interests in Castilla and the tenant of Carrión de los Condes, which strategic point then passed bloodlessly to León–Castilla. At the end of April further gains were easily made when the burghers of Burgos rose suddenly and successfully against their Aragonese garrison and delivered the town to Alfonso VII.

Since the entire Aragonese position in Castilla was on the edge of collapse, Alfonso of Aragón could not avoid taking the field. He advanced into Castilla with a strong force in July and took up a position south of Castrojeriz in a valley called Tamara. Neither side seems to have been anxious for a trial of arms. *El Batallador* had pressing concerns for the strengthening of his new conquest, the former taifa of Zaragoza. Alfonso VII had grave reservations about the trustworthiness of the Lara counts, who had finally joined his campaign, if it should come to actual battle. Under the circumstances, Viscount Gastón of Bearn and Viscount Centulle of Bigorre took the lead in proposing a compromise. Alfonso of Aragón agreed to return to the Leónese king within forty days all lands properly belonging to the latter but currently held by himself. If these were the terms, and we have them only from a Leonese source, they were not honored, but at least war was averted.

The Aragonese monarch returned to the south of his new territories to bolster its defenses on the frontier with Teruel. Alfonso VII had to settle for the moment for his recent gains. Everything in the Rioja continued in the hands of the king of Aragón, in addition to the controlling positions in the heights of the Sierra de la Demanda at Oca and Belorado, which controlled the pass between the Rioja and Castilla. But farther west in the lands of Castilla proper he was left nothing but the very strong position of Castrojeriz, on the pilgrim road, and the subsidiary fortresses around it. The long Aragonese occupation of Castilla was all but ended, and Castrojeriz itself was a nuisance, but an isolated one which could be reduced on some favorable occasion.

Having consolidated his gains in Castilla, Alfonso VII then turned his attention to the west and by October was in Galicia. He was responding to a new attempt of Teresa of Portugal to bolster her position in the south of Galicia around Túy. Alfonso, with the aid of local forces, drove into Portugal and devastated its lands for six weeks. Returning to Santiago de Compostela, he then recouped his expenses for the year's campaign by extorting some 1,000 silver marks from the church of the Apostol and his old mentor, Archbishop Gelmírez. At least, our source presents the action in that light; the archbishop may have been culpable in some respect. In any event, the king promised in return to surrender some properties to the church, to bestow upon it the offices of royal chancellor and treasurer in perpetuity, and to be himself buried in that shrine upon his death. In these charters of November 13, 1127, the king is seen accompanied by his cousin, Count Alfonso Jordán of Toulouse, and his sister Sancha. For good measure the latter also agreed to be interred at Compostela.[12]

Immediately upon granting those charters, the king must have left for León. It was in that province, at Saldaña we are told, that he was wed in November of that year. The bride was Berengaria, daughter of Ramón Berenguer III of Barcelona. The marriage sealed an alliance of Barcelona with León–Castilla which was directed against Alfonso I of Aragón. For the moment, however, her chief importance was to be domestic. From her Alfonso required that son who would bolster his position against his dynastic rivals.

The year following was spent by Alfonso attempting to harmonize the conflicting demands of the western and eastern frontiers for his attention. In March he was in the west at Zamora where once again he met with Teresa of Portugal. We do not know the substance of their conversations, but the probability is that Alfonso's foray into her dominions the past fall had seriously affected her dominion in Portugal and that she was seeking his neutrality or even his support. Whatever the outcome of the talks, Teresa's reign was to end abruptly on June 24, 1128, when she was defeated by her son, Alfonso Enríquez at the battle of San Mamed near Guimarães in northern Portugal and forced into exile.

---

[12] Falque Rey, ed., *Historia Compostellana*, pp. 395–410, relates the story. It is a highly partisan work, of course. The texts of the relevant grants are contained in Tumbo A of the chapter archive and have been published by Antonio López Ferreiro, *Historia de la Santa Apostólica Metropolitana Iglesia de Santiago de Compostela*, 11 vols. (Santiago de Compostela, 1898–1911), 4:12–15 append.

The beginning of the long reign of Alfonso Enríquez of Portugal (1128–1185) was associated with an internal *coup* in that territory. For the past decade his mother had been ruling with the support of Count Fernando Pérez of the Galician family of the Trastamara and the lesser noble families of the Portuguese south around Coimbra. Whether or not her liaison with the Galician count was ever solemnized as a formal marriage is unclear. Nevertheless, it threatened the position of her son by her earlier marriage to the Burgundian count Henry. He in turn made common cause with the greater magnate families of the northern territories between the Duero and Miño rivers. The battle of San Mamed which catapulted the nineteen-year-old into control was, therefore, an internal revolution, but it could not fail to affect León–Castilla. Teresa and Count Fernando fled into Galicia where they had powerful allies and from which they might be able to continue the struggle. They thus became a problem for both Alfonso VII of León–Castilla and Alfonso I of Portugal which would react upon the perennial question of the proper border of Portugal and Galicia. Even more serious was the question of the political relation of the two cousins. Was Alfonso of Portugal simply a cadet member of the dynasty of León–Castilla ruling a powerful *appanage* in the west, or was he the king of a new Iberian monarchy? For the moment, in his charters, Alfonso Enríquez was content merely to style himself *"infans."* However, by the end of the year he had imposed the choice of Bernard, former archdeacon of the church of Braga, as the new bishop of Coimbra to succeed the defunct Bishop Gonzalo, and the choice of bishops was the prerogative of kings.

In the meanwhile, Alfonso VII was preoccupied with the east. Alfonso I of Aragón was busy with a siege of Muslim-held Molina de Aragón which controlled a secondary route just north of the Sierra de Albarracín from Aragón into the eastern reaches of the territory of Toledo. His activities there threatened the Leonese positions to the north around Medinaceli, which dominated the main road from Aragón to Toledo, and Morón de Almazán which fronted Aragonese-held Almazán itself. In the late summer the Leónese monarch gathered what forces he could and marched into the area. As he advanced, the king of Aragón moved northward into Almazán in the Sorian highlands on the upper Duero. There in October of the year the two rivals decided once again not to risk a trial by battle. Alfonso VII contented himself with reinforcing defenses around Medinaceli and Morón. Alfonso of Aragón similarly reinforced Almazán and then went on to capture Muslim Molina de Aragón at the end of the year.

On the eastern front, then, the Leonese monarch had clearly been rebuffed and forced to withdraw, leaving the Sorian highlands in Aragonese possession. The cause of his embarrassment was, our source tells us, the counts of Lara who refused to participate in the campaign and encouraged others not to do so.[13] Alfonso VII would have to address their insubordination in a wider context. There was clearly a crisis in León–Castilla in 1129–1130, and we cannot be sure of its exact progression. Perhaps it was touched off by the birth of a male heir to the king. In April of 1136 Alfonso had the men of Zamora do homage to his son "Raimundo", otherwise unknown to history but clearly his firstborn.[14] He may have been born around 1129. Alternative potential heirs to the throne would therefore have been subjected to great pressure to act.

Alfonso VII seized the initiative in a great council held at Carrión in February of 1130. In attendance were the papal legate, Cardinal Humbert, Archbishop Olegario of Tarragona, and the Portuguese bishops of Oporto and Coimbra as well as most of the bishops of León–Castilla. Relations with Barcelona and with Portugal must have been on the agenda, but the most spectacular results had to do with Alfonso's realm itself. During its sessions three bishops of León–Castilla were deposed, those of Oviedo, Salamanca, and León itself. It was asserted by contemporaries that they had opposed the marriage of the king, which stance was of course tantamount to supporting a continuation of the dynastic tangle. We cannot tell from the surviving records whether Alfonso was carrying out a necessary preemptive *coup* or simply overreacting. In any event, the assistance of the powers of Galicia was necessary to carry it through, and Archbishop Gelmírez was rewarded by the selection of two of his canons to become the new bishops of León and Salamanca.[15]

Such drastic steps had reverberations throughout the realm. The Leonese magnate Pedro Díaz raised the standard of revolt in his castle not far from Mansilla, which latter was within 20 kilometers of León itself, and he was joined by Jimeno Jiménez, the castellan of the castle of Valencia de Don Juan only another 30 kilometers to the south. In Castilla proper Count Pedro González of Lara and Count

---

[13] Sánchez Belda, *Chronica Adefonsi Imperatoris*, pp. 15–19. The chronicle dates the campaign to 1129, and it probably did extend into that year in some fashion.

[14] Attention was first called to this scion of Alfonso by Hilda Grassotti, "Dos problemas de historia Castellano–Leonesa, siglo XII," *CHE* 49–50 (1969):144.

[15] The materials and intricacies of this council are explored in Bernard F. Reilly, "On Getting to Be a Bishop in León–Castile: The 'Emperor' Alfonso VII and the Post-Gregorian Church," *Studies in Medieval and Renaissance History* 1 (1978):48–53.

Bertrán de Risnel, the latter married to Alfonso's half sister Elvira, went into overt opposition and seized the city of Palencia. Count Rodrigo González, Pedro's brother, declared against the king in Asturias de Santillana, and Gonzalo Peláez rose in revolt in Asturias de Oviedo. Fortunately for the young king, the rebels seem to have been unable to coordinate their activities.

In the spring of the year Alfonso struck at Palencia and took both Count Pedro and Bertrán prisoner when that city declared instead for him. Both were stripped of their honors and taken to León. Count Pedro either fled or was exiled and took refuge with Alfonso of Aragón who was currently occupied with the siege of Bayonne. There he was sought out and challenged by Alfonso VII's cousin, Count Alfonso Jordán of Toulouse, and died as a result of that duel. Meanwhile, Count Rodrigo Martínez, the royal castellan in León, and his brother had been blockading Pedro Díaz in his fortress where he had been joined also by Pedro Froílaz. The king now advanced to that siege and the rebels shortly surrendered. Both were relieved of their commands and goods. When they collapsed, Jimeno Jiménez in Coyanza hastened to make his submission to the king as well.

The backbone of the revolt in León and Castilla was now broken, and Alfonso was able to advance during the summer into Asturias de Santillana and force the surrender of Rodrigo González after wasting the latter's possessions there.[16] In Asturias de Oviedo, Gonzalo Peláez continued his defiance, but the season was too far advanced to make an invasion of that mountain redoubt feasible. Because he would see an alternative opportunity in the following year, Alfonso allowed that revolt to continue to fester through 1131 as well. During the summer of the latter year, taking advantage of the continuing absence of Alfonso I of Aragón in Gascony, he mounted a major siege of Castrojeriz and its supporting fortresses. When the Aragonese commander, after six months of fighting, found himself unable to secure reinforcement from the *Batallador*, he surrendered his weary and starving troops in October. Another result of this victory was that the Hūddid heir to Zaragoza, Saif al-Dawla, now allied himself with the Leonese monarch against Alfonso of Aragón. The Muslim ruler's land around Rueda in the valley of the Jalón furnished Alfonso VII with an important potential passage to the valley of the Ebro itself.

With his position in the east thus considerably improved, the Leonese king invaded Asturias de Oviedo in 1132. Count Gonzalo Peláez and his supporters were quickly shut up and besieged in his

---

[16] Sánchez Belda, *Chronica Adefonsi Imperatoris*, pp. 19–23.

castles. However, resistance was sufficiently strong that the king agreed to a one-year truce. Alfonso took a mistress at this time, Guntroda Pérez, from an important family of the north in a move obviously designed to bolster his support in Asturias. There the matter stood, while in the summer of 1133 the king conducted a great and successful raid in Andalucía through the territories of Sevilla, Cadiz, and Jerez in company with Saif al-Dawla. During the interim Gonzalo Peláez had again risen in rebellion. This time Alfonso delegated the fight to Count Suero Vermudez and the latter's nephew, Pedro Alfónsez. After hard fighting Gonzalo finally surrendered, and was brought to the presence of Alfonso, who pardoned him. However, the rebellious count was not allowed to return to Asturias but was instead given another tenancy. When he revolted again he was again subdued, but this time he was allowed to go into exile in Portugal, where he finally died, being returned to Oviedo for burial.

By the year 1134, then, Alfonso VII established himself securely in most areas of his unwieldy realm. He had liberated Castilla from the Aragonese. He had resumed the *Reconquista* with notable success. His actions against those who would challenge his rule or his marriage and the revolts they initiated had been uniformly successful. Probably more important still, by that date Queen Berenguer had given him two sons, Raimundo and now Sancho, the latter having been born in either 1132 or 1133.[17] A regular succession to the king seemed thus to be assured, and further resistance to him futile.

Precisely at this point his great adversary and former stepfather, Alfonso of Aragón, died after the defeat at Fraga. It was under these circumstances that Alfonso VII was to march into the Rioja in the fall of 1134 to reclaim the remainder of his grandfather's possessions there and the long-coveted lands of the former taifa of Zaragoza. As we have already seen, the latter were finally to elude him. The three-cornered struggle which emerged there between himself, García Ramírez IV of Navarra, and Ramiro II of Aragón, as well as the marriage of the latter's daughter, Petronila, to Count Ramón Berenguer IV of Barcelona in 1137, would deny the Leonese anything like full success. Although he did recover the Riojan holdings of his grandfather, he was forced to settle for the homage of the new count–king of Aragón instead of Zaragoza. At the same time, however, he also obtained the Aragonese-held lands in the high valley of the Duero around Soria. Almost at the outset of this

---

[17] See the article by Luciano Serrano, "Berengere," *DHGE* 8 (1935), cols. 411–13, which is useful but now needs to be revised.

prolonged contest, when Zaragoza was temporarily in his hands, he had had himself crowned "emperor" in León on Pentecost, May 26, 1135.

This new imperial dignity was to provide the intellectual framework under which the emerging political realities of Christian Iberia could be assimilated. Since Alfonso VII was now more than simply king of León-Castilla, he would receive, as emperor, the homage of essentially independent kings such as Ramón Berenguer IV of Aragón–Barcelona in 1137 and García Ramírez IV of Navarra in 1140, without theoretical damage to their regal status but also with some recognition of his own overriding dignity.[18] This conception was to prove useful in the accommodation of a newly born Portuguese realm as well.

The Emergent Kingdom of Portugal

Without exploring the jungle of ethnography and linguistics beloved of Portuguese nationalists and some historians, suffice it to say that medieval Portugal appears first as a march of the kingdom of León against the Muslim of Andalucía. That was its status when Alfonso VI entrusted it in 1096 to his new son-in-law, Count Henry of Burgundy, and his natural daughter, Teresa. Although these two have sometimes been credited with the intention of constructing an independent Portuguese realm from the outset, it is clear that they did not even usually reside there until the death of Alfonso VI and that only the accession in León–Castilla of Urraca in 1109 led to their withdrawal from court.[19] From that date until the death of

[18] The meaning of the "imperial" dignity in Iberia has generated a great deal of controversy. For a reasonable and up-to-date guide to the major opinions, see Joseph F. O'Callaghan, "The Integration of Christian Spain into Europe: The Role of Alfonso VI of León–Castile," in Bernard F. Reilly, ed., *Santiago, St.-Denis, and Saint Peter* (New York, 1985), pp. 101–20.

[19] The most balanced and judicious account of their activities is to be found in Torquato de Sousa Soares, "O governo de Portugal pelo Conde Henrique de Borgonha: Sus relações com as monarquias Leonesa–Castelhana e Aragonesa," *RPH* 14 (1974):365–97, and "O governo de Portugal pela Infante-Rainha D. Teresa," *Colectanea de estudios im honra do Prof-Doutor Damião Peres*, (Lisbon, 1974), pp. 99–119. The only reliable general work on Portugal in English is A. H. de Oliveira Marques, *History of Portugal*, Vol. 1 (New York, 1972). Damião Peres, *Como nasceu Portugal* (Porto, 6th ed., 1967), résumés both the history and the scholarship up to that date. Peter Feige, "Die Anfänge des portugiesischen Königtums und seiner Landeskirche," *GAKS* 29 (1978):85–352, is a close study of the documents involved. Ludwig Vones, *Die "Historia Compostelana" und die Kirchenpolitik des nordwestspanischen Raumes* (Cologne, 1980), is often useful.

Count Henry in 1112 it is perfectly clear that the aim of the couple was somehow to gain control of the larger realm of León–Castilla or some portion of it.

After that date Teresa no longer had the resources to play the larger game and seems to have been content for the next four years simply to bide her time, waiting for some dynastic accident. After all, if her sister, Urraca, had a son and heir to Alfonso VI she too had a son and heir to him. It was the association of Urraca's son, Alfonso Raimúndez, in rule with her in 1116 that prompted Teresa to action. By early 1117 she had ceased to style herself "*infanta*" and had begun to use the title "*Regina.*" Yet the question remained of whom or what she was queen. There certainly was a Portuguese provincialism, or particularism, by this time. There was also a Portuguese geography, for those lands were thoroughly separated from León by a north–south mountain barrier of formidable proportions which ran from the Bay of Biscay to the basin of the Tajo. But also between that barrier and the Atlantic shores those lands from below Coimbra to Santarém and Lisbon on the Tajo were held by the Murābit, and those from the Miño River north to Cape Finisterre comprised rather Leonese Galicia.

History, language, and kinship locked Portugal more intimately with Galicia, and the border between the two had never been more than an administrative device. Moreover, Teresa lacked the military capability to initiate an assault on the Murābit. She began, then, to negotiate with the various factions in Galicia which so plagued her sister. By 1120 she formed a stable alliance with the great house of Trastamara, symbolized by her lover, Count Fernando Pérez. She also extended her control over the bishoprics of Túy and Orense and the influential monastery of Celanova in the valley of the Miño. Her power there endured well past the death of Urraca in 1126 despite the efforts of the latter to dislodge her. She also continued to style herself "*regina,*" although without specification as to realm.

In turn, as we have noted above, Teresa was herself dispossessed in 1128 by her son, Alfonso Enríquez and forced to flee into Galicia with her consort. Under Teresa's son, Portugal would become an independent monarchy. Nevertheless, at the outset of his reign, Alfonso Enríquez styled himself only "*infans*" and was careful to stress his descent from Alfonso VI of León–Castilla in his diplomas. Even less than his mother, it appears, he had given up hope of acceding to that larger realm. Like her, he also continued to be active in the valley of the Miño, patronizing the monastery of Celanova there in 1130.

Over the next few years the power of the young ruler of Portugal would slowly grow. In November of 1130 his mother died, and although she had a daughter, Sancha, by Count Fernando, neither daughter nor father seems to have mounted a serious threat to supplant him. However, in 1131, Vermudo Pérez, brother of Fernando and son-in-law to Teresa since 1125 by marriage to Urraca, her older daughter by Count Henry, went over into rebellion. He held the district around Viseu on the Upper Mondego northeast of Coimbra. The revolt was put down with ease, and he and his wife, the *Infanta*, had also to flee into Galicia. By 1135 Alfonso Enríquez had sufficiently consolidated his power to take two major steps. In March of that year, he began to style himself "Portugalensis Princeps" in his diplomas, although he also continued to cite his descent from Alfonso VI of León. One suspects that he was reacting to the plans of his cousin to be crowned emperor, to which ceremony he was likely invited although he did not attend. Also, in December of that year, he began the construction of a major fortress at Leiria, 70 kilometers southeast of Coimbra. Its purpose was to dominate the fertile plain and block the approach to Coimbra from Murābit Lisbon and Santarém.

That the rising power of Portugal and the established kingdom of León–Castilla should conflict at some point was almost inevitable. The lack of a real border and the interlocking family relationships between Galicia and Portugal were tinder for any spark. It may be that the grant made by Alfonso Enríquez to the Galician monastery of Tojos Outos in 1136 had some sort of triggering effect. We cannot be sure, but certainly it was startling that the *Infans* of Portugal should be courting the favor of a monastery so far north. It was only 30 kilometers southwest of Santiago de Compostela itself. What is clear is that in 1137 a border war erupted, and in the spring Alfonso Enríquez invaded Galicia, taking Túy. Both of our sources for the conflict at least agree that he also concerted his actions with those of García Ramírez IV of Navarra.[20] The king of León marched west, invaded and ravaged northern Portugal and retook Túy. In that town, on July 4, 1137, the *infans* of Portugal swore to be the faithful servitor of the *imperator* of Spain forevermore.[21] Despite both the defeat and the pact, Alfonso of Portugal continued to dabble in the politics of Galicia. In October of that very year he made a grant to the bishopric of Túy.

---

[20] Sánchez Belda, *Chronica Adefonsi Imperatoris*, pp. 58–62, and Falque Rey, ed., *Historia Compostellana*, pp. 519–21.
[21] The text is given in Romualdo Escalona, *Historia del real monasterio de Sahagún*, 1782, Reprint (León, 1982), pp. 527–28, who had it from the archive of that monastery. The text does not formally mention feudal homage but that is the sense of it.

Nevertheless, the border remained relatively peaceful for the next three years. Alfonso Enríquez turned his attention to the south where local Christian forces had suffered some setbacks in 1137. Doubtless by way of riposte to his activities, in 1139 the Murābit made a major effort, gathering troops from North Africa, Sevilla, and Badajoz, as well as from the south of Portugal, for an invasion of the north. The Portuguese monarch met them at Ourique, far to the south of his own territories in the Algarve, and defeated them decisively these on July 25, 1139.

Perhaps emboldened by that victory, Alfonso Enríquez in the following year launched another invasion of the border territories of Galicia along the Miño, scoring successes against the supporters of Alfonso VII. In retaliation, in the summer of 1141 the Leonese king struck into Portugal and down toward Braga. But his Portuguese cousin hurried to the scene and managed to shut him off from the valley of the Limia and to blockade him near Arcos de Valedevez. In the fighting that developed the Leonese got considerably the worst of it and finally appealed to the archbishop of Braga to arrange a settlement. The result was the conclusion of a peace which was to endure for some time to come, as well as the return of castles held by the emperor in Portugal and of castles held by Alfonso Enríquez in Galicia. Whether or not it was a thorough redrawing of the political lines of authority in the northwest is less than clear.[22] It should also be noted that it was at the time of this particular struggle that the royal title was assumed by Alfonso Enríquez. Certainly the first original charter in which he styles himself "Portugalensium rex" is dated July 7, 1140, and there are extant copies of earlier charters of that year that contain some variant of that title and which should likely be accepted.[23] Moreover, while the struggle was being waged in the north, Murābit forces assaulted and took the fortress of Leiria in the south, which was the key defensive position protecting the road to Coimbra.

Clearly there were ways in which mutual cooperation against the Murābit would be more advantageous to all of the Christian monarchs of the north than the continual sparring amongst themselves which had so marked the period between the death of the *Batallador* in 1134 and the conclusion of the peace between Aragón–Barcelona and Navarra in 1142. Such collaboration was to be the

[22] The sources are Sánchez Belda, *Chronica Adefonsi Imperatoris*, pp. 64–67, on the Leonese side, and the "Chronica Gothorum," pub. Monica Blöcker-Walter, *Alfons I von Portugal* (Zurich, 1966), pp. 154–55. The two are not entirely in agreement. For the best chronology, see Joaquim Veríssimo Serrão, *História de Portugal*, Vol. 1 (Lisbon, 1976), pp. 86–87.

[23] For the original of the charter dated July 7, 1140, see *DMP*, 1–1: 222–23.

Plate 6   Castle of Leiria, Portugal

major characteristic of royal policy in Christian Iberia in the eight years to come. As a result, all along the southern front there was a Murābit collapse, which led to one of the most spectacular and sustained Christian advances in the entire history of the *Reconquista*.

Nevertheless, the new characteristic of this advance was that it proceeded from radically different poles of Christian authority. In it the king of Portugal and the count–king of Aragón–Barcelona launched what were fundamentally their own offensives, which resulted in the aggrandizement of their own proper kingdoms. León–Castilla had finally lost the monopoly of the *Reconquista*. Christian Iberia was now composed of four independent monarchies. Each had its own identifiable territories, which would subsequently be associated with it until the appearance of a single Spanish monarchy in the 16th Century. These were not equals in power, to be sure, but each possessed the minimal *puissance* required to prevent its absorption by the others as well as to make it an attractive ally in the political jockeying of each of the others. Despite Alfonso VII's assumption of the imperial title, the hegemony of León–Castilla in Christian Iberia had been lost some two decades before that kingdom itself split in twain in 1157.

9

The Preponderance of the Christian North
(1143–1157)

When Alī ibn Yūsuf died on January 28, 1143, the Murābit Empire in North Africa and Iberia was already on the point of extinction. It had lasted the only for the reigns of his father and himself. In brief, that slight duration is explicable in two fashions. For one, the empire never had a formal structure other than that of a family and its allies. As with most governments in the dar al-Islam, the Murābit had been unable to imagine, much less construct, a legitimate, independent political authority capable of commanding respect on its own terms. Alī had been the supreme religious authority and therefore the supreme political one as well. The governors of the provinces were simply his brothers, his sons, his nephews, and his cousins. There was no separate political *res*.

By 1106, at the death of his father, Yūsuf ibn Tāshufīn, that personal empire had swept away all but one of the Iberian taifas, Zaragoza. Under Alī's rule it would also be subdued in 1110. By 1111 Alī had also reclaimed Santarém from the count of Portugal and Coria from the queen of León–Castilla. In the first five years of his reign the frontier between Christian and Muslim in the peninsula had been reestablished almost at the line which had prevailed in 1086 when the Murābit entered the Iberian world. The exception, of course, was Toledo. For two decades Murābit armies would march periodically to the assault of that bastion but would fail to reduce it.

Behind it, León–Castilla would continue with increasing intensity to repopulate the trans-Duero and the highlands around Guadalajara and Sigüenza to the northeast of Toledo. At the same time, the rising power of Aragón would wrest away the territories of the taifa of Zaragoza in the extreme northeast. Alfonso I of Aragón, after defeating every Murābit army Alī could spare, ravaged far south into Andalucía and even had the audacity to winter there in 1125–1126.

In 1126 the death of Queen Urraca of León–Castilla and the accession of her son would soon begin to allow for a more effective marshaling of the forces of León–Castilla against him. Fortunately for Alī, in the nine years preceding his death, the demise of Alfonso I of Aragón had set his Christian enemies against one another in one degree or another. But in January of 1143 that respite seemed about over.

If the Murābit Empire was crumbling for lack of an adequate political structure, the great strength which it had early exhibited as a religious reform movement was also failing. All fundamentalism is notoriously corruptible by its own success. The Murābit had begun by condemning music, song, poetry, wine, and soft garments and had ended by finding these things very pleasant indeed in their Andalucían delicacy. Seduced not merely by the physical and intellectual refinements of their Spanish brethren but by the seeming religious precision offered by the exacting Malikite interpretations of the *Koran* and the *hadīth*, they now would become the target of yet another fundamentalist reform movement which would sweep away the religious justification which was their sole *raison d'être*.

The new prophet, ibn Tūmart, was born among the mountain, Masmūda Berbers some time around 1075.[1] He seems early to have been marked as promising in religion and study, and left on the traditional journey to consult the theological masters of the east about 1107, just after Alī ibn Yusuf began his own reign in North Africa. Little is known of that pilgrimage, except that its formation seems to have occurred outside Bougie in modern Algeria where Alī began to recruit followers. Most prominent among these was Abd al-Mūmin, his general and eventual successor. This young man had also set out to seek enlightenment in the east, but got no farther than Bougie.

In that milieu ibn Tūmart began to preach the ordinary puritanism of Islam. That is, he demanded of his followers a strict segregation of the sexes, abstinence from alcohol, and the avoidance of such levities as music, dance, and poetry. He returned to his homeland about 1120, immediately running afoul of the Murābit authorities by refusing to pay a non-Koranic tax. He did dangerously well in a theological debate before Alī ibn Yusuf himself at Marrakesh. Warned that Alī was considering his execution, the prophet withdrew to

---

[1] On ibn Tūmart and the early Muwāhhid, see Charles-André Julien, *History of North Africa*, trans. John Petrie (London, 1970), pp. 93–110. The *UNESCO General History of Africa*, Vol. 4 (Berkeley, 1984), pp. 19–22, offers some refinement of Julien's views.

Aghmat and later retreated into the Atlas Mountains to Tinmāl. From that position he began to organize the surrounding tribes of Masmūda Berbers. This organization is difficult to distinguish from the other tribal confederations that arose from time to time. It had the typical great council and smaller auxiliary ones. Its procedures were unusual only in its asceticism, which, at least for a time, was more likely to be its distinguishing factor, rather than family and tribal considerations.

When a sufficient number of tribes had joined his ranks and accepted his absolute religious authority as *Imām*, ibn Tūmart declared himself to be the sinless *mahdi* sent by God to destroy the heretical Murābit and concocted an Arabian genealogy. The content of his theology was not very original. It stressed the absolute unity of Allāh, and allowed a figurative interpretation of the words of the *Koran* in order to avoid their implication of parts in the Godhead. Hence, he and his disciples were the "al-Muwāhhid," the believers in the one God. In its use of the device of the *mahdī*, it borrowed from Shia thought and allowed a certain leeway for Sufic mysticism. More important practically, however, was the condemnation of the literal interpretation and the legal accretions of the Malikites and their Murābit supporters. The doctrine of predestination which emerged naturally from the concentration upon the unity of God's knowledge and his will was also handy in its aptness for the stigmatization of the Murābit as already the condemned of Allāh.

Ibn Tumart combined this mixture of rigorous religion and astute politics with unflinching severity toward both individual opponents and entire tribes. Purges were commonplace, and the *Imām* emerged as the sole ruler of the Atlas peoples. Along with severity went active proselytism in which the *māhdi* both preached and wrote in Berber rather than simply in Arabic. As early as 1122 he attempted an assault on Marrakesh itself, but with little result other than to stimulate Alī to the raising of extensive fortifications there. Yet the Murābit could not allow the continued dominance of the mountain backbone of Morocco by their enemy. In 1128 a Murābit army ventured an expedition against Tinmāl but was soundly defeated. The Muwāhhid then advanced to lay siege to Marrakesh for better than a month. The hillmen, themselves in turn soundly beaten, returned to their strategy of infiltrating and spreading their authority and doctrine from mountain village to mountain village. It was a hill movement still when ibn Tūmart died in 1130.

Of necessity there was a hiatus in the rhythm of the Muwāhhid advance while the *mahdī*'s successor, Abd al-Mūmin, searched for a way to consolidate his own position. Finally, he took both the title of caliph and of "Amir al-Muminin," leader of the faithful. Either was a claim to absolute spiritual and political authority, but taking both was something less than styling himself the new *mahdi*. To that dignity he could not pretend, and so his position was always less than that of his patron and predecessor. Consequently, he would more and more be driven to rely on the traditional stuff of Muslim politics, the aggrandizement of family and tribe. That, however, lay somewhat in the future. For the next ten years he would concentrate on strengthening the mountain redoubts of southern Morocco and on moving gradually north into the High Atlas. Not until 1141 was Abd al-Mumin ready to descend into the plains to challenge the main Murabit power.

Meanwhile Ali ibn Yusuf had designated his son by a Christian slave, Abu Muhammad Sir, as his successor. Sir had proved his abilities in al-Andalus and was accepted by the entire dynasty despite the fact that he was not Ali's firstborn. The direction of the Murabit provinces in Iberia now fell largely to another of his sons, Tashufin ibn Ali, who was based at Sevilla. Fortunately Tashufin did not need to be greatly concerned about the northeast, where ibn Ganiya, another of Ali's sons, was governor of Valencia and would at least prove a bulwark against further Aragonese advance. But, on the central frontier, the contest would sway back and forth furiously for the next ten years.

In what seemed to be a continuation of the hammering at Toledo – a Murabit endeavor for the last twenty years – Tashufin in 1130 attacked the castle of Aceca, not 20 kilometers northwest of that city, took it, and then carried off the alcalde of Toledo to captivity. He also rode round the city itself and attacked its outlying castle of San Servando. In the following year Murabit forces ambushed and killed another governor of Toledo, Guter Armíldez, in the very environs of the city. Even so, the Muslim fortunes do not seem to have been all that bright if we consider that they were engaged with mostly local forces. Moreover, Toledan forces and allies from the town militias of the trans-Duero just to the north proved powerful enough to conduct extensive raids through Andalucía in 1132 and 1134. More ominously, in 1133 Alfonso VII himself had found an opportunity to do the same, penetrating all the way to the outskirts of Córdoba. Called away by other concerns in the north, the Leónese monarch would not return before 1137, at which time he would stage another great *razzia* through al-Andalus, which carried him all the way to the suburbs of Cádiz.[2] Clearly a dangerous

---

[2] Luis Sánchez Belda, ed., *Chronica Adefonsi Imperatoris* (Madrid, 1950). The unknown author devotes the entire second of two books to the theme of the Alfonsine reconquest.

disproportion was developing, which would become all the worse when Tāshufīn was called home to Morocco that same year by his half brother, Sīr, who was beginning to distrust his brother's growing reputation.

Alfonso VII would use his advantage to strengthen his own frontier over the next four years. In 1139 he laid siege to the Muslim fortress of Colmenar de Oreja 60 kilometers northwest of Toledo and north of the Tajo. The castle had threatened the flank of Toledo for thirty years. It fell to Alfonso late in the year despite frantic efforts of the governors of Córdoba and Sevilla to relieve it. Three years later the Leónese would lay siege to Coria at the western end of the frontier. This city, which lay in the gap between the Tajo basin and the plains of the trans-Duero, had also been seized in the dark days just after the death of Alfonso VI. For thirty years it had allowed the Murābit to succor the Muslim population in the extreme west of that plain and had always threatened the possibility of a major Muslim offensive. Once again neither Murābit North Africa nor Andalucía was able to offer any real assistance, and in June of 1142 the town fell to Alfonso.

Thus, upon the death of Alī ibn Yūsuf, the Murābit Empire was beset both in North Africa and in Iberia by those enemies who were to destroy it in a mere three years. In Algeria Abd al-Mūmin would strike against Tlemcen, defeating Tāshufīn ibn Alī there in 1145. In the course of his retreat, Tāshufīn was killed in an accident. The Murābit were now completely bereft of competent leadership. Leaving the siege of Tlemcen to subordinates, Abd al-Mūmin first attacked Fez, which surrendered after a siege of nine months, and then Marrakesh itself, which he took in 1146. The young son of Tāshufīn, who had been nominal leader of the Murābit since his father's death, was beheaded and the population of Marrakesh massacred. A Muwāhhid Empire now united all of Morocco, its mountain and Saharan hinterlands, and a portion of what was to become modern Algeria.

Meanwhile, across the Mediterranean, Alfonso VII had once again taken up the *Reconquista* in Andalucía proper. In 1143 he led an extensive raid through Andalucía, while in Portugal Alfonso Enríquez hammered valiantly at Lisbon, although with little success. Ramón Berenguer trenched steadily against the countryside about Lérida and Tortosa. In September a great council of the realm and church of León–Castilla met in Valladolid. Under the legateship of the Roman cardinal Guido it settled many of the questions outstanding among the Christian kings of Iberia. The papacy was preparing to accept the kingship of Alfonso Enríquez in Portugal, and Alfonso VII would have to do the same. In June of 1144 in León the marriage of Urraca, Alfonso's natural daughter, and King García Ramírez IV of Navarra would take place. It was to be uneasy peace, which did not bode well for Muslim Iberia. In September and October of 1144 Alfonso VII was once again conducting a raid at least up to the borders of Andalucía in the territories of Calatrava just north of the Sierra Morena.[3] What then followed was enormously facilitated, strengthened, and extended in its impact by two other developments.

In the first place, there was the beginning of a general revolt against the Murābit in Andalucía itself. Doubtless this was a reaction triggered in part by the death of Alī ibn Yūsuf in Morocco in 1143, as well as the news of the troubles besetting his successor, Tāshufin ibn Alī. On the other hand, the inability of the Murābit to defend al-Andalus against the increasing tempo of raids conducted by Alfonso VII must also have played a part. Involved as well was some sympathy for the Muwāhhid cause as a religious phenomenon. Still, plain and simple antipathy for the Murābit themselves seems to have been at least as important. In any event, during the summer of 1144 a serious revolt against their authority broke out in the Algarve, spreading from Silves, Mértola, and Evora through Huelva and Niebla into the territories of Sevilla itself. Ibn Gāniya, who had been given full authority in Iberia by Alī ibn Yūsuf just before the latter's death, left Sevilla to put down that insurrection, whereupon, in December of 1144 or January of 1145, a more serious revolt broke out in Córdoba.

In short order, Alfonso VII's ally, the Hūddite prince Saif al-Dawla, appeared in Córdoba and took control of the city. In March of 1145 he was expelled by the original rebels, whereupon he proceeded to Jaén, where he installed a nephew in power while he himself went on to seize control in Granada in the early spring. The local rebels there were able to tolerate him only until the end of the year, and at the beginning of January of 1146 he gravitated to Murcia where he again was able to put himself at the head of a local rebellion, but only very briefly. On February 5, 1146, his career came to an abrupt end when he was defeated and killed in a battle with a Leonese force operating in the area. Alfonso VII disavowed any responsibility for this action, but apparently his lieutenants in the south had decided to simplify a hopelessly tangled situation. Meanwhile, ibn Gāniya had defeated the Portuguese rebels and

---

[3] The Christian sources must be supplemented by the Muslim ones which are often more specific. For all of this period Francisco Codera y Zaidín, *Decadencia y desaparición de los Almorávides en España* (Zaragoza, 1899), remains indispensable, although some of it has to be corrected from Ambrosio Huici Miranda, *Historia musulmana de Valencia y su región*, Vol. 3 (Valencia, 1970).

regained control of Córdoba as well, but the whole of the east of Andalucía, as well as Granada and Málaga in the south, had become independent. Obviously the Christian powers of the north would not fail to make capital of the political musical chairs which had begun in al-Andalus.

The Reconquista and the Second Crusade

At the same time, but at much farther remove, the Muslim leader Zenghi was to march into a conquered city of Edessa in December of 1144 and shortly thereafter proceed to mop up the last remnants of the county of Edessa, the earliest of the crusading states established by the First Crusade in the Levant. That development would set off shock waves in Western Europe, which would have their repercussions in Iberia as well. The news of the fall of Edessa seems to have reached Europe only during the following summer, and not until December of 1145 did Pope Eugenius III (1145–1153) react to it by issuing a bull for a new crusade. Even then there was no reaction until the bull was reissued in March of 1146, until Louis VII of France managed to persuade the French to act, and the endorsement of Bernard of Clairvaux was secured at the end of that month. As it happened, Iberia was to become the singularly successful theater of that generally unhappy movement.

When precisely Alfonso VII of León–Castilla became aware of the projected crusade is difficult to say. Archbishop Raymond of Toledo had been in Rome during the summer of 1145 and may have learned of the fall of Edessa then. He may even have heard talk of a possible papal bull of crusade to come. He may also have been sent to attend Louis VII's Easter court at Vezelay in 1146 in order to determine what the French intended to do. Alfonso VII's first cousin, Count Alfonso Jordán of Toulouse, took the cross there and subsequently died in the Levant. In 1147 a new bull of Eugenius III would specifically list both Iberia and the eastern frontier of Germany as legitimate crusading arenas. In that same year a subsequent papal letter exhorted the Genoese to assist in this theater, and in 1148 the pope would bestow the dignity of a crusade upon Ramón Berenguer's campaign against Tortosa. These papal actions were, in fact, reactions to the initiatives of Alfonso VII, the Genoese, and Ramón Berenguer respectively. Alfonso Enríquez of Portugal seems to have sought no papal sanction and received none.

In all likelihood the initiative of Alfonso VII was the first, probably set in motion in the spring of 1146. Unlike the crusade to the

Holy Land, which did not officially start until 1147, the Leonese monarch marched almost immediately, rather than wait upon a reply. By the end of April, 1146, he was already in Toledo awaiting the rally of his host. By May Alfonso was in Córdoba, had seized part of the city, and forced the Murābit governor, ibn Gāniya, to hold the remainder as his vassal. By August he was back in Toledo, and in September a treaty was signed whereby the commune of Genoa pledged to supply a fleet, troops, and siege machinery for the reduction of the Muslim port city of Almería the following May. The agreement was conditional upon the adhesion to it of Ramón Berenguer IV of Aragón–Barcelona. In return, Alfonso pledged to pay 10,000 gold dinars immediately and another 10,000 by the following Easter, the money to be delivered to Barcelona. A subsequent treaty was also reached with Ramón Berenguer, who pledged to cooperate in the reduction of Almería and then was to secure the services of the Genoese for an attack upon Muslim Tortosa.[4] In mid-November Alfonso met with Ramón Berenguer and King García Ramírez IV of Navarra at San Esteban de Gormaz to coordinate the coming campaign.

Having made these arrangements, Alfonso then marched for a winter campaign against the Murābit fortress of Calatrava la Vieja which could not be left unreduced. By the beginning of January, 1147, that stronghold was his. He then retired north to attend to the ordinary life of the realm, but by May he was again in Toledo. Mid-July found the Leonese, having traversed the Sierra Morena by way of the pass of Despeñaperros, on the upper reaches of the Guadalquivir, laying siege to Andújar. The Almería campaign was underway.

Nevertheless, his cousin, Alfonso Enríquez of Portugal, had stolen a march on him. In mid-March the Portuguese king had made a swift thrust south from Coimbra and in a night attack surprised the Muslim town of Santarém. With its fall, he now controlled the passage of the Tajo against any but waterborne forces, and had isolated Muslim Lisbon and its environs from its coreligionists to the south. The feat was important in itself, but it became doubly so with the appearance of a crusading fleet upon the scene.

The first elements of this fleet had sailed from Cologne about the end of August bound for the Levant.[5] In the passage of the North

---

[4] Descriptions of the Almería campaign are to be found in Sánchez Belda, ed., *Chronica*; in Caffaro, *De Captione Almerie et Tortuose*, ed. Antonio Ubieto Arteta (Valencia, 1973); and in the usual scattered documents.

[5] The sources for these events are the "Chronica Gothorum" in Monica Blöcker-Walter, *Alfons I von Portugal* (Zurich, 1966), pp. 156–57; and Charles Wendell

Plate 7   The pass of Despeñaperros in the Sierra Morena

Sea and the Channel it was joined by equally strong formations of Flemish and English. On Pentecost, June 8, 1147, the combined force arrived off Galicia, and some of its complement celebrated that feast at Santiago de Compostela. From Galicia the crusaders sailed south to Oporto where they were met by its bishop, Pedro. That prelate convinced them to at least stop to parley with his king who was holding Lisbon to siege. The crusaders did just that, and Alfonso Enríquez persuaded them to join in the attack. The price of their adhesion was a treaty guaranteeing them the spoils of success and subsequent perpetual trading privileges in the entire realm. Lisbon put up a stubborn defense, but finally succumbed to the combined forces on October 24, 1147. Mopping up afterward turned all of Portugal north of the Tajo and south of Coimbra into Christian territory. It should perhaps be noted that the first bishop of a restored Lisbon was to be the Englishman Gilbert of Hastings.

David, ed., *De Expugnatione Lyxbonensi* (New York, 1936). Two particularly useful studies have been done by Giles Constable, "The Second Crusade as Seen by Contemporaries," *Traditio* 9 (1953):213–79; and "A Note on the Route of the Anglo-Flemish Crusaders of 1147," *Speculum* 28 (1953):525–26.

Alfonso VII, on the other hand, was still in western Andalucía at Baeza on the Guadalquivir in mid-August in the company of King García Ramírez IV of Navarra. They took that city as a base and support for their line of retreat and then commenced the terrible march through mountain and desert to Almería on the Mediterranean. When the two kings arrived they joined the Genoese, Ramón Berenguer IV of Aragón–Barcelona, Count William of Montpellier, and a host of others who had come by sea to that city, emporium, and pirates' nest. At that time Almería had a population of something like 28,000, and its walls covered approximately 79 *hectares*.[6] Nevertheless, its fleet had prudently withdrawn and help was not forthcoming from elsewhere. On October 17th the city surrendered and was turned over in early November to a Genoese, Ottone di Bonvillano, who was to hold it as a vassal of that commune. On November 25th the Leonese monarch was back in Baeza on his way north.

In the following year Alfonso himself undertook no campaign, but the momentum of the Christian offensive was not to slow. As agreed, the Genoese in 1148 joined with Ramón Berenguer in a siege of the major Muslim port city of Tortosa at the head of the delta of the Ebro.[7] There they were joined by the forces of the Templars and of the Hospitallers of the realm, by Counts William of Montpellier and Bertrán of Toulouse, and a variety of lesser warriors including even some veterans of the seafarers who had helped to subjugate Lisbon in the fall of 1147. These had coasted around all of Iberia and were ready for another contest. The siege began in July and continued until December. Tortosa was then forced to surrender, but with the understanding that its Muslim citizens were guaranteed the rights of freedom, property, and worship, as was traditional in Iberia. The town was sufficiently rich for the Genoese to be content with a third of it and the Templars with a fifth, while the Catalan seneschal, Guillem Ramón of Moncada, received a third of the remaining royal third. But for that port to realize its full potential, the Ebro had to be freed upstream.

For the past five years Ramón Berenguer IV had been nibbling away at the hinterlands of both Tortosa and Lérida. That helps to

---

[6] Leopoldo Torres Balbas, "Almería islámica," *Al-Andalus* 22 (1957):411–53, describes the city in the 11th Century. José Angel Tapia Garrido, *Historia general de Almería y su provincia*, 3 vols. (Almería, 1976–78), 1:433–34, is perhaps somewhat too sure of its further growth by the 12th Century.

[7] Rudolf Hiestand, "Reconquista, Kreuzzug und heiliges Grab," *GAKS* 31 (1984):136–57, is the most recent and the most complete treatment of the sources for the conquest.

explain the relative ease of conquest of Tortosa in 1148, and of the overrunning of Lérida in 1149. There again Ramón Berenguer was able to call upon the forces of the viscount of Bearn, the count of Urgel, and the Knights Templar of his kingdom. By June of 1149 the siege of Lérida, neighboring Fraga, and Mequinenza had begun. All three cities surrendered on October 24th on the usual terms. By this time Murābit authority had disintegrated everywhere and there was no leader of sufficient power in the Muslim world able to organize a relief force. Lérida was divided with the count of Urgel securing one-third and Ramón-Berenguer two-thirds. Of that the count–king gave a further one-fifth to the Templars. The "Count of Barcelona" and "King of Aragón" now took the further title of "Marquis of Lérida and Tortosa." The whole of the old lands of the taifa of Zaragoza in the basin of the Ebro had now passed definitively into Christian hands.

At the end of the year 1149 the Second Crusade was finally over. The German crusaders against the Wends beyond the Elbe had broken up and returned home without significant accomplishment. Another German army had found disaster on the plains of Asia Minor. Its survivors and the French army had ineffectually besieged Damascus and then gone home in their turn. Louis VII of France returned to Italy with plans to organize another expedition to the Levant, but would find little enthusiasm beyond his own. In Iberia the results had been much more encouraging. The Portuguese border had been carried permanently south from Coimbra on the Mondego to Santarém and Lisbon on the Tajo. The entire basin of the Ebro had fallen to Aragón–Barcelona in the east. León–Castilla had cleared the whole of the plain of Castilla la Nueva of the Murābit and had established a strong position in the upper basin of the Guadalquivir and Almería. But in this case, unlike the two former, a strong and continuing effort was needed to consolidate that advantage. Alfonso VII was to base his plans upon the continuance of help from the north of Europe, but he too would discover that the crusading spirit had vanished there.

Andalucía Fragmented and Contested

Even in the two years prior to the final demise of the Murābit North African empire in 1146, the Muwāhhid emir, Abd al-Mūmin, had begun to receive delegations from the Muslim of Iberia requesting his assistance. He had received them all politely and had offered assurances of his interest, but his essential concerns lay south of

Gibraltar. A modest expeditionary force was despatched in 1146, but for the present he was preoccupied with consolidating his position in newly conquered Morocco. Then, when he did feel strong enough to undertake again a course of conquest, Algeria was to be the target. In 1152, the Muwāhhid marched suddenly against the Hammādid kingdom taking both Algiers itself and then Constantine farther east. However, he had then to contend with the Bedouin Hilāl Arabs of the interior who had been loosely allied with the Hammādids. It required a great victory over them on the plain of Setif in 1153 before the diplomacy could begin which would reconcile them to the new state of affairs in the African northwest.[8]

Nevertheless, soon after these conquests which enlarged the power structure of the empire, Abd al-Mūmin was faced with a serious set of conspiracies which centered about the remaining members of the family of the former *mahdī*, ibn Tūmart. These were put down with considerable bloodshed, and the chief members of that family were placed under what amounted to protective custody in Fez. In 1156 in a great meeting at Sale in Morocco, the emir had his own firstborn son, Muhammad, recognized as his eventual successor. He then installed his other sons in the governorships of the major cities of the empire. Each governor was also to be accompanied by a *vizier*, or advisor, drawn from among the tribal sheiks. The power structure was being generalized beyond the original tribes of the High Atlas, but it was becoming ever more the typical familial and tribal confederacy, rather than a theological crusade.

Even when the Muwāhhid emir was sufficiently strong to begin another extension of his empire, the target was to be Tunisia, not Iberia. In that region the power of the Zīrīd rulers had been gradually curtailed by the aggressions of Roger II of Sicily. Intent upon securing control of as much of the Mediterranean trade as possible, Roger began in 1134 by securing the submission of Djerba and Mahdiya. In 1146 he took Tripoli and then Gabes, Sfax, and Sousse. His object was the ports of the region, and he had no intention of erecting a land empire. Roger was content to play the local Muslim powers off against one another and to continue to control their commerce. Still, the Christian power there was a scandal to Muwāhhid orthodoxy and its weakness a temptation to the latter's cupidity. In 1159 Abd al-Mūmin began an offensive which would sweep the Norman power entirely from the African littoral in the space of two years.

---

[8] Ambrosio Huici Miranda, *Historia política del imperio Almohade*, Vol. 1 (Tetuán, 1956), pp. 153–69. The book represents his usual exacting scholarship on the early years of the Muwāhhid.

With his hands shortly free finally to turn his attention to al-Andalus, and actually engaged in preparing a major expedition from Sale, the emir died in 1163. Those of his armies which he had thus far been able to spare had achieved considerable successes in Iberia. Nonetheless, his death without ever setting foot in Spain is symbolic of the altered interests of North African Islam. The Murābit before them had never quite managed to restore the status quo of Islam and Christianity in the peninsula that had existed at the fall of the caliphate in Córdoba in the early 11th Century. Coimbra and Toledo had remained beyond their grasp, and the last taifa, Zaragoza, had yielded to them less than a decade before they, in turn, would lose it to Aragón. Not only would their Muwāhhid successors fail to reclaim Lisbon, or Santarém, Lérida, or Tortosa, but they would be long unable to extinguish all independent Muslim authority in the peninsula.

With all that said, such Muwāhhid forces as could be spared from the African theater did make significant advances there. Landing in 1146, they secured the area around Algeciras, and then advanced northward, being welcomed first in Jérez de la Frontera, and then in an arc through the Portuguese Algarve in more of a parade than a campaign. Niebla, Mértola, and Silves yielded to them, and then Badajoz. They were now ready to advance against the Murābit forces in Sevilla itself, which they took with great slaughter in January of 1147. A little later in the year, when Alfonso VII was conducting his great campaign against Almería and reducing Baeza in the process, the Murābit ruler in Andalucía, ibn Gāniya, renounced the ties of vassalage to León which he had accepted and surrendered Córdoba and Jaén to the Muwāhhid. He himself then proceeded to Granada where he attempted without success to persuade the local Murābit governors to do the same. He died in Granada in January of 1149.

By the middle of 1147, then, the Muwāhhid forces had secured the Algarve and the lower basins of the Guadiana and the Guadalquivir for Abd al-Mūmin. Nevertheless, local Muslim feeling sometimes ran strong against these new African masters, causing occasional, often widespread, revolts against them in these regions and even supporting instead local Murābit rulers in Málaga, Granada, and many of the eastern regions. Most notable were the independent Muslim rulers in the Balearics, Valencia, and Murcia. The independent Balearic kingdom in particular was to become a center of violent reaction against the Muwāhhid which endured well beyond our period. However, it took the direction of offensives against the latter's African possessions and so does not concern us here.

On the mainland, the greatest of the new taifa kings was ibn Mardanish of Valencia. That city had risen against the Murābit in

March of 1145, and after the usual confusions and struggle had fallen to "el rey Lobo," as the Christian sources often refer to him, in 1147. A soldier of fortune and a man of uncertain ancestry, he is said to have been of Christian descent, which would not have been unusual for the period. He was, in any event, a ruler of considerable diplomatic as well as military skill and ordinarily found himself allied with the various Christian powers as a practical alternative to subjection to the Muwāhhid. He quickly agreed to pay *parias* to Ramón Berenguer of 100,000 gold dinars annually in order to avoid the fate of Tortosa, Lérida, or Almería. In return, the count of Barcelona agreed to furnish military aid as needed. In January of 1149 he also signed a ten-year peace with Pisa and granted that city factories in both Valencia and Denia. In June of the same year he struck a similar bargain with Genoa, granting factories in Denia and Valencia and promising not to attack their other trading stations in Almería and Tortosa. This pact, too, was to endure for ten years.[9]

During 1148 and 1149 when Tortosa and then Lérida were falling to Ramón Berenguer in the east, the activities of·Alfonso VII seem to have been limited to diplomatic efforts and internal politics. In all probability the great effort against Almería of 1147 had exhausted both his purse and his subjects. By 1150, however, he was ready to resume the offensive in Andalucía. Representatives of his cousin, Alfonso Enríquez, were in Toledo in May of that year to coordinate their efforts. Apparently the two monarchs realized that their own efforts might not be sufficient, and Bishop Gilbert of Lisbon was despatched to England to raise a new crusading fleet and army for the following year. By the end of May Alfonso VII was laying siege to Córdoba and struggling with Muwāhhid relief forces in its environs.

The contest was inconclusive, despite the presence and aid of King García Ramírez IV of Navarra and Count Armengol of Urgel in the Christian host. The most the Leonese could do was capture the fortress of Montoro on the Guadalquivir, which blocked the entrance of the Muwāhhid into upper Andalucía from the west. He then seems to have withdrawn to harass Jaén where he may have set up siege lines in August. From there he retired, first to Baeza and then back to Toledo by October. If Alfonso Enríquez made any sallies on his front, we do not know of them.

[9] The texts are found, respectively, in Michele Amari, ed., *I diplomi arabi del R. Archivio Fiorentini* (Florence, 1863), pp. 239–40; and Caesare Imperiale di Sant' Angelo, ed., *Codice diplomatico della Republica di Genova*, Vol. 1 (Rome, 1936), pp. 247–49.

 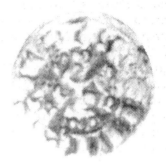

Plate 8   Coinage of Ramón Berenguer IV of Barcelona

The results of that campaign were modest, and Alfonso VII hoped for much greater successes in 1151. Those expectations are embodied in the Treaty of Tudején, which he signed with Ramón Berenguer IV on January 27th of that year. By the terms of the treaty, Alfonso VII recognized the right of Aragón–Barcelona to the Muslim territories of Valencia, Denia, and the greater part of Murcia, which the Catalan would hold as fief from Alfonso when it was conquered. The treaty also provided for an equal division between them of the lands of Navarra, for García Ramírez had died on November 21, 1150. For some reason, presently unknown to us, this pact was stillborn. No serious attempt was made to implement it. The Catalan monarch would not take up the *Reconquista* in Valencia, Denia, or Murcia, all of which continued to be subject to ibn Mardanīsh, who recognized the former's suzerainty and paid him *parias*. In Navarra, Sancho VI *el Sabio* (1150–1194) would succeed to his father's domains without noticeable challenge. Still, the treaty indicates the direction of Alfonso VII's ambitions just then and their dimensions.

By April, 1151, the Leonese monarch was in Toledo preparing a new campaign. During July and August he was carrying on a siege of Jaén, the gateway to the Sierra Nevadas and Granada, which eluded his grasp. That summer, his charters tell us, he was also awaiting news of the arrival of a crusading fleet and army to join him in an attack upon Sevilla which, of course, never arrived. The efforts of Bishop Gilbert of Lisbon to fan the embers of the Second Crusade in England had been fruitless. Moreover, while Alfonso Enríquez did assault the key position of Alcácer do Sal in the Muslim Algarve, he failed to take it, and so diverted no appreciable Muwāhhid forces from Andalucía. October found the Leonese monarch once again back in Toledo with no gain from the summer's fighting.

The following year Alfonso's aims in the south were more limited, perhaps scaled to the resources he could reasonably expect to muster at this point when fighting alone. Still his objective eluded him. This was the tiny taifa of Guadix, which occupied a key position at the mouth of that corridor, between the Sierra Nevada and the Sierra de Baza, which represents the best route from Baeza to Almería. The siege of Guadix occupied him in July and perhaps in August. At the beginning of September he was back in Toledo, but, we are told in his charters, he had come by way of Lorca in Murcia. We know that the former king of Guadix retired to Morocco in 1152 and that the city did not fall to Alfonso.[10] The best conjecture seems to be that the city surrendered to ibn Mardanīsh, king of Valencia and Murcia, instead of to the Leonese, and that the thwarted Christian ruler staged a punitive expedition through the lands of Murcia on his way back to Toledo.

After the exasperating episodes of the three previous years, Alfonso VII would mount no Andalucían offensives in 1153 and 1154. He was, in fact, rather too busy with diplomatic overtures in the north and with the internal affairs of the realm. However, the Muwāhhid forces of Andalucía would take advantage of that respite to overrun the taifa of Málaga, thus strengthening their own position in the west and further threatening the thus far independent taifa of Granada in the east.

The major events of these years for Alfonso VII were the negotiation of the marriage of his daughter, Constancia, to King Louis VII of France in 1153, which was consummated in 1154, and the visit of Louis VII in the fall of 1154. Although the motives of Alfonso would inevitably have been complex, it is unthinkable at this juncture that he would not have hoped to secure military assistance to

[10] Codera y Zaidín, *Decadencia*, p. 133.

complete his conquests in Andalucía, that is, a crusade of sorts. All that he did, in fact, realize was increased prestige for himself and the pilgrimage of the French king to Santiago de Compostela.[11]

The most assistance that Alfonso was able to muster came from the visit of the papal legate, Cardinal Hyacinth, in 1154–1155. The support of the papacy was enlisted for a variety of royal concerns about the organization of the peninsular church, and, in the council held at Valladolid in February of 1155, the legate and the assembled bishops issued a call for a renewed effort against the Muslim in the peninsula. Alfonso is likely to have realized some additional help, at least extraordinary revenues, as a result. In any event, in June he finally took the Muslim stronghold of Andújar on the Guadalquivir, which had impeded communications between his own advance point at Montoro to the west and his major base in Andalucía at Baeza. His hopes for the development of upper Andalucía are underscored by the fact that a bishop had been consecrated for Baeza, probably at the Council of Valladolid. In the same campaign Alfonso also captured Santa Eufemia and Pedroche, south of Almadén in the valley of the Guadiana, thus bolstering his position west of Calatrava la Vieja. It was not an unprofitable summer, and the Leonese spent most of September in Toledo and Talavera seeing to his strength on the middle Tajo.

Nonetheless, the next two years would see the collapse of the Leonese position in Andalucía. During the winter of 1156, since he was unable to involve the kings of Portugal, Aragón–Barcelona, Navarra, or France in the contest for Andalucía, Alfonso VII turned to the Muslim taifa king, ibn Mardanīsh, of Valencia, Murcia, and Guadix. In February they signed a treaty by which the Muslim would become his vassal and surrender the fortress of Uclés, south of the Tajo and northeast of Toledo, to the Leonese monarch.[12] Doubtless Alfonso was planning some sort of joint military action for the summer to come. To that end, the winter and spring were spent in the Toledo area. However, in late June, disaster struck. The emperor fell ill and had to abandon any thoughts of campaigning for the remainder of the year. That his illness was serious is attested to

---

[11] Marcel Pacaut, *Louis VII et son royaume* (Paris, 1964), pp. 38, 181, and 185, puts the marriage in the French perspective. The fullest medieval account of the entire episode is Lucas de Túy, "Chronicon Mundi ab Origine Mundi usque ad Eram MCCLXXIV," in *Hispaniae Illustratae*, Vol. 4, ed. Andreas Schottus (Frankfurt, 1608), pp. 104–05.

[12] Julio González, "Repoblación de las tierras de Cuenca," *AEM* 12 (1982):183–204, puts the treaty in 1149 but the transfer of Uclés in 1157. For these very difficult matters of chronology I prefer to follow the evidence of the charters of Alfonso when available. The first mentions of ibn Mardanīsh as a vassal commence in 1156.

by the fact that it was noted in the dating formula of at least one of his charters.[13] His condition probably also accounts for the presence at court during the fall and winter of his daughters, Queen Constancia of France and Queen Sancha of Navarra.

This incapacity of Alfonso VII at such a crucial moment was to result in a series of reverses in the south. By coincidence or design, the Muwāhhid conducted a series of major offensives there in 1156. The powerful taifa of Granada fell to them, and ibn Said, son of Emir Abd al-Mūmin, was despatched to become its governor, with orders to effect the recapture of Almería. Far to the west, a new Muwāhhid governor would launch a series of attacks across the Tajo at Portugal. Another new Muwāhhid governor at Córdoba would overrun the new Christian positions at Santa Eufemia, as well as at Pedroche and the older stronghold at Montoro, in the spring of 1156. The former royal *alférez*, Núño Pérez, who had commanded in Montoro, disappears from the documents at this time, and we must suppose a sizeable defeat.[14]

The following year, 1157, would see the fall of Almería and the death of Alfonso VII. In late April Alfonso was in Toledo in the company of his sons, Sancho and Fernando. He probably had not recovered completely from his illness of the previous year – Lucas of Túy tells us that he was sick prior to the expedition – but his participation in the coming campaign was essential.

The Muwāhhid forces, led by ibn Saīd of Granada, had begun to set up siege lines before Almería in the early spring. The defense seems to have been anything but spirited, and before help could arrive the garrison had lost control of the lower town and been forced back upon the *alcázar*. Alfonso VII had left Toledo sometime in May for the difficult 475-kilometer march. He was joined by his ally, ibn Mardanish of Valencia, probably at the latter's stronghold of Guadix. From there the last 110 kilometers stretched over nightmarish marching territory to the objective. By the middle of June they had apparently reached the vicinity of the city and would remain there for some little time, although it is difficult to see where they could have established themselves. Almería lies on the narrowest of coastal plains, and the approach from Guadix would have left the rescuers access to neither the city nor the strand without an unacceptable risk of being cut off from any line of retreat. Nor was

[13] Archivo Diocesano de León, monasterio de Gradefes, no. 80, a likely original. Pub. Aurelio Calvo, *El monasterio de Gradefes* (León, 1936), pp. 308–09.
[14] Ambrosio Huici Miranda, "Un nuevo manuscrito de 'al-Bayān al-Mugrib': Datos inéditos y aclaraciones sobre los ultimos años del reinado de Alfonso VII, el Emperador," *Al-Andalus* 24 (1959):63–84, dates most of these events to 1155 on the basis of that literary evidence. Again I prefer to follow the charters.

there a suitable area for bivouac to the northwest of the city for any considerable number of troops.[15]

The relieving force maintained itself in and about Almería for a period but was unable to break through to the *alcázar* or to defeat the besiegers. Indeed, without the support of a fleet offshore, relief must have been impossible against such a determined enemy. Apparently the Genoese had lost interest in Almería, withdrawn from the city at some point during the previous nine years, and were not now ready to commit a fleet to its rescue. By mid-July at the latest Alfonso VII took the only practicable course. He and ibn Mardanísh withdrew northwest to Guadix and from there launched a feint against Granada itself in the hope of drawing off the Muslim from Almería. That plan failed, for Granada was confident of its ability to withstand his forces.

The attempt on Granada was abandoned, likely because Alfonso had become gravely ill, and a withdrawal toward the north begun. His condition probably worsened quickly because it appears that the retreat came to involve the garrisons of Andújar, Baeza, and Ubeda as well. The entire Christian portion of upper Andalucía was being evacuated, and the loss of Almería itself by the end of August would by then be anticlimactic. Just to the north of the pass of Despeñaperros through the Sierra Morena, the emperor died at Las Fresnedas on August 21, 1157. He was only fifty-two years old, apparently worn out by thirty years of almost continual campaigning from Portugal to Pamplona and from Cádiz to Almería. With his death, the contest between Muslim and Christian in the center of the peninsula would resume in the valley of the Tajo, rather than the valley of the Guadalquivir or even the Guadiana. It would not be conducted on quite the same terms, however, for a full generation had passed in which the Christian repopulation of the Tajo had proceeded virtually unhindered.

The New Balance of Christian and Muslim in Iberia

The sixty years after the death of Alfonso VII were to be marked by the developing offensive of the Muwāhhid, North African power in the peninsula. Everywhere the initiative would be theirs.

[15] Tapia Garrido, *Historia de Almería* Vol. 3, pp. 10–23, describes the campaign and its environs more or less well, but gives as 18,000 the number of troops in the joint army. A force of such size would have been impossible to provision, either on the march from Guadix or in and around Almería itself. Ibn Idari, *Al-Bayān al-Mugrib*, trans. Ambrosio Huici Miranda (Valencia, 1963), pp. 310–12, is the major source for the campaign.

Nonetheless, too much time had been lost in the consolidation of their African possessions, and the Muwāhhid were never able to achieve for themselves that position in Iberia which the Murābit had so recently held. In the east, some fifteen years were to pass before they could absorb Valencia and Murcia. Ibn Mardanīsh, for as long as he lived, did not simply hold them at arm's length, but often campaigned deep into Andalucía and even dared to lay siege to Sevilla itself. Then, on that formidable adventurer's death in 1172, when the Africans were finally able to secure his territories for themselves, they found it still impossible to undo the work of Alfonso *el Batallador* and of Ramón Berenguer IV to the north. The 85,000-square-kilometer basin of the Ebro, with its great, and recently Muslim, cities of Zaragoza, Tudela, Lérida, and Tortosa, had been permanently lost to the dar al-Islam.

In the extreme west, they were able to restrain the Portugal of Alfonso Enríquez at the line of the Tajo, but again, to recover either the so-recently-Muslim Lisbon or Santarém proved permanently beyond their grasp. Instead, the tide of battle was to sway back and forth across their dominions, not those of their rival. In the center of the peninsula, the brief dominion of León–Castilla in upper Andalucía had collapsed with the death of Alfonso VII. Over the next sixty years Muwāhhid forces would operate most often on the plain of Castilla la Nueva. At different times they would even thrust as far north as Talavera de la Reina and Huete. Yet even then they would not threaten the key position of Toledo as had the Murābit. That city remained even further from the grasp of Muwāhhid than from that of Murābit. And behind that shield, the plains of the trans-Duero and the valley of the Tajo were being steadily repopulated from the north in a fashion which they were powerless to prevent. Even before the great watershed of Las Navas de Tolosa in 1212, the critical mass of the peninsula was filling up with a European population ultimately hostile to Islam. The new Muwāhhid power could forestall the immediate effects of that phenomenon, but it lacked the resources to reverse it.

Indeed, part of their success in delaying it must be credited to the lassitude of the Christian powers of the north in pressing their growing advantage. It was a lassitude born in part of other preoccupations. Alfonso Enríquez of Portugal was perhaps never quite so mesmerized by the possibility of acceding to the throne of León–Castilla as had been his mother. Although he never stopped alluding in his charters to his own descent from Alfonso VI, he pursued more actively a singular identity for Portugal among the powers of Iberia. If it was only in 1140 that he had begun to style himself "king" rather than *"infans"*, nevertheless by the end of 1143 Alfonso had secured papal recognition of that new dignity at the price of surrendering his lands to the Roman authority and accepting them back as a papal vassal.[16]

Alfonso Enríquez had underscored that blossoming independence in 1146 when he married Matilda, the daughter of Count Amadeus III of Savoy, and so brought the lustre of a foreign marriage to his growing court. Only a year later he would have a son by that marriage and would increasingly be preoccupied with the territorial definition of the realm to which his heir would sooner or later accede. After 1157, he returned to those attempts to annex the Miño valley in southern Galicia which had been the constant ambition of his mother's reign. To be sure, although the struggle against the growing Muwāhhid presence in the Algarve was never to end entirely, it would for a long time take second place to other royal concerns.

In the east of Iberia, the situation was similar. Navarra, under Sancho VI, remained the object of both Castilian and Aragonese ambitions. Although they did not manage to realize them until the early 16th Century, their attempts to do so were predictable, constant, and distracting. Moreover, after the conquest of Tortosa in 1148 and Lérida in 1149, Ramón Berenguer's interests in further reconquest were extremely limited. He concentrated to some extent upon reducing minor Muslim strongholds in the lower valley of the Ebro, and he gave steady support to ibn Mardanīsh at Valencia. His actions can be seen as the better part of wisdom. His earlier successes had given him a very large territory to consolidate, and the *parias* paid by the Valencian were more valuable, in the short run, than the expense of conquering him.

The ruler of Aragón–Barcelona had two more pressing concerns. One of these was the consolidation of his unlikely realm. We can follow the process only imperfectly in the present state of knowledge. In 1150 the Aragonese *infanta*, Petronila, reached the age of fourteen and was promptly married to the count of Barcelona. Then, in 1152, it appears that some sort of accident of birth took place sufficient to alarm Ramón Berenguer as to the likelihood of his Aragonese bride either to survive or to give birth to another child. As a result, she was required to make a will which would leave her territories to him in the absence of an heir. Petronila would survive her husband as it turned out, and, in the process, provide him with

<hr />

[16] Carl Erdmann, *Das Papsttum und Portugal in ersten Jahrhundert de portugiesischen Geschichte* (Berlin, 1928), is still the best source for their relationship.

the necessary male heir, the future Alfonso II, in 1157. Nevertheless, at the death of the count–king in 1162, his only surviving son was but five years of age, and a considerable regency would militate against any energetic policy.[17]

Ramón Berenguer's second concern was to take advantage of the opportunities created in the south of France in 1147 by the death of Count Alfonso Jordán of Toulouse while on the Second Crusade. Regent since 1144 for his young nephew in Provence, he now managed to thoroughly outmaneuver the inexperienced new count of Toulouse. Using the devices of bluff, intimidation, and cupidity, he secured in turn the feudal submission of Béziers, Carcassonne, and Razès, long an ally of Montpellier, and of the comital house of Comminges by 1150. In 1154 he was also named regent for the young scion of the viscounties of Bearn and Bigorre, and so became the most powerful ruler in all of the Languedoc south of Toulouse itself. Therefore, when Eleanor of Aquitaine married the count of Anjou and Maine, soon to become king of England as well, in that same year, Ramón Berenguer sought an alliance with Henry Plantagenet in the southwest. In 1156, the count–king of Aragón–Barcelona and the king of England would be conducting a joint siege of Toulouse itself.[18] This new chapter of Aragón–Barcelona's pursuit of empire in the Languedoc, which would come to a bloody end on the field of Muret in 1214, would for long divert its attentions from the possibilities of the *Reconquista* in the south.

That the *Reconquista* ground to a halt in the middle of the 12th Century was more a result of the division of León and Castilla into two competing realms upon the death of Alfonso VII than any other single factor. For a century the León–Castilla of Fernando I, Alfon-

---

[17] Antonio Ubieto Arteta, *Historia de Aragón: Creación y desarrollo de la corona de Aragón* (Zaragoza, 1987), pp. 177–202, devoted the better part of a chapter trying to reconcile the documents that treat these events, the identity of the various children of the match, and even the proper name of Alfonso II, sometimes identified as Ramón, other times as Pedro. He was unsuccessful because he was reluctant to accept the obvious fact that many, if not all, of the documents that survive were later tampered with if they are not outright forgeries. Someone is going to have to do the job again, beginning with one eye on the history of the skullduggeries of the regency of the early reign of Alfonso II.

[18] The history of the Languedoc needs a new author. One must rely on the century-old work of J. Vaissette and Claude Devic, *Histoire de Languedoc*, Vol. 3 (Toulouse, 1872), or piece events together from the histories of the surrounding regions. Ferran Soldevila, *Historia dels Catalans*, Vol. 1 (Barcelona, 1962) is useful. For these particular times, from the French view, see Pacaut, *Louis VII*, pp. 184–85. Charles Higounet, "Un grand chapitre de l'histoire du XII siècle: La rivalité des maisons de Toulouse et Barcelone pour la preponderance meridionale," in *Mélanges d'histoire du Moyen Age Louis Halphen* (Paris, 1951), pp. 313–22, is more detailed.

so VI, and Alfonso VII had been the prime force of the Christian advance. Even when temporarily on the defensive, the kingdom had engaged the major energies of the Muslim south, and to that extent allowed the gains on its flanks of Portugal and Aragón. First the conquest and then the retention of Toledo had been the sine qua non of all subsequent Christian gains in Iberia. When Sancho III (1157–1158) inherited a separate Castilla and Fernando II (1157–1188) a separate León, the balance of power in the peninsula could not but be radically altered by that very fact.

Political devolution of that kind, strange as it is to the modern political sense, was always a possibility under the monarchy. When realm and ruler were so closely identified as to be almost indistinguishable, the rules of private property could all too easily be applied to what we see instinctively as the public *res*. After all, the king was, above all and always, the eldest male member of that dynasty which the aura of divine election had predestined to the rule of certain territories. Therefore, when a failing king had two or more adult sons, the tension for mastery of those various properties which constituted the royal fisc was, in a very real sense, natural. This would be even more true in an age when royal government possessed only the slightest institutional skeleton and a tradition that reached back no more than a century. The kingdom was nowhere to be found. The king was the most obvious fact of life. Permutations of the dynasty had gradually produced a new Portuguese kingdom, beginning in 1109. They had resulted in the gradual solidification of the new realm of Aragón–Barcelona, beginning in 1137.

Nonetheless, such dynastic factors seldom worked in abstraction from other determinants. We think automatically of underlying national realities, forgetting that the monarchy had not yet created nationality. "Particularism" is a better name for what was at work. In the case at hand, León–Castilla was at the death of Alfonso VII an imperial realm of about 250,000 square kilometers. Major mountain ranges separated it, from east to west, into littorals on the Bay of Biscay and the Atlantic, a northern *meseta* of Castilla la Vieja, and a southern *meseta* of Castilla la Nueva. To delegate authority to various members of the dynasty for one or another province of this sprawling, awkward realm was already a time-honored practice. In the absence of most other machinery of government, it was a practical device to bring the dynastic charisma to bear on its scattered subjects. From there it was but a short step to partition itself if dynastic developments were to encourage it.

Finally, there was the local dynamic. Although all of the great noble houses of the kingdom were, in some degree, court families,

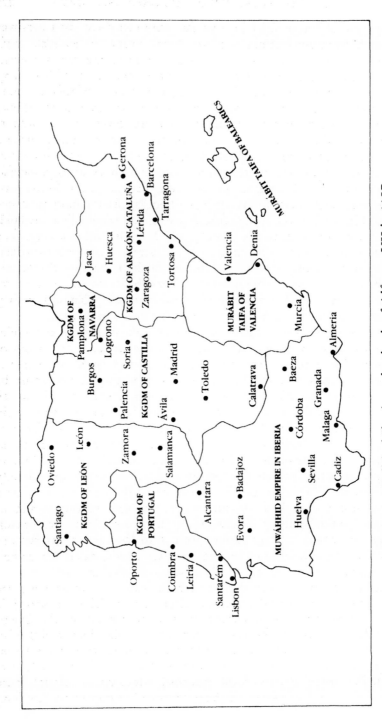

Figure 6 Political Iberia at the death of Alfonso VII in 1157

they remained rooted in regions that supplied them with a power most imperfectly conjoined to the regal authority. And although they were not infrequently related by blood to the dynasty itself, regional considerations were usually more important to them than those of the entire realm. As a result, they were perfectly at home attempting to manipulate their royal cousins for personal or regional advantage when divisions appeared in the narrower dynasty proper.

Alfonso VII had five sons who survived long enough to make a mark in the surviving records. Of those only two were still alive at his own death. Both had had a considerable political history. Sancho was born about 1133 and Fernando three years later. The former had begun to be associated with his father in the intitulation of documents by 1142, was cited as king by 1149, and was knighted in 1152. For Fernando, the pertinent dates are 1144, 1152, and 1155. The earliest charter of Sancho himself that survives dates to 1149 and that of Fernando to 1155. That is, well before the death of Alfonso VII his two sons were actively associated in the government of the realm, and both had control of portions of the royal fisc from which they could make alienations and support courts of their own.

That peculiar division of the realm, then, into a Castilla under Sancho's control and a León under Fernando's, must be the work of Alfonso VII himself. As drawn, Sancho III of Castilla controlled the Rioja, Asturias de Santillana, those Basque territories that could be said to be under at least nominal control, and Castilla la Vieja as well as Castilla la Nueva. The latter had come to include the overlordship of Zaragoza, Calatayud, and Daroca in the east as well as the lands of the Tajo basin. But in the west "Castilla" also stretched as far as Sahagún, and then south through Medina del Campo, Arévalo, and Avila. In other words, it included much territory traditionally associated with León rather than Castilla. Fernando II of León controlled only Galicia, Asturias de Oviedo, a reduced realm of León itself, and the new Leónese Extremadura from Zamora on south through Salamanca and Coria. His was certainly the portion of a younger son, one not generous enough to compel his willing acceptance of his father's boundaries as permanent.

Given the present state of research, it is difficult to isolate those factors that must have determined such a novel division. It is possible that linguistic and local factors of settlement south of the Duero prevailed. Certainly, it seems clear that the Castilian and Riojan emigration had been sliding southwest for some time in the trans-Duero, and it may also have been predominant in Castilla la Nueva, although that is less clear. Rather more important, I suspect, were the ambitions and power of those great noble houses already long associated with each of the heirs. Sancho had been raised in the household of Guter Fernández of Castro, the greatest of the Castilian magnates with powerful allies in León by virtue of his father's marriage to the daughter of Count Pedro Ansúrez. His own marriage linked him with the Ordóñez of the Rioja. He had been *majordomo* in the courts of Urraca and Alfonso VII, and would be of Sancho III as well. But Alfonso and Sancho also had to come to terms with Count Manrique of Lara, son of that count Pedro González who had been the consort of Sancho's grandmother, Queen Urraca. Manrique's uncle, Count Rodrigo González, had held Asturias de Santillana, Segovia, and Toledo under Alfonso VII. Manrique himself had been royal *alférez*, and had held Atienza, Avila, Madrid, Toledo, and finally Baeza.

On the other hand, Fernando II had been raised in the court of the great Trastamara magnate of Galicia, Fernando Pérez, son of the former guardian of Alfonso VII. Although the Trastamara were practically monarchs in Galicia, their influence was relatively more limited at court and in the east of the realm. Their influence had also been large in Portugal, but the growing independence of that realm reacted on their own power after 1137. Outside of Galicia, they were allied by marriage to the powerful Leonese magnate, Suero Vermúdez, and so also to his nephew, Pedro Alfónsez of Asturias. When all is said, it appears that the "León" of Fernando II followed fairly closely the spheres of influence of those houses bound to him as well as that current of migration from Galicia, León, and the Bierzo which had worked its way down through Zamora and Toro, to Salamanca and even to Coria.

Fernando's appetite and discontent nevertheless remained great, and, given the sudden demise of Sancho III at no more than twenty-five years of age and the succession of his three-year-old son, Alfonso VIII (1158–1214), he would have opportunity and motive for a series of attempts against Castilla which would present equal opportunities to the Muwāhhid in the south. That under these circumstances the African Empire was unable to wrest control of the valley of the Tajo away from Castilla is a commentary on the underlying disparity between the two societies that then shared the Iberian Peninsula. The power of Islam had eroded to the point at which it could sometimes win battles but could not occupy the land on which it fought. The power of Christianity had swelled to that point at which it could often lose battles and yet continue to claim the soil over which they raged. The first was the measure of the decline which had occurred. The second was the measure of the growth that still continued.

10

The Two Cultures of 12th-Century Iberia

In Muslim and Christian Iberia the balance of power had shifted by the middle of the 12th Century. In addition, the two were growing in radically different fashions and directions. In their external relations, in their internal structures, and in their address to reality, both were diverging one from the other with increasing speed. If the 8th-Century promise of Muslim Iberia had never been entirely realized, it was increasingly evident that some four centuries later a distinct society with quite separate intents had taken irreversible form in the Christian north. The old quasi-tutelage to the Islamic south had gone, and the question for the future was the nature of the final balance between the two rival worlds.

Politically, Muslim Spain had been altered much more drastically than the Christian north. It had become a province of one or the other North African empires and would remain so down to the catastrophe of Las Navas de Tolosa in 1212. Attempts to remain independent of the Berber world of the south, or to regain that independence once lost, proved uniformly abortive until the crushing Christian successes of the 13th Century provided the conditions for the final emergence of the Muslim Granadan enclave of the Late Middle Ages.

That later development illustrates well the central dilemma of Muslim Iberia. From the fall of Coimbra in 1064 it was constantly being cannibalized by the emerging realms of the Christian north, yet, when it turned to North Africa for succor it found only an alternative master. Muslim rulers, from al-Qadir of Toledo to ibn Mardanish of Valencia, found willing Christian allies to help defend them either against one another or against the Berbers of the south, but the price was always the hated *parias* and the spectre of outright conquest from that quarter. So it was that the great taifas of Toledo and Zaragoza had been absorbed into the growing Christian world along with the northern third of Portugal, this latter amputated from the taifa of Badajoz. But the new African rulers, Murābit or Muwāh-hid, were unable to reverse this development in its main lines. At best they reclaimed some of the southern borderlands and retarded the Christian advance.

At the same time, therefore, that Muslim Andalucía was becoming an appendage of North Africa it was also shrinking in extent. The basin of the Duero had perhaps never been an integral part of it, but the 11th-century Christian occupation of its southern reaches represented a strategic reverse of the first magnitude. The 12th-century losses of the Ebro basin and of central Portugal were simply irrevocable amputations. The 11th-century loss of Toledo and the Tagus basin was disputed long and hard, but that process scarcely disguised the slow but accumulating enemy advance up to the very borders of Andalucía itself. Some small gain was realized out of all this as Muslim refugees from the north settled within the reduced areas of the south. We are unable to gauge the volume of such immigration, and the likelihood is that any net gain in population was more than offset by the flight of its Mozarab population in increasing numbers to the now visibly potent northern realms of their coreligionists. Nor is there any indication that the Muslim population of Andalucía itself was growing in absolute numbers at this time, and the influx of Berbers from North Africa seems to have been almost exclusively composed of administrators, soldiers, and a few merchants. In demographic terms, Muslim Iberia was a static society if an increasingly homogeneous one in religious character.

The new Berber dominance itself, Murābit or Muwāhhid, introduced little change or development beyond the obvious. The fact is that the contact between North Africa and Andalucía visibly improved the agriculture and the practical arts of the former, but they, were relatively too primitive to contribute much in return. Beyond its centralization in the hands of the sons, grandsons, nephews, and cousins of the reigning North African emir, government changed almost not at all. It still remained familial in character, with its legitimacy resting upon the essentially religious credentials of the ruling house. This unity, combined with the ability to draw upon human resources from beyond the Straits, increased the military potential of Iberian Islam spectacularly, but it also reduced the ability of the government to respond to local needs or conditions. In institutional terms, one can detect virtually no change in the internal government of Andalucía, beyond, perhaps, an increased reliance upon written communication and instructions which followed upon the greater distances now involved.[1]

The same sort of *stasis* appears also to characterize the economic life of Andalucía. The contemporary geographer and indefatigable traveler, al-Idrisī, described it as thriving, varied, and prosperous, but he does not mention innovations.[2] Nor does one find elsewhere evidence of that geographical expansion into new territories and previously uncultivated tracts which was so typical of the Christian north during the period. Such expansion in the world of farming did take place notably in North Africa, on the other hand, with the importation of Andalucian techniques. The frontier, so to speak, of Iberian Islam had become the plains of Morocco and Algiers. At the same time, the increase of Andalucían trade responded to the new opportunities in the markets of North Africa. It was also stimulated by the increased availability of gold from central Africa, flowing from the Berber hegemony there. The fourteen known mints for gold coinage which functioned in early 12th-century Andalucía afford striking proof of the continuing wealth of this society.

The general cultural and intellectual vigor of Iberian Islam is also evident, although there were some inevitable reversals. The taifa courts disappeared after 1090, and patrons, indeed practitioners, of the life of the mind like the poet–king al-Mutamid of Sevilla or the historian–king Abd Allah of Granada would pass from the scene. Then, too, although the dynamic that may have created them was nurtured partially in the lost world of Islam, the intellectual phenomenon of Toledo, Zaragoza, or Barcelona will now be displayed within a northern, Christian context. Nevertheless, it is difficult to speak of the cultural life of Spanish Islam during the 12th Century without resorting to the term "brilliant." In general, fashion dictates that the Muwāhhid get better marks for the patronage of culture than the Murābit. That seems less than just. The movements were essentially the same, at least to the non-Muslim. Although they can and should be distinguished theologically, both were, for example, intransigently opposed to such frivolities as poetry, music, and polite court life during their formative periods yet came to indulge all of these shortly after they achieved imperial power. Both insisted, to

---

[1] This condition makes a general survey such as Anwar G. Chejne, *Muslim Spain: Its History and Culture* (Minneapolis, 1974) largely adequate in its description of governmental structures and practices, even though that author does not attend to the chronological background as well as he does his coverage of intellectual trends.

[2] Al-Idrisī, *Description de l'Afrique et de l'Espagne* (Paris, 1866), translated from the Arabic by Reinhart Dozy, is still fresh and readable.

the extent possible, on fundamentalist religious orthodoxy among Muslims, and were sometimes guilty of persecution, exile, and even judicial murder of religious deviants from it. If anything, the record of the Muwāhhid is worse, in that they were also much less tolerant of the other "people of the book." However much they might patronize the Muslim artist or thinker, it is indisputable that they bore the responsibility for the increasing emigration of Mozarabs and Jews from Andalucía which resulted from their harsher policies. The loss of variety in cultural and intellectual life that ensued must be laid at their door.

In general, the 12th-century artistic and mental life of Iberian Islam was highly traditional; that is, its tutelage to the Near Eastern masters continued, although with local refinements. Literary as well as religious pilgrimage to the Near East remained important. Education became even more dominated by the mosque with the reduction of princely patronage, which could only mean that its purpose and activity remained largely exegetical. Grammatical and literary studies functioned as auxiliaries to this type of learning and therefore, were also prominent. Even science and philosophy emphasized mastery of the Greek, antique heritage, its practical application, and its development. The same approach characterized the utilization of Indian and Persian mathematics and astronomy.

Poetry – of love, nature, and heroics – continued to occupy central place, usual in a court setting where recitation was much more common than reading. Even philosophers – ibn Bājjah, for example – composed poetry; it was the traditional mark of an educated man. Still, the classical language and meters were being modified. Especially noteworthy was the rise of two new forms, which employed, to some extent, the meters and even the language of the Romance tongue. These were the *muwashshah* and the *zajal*, which first achieved wide popularity in the Murābit period. The Córdoban, ibn Quzman (1100–1160), made his reputation in this genre.

Nevertheless, perhaps the finest flowering of the culture of al-Andalus appeared in prose; a sign of a more widespread literacy among the elite. The most familiar of these works are religious and philosophical ones. Indeed, the central intellectual problem of this period produced a series of thinkers preoccupied with the relationship of faith and reason. For ibn Bājjah of Zaragoza (1070–1138), this conundrum inspired a work, called *The Rule of the Solitary*, which advocated a withdrawal from the society of the day whose behavior rarely matched its religious ideal. Alone, the superior individual could construct for himself a truly ethical life based upon the prescriptions of logic and the study of human nature. Although not itself a theological *Summa*, the work of Avempace, as he came to be called in the Latin West, had notable impact on the development of the thought of individuals as diverse as Albertus Magnus, Ramon Llull, and Averröes.

Ibn Tufayl (1105–1185), born in Almería, was an admirer of ibn Bājjah, but chose to cast his own work, *Alive, Son of Awake*, in the form of a romance. One protagonist, Hāyy, grows up in solitude on a desert isle and constructs his own religion based on natural philosophy; the other, Asal, is raised in the tradition of Islam. Together, the two attempt a reform of religion in a neighboring society. Their failure convinces them that the masses can only be ruled by the dictates of faith. On the other hand, exceptional individuals will find, that philosophic and religious truth are different paths to the same God and that this understanding can be acted upon only in relative solitude. The two friends will retire to an uninhabited island to live and worship together.

Unlike his heroes, ibn Tufayl stood squarely in the midst of the political life of the day. He held a variety of administrative posts in the Muwāhhid government, becoming finally the *vizier* and personal physician of the Muwāhhid emir Abū Yakūb (1163–1184). Like many of the intellectuals, he wrote not only on religion and philosophy but also on astronomy and medicine, and was the sort of person who would both grace and prove useful in a royal court. The central conceit of his romance, the device of a human being growing up in near-complete isolation from others of his kind, was destined to have a long history in subsequent European literature. He was also the court patron of the more famous ibn Rushd, or Averröes (1126–1198), to the Latin West.

The latter was a Cordoban and, like most of his fellows, a polymath. He wrote not only on religion and philosophy but on medicine, astronomy, philology, and law. Thanks to his patron, ibn Tufayl, he was also involved in political life as a *qādī* in Sevilla, as a chief *qādī* in Córdoba, and finally as court physician himself. He was prominent under Abū Yakūb, and, for a time, under his successor, Abū Yūsuf (1184–1199); but he was accused of heresy, his books were burned, and he was forced into exile in 1195 by pressure from the *faqīh*, who were alarmed by the tenor of his thought. This was expressed chiefly in his *Commentaries* on the various philosophical works of Aristotle, which maintained the integrity of the philosophical road to truth, even when it appeared to conflict with the data of Revelation. He was prepared to accept the eternity of matter and the unity of the active intellect in all rational beings. His identification of the problems and the fashion in which he posited them would contribute to much of the intellectual fireworks of the Christian west during the 13th and 14th Centuries. Thomas Aquinas and Siger of Brabant were extensively influenced by his work, and many of his positions, restated, were condemned at the University of Paris in the late 13th Century.

The career of Averröes represents the high water mark of the attempt at a philosophical expression of Islam. The future belonged, as did in large measure the 12th Century itself, to fundamentalist reaffirmations of the traditional theology, as represented by the Murābit and Muwāhhid movements. But other attempts to enrich or enlarge that theology were also ultimately rejected. The Almerian theologian ibn Árif (1088–1141) would gain temporary fame, which resulted in a teaching career in Zaragoza and then in Valencia for a time. However, he was a leading exponent of Sufism – the practice of asceticism and contemplation that led one to a direct experience of God – and so was exiled from Iberia, first to Ceuta, and then to Marrakesh. At the latter he enjoyed the favor of the emir for a time, but died, nonetheless, in exile, reputedly of poison.[3]

A combination of disciplines, we should say, of religion, philosophy, and humane letters, dominated the learning of the day, but other subjects were pursued and often by the same figures. The Cordoban al-Mawāīnī (d. 1168), who worked in Granada, provided a schema in seven parts, *The Comfort of Hearts and the Protection of Youth*, of the branches and hierarchy of learning. Islamic medicine in particular knew the Greeks Galen and Hippocrates and made significant advances from that point in botanical classification, pharmacology, and medical diagnosis. In geography al-Idrisī (1100–1166), born in Ceuta and educated in Córdoba, settled finally in the Sicily of the Norman king Roger II. There he compiled the results of his travels, those of contemporaries, and the Greek sources to construct a geography of the world useful still to the historian. A considerable corpus of historical works existed, but much is known only through later excerpting or mention. The *Djahira* of ibn Bassām of Santarém (d. 1147) provided vivid portraits of the political and literary world of his time in the tradition of the *adab* genre.

In astronomy and mathematics, the greatest work had already been done in the taifa period by figures who are usually discussed in connection with the transmission of their work to the Latin West. But al-Bitruji, a disciple of ibn Tufayl, produced a work on astronomy which had contemporary as well as subsequent importance. In

---

[3] W. Montgomery Watt, *Islamic Philosophy and Theology* (Edinburgh, 1962), furnishes a clear guide to a complex and controverted subject.

the realm of applied botany, mention needs to be made of the *Book of Agriculture* by al-Zakariyya.[4]

The continuity of African dominance is also illustrated by the close ties between Muslim and Jewish culture. Thus, Abraham bar Hayya (1065–1136) drew on Islamic science in his mathematical and astronomical works which circulated among the Jews of Cataluña. Moses ben Ezra (1055–1138), who served the Granadan taifa before the Murābit annexation but sought refuge in the Christian north after 1090, was an accomplished poet in the Arabic fashion and composed *muwashshah* on the theme of love as well as *adab*, or collections of biographies of literary figures.

However, the greatest of the contemporary Jewish scholars was Moses Maimónides of Córdoba (1135–1204). Some of his writings included the *Misneh Torah*, or Hebrew law code, a commentary on the *Mishnah*, written in Arabic, and his most famous *Guide for the Perplexed*, also in Arabic. In the latter he took up the central question of the times – the relation of philosophy and theology – which so exercised his older contemporary, ibn Rushd. In a philosophy based upon Aristotle as well as contemporary thinkers, Moses established the independence of that discipline but also attempted to employ it to defend a natural religion, based upon reason rather than Revelation. Although he recognized that the latter was essential to the faith of Israel, as it actually existed, his distinction between that faith and human reason, which was unable to affirm or deny particular aspects of the former, outraged many of the rabbis and the Jewish community. Ultimately, Maimónides's philosophical thought was to find its most lasting effects in the thought of the Christian, scholastic philosophers, and Judaism would turn away from philosophical exegesis and natural religion as would Islam.

Maimónides's life was illustrative of the troubled state of Andalucía under the Berber dynasties. His family and himself became refugees after the conquest of Córdoba by the Muwāhhid in 1148 and spent some years wandering in the peninsula. In 1160 the partial relaxation of the harassment of the Jews encouraged the family to settle in Fez in Morocco. Yet these surroundings were far from congenial, and Maimónides eventually left for the Near East in 1165. There his fame increased enormously, and he would spend the latter years of his life as physician to the court of the new master of Near Eastern Islam, Saladin, for his work in medicine and pharmaceutics was even more famous than his philosophy among contemporaries.

[4] Juan Vernet, *La cultura hispanoárabe en Orient y Occidente* (Barcelona, 1978), is an authoritative survey both of the sources of Iberian science and of its transmission to the Latin world.

The difficulties of the time would promote still another attitude which would gradually gain strength within the Iberian Jewish community. It is reflected by Moses ben Ezra (d. 1135), a poet of no small merit, who fled the Murābit advance to take refuge in León–Castilla. There he reacted strongly against the tendency of the Jewish community to assimilate much of the manners and mores of the Christians among whom they lived. This reaction in favor of a more thoroughgoing cultural separatism was heard even more strongly in the words of a fellow poet, Judah Halevi of Toledo (d. 1150). Halevi rejected attempts to explore natural theology in favor of a strict dependence upon Revelation. In his major work, *Kusari*, he compared the three religions of Christianity, Islam, and Judaism in a series of imaginary dialogues set in the 10th-century kingdom of the Khazars. Of course, the palm is awarded to Judaism and to Revelation. Judaism is both peculiar and superior by reason of the Covenant, the sacred *Torah*, and the special bond to Palestine. Halevi urged Jews to recognize their uniqueness and to reject accommodation with either Christian or Muslim. Shortly before his death, he came to the conclusion that he must return to Palestine. He did in fact die in the Near East. Now obviously some of these ideas were regarded as extreme by the contemporary Jewish community. Nevertheless, their influence boded ill for that extraordinarily fecund intellectual affinity between Muslim and Jew which had marked the previous three centuries in al-Andalus.

Christian Iberian Society in the Mid–12th Century

Perhaps the most significant difference in the respective evolutions of Muslim and Christian Iberia is that while the former lost control of its own political life the latter did not. The north of the peninsula experienced the most powerful of influences and major assistance from Europe beyond the Pyrenees, but at no point was its own independence of action even threatened. On reflection, that fact seems all the more remarkable because the societies to its north were somewhat more developed in many respects, and the flow of cultural borrowing was certainly from north to south. The artistic and technological superiority of Andalucian to Berber produced just the opposite effect, as it had become the tutor of North Africa. Christian Iberia was as fortunate in the heterogenous character of the European world as Andalucía was unfortunate in the newfound unity of the African West.

Then, too, Christian Iberia gradually took on a political diversity that mirrored that of Europe generally. While the taifas were being absorbed into one or the other Berber empire, León–Castilla, Aragón–Barcelona, Portugal, and Navarra were establishing themselves as independent realms, each with a vigorous political life of its own. The northern Iberian kingdoms may have begun the period as scarcely more than the reflections of able and determined warlords, much like the taifa kingdoms, but, by its end, each had gone far toward becoming a realm identified with a particular dynasty whose legitimacy was increasingly difficult to challenge. Monarchical institutions in each might as yet be exceedingly few, and those structured only in the loosest of fashions, but each had its *curia regis* of king, family, officials, churchmen, and nobles. A recognizable chancery had appeared everywhere with its own style, if precious few clerks. Even its chief was not yet uniformly styled "chancellor." The chief instrument of royal government was the royal fisc, and a *majordomo* was the court official theoretically in charge of it, while local *merinos* actually enjoyed great independence in the care of both the king's property and the king's business in their jurisdictions. The royal army was, unless the host was mustered for a campaign, the royal bodyguard. The *alférez* who commanded it, under the king, was also a court official. Coinage was a royal prerogative, but it was farmed. Justice was supposed to be a royal prerogative as well, but it had either been sold or farmed, as had the tolls of roads, bridges, and ports. In brief, royal government was short of reach and spastic in application but it enjoyed a unique prestige which any taifa king would have envied. When it could divine the real interests of its subjects and assume the initiative in their realization, the royal person could become well-nigh irresistible, at least for a time.

The greatest and most significant illustration of that fact was the royal role in the repopulation so characteristic of the period. The king's action was crucial in two respects. Everywhere he was the sole source of legitimate title to lands not previously occupied and of the civil order which prevailed in them. In addition, the king was just as obviously the one person who could ordinarily muster the force and following necessary to wrest major new lands from the Muslim. But the crown did not create the excess of population which flowed into those territories. Moreover, as they were in virtually everything else, the great nobles of the realm were the crown's indispensable lieutenants in the carrying through of the work so begun. They became the castellans of fortresses in liberated territories, the organizers of great estates therein, and even the promoters of peasant migration into them. This is, indeed, the period of the formation of many of those great noble houses whose names will resound thereafter in the history of the Iberian kingdoms. From the Moncada of Cataluña, to the Haro of la Rioja, the Lara and the Castro of Castilla, or the Trastamara of far Galicia, it is one of the great ages of the formation of noble lineages based upon a new propertied and political *puissance*.[5]

Both the Muslim south and the Christian north were basically agricultural societies, and Andalucía was still, at this period, the possessor of the more sophisticated agricultural technology. Still, the north had learned enough of the techniques of irrigation, of dry farming, of milling, and all the rest, to be able to exploit its more varied environment and to appropriate additional lands on its borders as opportunity offered. In contrast to the static society of Iberian Islam, it was most clearly an expanding world, in the most direct meaning of the phrase.

Beginning with the river basin of the Mondego in the reign of Fernando I, the Galician–Portuguese peasants had successively occupied the basin of the Lis, and were engaged in appropriating the northern half of the basin of the Tajo itself during the reign of Alfonso Enríquez. The population of León–Castilla had drifted massively into the southern basin of the Duero during the reign of Alfonso VI, calling into renewed being centers such as Segovia, Salamanca, and Avila. Despite subsequent setbacks, during that of Alfonso VII it was also filling up the plain north of the Tajo and pushing small settlements south of that river itself.[6] In the east Christian farmers had finally broken out of upland Aragón and coastal Barcelona and taken command of the agriculture of the entire basin of the Ebro by the period of Ramón Berenguer IV.

In the realm of commerce, however, a comparison reveals that much of the old inferiority to Andalucía still prevailed. Trade in the north still is best described as local. With few exceptions towns were little more than redistribution points for the agricultural products of their environs. While they were clearly growing in extent, their government was largely in the hands of their bishop in the case of episcopal sees, or the king or a local magnate for noncathedral towns. That they should have their local customs or law codified in

[5] Salvador de Moxó, "De la nobleza vieja a la nobleza nueva," in *Cuadernos de Historia* 3 (1969):1–210, and *Repoblación y sociedad en la España cristiana medieval* (Madrid, 1979), has made the essential beginning to the renewed study of this phenomenon.
[6] Julio González, *Repoblación de Castilla La Nueva*, 2 vols. (Madrid, 1976), has done a masterly survey of the phenomenon in the basin of the Tajo. Earlier he had assembled much of the evidence for that of the southern half of the basin of the Duero in a long series of articles in a variety of journals.

fueros was increasingly common. Still, while such a document made explicit some particular local statutes and specified some local offices, town officers were chosen by their respective superiors who were the source of the law which the former administered. In this respect it would be misleading to speak of town government as such.[7] Tradesmen and artisans had clearly so increased in number that the authorities began to treat them as a separate social group. They sometimes even possessed strength sufficient to revolt against their superiors, especially when times were otherwise troubled, but they were not yet so wealthy or essential as to make good a permanent government of their own.

Nevertheless, the new trans-Duero region had become the focus of a thriving *transhumance* which brought the livestock of Asturias and the Rioja seasonally into the regions of Segovia, Avila, and Salamanca. Already it was sufficiently important for al-Idrisī to take note of it, and at some point it would change the social complexion of the eastern two of these territories, filling them up with speakers of the Castilian rather than Leonese. At the same time, a corridor of some long-distance trade had grown up along the *camino de Santiago*. The pilgrim traffic from the north had stimulated modest development in cities from Jaca and Pamplona in the east to Burgos, León, and Santiago de Compostela in the west.

Such seaborne trade as existed was largely carried in the ships of others. On the Atlantic coast the tiny ports of Portugal and Galicia doubtless had their modest fishing fleets but little more. The chronicles record the occasional presence of both foreign pirates and foreign traders, from England to the north and Muslim Andalucía to the south, but the region had not begun to develop an active Atlantic trade of its own. Along the Bay of Biscay in the north the situation was similar. The spectacular development of the Basque ports was more than a century away still, and local fishing was the norm. Only on the coast of Cataluña do we find something more, but even there it is hard to gauge the active contribution of Iberians themselves.

The most prominent seamen along the eastern coast were the Genoese. By mid-century they had their factories in Catalan Barcelona and Tortosa, and in Muslim Valencia, Denia, and Almería to the south. The Italians reluctantly shared their dominance with the

[7] The chapter on "The Government of Towns" in Bernard F. Reilly, *The Kingdom of León–Castilla under Queen Urraca, 1109–1126* (Princeton, N.J., 1982), pp. 314–51, is probably still as good a short summary of their status as currently exists in English. The question of the *fueros* is still bedeviled by the medieval practice of simply rewriting the original document when one's rights would be subsequently amplified.

Muslim seafarers of the Balearics, where the last of the Murābits enjoyed a genuine, if autumnal, brilliance in the late 12th Century. Those Muslim islets had withstood the attempts made against them by the combined fleets of Pisa, the Languedoc, and Cataluña between 1114 and 1116 and would see another century yet of independence. But Catalan ships had participated in that attempt and Raman Berenguer III had captained it. That fact alone argues that the naval capacity, hence the trade, of Cataluña had progressed beyond simple fishing. Although its presence in the western Mediterranean is almost impossible to detect so early, a seaborne, coasting trade with the Muslim south and the French littoral to the north is the least indicated by the episode. However, the formation of a Catalan sea empire in those waters still lay some seventy years in the future.

Institutional Change and Diversification in Christian Iberia

Beyond the dynasty, that permanent reality most pervasive and influential within each of the northern kingdoms was the Christian church. Yet that church itself was both a dynamic and complex structure and cannot be understood as a simple unity. Its most essential organizational element was the episcopal diocese, but that geographical grid had to be radically adjusted to fit the new political reorganization as well as the expansion southward of the Christian realms. By the mid–12th Century much of that had been accomplished, although, of its nature, completion would wait on the final extinction of Muslim political power in the peninsula.

With the emergence of an independent Portugal under Alfonso Enríquez after 1128, the archbishops of Braga found an essential ally in the struggle they had been waging with the prelates of Santiago de Compostela for the past four decades. In Late Antiquity Braga had been the metropolitan see of all of Galicia and Astorga as well. But in the new world of the kingdom of León–Castilla it was little more than a frontier bishopric of modest importance. Against it was arrayed the growing influence of the great shrine–church of Saint James which sought and obtained both independence of Braga for itself in 1095 and then the very metropolitan dignity in 1120, both by the invocation of growing papal authority. The emergence of Santiago de Compostela as a rival in its own jurisdiction was fought but inevitably lost by Braga, which had meanwhile become the chief see of an emerging Portugal. Alfonso Enríquez would successfully employ his own power and influence after 1128 to keep Braga independent of both the Leonese church and the Leonese kingdom. He would make it the metropolitan church of his new Portugal. In that process he would himself, enlist, the aid of the papacy to secure a new ecclesiastical province for Braga, composed of the bishoprics of his realm from Oporto in the north to Lisbon in the south.[8]

The Leonese kings and church had even more complicated problems. After the conquest of Toledo in 1085, Alfonso VI obtained papal recognition of that diocese's metropolitan rank and its position as primatial see for the entire peninsula. He also obtained papal recognition for the sees of Burgos, Oviedo, and León, which had not existed in antiquity but were autochthonous creations of the *Reconquista*. He had secured, as well, the independence of the diocese of Burgos from a restored Catalan metropolitanate of Tarragona. In 1120 his daughter and successor, Urraca, reluctantly had to accept the papal award of metropolitan status to Santiago de Compostela and the simultaneous concession to the latter of suffragan sees in Avila and Salamanca. This erection of another metropolitan church within the kingdom complicated and contravened royal policy which had made Toledo its chosen instrument of ecclesiastical control since 1085. Urraca did have the satisfaction of seeing a new bishopric at Zamora formed out of former territories of Braga in 1122 and papal recognition of that process. Still, Alfonso VI, Urraca, and Alfonso VII, in turn, failed in the attempt to make good an effective primatial dignity of Toledo over all the Christian churches of Iberia. That ecclesiastical failure was the echo of their inability to make their secular authority over the entire peninsula, embodied in the imperial title, a political reality.[9]

Alfonso VI seems to have made it one of the pillars of his claims in response to the assertion of Pope Gregory VII of papal suzerainty in

[8] Unfortunately, modern church histories tend to project present organizational realities and political prejudices back upon a period which knew little of either. With that in mind, Fortunato de Almeida, *História da Igreja em Portugal*, Vol. 1 (Oporto, new ed., 1967), is useful. Carl Erdmann, ed., "Papsturkunden in Portugal," in *AGWG*, Philologisch-historische Klasse, N.S. Vol. 20 (Berlin, 1927), is essential to an understanding, as is the same author's *Das Papsttum und Portugal in ersten Jahrhundert der Portugiesischen Geschichte* (Berlin, 1928). Antonio López-Ferreiro, *Historia de la Santa Apostólica Metropolitana Iglesia de Santiago de Compostela*, 11 vols. (Santiago de Compostela, 1898–1911), is the venerable and still indispensable guide to the fortunes of that institution. A lively guide in English to that church in this period is Richard A. Fletcher, *Saint James's Catapult: The Life and Times of Diego Gelmírez of Santiago de Compostela* (Oxford, 1984).

[9] Again with much care for the detection of modern bias, Javier Fernández Conde, ed., *La historia de la iglesia an España*, Vol. 2 (Madrid, 1982), is an adequate if uninspired guide. The papal documents for León–Castilla have not been edited, although Demetrio Mansilla, *La documentación pontificia hasta Innocencio III, 965–1216*, (Rome, 1955), made a strong start.

the peninsula in 1073 and again in 1077. Precisely what the pope had in mind is difficult to fathom, but his claims were never admitted. Instead, in 1077 Alfonso himself began to adopt the style of "imperator totius ispanie" in his diplomas.[10] It was a style he maintained down until his death in 1109, and its use must then have seemed reasonable in view of his commanding position among the Christian realms of the peninsula. During the contest of Urraca and Alfonso I of Aragón it fell on hard times by the very nature of things. With the accession of Alfonso VII the imperial title again became central to the attempt to reassert the hegemony of León–Castilla. Alfonso VII staged an imperial coronation in León in 1135 and insisted that the new kings of Portugal and Navarra and the count–king of Aragón–Barcelona do homage to him. He also exacted homage from such Muslim rulers as were subject to him from time to time. The papacy never reasserted its own claims to suzerainty but appears to have ignored those of León–Castilla. On the latter's division after the death of Alfonso VII in 1157, the question became moot.

In the northeast an especially complicated situation saw many of the ancient sees, which had migrated north into the mountains during the long period of Muslim dominance, return to their traditional sites as the Aragonese reconquest overwhelmed the taifas of Zaragoza, Lérida, and Tortosa in turn. Also, the counts of Barcelona had long been eager to pry the Catalan bishoprics free of the authority of Narbonne. They succeeded finally when Urban II in 1089 allowed the reestablishment of the old metropolitan see of Tarragona, even if the new prelates had to wait another half century before they could actually take up residence in their archiepiscopal city on the frontier. When the counts of Barcelona became the count–kings of Aragón and Barcelona after 1137, Tarragona also became the metropolitan see of Aragón, and the churches of each of the Iberian kingdoms had become organizationally coterminous with their respective realms. Their ecclesiastical authority would march south in step with the secular authority of their monarchs.[11]

This fundamental recasting of the Iberian church involved bitter local quarrels, which in many cases continued into the 13th Century.

---

[10] The use of the imperial title and the rationale behind that use has been the subject of long, often acrimonious debate among historians, usually with a most imperfect knowledge of the royal documents in which it was alone expressed. For the most recent summation of its reappearance in this period, see Bernard F. Reilly, ed., *The Kingdom of León–Castilla under King Alfonso VI, 1065–1109* (Princeton, N.J., 1988), pp. 95–115.

[11] The tiny realm of Navarra is the obvious exception. Its sole bishopric, Pamplona, remained subject to Tarragona.

To solve them in terms of a legitimacy that everyone could respect led both the monarchs and the bishops to appeal with ever-increasing frequency to the emerging papal power at Rome. Thus, local imperatives combined with the general church reform movement of the 11th and 12th Centuries to establish Roman authority as a regular element of ecclesiastical government and politics in the peninsula. In particular, Toledo, and even Santiago de Compostela, would sometimes be commissioned as papal legates for parts of Iberia, but special legates from Rome itself had been frequent there since 1090. The increasing ties to the Roman pontiff would also change the complexion of the Iberian church in other fashions to bring it more into conformity with practice elsewhere in Europe.

One distinctive feature of Iberia was the possession of a local Christian liturgy, the Mozarabic Rite. The Roman reformers had early fastened upon this practice as offensive, even vaguely suspect in doctrinal terms, and demanded that it be conformed to Roman practice as part of the price of their cooperation in the general reorganization of the Iberian church. In the second half of the 11th Century the kings of Aragón, Navarra, and León–Castilla capitulated to this demand, the latter kingdom in 1080. One may wonder if the actually modest liturgical changes involved were proportionate, religiously, to the ecclesiastical revolution which was worked in many of the peninsular churches, at least partially in their name.[12] In this, as in so many other cases, papal authority in the peninsula was sufficiently potent to initiate change there, but was seldom able to control or direct the real alterations then effected by local ambitions in its name.

Given its then vastly greater extent and influence, the most important effects were worked in the Leonese kingdom. The enforced change of rite may have been involved, in the *interregnum*, in the episcopate at Astorga (1080–1082), in the revolt in Galicia led by the bishop of Compostela (1086), with the deposition of the archbishop of Braga (1091), and certainly with the anarchy in the see of Coimbra (1088–1091). But it seems that these events paled with the changes worked on the southern frontier as the *Reconquista* advanced. Everywhere, in all likelihood, the local prelate was ousted and one of the conquerors installed in his stead as the sees involved were treated as part of the spoils of a successful campaign. Here, as in the Near East of the Crusaders, the difference of rite must have been the

[12] A series of studies in English dealing with this question is found in Bernard F. Reilly, ed., *Santiago, St.-Denis, and Saint Peter* (New York, 1985). For a briefer but more recent account, see Reilly, *Alfonso VI*, pp. 95–115.

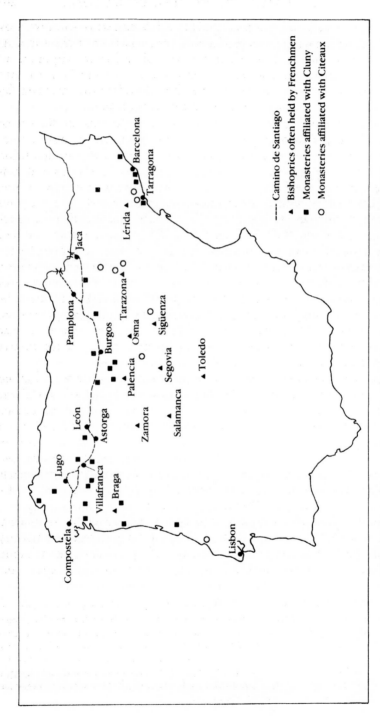

Figure 7 Avenues of French influence in 12th-century Christian Iberia

handiest excuse. In Toledo after 1085, the conquest was followed by the installation of the French Cluniac Bernard as new archbishop. At Valencia, the conquest of the city by the Cid led to the appointment of the French Cluniac Jerome as bishop. At Lisbon in 1147 Alfonso Enríquez repaid his debt to the English Crusaders for their help by naming the Englishman Gilbert, as the new prelate.[13]

The *Reconquista*, then, as it advanced southward to subject or drive out the Muslim population, also resulted in the modification of the religious practices of the liberated Mozarabs and the imposition of new religious superiors as well as new secular leaders and customs. We cannot follow the latter two as closely as we might like, but it is very clear that the imposition of French bishops took place more generally in León–Castilla. That process began with the selection of the French Cluniac Bernard of Sauvetot as the archbishop of Toledo in 1086. Over the next four decades Bernard would be the chief counsellor and support of Alfonso VI and then of his daughter, Urraca. From his commanding position as archbishop, primate of Iberia, sometimes papal legate, and royal *confidant*, he would be instrumental in filling up the sees of the realm with prelates of largely French Cluniac extraction. Many of these were Cluniac monks whom he recruited in visits to France and installed first as canons in the cathedral chapter of Toledo.

Of the archepiscopal sees, Toledo was held by Bernard himself (1086–1125) and then by his protégé Raymond (1125–1151). Braga went to the French Gerald (1096–1108), succeeded by the French Maurice Bourdin (1109–1118); henceforth an effectively independent Portugal would give that prize to scions of the local nobility. In Galicia, again, the strength of regional particularism largely shielded the bishoprics from such appointments, but Santiago de Compostela was held briefly by the Dalmatio (1094–1095), Berenguer (1150–1151), and Bernard (1151–1152), all Frenchmen.

In general, one may say that in the older lands of Asturias, Galicia, León, and Castilla la Vieja, local power structures were sufficiently strong to prevent the imposition of candidates totally from without. But in the restored sees coming into being on the frontier, the

[13] The subject has not received the attention it deserves. Traditional church historians have simply assumed that such sees were empty at the time or that the incumbent was killed in the siege. Even if such unfounded assertions should be true, it is clear that the local Christian communities lost control of their own church in the process. At Toledo the Mozarabs at least maintained a series of parishes in the city which continued to employ the old rite; but that community possessed unusual strength, and the danger of Muslim reconquest had for so long been a real one that their interests had to be placated in some degree.

process had full rein. Installed by the Cid at Valencia (1097–1102), after the fall of that city Jerome was transferred and became bishop of Salamanca (1102–1120), from which position he also administered the sees of Avila and Zamora. Salamanca was again in the hands of a Frenchman, Berenguer, from 1135 to 1150. Burgo de Osma from its restoration in 1102 was in the hands of the French Peter (1101–1109), succeeded by the French Raymond (1109–1126), and the French Bertrand (1128–1140), and the French Stephen (1141–1147), before passing to Juan Téllez in 1148. Segovia and Palencia followed the same pattern.[14]

Still, it must be said that these south French prelates quickly took on the advocacy of the traditional privileges of those churches which they inherited. They did not form a cabal in any sense that we can detect. Nonetheless, they could not have been but united by a certain sympathy in their shared exile and marked by the same set of convictions deriving from their common, early experiences. The presence of these outsiders may have been influential in speeding the process of formation of cathedral chapters in the peninsula. These typical institutional growths were common to the church structure all over Western Europe in the 11th and 12th Centuries. In an earlier period the liturgical needs of cathedrals seem most often to have been met by a monastic community attached to the cathedral. Loosely related to the reform movement of those centuries was the formation of a corporation of resident canons who saw to the chanting of the liturgical hours, the saying of solemn Masses, and such. This new ecclesiastical corporation was shortly to develop its own offices and officers, its own procedures, eventually its own seal, and, quite early on, its own claim to a portion of the revenues of the cathedral. By the middle of the 12th Century the cathedral chapter will have become the electoral college of its bishopric, at least in canon law.

Now, like so much of the history of the Iberian church, the emergence of the cathedral chapter has been insufficiently studied. Documents forged to settle later property disputes have often been taken at their face value.[15] However, it is eminently clear that chapters emerged everywhere in Iberia in the first half of the 12th

---

[14] Richard A. Fletchere, *The Episcopate in the Kingdom of León in the Twelfth Century* (Oxford, 1978), is enlightening for the geographical area treated. Bernard F. Reilly, "On Getting to be a Bishop in León–Castile: The 'Emperor' Alfonso VII and the Post-Gregorian Church," *Studies in Medieval and Renaissance History* 1 (1978), pp. 37–68, is another partial study.

[15] Tomás Villacorta Rodríguez, *El cabildo catedral de León* (León, 1974), or Juan Ramón López-Arevalo, *Un cabildo catedral de La Vieja Castilla, Avila* (Madrid, 1966), are studies valuable for the latter 12th Century and subsequent periods.

Century. Their formation was motivated by the desire to reform the moral and educational levels of the bishop's *familia*, at least in part. But at Toledo, for example, the chapter came into being as a "French" innovation, intended to support Archbishop Bernard against the Mozarabic clergy of the see. At Santiago de Compostela, on the other hand, the chapter emerged as the first instrument of Bishop Gelmírez's consolidation of his control in that troubled see. The Iberian bishops were, after all, only, doing exactly what the reform party had itself done at Rome in the mid–11th Century when they installed themselves as the cardinals of that church and then voted themselves the electoral college of the papacy in 1059. The richness of the development is the main point, however. Like the society in which it inhered, the Iberian church was becoming more and more complex and its power more widely shared. While that growth could be enormously productive of quarrels, it also gave a great latitude to local initiative in an age whose conditions rewarded just that.

This elaboration of structures in Christian Iberia, which at the same time enriched their own experience and linked them more closely with Europe beyond the Pyrenees, is nowhere more marked than in the case of the new religious orders. The Burgundian abbey of Cluny enjoyed great prestige with the dynasty of León from the time of Fernando I, who initiated an annual subsidy of 1,000 dinars to it about 1050. But his son, Alfonso VI, not only doubled that subsidy but began the donation of royal monasteries in León–Castilla to Cluny. Between 1073 and 1079 he ceded no fewer than five monasteries of the realm to that house. The example of the Leónese crown was imitated by the noble houses of the kingdom and in neighboring realms, so that, by the mid–12th Century, the possessions of Cluny formed a chain of dependencies of some twenty-two houses stretching from Barcelona to Coimbra. These centers were linked to Burgundy by ties of personnel, administration, finance, and spiritual affinity. They were points from which European and French influence radiated in not inconsiderable fashion.[16]

But from the beginning of the 12th Century the Black Monks of Cluny increasingly had to share their prestige and influence as reformers with the White Monks of Citeaux. When the sons of Saint

[16] The indispensable modern source for this development is Charles J. Bishko, "Fernando I and the Origins of the Leónese–Castilian Alliance with Cluny," in *Studies in Medieval Spanish Frontier History* (London, 1980), pp. 1–136. It was published earlier in Spanish; see *CHE* 47–48 (1968):31–135; and 49–50 (1969):50–116.

Bernard of Clairvaux did begin to make their presence felt, an influx of the Cistercian order would result in Iberia as well as in other parts of Europe. In 1140 Alfonso VII drew on the new monks, from the Gascon house of l'Escale-Dieu, to organize the community of Fitero. Some nine years later the first Catalan houses, the equally famous Poblet and Santes Creus, were established. Portugal had to wait until Alfonso Enríquez installed the Cistercians in Alcobaça, between Lisbon and Coimbra, in 1153. By that time the number of such houses had grown to seven,and still another organizational thread would tie Iberia to Europe.

A third type of monasticism, again tied to the elaboration of French influence in the peninsula, was that of the new military orders – the Templars, the Hospitallers, and the Order of the Holy Sepulcher. However, their appearance was not as spectacular as originally planned in 1134. The will of Alfonso I *el Batallador* of Aragón had been set aside, and so the kingdom of Aragón was not to be divided among them. Nevertheless, in the subsequent decade the new count–kings of Aragón–Barcelona would grant them substantial concessions of property in the southern reaches of their realm. Even more so than Cluny and Citeaux, the crusading orders were great international organizations, and their spread in Iberia would bring that region into contact with a world well beyond even France. Although their beginnings in Aragón–Barcelona were spectacular, there are evidences of a humbler penetration into the other Christian realms of the north. This subject, too, is bedeviled by the crucial lacunae in critical studies of the royal charters of the period, although that is being remedied gradually.[17] In the latter 12th Century the European military orders were to inspire their Iberian counterparts, most notably, the Order of Santiago.

Iberia and the Making of the Medieval Western Mind

If generally during this period the Iberian peninsula was the beneficiary of political, economic, and cultural currents originating elsewhere, there is one striking exception in the realm of matters intellectual which deserves careful attention. This is the wholesale transmission of Greek, Roman, Indian, Persian, Jewish, and Muslim learning to the learned world of Western Europe north of the Pyrenees. In this transcendentally important labor the representatives

---

[17] For example, Alan J. Forey, *The Templars in the Crown of Aragon* (London, 1973), and Santos García Larragueta, *El gran priorado de Navarra de la Orden de San Juan de Jerusalén*, 2 vols. (Pamplona, 1957).

of all three communities, Jewish, Muslim, and Christian, collaborated in what was practically the final and, perhaps, the greatest product of their mutual experience.

Although this transfer of knowledge took place principally, under the aegis of León–Castilla, it would have been impossible without the assistance of scholars of the Muslim and Jewish communities, among whom literacy was so much more common. In the 11th and 12th Centuries the princes, nobles, and great merchants of Iberian Islam and Judaism were also men of letters who at least played at composing poetry and dabbled in philosophy and letters. Some of them were truly poets and philosophers, as we have seen. In the Iberian north, on the other hand, it will be the 13th Century before we can be sure of a king who could read and write. The nobility, as a class, were warriors rather than courtiers, and were wholly bereft of a cultural tradition of letters so far as we can determine. The merchant class had hardly begun to flower. Formal learning was a practical monopoly of the clergy.

The traditional learning of the Early Middle Ages continued, that is, the learning of "The Book." The clergy, some of them, learned Latin because it was the language of the Bible, and of the Psalter in particular, which supplied so many of the prayer texts of the liturgy, and of the Ordinals, that is, liturgical books of prayers and rubrics for the celebration of the Mass and the sacraments. In the course of mastering Latin they used some of the Latin texts of antiquity and in the process absorbed some of the classical letters, history, and philosophy. In addition to Sacred Scripture, their professional life almost demanded that they know something of the Latin Fathers and their commentaries on that text and on Christian life in general. Therefore, Augustine, Jerome, Ambrose, Gregory the Great, Boethius, Orosius, and Isidore of Sevilla were likely to be a part of their mental sustenance, in some degree at any rate.

If one asks what they then did with this intellectual training, the answer must be that they wrote professional literature when they wrote at all. If we exclude copying of sacred and religious texts, which was probably the most constant literary task to occupy them, then we must assume that they wrote biblical commentary of their own. They certainly wrote hymns and sermons. A series of translations of Latin sermons into Catalan, together with a commentary, survives from the early 12th Century.[18] In addition, they wrote saints' lives. A contemporary wrote a life of Archbishop Gerald of

[18] Roger Wright, *Late Latin and Early Romance in Spain and Carolingian France* (Liverpool, 1982), is one of the easier and most effective ways to get a quick sense of what was going on.

Braga; and a *vita* was done on Archbishop Bernard of Toledo, which was utilized by the 13th-century historians but seems not to have survived independently.[19] The more ambitious works that survive today, were undertaken to celebrate the pontificate of Archbishop Diego Gelmírez at Santiago de Compostela and the reign of Alfonso VI of León–Castilla.[20] Surely more general histories in the chronicle tradition were also written; however, at this writing, they do not appear to have survived, although their footsteps can be traced in the 13th-century practitioners of that genre.

What is to be remarked here is the absence of anything that might be called a court literature. In this regard, contrast with the contemporary literature of Andalucía is stark. But then, perhaps, we are looking, in the wrong place. A courtly literature was coming into existence, but it was a vernacular, unwritten form. In the first half of the 13th Century the historian Lucas of Túy would include in his chronicle materials plainly based on epic materials. These dealt, for example, with the legendary beginnings of the *Reconquista*, the victory of Pelayo over the Muslim at Covadonga in the mountains of Asturias in the 8th Century, and the warrior exploits of Bernardo del Carpio in the 9th. In the first half of the 12th Century the author of the *Historia Silense* was already employing elements from what appear to be Romance *gestae*, whose subjects were the tragic death of Sancho II of Castilla in 1072 before the walls of Zamora and the early adventures of his brother, Alfonso VI of León–Castilla.

Nevertheless, the most famous portion of this literature was of the career of Rodrigo Díaz de Vivar, *El Cid*. The scholarly tangle about the dating of these works reflects the complexities of the period itself.[21] The earliest, the *Carmen Campi Doctoris* and the *Historia Roderici*, are certainly learned Latin renderings of what were popular tales which may or may not have been previously written down. While these two pieces derive, as we have them, from the latter 12th

[19] Bernard F. Reilly, "Sources of the Fourth Book of Lucas of Tuy's 'Chronicon Mundi.'" *Classical Folia* 30 (1976):127–37, is one introduction into the mysteries of 12th-century literature in the peninsula. So much remains to be done that scholars may be happily occupied by it for the next half century.

[20] Emma Falque Rey, ed., *Historia Compostellana* (Turnholt, 1988), is a much needed edition of a work that is part diocesan register of properties and privileges, part hagiography, and part official biography, along with patches of independent works stitched into the fabric. Justo Pérez de Urbel and Atilano González Ruiz-Zorilla, eds., *Historia Silense* (Madrid, 1959), is a wayward history which devoted so much time to an introduction that it apparently never got beyond the initial seven years of Alfonso's forty-five-year reign.

[21] Richard A. Fletcher, *The Quest for El Cid* (New York, 1990), is a relatively painless introduction to these questions.

Century, the materials on which they were based likely belonged to the first half of the century. Of course, with the appearance of the *Cantar de mio Cid* itself in the first decade of the 13th Century we have an even newer phenomenon, the use of Old Spanish in a long written work. Literacy in it had obviously been achieved somewhat earlier and would soon triumph even in the royal chanceries when royal charters would begin to employ it. For our purposes, however, what matters is that the Cid tradition clearly has long roots, and that the courtly literature of the north was a vernacular one and quite different in content and much simpler in style than that of Andalucía.

Of course, the learned and the popular literatures of the north interacted and would do so increasingly. The mechanics of that process are difficult to follow, but the Latin learning of the monasteries and the cathedral chapters must always have had some effect upon the secular world about them. Prescriptions in canon law that the parish priest was responsible for the education of the local children had long existed, and when monks became parish priests, as they sometimes did, they would have been able to give at least rudimentary education in "letters," that is, the Psalter, the Pater Noster, and the Nicene Creed, together with the alphabet and grammar needed to understand them at some level. By the 12th Century the new institutional stability and wealth provided by the emergence of the cathedral chapters provided the opportunity to educate not just the clergy of the cathedral but also even some of the diocesan clergy. In addition, at all times and ages, there have been those whose taste proved not to be for the monastery or the priesthood even after they had done some preparation for it. Once again in the world, such men's most obvious resource was likely to be a literacy which could gain them a livelihood as tutor, notary, or schoolmaster. While the resulting diffusion of literacy in the lay society of the times should not be exaggerated, it did exist.[22]

At the same time, none of these developments prepares us for what began to take place in the intellectual realm in Barcelona, in Tarazona, and above all in Toledo in the first half of the 12th Century; that is, the collaboration of scholars drawn from Europe beyond the Pyrenees with local scholars, Muslim, Jew, and Christian, in a sprawling work of translation of the treasures of Greece, Rome, India, Persia, and Islam into Latin for the education of the Western European world. What specifically drew these scholars to

[22] Michael Clanchy, *From Memory to Written Record* (Cambridge, Mass., 1979), is a brilliant study of the conditions and realities of such a transition.

Iberia is impossible to say. One can only conjecture that the increasing popularity of the pilgrimage to Santiago de Compostela provided the vehicle which would put northern clerics in touch with the increasingly learned clerics of Spanish monasteries and cathedral chapters. We also hear of cathedral chapters which began to send at least an occasional canon north to be further educated in the schools of France. Cluniac and Cistercian monasteries must have done much the same thing with especially promising novices. In whatever fashion, the word got out that the riches of antiquity were accessible in Iberia.

Illustrative of the movement which was now to develop, the Italian Plato of Tivoli worked in Barcelona during the reign of Ramón Berenguer IV (1131–1162) to produce a translation of the *De Motu Stellarum* of the 10th-century al-Battānī. The work was important for trigonometry as well as for astronomy. He also translated the 11th-century work on the astrolabe of ibn al-Saffar and Ptolemy's *Quadripartitum*. That is to say, he translated these from the vernacular into Latin after the Jewish scholar with whom he collaborated, Abraham bar Hiyya, had rendered them from Arabic into that tongue. But Plato also translated the work of his collaborator. That is, Abraham himself was the author of the *Liber Embadorum*. This work contained the first published solution of a quadratic equation in the Medieval West, and would be utilized later in the century by Leonardo Fibonacci in his *Practica Geometriae*.

About the same time, Hugh of Santalla at Tarazona was preparing a translation of Arabic astronomical tables. That this activity was not simply pure gain is illustrated by the fact that Hugh also busied himself translating works of astrology and alchemy. Hugh was an Iberian, probably from western Asturias, who seems to have worked alone under the patronage of the bishop of Tarazona.

The greatest center for such translations, however, was the frontier town of Toledo during the pontificate of Archbishop Raymond (1126–1151). There the Italian Gerard of Cremona labored long and outlived his initial episcopal patron, disappearing not until about 1187. In the course of that period he is responsible for no fewer than eighty-seven translations, including Aristotle's *Physics*, Euclid's *Elements*, Ptolemy's *Almagest*, and al-Kindi's *De Intellectu*, and *De Quinque Essentiis*. During the earlier part of Gerard's career in Toledo he was contemporary with the Jewish convert to Christianity John of Sevilla, and the latter's co-worker, Domingo Gonzálvez, sometime archdeacon of Segovia. Their activity ranged over mathematics, astronomy, medicine, and philosophy. It included the *Liber Alghoarismi* of unknown Muslim authorship, al-Battānī's

Liber de Consuetudinibus, the medical *Secretum Secretorum* by the 9th-century Sir al-Asrār, some of the works of the Muslim philosophers al-Fārābī (10th Century), ibn Sīnna (11th Century), ibn Gabirol (11th Century), and al-Ghazālī (11th Century).

Also during this period, 1138–1142, the above were joined for a time by the much-traveled Herman of Carinthia. Herman had studied at Chartres, visited Spain, and then went north again to the Languedoc. Among the works which he translated were the *Planisphere* of Ptolemy, a variety of books on astronomy by Muslim and Jewish authors, probably including the famous astronomical tables of al-Khwārizmī. He also translated two religious works, the *Doctrina Mahumet* and the *De Generatione Mahumet*, the first of which presented some Muslim teachings in dialogue form. The second traced the genealogy of the prophet from Adam.[23]

As the reader will have noticed, the interests of these translators ran very heavily to mathematical and scientific materials and to philosophy, which latter would not have been rigidly distinguished from science during the times. In this they were largely following the lead of Islam itself, which had been much more interested in the science and thought of the world of antiquity than it had been in its letters. In general, one may say that the Greek literary inheritance would wait upon the age of the Italian Renaissance for its recovery. As for the literature of Islam, its effects upon vernacular Iberian letters had been direct and seemingly continuous and had no need of such cumbersome machinery.

There was to be another great period of translations at Toledo in the 13th Century. Such translations were also being made, in much lesser numbers, in Sicily during the 12th Century and in the Balkans during the 13th Century. By the end of that latter time, it is fair to say that the European West had recovered virtually as much of the corpus of Greek scientific knowledge as is known to us down until today. It had also borrowed the very considerable additions to Greek astronomy, geometry, physics, and medicine, made by generations of Muslim and Jewish scholars. But the Greeks had done very little in mathematics. Here Islam had built rather on the achievements of Indian mathematicians. As a result, the 12th-century West came into possession of what we usually call "Arabic" numerals to replace the clumsy Roman numerals, the concept of zero, and the indication of

---

[23] The still essential catalog to all of this activity is George Sarton, *Introduction to the History of Science*, Vol. 2 (Baltimore, 1931). It becomes even more comprehensive by reason of the author's generous inclusion of history, geography, law, and philosophy under this rubric. A briefer, more manageable introduction is cast into a narrative by Alistair C. Crombie, *Medieval and Early Modern Science*, Vol. 1 (New York, 1959).

value by place. Combined, these factors did not so much revolution-
ize as they did create the Western mathematics which would have
such a brilliant future before it.

As part of the same process, the West would recover the entire
corpus of the works of Aristotle, of which only the *Logic* had
previously been known. Here, too, the Greek legacy came not of
itself solely but in combination with the commentaries, additions,
and modifications of generations of Jewish and Muslim philosophers,
among whom Moses Maimónides, ibn Sīnna, and ibn Rushd are the
most outstanding. On the foundation established by this particular
borrowing, the Western scholastics would build the whole of that
method of reasoning and investigation which was to mark the life of
the mind there for the following centuries. The first great age of this
appropriation of knowledge centered precisely upon the Christian
Iberia of the 12th Century.

Another associated phenomenon which should be noted was the
contemporary translation of the *Koran*. Here we can follow the
process rather well for a change. The task was carried out by a group
between 1141 and 1143. The central figure was an English monk,
Robert of Ketton, who had studied with Plato of Tivoli in Barcelona,
subsequently became archdeacon of the church of Pamplona, and
seems to have ended his life back in England. Robert has a variety of
other translations in astronomy and mathematics to his credit and,
in addition, himself composed a set of astronomical tables for the
longitude of London. He was assisted in the work on the *Koran* by
a Muslim named Muhammad who cannot be further identified.
Further collaborators were one Peter of Toledo, also unidentifiable
outside of this context, Herman of Carinthia, an old friend and
previous associate of Robert, and Peter of Poitiers, secretary and
notary of Abbot Peter the Venerable of Cluny (1122–1156).

In the years 1142–1143 Peter the Venerable traveled to León–
Castilla to negotiate with Alfonso VII some financial settlement in
lieu of the annual subsidy paid to that kingdom by Cluny but
actually then long in arrears. An agreement was reached. Far more
important, however, Peter had already met, probably at Nájera in
the Rioja, at least some of the translators-to-be and had conceived
the idea of rendering the *Koran* into Latin. His secretary, Peter of
Poitiers, seems to have served as the general director of the project
and Peter of Toledo as the editor. When completed, the translation
of the *Koran* was part of a collection intended to elucidate the
doctrine of Islam as well as to present its fundamental text. Herman
of Carinthia two translations of Muslim works, mentioned above,
served as part of the whole. Peter the Venerable had previously been

interested in the study of the beliefs of religions competing with Christianity with an aim to the conversion of their adherents. It was the circumstance of the journey to Iberia, for wholly other purposes, which familiarized him with the resources offered by that time and place and so suggested the initiative which eventuated so remarkably. As such it offers a spectacular example of the imagination and initiative of the times, and is a precious illustration of the various factors that combined to allow both to be realized.[24]

Christian Iberia in Western Europe

If the first half of the 12th Century was to see this extraordinary cooperation of what we may call the old Iberian complex of Muslim, Jew, and Christian, which gave so much to Western Europe, it was also the period during which the Christian portion of that triad was increasingly asserting itself. Simultaneously it adopted practices and institutions that linked it ever more closely with the world to its north. The foundations were being laid for the new Iberia of the High and Late Middle Ages. That would be a changed world in which the Jewish and Muslim elements remained important but now existed by sufferance within a predominantly Christian European society.

In a sense we have been discussing just that process, as it emerged from the war, politics, ecclesiastical change, and cultural borrowing, in everything that has been said up to this point. However, we might well for a moment or two contemplate the same phenomenon as it would have impinged most directly on the consciousness of that lowly mass of Christian Iberians who were neither nobles nor clerics, merchants nor warriors, but simply farm folk who followed the plow and the seasons. Even there, in that almost unvarying round, change was now noticeable, even if its intensity and components might alternate from region to region.

For those who lived, the majority surely, on the great northern *meseta* of Castilla la Vieja, the new reality was, above all, the hustle and bustle of the pilgrimage to Santiago de Compostela. One may fairly say that sometimes a difference in degree does make a difference in kind, purists to the contrary. The pilgrimage was hardly new in any absolute sense. Most things are not. But every indication is that its popularity in the 12th Century far surpassed anything in its

---

[24] James Kritzeck, *Peter the Venerable and Islam* (Princeton, N.J., 1964), is the fundamental study of the venture and its issue.

past. Part of that new prestige is reflected in the willingness of Rome itself to raise Santiago's church to archepiscopal status in 1120 in defiance of tradition and canon law. Part of it is reflected in the dizzy career of Bishop-archbishop Diego Gelmírez as organizer, builder, reformer, and even aspiring king-maker. Still another reflection of it was the great, new Romanesque cathedral raised over the relics of the Apostle.

A different measure is the procession of the great ones of the world to the shrine of Santiago in the first half of the 12th Century. That Stephen, the treasurer of Cluny, or Guido, cardinal and legate of Rome, should visit there in 1121 is not too surprising but none the less important for all that. Matilda, daughter of Henry I of England, came in 1125; in 1127, Duke William X of Aquitaine was to die in Compostela while on pilgrimage. Count Alfonso Jordán of Toulouse made the trip in 1140, Bishop Henry of Winchester in 1151, Bishop Nicholas of Cambrai in 1153. In the following year, 1154, the king of France himself, Louis VII, found time to bend the knee to Santiago. All of these with their cortege traveled through and past the farm villages of the northern *meseta*, bringing a glimpse of what was, otherwise, only the stuff of travelers' tales. But the most lasting effects must have come from the more intimate contacts with the thousands of more ordinary folk who trudged the same dusty trail from the Pyrenees to the Atlantic, needing food, shelter, supplies, and amusement at every turn. Such contacts made Europe familiar to the generality of Iberians, while Andalucía receded further and further from everyday experience.

Finally, the surest sign of success is imitation. One of the most famous men of the first half of the 12th Century was Bishop Pelayo of Oviedo (1100–1130), the biographer of Alfonso VI. The bishop was a determined promoter of the fortunes of his see and the author of a series of well-known forgeries, all directed to that end. Among these was a forged charter dated to 1075 which placed Alfonso VI in Oviedo and presiding at the opening of the *Arca Sancta*. This latter contained a fantastic collection of relics deriving from all over the known world which were purported to have journeyed from Toledo to Oviedo in a flight from the 8th-century Muslim conquest. The good bishop was clearly attempting to divert some of the lucrative pilgrim traffic from Compostela to his own Oviedo by advertising the latter's spiritual treasures.

Yet the pilgrimage to Santiago did not exhaust the ways in which Europe was impinging on Iberia at the humblest levels. To be sure, some of the pilgrims never did return home, which left a sprinkling

of northerners among the native population whom the documents
sometimes disclose. In the late 11th Century the French Burgundian
counts Raymond and Henry, who were to become the male progeni-
tors of the ruling dynasties of León–Castilla and Portugal, must have
been accompanied by some little court of their countrymen, but no
trace of that can be detected. Nevertheless, in the 12th Century,
Burgos, Carrión de los Condes, and León on the pilgrim road had
their identifiable *barrios* of "francos." So did Villafranca del Bierzo
far up in the mountains to the west, and, of course, Santiago de
Compostela at the terminus of that highway. Somewhat more to the
south, Zamora and Salamanca also had French colonies of some size,
perhaps recruited in part through the efforts of Count Raymond
who was actively involved in their repopulation. Even Toledo at the
leading edge of the southern frontier had its French *barrio*. In the
course of time these immigrants would intermarry with the local
population and lose their distinctiveness, but in the interim they
would have constituted a most potent reminder of the greater world
to the north.

Except for Counts Raymond and Henry and a few fighting men
who may have accompanied them, there was no detectable influence
of French or other noblemen in Iberia west of the Ebro. Even the
disaster at Zalaca in 1086 called northern nobles only so far west as
Tudela. In Aragón and Cataluña, however, the case is quite different.
Here the French were actively involved in the reconquest of Huesca
in 1096, of Zaragoza in 1118, Tudela in 1119, Tortosa in 1148, and
Lérida in 1149. Men like the Gascon Viscount Gaston of Bearn and
the Norman Robert Burdet not only came as permanent settlers
themselves but brought with them wives, body servants, grooms,
falconers, masters of hunt, blacksmiths, fools, jugglers, and all that
motley lot of hangers-on which the great attract in any age. If they
never quite constituted an army of occupation, still, to the tiny
villages of the northeast, these bands must have had something of
that impact. Then, too, the frequent papal calls to crusade, with its
multiplicity of lures from salvation, to adventure, to plunder, surely
drew large numbers of lesser nobles from the more crowded com-
petitions for land in the Languedoc and Gascony.

Northeastern Iberians were in almost daily contact with the world
of Europe by reason of trade long established through the passes of
Roncesvalles and Somport with the great Muslim emporiums of
Tudela and Zaragoza. Pamplona and Jaca, where these natural road-
ways debouched onto the Iberian plain, had long had their French
barrios as places convenient for reststops and storage of goods for

transshipment. Farther east, Barcelona enjoyed a similar placement for land traffic through the inland valley of the Penedès from Narbonne southward toward Valencia and Tortosa. In addition to its French colony, Barcelona must have also had at least a small settlement of Italians, for the Genoese and Pisans had begun the development of factories along the eastern coast in the 12th Century. What was true of Barcelona was true, in lesser extent, of places like Gerona, Perpignan, and even Vich and Urgel.

Given the influence of a constant parade of pilgrims, royal marriages, ecclesiastical persons and policies, and noble, merchant, and artisan neighbors, perhaps the most pervasive symbol to the average Iberian of the new European world coming into being was the massive alteration of the very church within which he worshipped weekly. Everywhere, it seems, in the late 11th and 12th Centuries, old cathedral, town, and monastic churches were being torn down and new ones erected in their places. This activity is the most evident and basic index of the growing prosperity of Christian Iberia as well as of the increasing power and resources of its ecclesiastical corporations. Invariably these new churches were larger, grander, and richer than the ones that had preceded them. They were designed to house a larger population and to accommodate a more splendid liturgy.

Still, the most obvious thing about these new churches was that they were different, visually different, even to the most careless peasant observer. The older, Mozarabic style was disappearing, and a new, Romanesque style was replacing it. Architectural arguments quickly become too technical for the layperson. In general, however, one may distinguish the Mozarabic church with its single nave, square apse, horseshoe arch, and mosaic decoration from the Romanesque church with its nave and two side aisles, semicircular apses, its transept, barrel vaults and rounded arches, and elaborately carved statuary. Aside from their usual difference in size, the two are simply quite remarkably different buildings, even to the most untrained eye. These new structures were going up virtually everywhere, and they were to furnish even the most remote neighborhoods with the sort of unavoidable, visual, and shocking evidence that their world was indeed changing.

The full analysis of the change is complicated, of course, by the fact that the Romanesque churches were built on the same site as the one, or two, or three Mozarabic churches which had preceded them. The problem of defining the Mozarabic is bedeviled by the survival of examples of mainly monastic or parish churches at best, not cathedrals. In lesser degree, the same is true of the Romanesque, which would be replaced by the newer Gothic, beginning at the end of the 12th Century. Yet enough remains to catch the difference in flavor and the scale of the change.

All along the pilgrimage road to Santiago one can still see the Churches, and their distribution and numbers continue to impress. The cathedral of Jaca, at the foot of the Somport Pass, was built in the latter 11th Century but is unmistakeably Romanesque. Farther west, on the way to Pamplona, is the monastic church of Leyre. Westward again at Frómista, on the *meseta* between Burgos and Carrión de los Condes, is the church of San Martín, as French in its name as in its style, probably a parish church from its beginnings. In the old royal city of León is the church of San Isidoro, probably an urban, monastic church in its beginnings but then converted into a species of royal chapel and center of the cult of its famous patron, and rebuilt, at some point, in the "sweet new style." Well up into the mountains in the Bierzo still stands an impressive, early, and probably originally monastic church, product of the same ubiquitous building program. And, of course, within the husks of centuries of additional additions and accretions, the great Romanesque cathedral begun in 1076 at Santiago de Compostela itself still perdures.

Far to the south of the "Way of Saint James," the cathedral in Zamora, begun about 1151, is an example of how eclectic a still-unmistakeably-Romanesque structure could be. And further south again, the old cathedral of Salamanca, begun a little earlier, was unknowingly preserved for us today by the somewhat lunatic notion in the 13th Century of building a new, Gothic cathedral next to it without demolishing the older structure. In the west, almost on the Atlantic, the Romanesque monastery of Santa Cruz de Coimbra was begun about mid-century under the patronage of the new Portuguese king, Alfonso Enríquez.

As is so often the case, Cataluña marched to its own rhythms and the rebuilding in Romanesque had begun there earlier. Correspondingly, less of it survived the later popularity of the Gothic. At Gerona the old Romanesque cathedral had already been consecrated in 1038 and would stand into the 14th Century. In Barcelona, the urban, Romanesque church of Santa Eulalia was consecrated in 1101 but later rebuilt. However, one can still see the original Romanesque at San Pablo del Campo.

Virtually everywhere in northern Christian Iberia, then, one saw the very physical milieu change in the most dramatic and sustained of fashions. Kings, churchmen, and the greater nobles played the active role in this transformation and were most conscious of the new rules of the game, its restraints and opportunities. But if the intricacies of the causal chain eluded them, the commonality of

Christians had visible evidence of its end effect and significance. The unchanging church itself was changing. Although they might have been hard-pressed to formulate it so, all must have been aware that the new Christian society of northern Iberia was destined to take shape within a European matrix rather than a Mediterranean one.

Bibliography

Primary Published Sources

Abd Allāh. *El siglo XI en 1a persona: Las "Memorias" de Abd Allāh, ultimo rey Zirī de Granada destronado por los Almorávides (1090)*. Trans. Évariste Lévi-Provençal and Emilio García Gomez. Madrid, 1980.

Al-Idrisī. *Description de l'Afrique et de l'Espagne*. Trans. Reinhart Dozy. Paris, 1866.

Al-Kardabus. "Kitab al-Iqtifa." In al-Maqqarī, *The History of the Mohammedan Dynasties in Spain*. Trans. Pascual de Gayangos. Vol. 2, append. C, pp. xxii–xlvii. 1843. Reprint. New York, 1964.

Al-Maqqarī. *The History of the Mohammedan Dynasties in Spain*. Trans. Pascual de Gayangos. 2 vols. 1840–43. Reprint. New York, 1964.

Amari, Michele, ed. *I diplomi arabi del R. Archivio Fiorentini*. Florence, 1863.

Azevado, Rui Pinto de, ed. *Documentos medievais Portugueses*. Vol. 1. Lisbon, 1958.

Blanco Lozano, Pilar, ed. "Colección diplomática de Fernando I (1037–1065)," *AL* 40 (1986), pp. 7–212.

Caffaro. *De Captione Almerie et Tortuose*. Ed. Antonio Ubieto Arteta. Valencia, 1973.

"Chronica Gothorum." In *PMH, Scriptores*, pp. 5–17. Lisbon, 1856.

David, Charles Wendell, ed. *De Expugnatione Lyxbonensi*. New York, 1936.

Durán Gudiol, Antonio, ed. *Colección diplomática de la catedral de Huesca*. Vol. 1. Zaragoza, 1965.

Erdmann, Carl, ed. "Papsturkunden in Portugal." In *AGWG*. Philologisch-historische Klasse. N.S. Vol. 20. Berlin, 1927.

Falque Rey, Emma, ed. *Historia Compostellana*. Turnholt, 1988.

"Historia Roderici." In Ramón Menéndez Pidal. *La España del Cid*, Vol. 2, pp. 901–67.

Huici Miranda, Ambrosio, ed. *Las crónicas latinas de la reconquista*. 2 vols. Valencia, 1913.

Ibn Idarī. *Al-Bayān al-Mugrib*. Trans. Ambrosio Huici Miranda. Valencia, 1963.

Imperiale di Sant' Angelo, Caesare, ed. *Codice diplomatico della Republica di Genova*. Vol. 1. Rome, 1936.

Jiménez de Rada, Rodrigo. *De Rebus Hispaniae*. Ed. Juan Fernández Valverde. Turnholt, 1987.

Kehr, Paul, ed. "Papsturkunden in Spanien, II: Navarra und Aragon." In *AGWG*. Philologisch-historische Klasse, N.f. Vol. 22. Berlin, 1928.

Lucas de Túy. "Chronicon Mundi ab Origine Mundi usque ad Eram MCCLXXIV." In *Hispaniae Illustratae*. Ed. Andreas Schottus. Vol. 4, pp. 1–116. Frankfurt, 1608.

Mansilla, Demetrio, ed. *La documentación pontificia hasta Innocencio III, 965–1216*. Rome, 1955.

Menéndez Pidal, Ramón, ed. *Cantar de mio Cid*. 3 vols. Madrid, 1954.

——, ed. *Primera cronica general de España*. 2 vols. Madrid, 1955.

Múñoz y Romero, Tomás, ed. *Colección de fueros y cartas pueblas*. Madrid, 1847.

Núñez Contreras, Luis, ed. "Colección diplomática de Vermudo III, rey de León." *Historia, instituciones, documentos* 4 (1977):381–504.

Pérez de Urbel, Justo, and Ruiz-Zorilla, Atilano González, eds. *Historia Silense*. Madrid, 1959.

Puyol y Alonso, Julio, ed. "Las crónicas anónimas de Sahagún." *BRAH* 76 (1920):7–26, 111–22, 242–57, 339–56, and 512–19; and 77 (1921):51–59 and 151–61.

Robert, Ulysse, ed. *Bullaire du Pape Calixti II*. 2 vols. Paris, 1891.

Rosell, Francisco M. ed. *Liber Feudorum Maior*. Barcelona, 1945.

Sánchez Alonso, Benito, ed. *Crónica del Obispo Don Pelayo*. Madrid, 1924.

Sánchez Belda, Luis, ed. *Chronica Adefonsi Imperatoris*. Madrid, 1950.

Santos Coco, Francisco, ed. *Historia Silense*. Madrid, 1921.

Ubieto Arteta, Antonio, ed. *Colección diplomática de Pedro I de Aragón y Navarra*. Zaragoza, 1951.

——, ed. *Crónica Nájerense*. Valencia, 1966.

——, ed. *Documentos de Ramiro II de Aragón*. Zaragoza, 1988.

Secondary Works

Aguadé Nieto, Santiago. *De la sociedad arcaica a la sociedad campesina en la Asturias medieval*. Madrid, 1988.

——. *Ganadería y desarrollo agrario en Asturias durante la Edad Media, siglos IX–XIII*. Barcelona, 1983.

Aguirre Sabada, F. Javier, and Jiménez Mata, María del Carmen. *Introducción al Jaén islámico*. Jaén, 1979.

Almeida, Fortunato de. *História da Igreja em Portugal*. Vol. 1. Oporto, new ed., 1967.

Ashtor, Eliyahu. *The Jews of Moslem Spain*. Trans. Aaron Klein and Jenny Machlowitz Klein. 2 vols. 1966. Reprint. Philadelphia, 1973–79.

Baer, Yitzhak. *Historia de los judios en la España cristiana*. José Luis Lacave. Madrid, 1981.

Barrios García, Angel. *Estructuras agrarias y poder en Castilla: El ejemplo de Avila, 1085–1320*. Salamanca, 1983.

Bishko, Charles J. "The Abbey of Dueñas and the Cult of Saint Isidore of Chios in the County of Castile (10th–11th Centuries)." In *Homenaje a Fray Justo Pérez de Urbel, OSB*. Vol. 2, pp. 345–64. Silos, 1977.

———. "Fernando I and the Origins of the Leonese–Castilian Alliance with Cluny." In *Studies in Medieval Spanish Frontier History*, pp. 1–136. London, 1980.

Bisson, Thomas N. *The Medieval Crown of Aragon*. Oxford, 1986.

Blöcker-Walter, Monica. *Alfons I von Portugal*. Zurich, 1966.

Bofarull y Mascaró, Prospero de. *Historia de los condes de Urgel*. Barcelona, 1853.

Bonnassie, Pierre. *Cataluña mil anos atrás, siglos X–XI*. Barcelona, 1988.

Bosch Vilá, Jacinto. *Historia de Sevilla: La Sevilla islámica, 712–1248*. Sevilla, 1984.

Brignon, Jean, Amine, Abdelaziz, Boutaleb, Brahim, Matrinet, Guy, and Rosenberger, Bernard. *Histoire du Maroc*. Paris, 1967.

Buesa Conde, Domingo J. *El rey Sancho Ramírez*. Zaragoza, 1978.

Bulliet, Richard W. *Conversion to Islam in the Medieval Period*. Cambridge, Mass., 1979.

Calvo, Aurelio. *El monasterio de Gradefes*. León, 1936.

The Cambridge History of Islam. Vol. 2. Cambridge, 1970.

Castro, Americo. *The Spaniards: An Introduction to Their History*. Trans. W. F. King and S. Margaretten. Berkeley, 1971.

Chejne, Anwar G. *Muslim Spain: Its History and Culture*. Minneapolis, 1974.

Clanchy, Michael. *From Memory to Written Record*. Cambridge, Mass., 1979.

Codera y Zaidín, Francisco. *Decadencia y desaparición de los Almorávides en España*. Zaragoza, 1899.

Conde, Francisco Javier, ed. *Historia de la iglesia en Espana*. Vol. 2. Madrid, 1982.

Crombie, Alistair C. *Medieval and Early Modern Science*. Vol. 1. New York, 1959.

David, Pierre. *Études historiques sur la Galice et le Portugal du VIe au XII siecle*. Paris, 1947.

Defourneaux, Marcelin. *Les Français en Espagne aux XIe et XIIe siècles*. Paris, 1949.

Diaz y Diaz, Manuel C. *Index Scriptorum Latinorum Medii Aevi Hispanorum*. 2 vols. Salamanca, 1958.

———. *Libros y librerías en La Rioja altomedieval*. Logroño, 1979.

Diccionario de historia eclesiástica de España. 4 vols. Madrid, 1972–75.

Dictionaire d'histoire et de géographie eccleiastiques. 21 vols. Paris, 1912– .

Durany Castrillo, Mercedes. *San Pedro de Montes: El dominio de un monasterio benedictino de El Bierzo, siglos IX al XIII*. León, 1976.

Duro Peña, Emilio, ed. *Catálogo de los documentos privados en pergamino del archivo de la catedral de Orense, 888–1554.* Orense, 1973.

Erdmann, Carl. *Das Papsttum und Portugal in ersten Jahrhundert der Portugiesischen Geschichte.* Berlin, 1928.

Escalona, Romualdo. *Historia del real monasterio de Sahagún.* 1782. Reprint. León, 1982.

Estepa Díez, Carlos. *Estructura social de la ciudad de León, siglos XI–XIII.* León, 1977.

Fernández Conde, Javier, ed. *La historia de la iglesia en España.* Vol. 2. Madrid, 1982.

Fletcher, Richard A. *The Episcopate in the Kingdom of León in the Twelfth Century.* Oxford, 1978.

———. *The Quest for El Cid.* New York, 1990.

———. *Saint James's Catapult: The Life and Times of Diego Gelmírez of Santiago de Compostela.* Oxford, 1984.

Flórez, Enríque. *Memorias de las reinas católicas de España.* 2 vols. 1761. Reprint. Madrid, 1964.

Forey, A. J. *The Templars in the Corona de Aragón.* London, 1973.

Gams, Pius Bonifacius, ed. *Series Episcoporum Ecclesiae Catholicae.* Ratisbon, 1873.

García Calles, Luisa. *Doña Sancha.* León, 1972.

García de Cortázar y Ruiz de Aquirre, josé Angel. *El dominio del monasterio de San Millán de La Cogolla, siglos X al XIII.* Salamanca, 1969.

———. *Historia de España Alfaquera.* Vol. 2. Madrid, 1973.

García de Valdeavellano, Luis. *Historia de España de los orígenes a la Baja Edad Media.* Vol. 1, pt. 2. Madrid, 2nd ed., 1955.

García Gallo, Alfonso. "Las redacciónes de los decretos del concilio de Coyanza." *El concilio de Coyanza, miscelanea,* pp. 25–39. León, 1971.

García Larragueta, Santos A. *El gran priorado de Navarra de la Orden de San Juan de Jerusalén.* 2 vols. Pamplona, 1957.

Glick, Thomas F. *Irrigation and Society in Medieval Valencia.* Cambridge, Mass., 1970.

———. *Islamic and Christian Spain in the Early Middle Ages.* Princeton, N.J., 1979.

Goñi Gaztambide, José. *Historia de la Bula de la Cruzada en España.* Vitoria, 1958.

Gonzaga de Azevedo, Luiz. *História de Portugal.* Vol. 3. Lisbon, 1940.

González, Julio. *Repoblacion de Castilla La Nueva.* 2 vols. Madrid, 1975.

González Palencia, Angel. *El arzobispo D. Raimundo de Toledo.* Barcelona, 1942.

Gonzálvez, Ramón. "The Persistence of the Mozarabic Liturgy in Toledo after 1080 A.D." In Bernard F. Reilly, ed., *Santiago, St.-Denis, and Saint Peter,* pp. 157–85. New York, 1985.

Grunebaum, Gustave E. von. *Medieval Islam.* Chicago, 2nd ed., 1953.

Higounet, Charles. "Un grand chapitre de l'histoire du XII siècle: La rivalité des maisons de Toulouse et Barcelone pour la preponderance meridionale." In *Mélanges d'histoire du Moyen Age Louis Halphen.* Paris, 1951.

Hill, John H, and Hill, Laurita L. *Raymond IV de Saint-Gilles*. Toulouse, 1959.

Huici Miranda, Ambrosio. "Contribución al estudio de la dinastía almorávides: El gobierno de Tasfīn ben Alī ben Yūsuf en el-Andalus." In *Etudes d'orientalisme dédiees a la memoire de Lévi-Provençal*. Vol. 2, pp. 605–21. Paris, 1962.

——. *Las grandes batallas de la Reconquista durante las invasiones africanas*. Madrid, 1956.

——. *Historia musulmana de Valencia y su región*. 3 vols. Valencia, 1969–70.

——. *Historia política del imperio Almohade*. Vol. 1. Tetuán, 1956.

Julien, Charles-André. *History of North Africa*. Trans. John Petrie. London, 1970.

Kritzeck, James. *Peter the Venerable and Islam*. Princeton, N.J., 1964.

Lacarra, José María. *Historia del reino de Navarra en la Edad Media*. Pamplona, 1975.

Lévi-Provençal, Évariste. *Historia de España*. Vols. 4–5 Madrid, 1957–65.

——. *L'Espagne musulmane au Xeme siècle*. Paris, 1932.

Linage Conde, Antonio. *Los orígenes del monacato benedictino en la península Iberica. 3 vols*. León, 1973.

Lomax, Derek W. *The Reconquest of Spain*. London, 1978.

López Alsina, Fernando. *La ciudad de Santiago de Compostela en la Alta Edad Media*. Santiago de Compostela, 1988.

López-Arevalo, Juan Ramón. *Un cabildo catedral de La Vieja Castilla, Avila*. Madrid, 1966.

López-Ferreiro, Antonio. *Historia de la Santa Apostólica Metropolitana Iglesia de Santiago de Compostela*. 11 vols. Santiago de Compostela, 1898–1911.

Martín, José Luis. *La península en la Edad Media*. Barcelona, 1976.

Martínez Díaz, Gonzalo. *Alava medieval*. Vol. 1. Vitoria, 1974.

Mayer, Hans Eberhard. *The Crusades*. Trans. John Gillingham. Oxford, 1972.

Menéndez Pidal, Ramón, ed. *La España del Cid*. 2 vols. Madrid, 4th ed., 1947.

——. *Orígenes del Español*. Madrid, 5th ed., 1964.

Miranda Calvo, José. *La reconquista de Toledo por Alfonso VI*. Toledo, 1980.

Moreta Velayos, Salustiano. *El monasterio de San Pedro de Cardeña*. Salamanca, 1971.

Moxó, Salvador de. *Repoblación y sociedad en la España cristiana medieval*. Madrid, 1979.

Nieto Cumplido, Manuel. *Historia de Córdoba*. Córdoba, 1984.

O'Callaghan, Joseph F. *A History of Medieval Spain*. Ithaca, N.Y., 1975.

——. "The Integration of Christian Spain into Europe: The Role of Alfonso VI of León–Castile." In *Santiago, St.-Denis, and St. Peter*. Ed. Bernard F. Reilly. Pp. 101–20. New York, 1985.

Oliveira Marques, A. H. de. *History of Portugal*. Vol. 1. New York, 1972.

Pacaut, Marcel. *Louis VII et son royaume*. Paris, 1964.

Peinado Santaella, Rafael Gerardo, and López de Coca Castañer, José Enríque. *Historia de Granada: La época medieval.* 2 vols. Granada, 1987.

Peres, Damião. *Como nasceu Portugal.* Porto, 6th ed., 1967.

Pérez de Urbel, Justo. *El condado de Castilla.* 3 vols. Madrid, 2nd ed., 1969.

———. *Los monjes españolas en la Edad Media.* 2 vols. Madrid, 2nd ed., 1945.

———. *Sancho el Mayor de Navarra.* Madrid, 1950.

Powers, James F. *A Society Organized for War: The Iberian Municipal Militias in the Central Middle Ages, 1000–1284.* Los Angeles, 1988.

Ramos y Loscertales, José María. *El reino de Aragón bajo la dinastía pamplonesa.* Salamanca, 1961.

Reilly, Bernard F. *The Kingdom of León–Castilla under King Alfonso VI, 1065–1109.* Princeton, N.J., 1988.

———. *The Kingdom of León–Castilla under Queen Urraca, 1109–1126.* Princeton, N.J. 1982.

———. ed. *Santiago, St.-Denis, and Saint Peter.* New York, 1985.

Russell, Josiah Cox. *Medieval Regions and Their Cities.* Bloomington, Ind., 1972.

Säbekow, Gerhard. *Die päpstlichen Legationen nach Spanien und Portugal bis zum Ausgang des XII Jahrhunderts.* Berlin, 1931.

Sagredo Fernández, Felix. *Briviesca antigua y medieval.* Madrid, 2nd ed., 1979.

Sánchez-Albornoz, Claudio. *Despoblación y repoblación del valle del Duero.* Buenos Aires, 1966.

———. *España, un enigma histórico.* 2 vols. Buenos Aires, 1957.

———. "La primitiva organización monetaria de León y Castilla." In *Viejos y nuevos estudios sobre las instituciones medievales españolas.* Vol. 2, pp. 887–928. Reprint. Madrid, 2nd ed., 1976.

———. *Sobre la libertad humana en el reino astur-leonés hace mil años.* Madrid, 1976.

———. "La sucesión al trono en los reinos de León y Castilla." In *Viejos y nuevos estudios sobre las instituciones medievales españolas.* Vol. 2, pp. 1107–72. Madrid, 2nd ed., 1976.

Sánchez-Candeira, Alfonso. *El "Regnum-Imperium" leónes hasta 1037.* Madrid, 1951.

Sarton, George. *Introduction to the History of Science.* Vol. 2. Baltimore, 1931.

Serrão, Joaquim Veríssimo. *História de Portugal.* Vol. 1. Lisbon, 1976.

Sobreques i Vidal, Santiago. *Els grans comtes de Barcelona.* Barcelona, 1961.

Soldevila, Ferran, ed. *Historia de España.* Vol. 1 Barcelona, 1952.

———. *Historia dels Catalans.* 3 vols. Barcelona, 2nd ed., 1962–64.

Sousa Soares, Torquato de. "O governo de Portugal pela Infante-Rainha D. Teresa." In *Colectanea de estudios im honra do Prof-Doutor Damião Peres.* Pp. 99–119. Lisbon, 1974.

Tapia Garrido, José Angel. *Historia general de Almería y su provincia.* Vol. 2. Almería, 1978.

Terrón Albarrán, Manuel. *El sólar de los Aftásids.* Badajoz, 1971.

Turk, Afif. *El reino de Zaragoza en el siglo XI de Cristo, V de la Hégira.* Madrid, 1978.

Ubieto Arteta, Antonio. *Historia de Aragón: Creación y desarrollo de la corona de Aragón.* Zaragoza, 1987.

——. *Historia de Aragón: La formación territorial.* Zaragoza, 1981.

——. "Los primeros años de la diocesis de Sigüenza." In *Homenaje a Johannes Vincke.* Vol. 1, pp. 135–48. Madrid, 1962.

UNESCO General History of Africa. Vols. 3–4 Paris and Berkeley, 1984–1988.

Vaissette, J., and Devic, Claude. *Histoire de Languedoc.* Vol. 3. Toulouse, 1872.

Vajay, Szabolcs de. "Ramire II le moine, roi d'Aragón, et Agnés de Poitou dans l'histoire et dans la legende." In *Mélanges offerts a René Crozet.* Vol. 2, pp. 727–50. Poitiers, 1966.

Vázquez de Parga, Luis; Lacarra, José María; and Uría Ríu, Juan. *Las peregrinaciones a Santiago de Compostela.* 3 vols. Madrid, 1948–49.

Vernet, Juan. *La cultura hispanoárabe en Orient y Occidente.* Barcelona, 1978.

Viguera, María J. *Aragón musulman.* Zaragoza, 1988.

Villacorta Rodríguez, Tomás. *El cabildo catedral de León.* León, 1974.

Vones, Ludwig. *Die "Historia Compostelana" und die Kirchenpolitik des nordwestspanischen Raumes.* Cologne, 1980.

Wasserstein, David. *The Rise and Fall of the Party-Kings: Politics and Society in Islamic Spain, 1002–1086.* Princeton, N.J., 1985.

Watt, W. Montgomery. *A History of Islamic Spain.* Edinburgh, 1965.

——. *Islamic Philosophy and Theology.* Edinburgh, 1962.

Wright, Roger. *Late Latin and Early Romance in Spain and Carolingian France.* Liverpool, 1982.

Periodical Literature

Bishko, Charles Julian. "Count Henrique of Portugal, Cluny, and the Antecedents of the Pacto Sucessorio." *RPH* 13 (1970):155–88. Now reprinted in his *Spanish and Portuguese Monastic History, 600–1300,* pp. 155–190A. London, 1984.

Constable, Giles. "A Note on the Route of the Anglo-Flemish Crusaders of 1147." *Speculum* 28 (1953):525–26.

——. "The Second Crusade as Seen by Contemporaries. *Traditio* 9 (1953): 213–79.

Engels, Odilo. "Papsttum, Reconquista, und spanisches Landeskonzil im Hochmittelalter." *AHC* 1 (1969):37–49 and 241–87.

Feige, Peter. "Die Anfänge des portugiesischen Königtums und seiner Landeskirche." *GAKS* 29 (1978):85–352.

Fita, Fidel. "Concilio nacional de Burgos (18 febrero, 1117)." *BRAH* 48 (1906):394–99.

Gago, Elías, and Díaz-Jiménez, Juan Eloy. "Los restos mortales de Alfonso VI y de sus cuatro mujeres." *BRAH* 58 (1911):36–55.

García Gallo, Alfonso. "Los fueros de Toledo." *AHDE* 45 (1975):341–488.

González, Julio. "Repoblación de las tierras de Cuenca." *AEM* 12 (1982): 183–204.

Grassotti, Hilda. "Dos problemas de historia Castellano–Leonesa, siglo XII." *CHE* 49–50 (1969):135–97.

Hiestand, Rudolf. "Reconquista, Kreuzzug und heiliges Grab." *GAKS* 31 (1984):136–57.

Huici Miranda, Ambrosio. "Los Banū Hūd de Zaragoza, Alfonso el Batallador y los Almorávides." *EEMCA* 7 (1962):7–32.

——. "Un nuevo manuscrito de 'al-Bayan al-Mugrib': Datos ineditos y aclaraciones sobre los ultimos años del reinado de Alfonso VII, el Emperador." *Al-Andalus* 24 (1959):63–84.

Kehr, Paul. "Cómo y cuando se hizo Aragón feudatorio de la Santa Sede?" *EEMCA* 1 (1945):285–326.

——. "El papado y los reinos de Navarra y Aragón hasta mediados del siglo XII." *EEMCA* 2 (1946):74–186.

Kofman, Lydia C., and Carzolio, María Inés. "Acerca la demografía asturleonésa y castellana en la Alta Edad Media." *CHE* 47–48 (1968):136–70.

Lacarra, José María. "Alfonso el Batallador y las paces de Tamara. Cuestiones cronologicas (1124–1127)." *EEMCA* 3 (1949):461–73.

——. "La conquista de Zaragoza por Alfonso I, 18 diciembre, 1118." *Al-Andalus* 12 (1947):65–98.

Lourie, Elena. "The Will of Alfonso I 'El Batallador,' King of Aragon and Navarre: A Reassessment." *Speculum* 50 (1975):635–51.

Mañaricua, Andrés E. de. "Provisión de obispados en la Alta Edad Media española." *Estudios de Deusto* 14 (1966):61–92.

Martínez Diez, Gonzalo. "El concilio compostelano del reinado de Fernando I." *AEM* 1 (1964):121–138.

Moxó, Salvador de. "De la nobleza vieja a la nobleza nueva." *Cuadernos de Historia* 3 (1969):1–210.

Ramos y Loscertales, José Mariá. "La sucesión del rey Alfonso VI." *AHDE* 13 (1936–41):36–99.

Rassow, Peter, ed. "Die Urkunden Kaiser Alfonso VII von Spanien." AU 10 (1928):327–468, and 11 (1930):66–137.

Reilly, Bernard F. "The Chancery of Alfonso VII of León–Castilla: The Period 1116–1135 Reconsidered." *Speculum* 51 (1976):243–61.

——. "On Getting to Be a Bishop in León–Castile: The "Emperor" Alfonso VII and the Post-Gregorian Church." *Studies in Medieval and Renaissance History* 1 (1978):37–68.

——. "Sources of the Fourth Book of Lucas of Túy's 'Chronicon Mundi." *Classical Folia* 30 (1976):127–37

Serrano, Luciano. "Berengere." *DHGE* 8 (1935):411–13.

Slaughter, John E. "De nuevo sobre la batalla de Uclés." *AEM* 9 (1974–79):393–404.

Sousa Soares, Torquato de. "O governo de Portugal pelo Conde Henrique de Borgonha: Sus relações com as monarquias Leónesa–Castelhana e Aragonesa." *RPH* 14 (1974):365–97.

Torres Balbas, Leopoldo. "Almería islámica." *Al-Andalus* 22 (1957):411–53.

Ubieto Arteta, Antonio. "La creación de la cofradía militar de Belchite." *EEMCA* 5 (1952):427–34.

——. "Homenaje de Aragón a Castilla por el condado de Navarra." *EEMCA* 3 (1947–48):1–28.

Index

Abbādid, 3, 12
Abd al-Azīz, 5
Abd al-Malik, king of Valencia, 37
Abd al-Malik, son of al-Mansūr, 2–3
Abd al-Malik, son of al-Mustain, 131,
 159, 161
Abd al-Mūmin, 207–8, 209, 215–7,
 222
Abd al-Rahmān, 3, 25
Abd Allāh, king of Granada, 75, 88,
 91, 103, 104, 105, 233
Abd Allāh ibn Mazdali, 145, 160
Abd Allāh ibn Yāsīn, 100–1
Abengania, see ibn Gāniya
Abraham bar Hayya, 237, 254
Abū al-Walīd Marwān ibn Djanah, 22,
 24
Abū Bakr, king of Valencia, 76, 86–7
Abū Bakr ibn Alī, 164, 167
Abū Bakr ibn Umar, 101–2,
Abū Imrān al-Fāsī, 100
Abū Muhammad Sir, 167, 208
Abū Yakūb, 235
Abū Yūsuf, 235
Aceca, 208
adab, 236, 237
Adrian IV, 190
Aftásid, 4, 104
Agde, 48, 119
Aghmat, 206–7
Agnes of Aquitaine, 185, 187, 188
Agreda, 146
Aimery of Thouars, 185
al-Bāttānī, 23–4, 254–5

al-Bitruji, 236
al-Fārābī, 254
al-Ghazālī, 255
al-Hakam, 23
al-Idrisī, 233, 236, 241
al-Khwārizmī, 23, 255
al-Kindi, 254
al-Mamūn, 5, 7, 37, 41, 75–6, 120
al-Mansūr, 2, 3, 5, 11, 13, 18, 25, 64,
 94
al-Maqqarī, 82
al-Mawāīnī, 236
al-Muqtadir, 36–7, 43–4, 49, 74, 76–8,
 106–9, 119
al-Mustain, 43, 86–88, 94, 105,
 109–18, 121, 131, 158–9
al-Mutadid, 22, 65, 83
al-Mutamid, 22, 75–6, 80, 82–4, 86,
 88, 92, 103–4, 120, 233
al-Mutamin, 86, 109, 120
al-Mutawakkil, 80, 88, 91–2, 103, 104
al-Muzaffar, see Yūsuf al-Muzaffar
al-Qādir, 76, 80–1, 84–5, 87, 120–1,
 124, 231
al-Zakariyya, 237
Alava, 27, 77–8, 107–8, 169, 185, 188
Albacete, 5, 7, 11, 80, 86, 161
Albarracín, 123
Alberta of England, 71
Albertus Magnus, 235
Alcácer do Sal, 220
Alcala de Henares, 37, 145
Alcira, 92, 124
Alcobaça, 250

Alcoraz, 115
Aledo, 87, 91, 92, 103, 124
Alexander II, 69
Alfaras, 117–8
alférez, 56, 108, 222, 230, 239
Alfonso III, 62
Alfonso V, 25–6
Alfonso VI, 20, 40–2, 51, 53, 58, 67, 71, 74–98, 103–5, 107–8, 109–15, 116–117, 120–1, 123, 124, 125, 126–7, 134, 135, 143, 153, 169, 171, 190, 200–1, 202, 209, 224, 226–7, 240, 243–4, 247, 249, 252
Alfonso VII, 51, 96–8, 127, 130, 132–4, 137–40, 142, 146–56, 168–72, 180, 183, 184–5, 186–9, 190–200, 201–30, 224, 226–7, 230, 240, 244, 250, 256
Alfonso VIII, 230
Alfonso I of Aragón, 20, 97–8, 113, 117–8, 127, 129–41, 145–6, 152–4, 158–74, 175, 179–80, 181–2, 183–4, 186, 194–5, 196–7, 198, 199, 203, 205–6, 224, 244, 250
Alfonso I Enríquez of Portugal, 127, 142, 148, 152, 154, 156, 171, 187, 192–3, 195–6, 200–4, 209, 211–3, 218, 220, 224–5, 240, 242–3, 250, 261
Alfonso Jordan of Toulouse, 129, 171, 177, 185, 191, 195, 198, 211, 226–258
Alfonso, bishop of Túy, 151–2
Alfonso of Toledo, 62
Alfonso Núñez, 148
Algeciras, 3, 11–12, 88, 102–3, 104, 110, 217
Algiers, 216
Alī Bakr, 135
Alī ibn Yūsuf, 95, 97, 105, 126, 131, 143, 161, 170, 176, 205–6, 208, 209, 210
Alicante, 48
Aljáferia, 160
Almadén, 221
Almazán, 169, 196
Almenar, 109, 120
Almenara, 123
Almeria, 4–5, 11, 12, 19, 48, 88, 124, 212, 217, 218, 220, 222–3, 235, 236, 241

Alive, son of Awake, 235
Almodis, wife of Peter of Melgueil, 48
Almodis, wife of Pons of Toulouse and Ramoń Berenguer I, 48–9, 52, 67, 71, 119
Alpenes, 116
Alpuente, 123
Alquézar, 107, 110
Alvar Fáñez, 87–8, 120–1, 135–6
Alvarez, 40
Amadeus III of Savoy, 225
amir al-muminin, 208
Anacletus II, 186
Andújar, 212, 221, 223
Anjou, 226
Aquitaine, 75, 90, 108, 171, 185, 187, 226
Arabic numerals, 23, 63, 255–6
Aranda del Duero, 29
Aranjuez, 97
Arca Sancta, 258
Arconada, 65
Arcos, 3
Arcos de Valedevez, 203
Arévalo, 79, 229
Arguedas, 109
Aristotle, 24, 235, 237, 254, 256
Armagnac, 75
armed forces, 88–9, 97, 114–5, 123–4, 161, 163–7, 222–3, 239
Armengol III, 46, 107
Armengol IV, 120
Armengol V, 94, 116
Armengol VI, 117, 185, 218
Arnaud of Lavedan, 160
Arnold, bishop of Huesca, 173
Arnisol, 164
Asal, 235
Astorga, 30, 131, 133–4, 245
Atapuerca, 27, 44
Atienza, 94, 153, 230
Augier of Miramont, 160
Ausona, *see* Vich
Avempace, *see* ibn Bājjah
Averroes, *see* ibn Rushd
Avicebron, *see* ibn Gabirol
Avicenna, *see* ibn Sīnna
Avila, 79, 84, 94, 229, 230, 243
Ayerbe, 109

Badajoz
  city, 9, 11, 217
  taifa, 4, 6, 11, 35, 39–40, 58, 76, 80,
    88–9, 91–92, 103–4, 125, 143, 232
Baeza, 214, 217, 218, 220, 221, 223,
  230
bailli, see merino
Balaguer, 117–8, 121, 158
Balearic Islands, 5, 11–12, 48, 72, 174,
  176, 177, 217, 242
Banū Hilāl, 102, 216
Barbastro, 37, 44, 69, 75, 112, 116,
  117–8, 158, 169, 183
Barcelona, city, 2, 11, 30, 47–8, 54–5,
  72, 174, 176, 177, 233, 241–2, 249,
  253, 254, 256, 260, 261
Baux, lineage, 176–7
Bayonne, 170–1, 181, 198
Baza, 20
Bearn, 46, 75, 111–2, 114, 160, 164,
  168–9, 170–1, 194, 215, 226
Beatus de Liébana, 62
Belmonte, 93–4
Belorado, 194
Berbers, 4, 9, 13, 99–102, 231–3, 237
Berengaria, 168, 180, 199
Berenguer, bishop of Barcelona, 116
Berenguer, bishop of Salamanca and
  archbishop of Compostela, 248
Berenguer Ramón I, 26, 49
Berenguer Ramón II of Barcelona,
  119–21
Berenguer Ramón II of Provence, 177,
  180
Berga, 175
Berlanga, 37, 135
Bernard, bishop of Coimbra, 196
Bernard, archbishop of Compostela,
  247
Bernard, archbishop of Toledo, 129,
  131, 139, 145, 146–7, 150–52, 154,
  155, 191, 247, 252
Bernard, bishop of Sigüenza, 152
Bernard, bishop of Zamora, 154
Bernard of Comminges, 160, 185
Bernard Atto of Carcassonne and
  Béziers, 160, 175
Bernardo del Carpio, 252
Bernat III of Besalu, 174–5
Bernat Guillem of Cerdanya, 175

Berta, wife of Alfonso VI, 93, 96
Berta, wife of Pedro I of Aragón, 115
Bertrán, bishop of Burgo de Osma,
  248
Bertrán of Risnel, 136, 141, 168, 194,
  198
Bertrán of Toulouse, 214
Besalu, 174–5
Béziers, 48, 119, 160, 175, 226
Bierzo, 40, 90, 192, 261
Bigorre, 46, 71, 160, 173, 194, 226
Boethius, 251
Book of Agriculture, 237
Bordeaux, 114
Borja, 161
Boso, cardinal, 140, 150–1, 159–60
Bougie, 206
Braga, 19, 136, 145, 148, 203, 242–3,
  245, 247, 251–2
Bureba, 27, 36
Burgo de Osma, 146, 248
Burgos, 2, 135–7, 140–1, 145, 149,
  154, 158, 159, 168, 183, 194, 241,
  243, 259, 261

Cáceres, 4, 88
Cádiz, 11, 208
Calahorra, 19, 36, 43, 77
Calasanz, 116, 158
Calatayud, 43, 149, 157, 161–2, 186,
  229
Calatrava, 86, 95, 210, 212, 221
Calixtus II, 97, 146–7, 149–51, 154,
  179
camino de Santiago, see Santiago de
  Compostela, pilgrimage
Candespina, 132
Cantar de mio Cid, 122, 253
Cantuarias, 81
Capcir, 175
Carcassonne, 48, 119, 171, 175, 226
Carmen Campi Doctoris, 252
Carmona, 3, 15, 91
Carrión de los Condes, 65, 135, 141,
  158, 168, 188, 194, 197, 259, 261
carta de arras, 130
Cartagena, 11, 87
castellan, 53–5, 57, 59, 239
El Castellar, 112
castellariam, 57

Castro, lineage, 146–7, 230, 240
Castrojeriz, 141, 158, 168–9, 171–2, 194–5, 198
cathedral chapters, 248–9, 253, 254
Celanova, 32, 152, 201
Cella, 169
censor, 17
Centulle IV of Bearn, 112
Centulle V of Bigorre, 160, 168, 173, 194
Cerdanya, 175
Cervera, 118
Ceuta, 9, 82, 84, 102–3, 236
chancery, 51–2, 56, 239
el Cid, see Rodrigo Diaz de Vivar
Cistercians, 249–50
Cidellus, see Joseph Ferrizuel
Clement II, 67
Cluny, 66–7, 75, 93, 139, 151, 247, 249, 250, 256, 258
Coca, 79
Cofradía of Belchite, 162
Coimbra, 20, 36, 39–41, 127, 143, 152, 154, 196, 197, 201, 202, 212, 213, 217, 231, 249, 250
coinage, 48, 58, 233, 239
Collectio Hispana, 62
Colmenar de Oreja, 135, 209
The Comfort of Hearts and the Protection of Youth, 236
Commentaries, 235
Comminges, 160, 185, 226
Conflent, 175
Constance of Burgundy, 90, 93, 96
Constancia Alfónsez, 220–1
Constantine, 216
Consuegra, 93–4
Córdoba
  bishopric, 19
  caliphate, 1–3
  city, 3, 9, 11, 22, 30–1, 64, 76, 91, 208, 210–11, 212, 217, 218, 234, 235, 236, 237
  taifa, 3, 37, 75–6, 80
Coria, 4, 7, 80, 88–9, 94, 103, 205, 209, 229–30
Corsica, 72
Couserans-Foix, 71
Coyanza, 70, 197–8
countship, 17, 59–60

Covadonga, 252
Crónica Najerense, 82
Cuart de Poblet, 92, 125
Cuéllar, 79
Cuenca, 7, 19, 80–1, 84, 135, 187
Cuixa, 67
Cullera, 170
curia regis, 55–6, 239
Cutanda, 149, 161, 167, 179

Dalmatio, bishop of Compostela, 247
Daroca, 149, 157, 161–2, 186, 229
De Generatione Mahumet, 255
De Intellectu, 254
De Motu Stellarum, 254
De Quinque Essentiis, 254
demography, 9, 15, 17–20, 30–1, 32–3, 85, 113, 157, 162, 190, 232
Denia, 5, 11–12, 48–9, 74, 80, 91, 92, 94, 120, 123, 124, 164, 165, 218–9, 241
Despeñaperros, 212, 223
Deusdedit, cardinal, 154
dhimmi, 14, 15, 17
Diego, bishop of Orense, 151–2
Diego Alvarez, 77
Diego Gelmírez, bishop-archbishop of Compostela, 129, 133, 136, 138–40, 143–4, 146–51, 154–5, 192–3, 195, 197, 249, 252, 258
Diego López, 141
Diego Peláez, bishop of Compostela, 77, 90–1, 115
Djahira, 236
Djerba, 216
Doctrina Mahumet, 255
Dolce of Provence, 175–6
Domingo Gonzálvez, 254

Ebles of Roucy, 47, 69, 71, 107
Ebro basin, 6, 43
Edessa, 211
Ejea de los Caballeros, 117, 158
Eleanor of Aquitaine, 226
Elements, 254
Elisabeth, wife of Alfonso VI, 96
Elvira, city, 20
Elvira Alfónsez, daughter of Alfonso VI by Elisabeth, 129
Elvira Alfónsez, daughter of Alfonso

VI by Jimena Munoz, 90, 129, 136–8
Elvira Fernández, 41, 96
Elvira Pérez of Lara, 141, 147, 193, 198
Empuries, 175
Ermesinda of Carcassone, 52, 71
Ermesinda of Navarra, 76–7
l'Escale-Dieu, 250
Estadilla, 112, 116
Esteban, bishop of Huesca, 170
Estefania of Couserans-Foix, 71
Estefania of Navarra, 65
Estella, 77, 186
Euclid, 23, 254
Eudes I of Burgundy, 90, 110
Eugenius III, 211
Eugenius of Toledo, 62
Evora, 210

faqīhs, 103, 167, 235
Fatimid, 9, 12
fatwāhs, 103
Felicia of Roucy, 107
Fernando I, 26, 27, 28, 35–7, 39, 42, 44, 51, 53, 58, 65–6, 69, 70, 74, 106, 123, 226, 240, 249
Fernando II, 222, 227, 229–30
Fernando Pérez of Lara, 141, 147, 193
Fernando Pérez of Traba, 147–8, 152, 171, 192, 196, 201–2, 230
Fernando Yáñez, 151, 154, 193
Fez, 102, 209, 216, 237
Fitero, 250
fossateria, 57
fossatum, 57
The Fountain of Life, 24
Fraga, 162, 173, 180, 181, 183, 184, 185, 187, 199, 215
Fresno de la Fuente, 152
Frómista, 261
Fuente el Olmo de Iscar, see Iscar
fueros, 57, 77, 145, 167, 240–1

Gabes, 216
Galen, 23, 24, 236
García I, 40–2, 71, 74, 90–1, 151
García, bishop of Burgos, 136
García, bishop of Jaca, 110
García, bishop of Zaragoza, 185, 186

García Ordóñez, 77, 108, 115
García Ramírez IV, 183, 184–6, 188–9, 199, 200, 203, 210, 212, 214, 218–9
García Sánchez III, 27, 35, 43, 45, 53, 65, 71
García Sánchez, count of Castilla, 26
Garsenda of Bigorre, 71
Gastón of Bearn, 160, 164, 168, 170–1, 173, 194
Gautier of Gerville, 160
Gelasius II, 146, 160, 179
Genoa, 72, 91, 176, 177, 211–2, 214–5, 218, 223, 241–2, 260
Gerald, bishop-archbishop of Braga, 247, 251–2
Gerald of Cremona, 254
Gerbert of Aurillac, 64
Gerona, 47, 72, 260, 261
Ghana, 101
Gilbert, bishop of Lisbon, 213, 218–9, 247
Gilbert of Hastings, see Gilbert, bishop of Lisbon
Giselberga of Couserans-Foix, 71
Godescalius of Le Puy, 64
Golpejera, 41, 53
Gomez Díaz, 65
Gomez González, 98, 132
Gomez Núñez, 151, 154
Gonzalo, bishop of Coimbra
Gonzalo Núñez, 115
Gonzalo Peláez, 198–9
Gonzalo Salvadórez, 77, 84
Gonzalo Sánchez, 27, 45
grammaticus, 61
Granada
  bishopric, 20
  city, 9, 16, 164–5, 210–11, 217, 223, 233, 236
  taifa, 4, 12, 58, 75–6, 88, 91, 103–4, 120, 220, 222, 231
Graus, 36, 46, 106, 109, 116
Gregorian reform, 68
Gregory I the Great, 62, 251
Gregory VII, 46–7, 107, 243–4
Guadalajara, 7, 94, 131, 205
Guadalquivir basin, 3–4
Guadiana basin, 4
Guide for the Perplexed, 237

Guadix, 19, 20, 164, 165, 220, 221, 222–3
Guido, cardinal, 209, 258
Guillem Ramón of Moncada, 214
Guillermo, bishop of Zaragoza, 186
Guillermo of Vich, 49
Guipúzcoa, 77–8, 107–8, 185, 188
Guntroda Pérez, 199
Guter Armíldez, 208
Guter Fernández, 146–7, 230
Guy, bishop of Lescar, 160, 173, 185
Guy of Vienne, 97, 146

ḥājib, 12
Hammudid dynasty, 12, 102
Haro, 44, 141, 240
Hasan ibn Mar Hasan, 24
Hayy, 235
Henry I of England, 258
Henry II of England, 226
Henry V of Germany, 176
Henry of Burgundy and Portugal, 90, 92, 94, 96–8, 114, 127, 131–4, 196, 200–1, 259
Henry, bishop of Winchester, 258
Herman of Carinthia, 255, 256
Hippocrates, 236
Hishām II, 2, 3, 12
Hishām III, 2
Historia Roderici, 252
Historia Silense, 252
Holy Sepulcher, order of, 181–3, 186, 189–90, 250
Honorius II, 154
Hospitallers, 181–3, 186, 189–90, 214, 250
Hūddid dynasty, 6, 119, 157–8, 159, 161, 172, 198, 210
Huelva, 3, 210
Huermeces, 37
Huesca, 43, 47, 49, 105–6, 109, 110, 112–5, 118, 119, 157, 159, 164, 173
Huete, 80, 224
Hugh, abbot of Cluny, 67, 93
Hugh, bishop of Oporto, 140
Hugh of Santalla, 254
Hugh the White, 68–9
Humbert, cardinal, 197
Hyacinth, cardinal, 221

ibn al-Saffar, 254
ibn Arif, 236
ibn Bājjah, 234–5
ibn Bassām, 236
ibn Gabirol, see Solomon ben Judah ibn Gabirol
ibn Gāniya, 173, 185, 187, 208, 210–11, 212, 217
ibn Hazm, 22, 24
ibn Mardanish, 217–8, 219, 220–1, 222–3, 224, 231
ibn Quzman, 234
ibn Rashīq, 103
ibn Rushd, 235–6, 237, 256
ibn Saīd, 222
ibn Shalib, 82
ibn Sīnna, 23, 255, 256
ibn Tufayl, 235, 236
ibn Tūmart, 206–7, 216
ibn Yahhaf, 125
Ibrahim ibn Yūsuf, 161
imām, 207–8
imperial dignity, 134, 200, 202, 204, 243–4
Inés of Aquitaine, wife of Alfonso VI, 75, 77, 90
Inés of Aquitaine, wife of Pedro I of Aragon, 108, 110, 115
Innocent II, 186
Iria Flavia, 54
irrigation, 8, 33, 44, 47
Isabel of Gascony, 71
Isabel of Urgel, 107
Iscar, 79

Jaca, 45–6, 58, 71, 106, 110, 113, 184, 185, 241, 259
Jaén, 91, 210, 217, 218, 220
Játiva, 87, 92, 123, 124
Jérez de los Cabelleros, 88
Jérez de la Frontera, 9, 217
Jérica, 123
Jerome, bishop of Valencia, Salamanca, Avila, and Zamora, 94, 247
Jimena Díaz, wife of Rodrigo Diaz de Vivar, 94, 105, 125
Jimena Múñoz, mistress of Alfonso VI, 90, 129
Jimeno, bishop of Burgos, 145, 154

Jimeno Jiménez, 197–8
Jimeno López of Alava and Vizcaya, 77
John XV, 67
John of Sevilla, 254
Joseph Ferrizuel, 98n
Juan Téllez, bishop of Burgo de Osma, 248
Joseph ibn Naghrila, 16
Judah Halevi, 238
Julian of Toledo, 62

Kairouan, 100
Khazars, 238
Koran, translation, 256–7
Kusari, 238

Lamego, 35
Lamtuna Berbers, 99–102
Lanhoso, 148
Lara, lineage, 40, 77, 84, 98, 115, 132, 141, 155, 169–71, 194, 197–8, 230
Las Fresnedas, 223
Las Navas de Tolosa, 1, 224, 231
Latro of Vizcaya, 188
Leiria, 202, 203
Leire, 45
León, city, 2, 30, 31, 35, 40–1, 54, 96–7, 145, 146, 191, 192, 197, 200, 209, 241, 243, 259, 261
Leonardo Fibonacci, 254
Lerida, 6, 19, 43, 49, 59, 87, 94, 107, 109, 112, 113, 116, 117–8, 119, 120–1, 123–4, 157–8, 162, 172–3, 179–80, 181, 187, 209, 214–5, 217, 218, 224–5, 244, 259
Lescar, 114, 160, 173, 185
Liber Alghoarismi, 254
Liber de Consuetudinibus, 255
Liber Embadorum, 254
Liber Judiciorum, 24, 62
Liria, 123
Lisbon, 11, 36, 92, 143, 201, 202, 209, 212–3, 217, 218, 224, 243, 247, 250
Logic, 256
Logroño, 6
Lop Jiménez of Alava and Vizcaya, 77, 107–8
Lorca, 220
Louis VII of France, 211, 220–1, 258

Lubb, 43
Lucas of Túy, 222, 252
Lucena, 22, 164
Lugo, 30, 90, 136, 192
Luna in Aragón, 112
Luna in León, 42, 90
Llantadilla, 40

Madrid, 81, 131, 135, 230
magister scolarum, 61
mahdī, 207–8, 216
Mahdiya, 216
Maine, 226
Majorca, *see* Balearic Islands
Málaga, 4, 5, 11, 20, 91, 94, 165, 211, 217, 220
mālik, 12
Malikite, 12, 100, 206–7
Manrique, 230
Mansilla, 146, 197
Manzanares, 11
María, daughter of Ramón Berenguer III, 174
Marrakesh, 102, 206, 207, 209, 236
Martín Sánchez, 77
Masmūda, 206–7
Matilda of England, 258
Matilda of Savoy, 225
Maurice Bourdin, archbishop of Braga, 247
mayordomus, 55–6, 146, 239
Mazdali, 94, 116, 135, 137
Medina del Campo, 79, 152, 229
Medinaceli, 6, 7, 11, 81, 94, 95, 153, 162, 169, 196
Melilla, 9
Mendo Goncalves, 145
Mequinenza, 173, 187, 215
merchant marine, 11–12, 48–9, 54–5, 72, 176, 241–2
Merida, 4, 11, 147, 154
merino, 52, 55, 59, 77, 239
Mertola, 3, 4, 210, 217
Mir Geriberto, 53
Mishnah, 237
Misneh Torah, 237
Molina de Aragón, 169, 196
Mollerusa, 94, 116, 174
Moncada, lineage, 214, 240
Mondoñedo, 192

Monreal del Campo, 161–2
Montearagón, 110
Montpellier, 119, 176, 214, 226
Montoro, 218, 221, 222
Montserrat, 67
Monzón in Aragón, 112, 117, 169, 171
Monzón in Castilla, 129–30
Morella, 109
Morón, 3, 196
Morón de Almazán, 196
Moses ben Ezra, 237–8
Moses Maimónides, 237, 256
Motril, 165
Mozárabic rite, 68–9, 245, 247
Muhammad, king of Calatayud, 43
Muhammad ibn Abi Amir, see
    al-Mansur
Muhammad ibn Āisa, 92, 124
Muhammad ibn Mazdali, 137
Muhammad, son of Abd al-Mūmin,
    216
Mujāhdid, 12
Mundir, 43, 87, 88, 109, 120–1
Murcia, 5, 9, 11, 87, 91, 103, 120,
    164–5, 170, 210, 217, 219, 220, 221,
    224
Murviedro, 123
Muwāhhid, 167, 206–8, 210, 215–7,
    218, 220–4, 224–5, 230, 231, 232,
    233–4, 235, 236, 237
muwāllad, 14, 18
muwashshah, 234, 236, 237

Nájera, 27, 36, 44, 65, 77, 184, 185,
    256
Narbonne, 48, 176, 244
nasi, 14, 15
Nicholas, bishop of Cambrai, 258
Niebla, 3, 210, 217
Nimes, 176
noria, 8, 29, 33
Nuño Pérez, 222

Odilo of Cluny, 66
Oca, 77
Olegario, bishop of Barcelona and
    archbishop of Tarragona, 179–80,
    185, 197
Oliva of Ripoll, 66
Olmedo, 79, 152

Oloron, 114
Oña, 32, 67
Oporto, 4, 19, 28, 29, 35, 142–3, 197,
    213, 243
Oran, 102
Ordóñez, lineage, 40, 230
Ordoño I, 17
Oreja, see Colmenar de Oreja
Orense, 151–2, 153, 192, 201
Oriel, 137
Orense, 35
Orosius, 62, 251
Otto di Bonvillano, 214
Ourique, 203
Oviedo, 17, 30, 197, 243, 258

Paio Mendes, 145
Palencia, 135, 171, 198
Pallars, 48, 175
Pamplona, 27, 30, 36, 44–5, 77–8, 106,
    111, 113, 183, 184, 185, 241, 244n,
    256, 259, 261
parias, 36–7, 39–40, 49, 58–9, 67, 74,
    76, 82, 87, 91, 105, 109, 114, 120,
    121, 123–4, 141, 172, 179, 218, 225,
    231
Paschal II, 116, 137, 159, 176–9, 179
Paschal, bishop of Burgos, 136, 140,
    145
Paschal, bishop of Toledo, 37
Pedro I of Aragón, 88, 93, 108, 110,
    112–17, 118, 157–8
Pedro, bishop of Cardeña, 91
Pedro, bishop of León, 131
Pedro, bishop of Oporto, 213
Pedro, bishop of Palencia, 152
Pedro, bishop of Rota, 173
Pedro, bishop of Segovia, 147, 152
Pedro, son of Ramón Berenguer I, 49,
    119
Pedro Alfónsez, 199, 230
Pedro Ansúrez, 77, 117–8, 230
Pedro Díaz, 197–8
Pedro Froílaz, 129, 131–3, 137–9, 144,
    148–9, 152–3, 192–3, 198
Pedro González, 141, 146–7, 155,
    169–71, 182, 193, 197–8, 230
Pedro Talesa, 183
Pedroche, 221, 222

Pelayo, bishop of Oviedo, 79, 82, 131, 197, 258
Peñafiel, 29, 79, 132, 141
Peñalen, 76
Peñaranda del Duero, 29
Perpignan, 72, 260
Peter, abbot of Cluny, 256–7
Peter, bishop of Burgo de Osma, 248
Peter of Gaberet, 160
Peter of Melgueil, 48
Peter of Poitier, 256
Peter of Puy in Velay, 65
Peter of Toledo, 256
Petronila, 186–7, 199, 225–6
Physics, 254
Pisa, 72, 176, 177, 242, 260
Planisphere, 255
Plato of Tivoli, 254, 256
Poblet, 250
political authority
   Christian, 50–2, 55, 226–7, 239
   Islamic, 2, 12–13, 205, 233–4
Pons, bishop of Barbastro, 116
Pons of Toulouse, 48
portaticum, 57
Practica Geometriae, 254
Primera cronica general, 86–7, 122
primicerius, 61
Provence, 175–7, 226
Ptolemy, 234, 254, 255
Puente Sampayo, 151

qādis, 12, 103, 125, 235
Quadripartitum, 254

Raimundo Alfónsez, 197, 199
Rainaud of Bailleul, 160
Ramiro I, 27, 36, 45–6, 71, 106
Ramiro II, 137, 140–1, 181–87, 199
Ramiro Sanchez, 77, 84
Ramón Berenguer I, 48–9, 53–4, 67, 71, 72, 74, 119
Ramón Berenguer II, 119–20
Ramón Berenguer III, 117–8, 121–2, 168–9, 173, 174–80, 195, 242
Ramón Berenguer IV, 173, 181, 187–90, 199, 200, 211–2, 214–5, 218–9, 225–6, 240, 254
Ramón Borell I, 58
Ramón Borell II, 71

Ramón García of Navarra, 76–7
Ramón Llull, 235
Raymond IV of Toulouse, 90, 129
Raymond, archbishop of Toledo, 247, 254
Raymond, bishop of Burgo de Osma, 146, 248
Raymond of Burgundy and Galicia, 90–1, 92–3, 94–5, 96, 98, 114, 129, 259
Razes, 48, 175, 226
el rey Lobo, *see* ibn Mardanish
Ribagorza, 26, 27, 45–6, 106–7, 110
ribāt, 101
Richard of Saint-Victor, *116*
Ricobayo, 192
The Ring of the Dove, 22
Ripoll, 63–4, 66–7
Robert Burdet, 160, 180, 259
Robert of Ketton, 256
Rodrigo Díaz de Vivar, 42, 80–2, 92, 93, 94, 105, 108, 109, 112, 116, 120–1, 122–5, 158, 174, 247, 248, 252
Rodrigo González, 141, 169, 171, 193, 197, 230
Rodrigo Martínez, 198
Rodrigo Ordóñez, 108
Rodrigo Ovéquez, 90–1
Rodrigo Vélaz, 146
Roger II of Sicily, 216, 236
Roger Bernard of Couserans-Foix, 71
Roncesvalles, 64, 259
Ronda, 3
Roussillon, 175
Rota, *see* Rueda de Jalón
Rotru of Perche, 160, 164
Rueda de Jalón, 83, 131, 159, 172
Rule of Benedict, 66
The Rule of the Solitary, 234–5

Sagunto, 123
Sahagún, 20, 32, 67, 126–7, 135, 136–7, 140, 150–1, 158, 183, 191, 229
sāhib, 12
Saif al-Dawla, 172, 198, 199, 210
Saint Ambrose, 251
Saint Augustine of Hippo, 62, 251

Saint Bernard of Clairvaux, 211,
    249–50
Saint James the Great, *see* Santiago de
    Compostela
Saint Jerome, 62, 251
Saint-Foy de Conques, 116
Saint-Gilles, 116
Saint-Maur, 67
Saint-Pons de Thomières, 67, 114, 116,
    183
Saint-Victor, 67
Saladin, 237
Salamanca, 79, 94–5, 154, 197, 229,
    230, 240–1, 243, 248, 259
Saldaña, 155, 195
Sale, 216, 217
Sampiro of Astorga, 62–3
Samuel ibn Naghrila, 16
San Benito del Campo, 54
San Esteban de Gormaz, 37, 81, 212
San Esteban de Litera, 117–8
San Facundo, 67
San Felix de Lovio, 54
San Fructuoso, 62, 66
San Isidoro, 62, 65–7, 251, 261
San Mamed, 195
San Martin de Albelda, 63–4
San Martin Pinario, 54
San Miguel de Cisterna, 54
San Millán de La Cogolla, 32, 34, 63,
    74, 184
San Pablo del Campo, 261
San Pedro de Cardeña, 34, 91, 125
San Pedro de Montes, 34
San Pedro el Viejo, 183
San Pelayo de Antealtares, 54
San Primitivo, 67
San Servando, 208
Sancha Alfónsez, daughter of Alfonso
    V, 26, 40
Sancha Alfónsez, daughter of Alfonso
    VI, 129, 136, 138
Sanch Alfónsez, daughter of Alfonso
    VII, 222
Sancha Fernández of Traba, 210
Sancha Ramírez, daughter of Ramiro
    I, 46
Sancha Raimúndez, 129, 138, 195
Sancho II of Castilla, 39–42, 44, 52–3,
    67, 71, 74, 106, 123, 252

Sancho III of Castilla, 187, 199, 222,
    227, 229–30
Sancho VI of Navarra, 219, 225
Sancho, count of Gascony, 71
Sancho *el Mayor*, *see* Sancho García
    III *el Mayor*
Sancho García III *el Mayor*, 25, 26,
    27, 35, 43–5, 66, 71, 98, 105–6,
    183
Sancho García IV, 28, 36, 40, 44–5,
    52–3, 71, 74, 76–7, 106
Sancho Ramírez I, 40, 44, 46–7, 58,
    69, 71, 75, 77–8, 88, 91, 106–12,
    118, 120, 157
Sancho Alfónsez, 92–3, 96–7, 126–7
Sanchuelo, *see* Abd al-Rahman
Sanhāja Berbers, 99–102
Santa Cruz, 261
Santa Eulalia, 261
Santa Eufemia, 221, 222
Santa Gadea, 42
Santa Justa, 65
Santa Maria el Real de Najera, 65
Santamara, 37
Santarém, 36, 41, 92, 131, 143, 201,
    202, 205, 212, 217, 224, 236
Santes Creus, 250
Santiago, order of, 251
Santiago de Compostela
    bishopric-archbishopric, 40–1,
        53–4, 77, 90–1, 97, 115, 132,
        136, 146–50, 154, 192–3, 242–3,
        245, 247, 249, 252
    city, 2, 30, 46, 143–4, 241, 259
    pilgrimage, 64–7, 187, 213, 221, 241,
        254, 257–8, 261
Santiuste, 37
Sardinia, 72
Sariñena, 181
Savoy, 225
Secretum Secretorum, 255
Segorbe, 123
Segovia, 79, 95, 136, 145, 147, 240–1,
    248, 254
Sepúlveda, 79
Setif, 216
*Seven Books of History against the
    Pagans*, 62
Sevilla
    bishopric, 19

city, 3, 9, 11, 15, 30, 65, 210, 217, 220, 224, 233, 235, 254
taifa, 3, 5, 6, 12, 41–3, 58, 75–6, 80, 82–3, 84, 86, 88–9, 92, 103–4, 120
Sfax, 216
Siger of Brabant, 236
Sigüenza, 19, 94, 152–4, 162, 205
Sijilmasa, 101
Silos, 32, 155
Silves, 3, 4, 217
Simancas, 29
Singra, 162
Sintra, 92
Sir al-Asrār, 255
Sir ibn Abū Bakr, 91–2
Sobrarbe, 26, 27, 45–6, 106–7, 110, 117
Sobroso, 138
Solomon ben Judah ibn Gabirol, 22, 24, 255
Somport, 45–6, 64, 71, 111, 160, 259, 261
Sousse, 216
Stephen, bishop of Burgo de Osma, 248
Stephen, treasurer of Cluny, 258
Suero Vermúdez, 199, 230
Sufism, 207, 236
Sus, 100, 101
Sylvester II, see Gerbert of Aurillac

Tajo basin, 6–7
Talamanca, 37
Talavera de la Reina, 7, 95, 131, 221, 224
Tamara, 168, 195
Tamarite de Litera, 117–8
Tamarón, 27, 51
Tamīn, king of Malaga, 103–4
Tamīn ibn Yusuf, 97
Tangier, 9
Tarazona, 145, 157, 160–2, 253, 254
Tarifa, 84, 91
Tarragona, 6, 11, 12, 19, 48–9, 119, 177–8, 179–80, 243, 244
Tashufin ibn Alī, 208–9, 210
Templars, 181–3, 186, 189–90, 214–5
Teresa I of Portugal, 90, 92, 96, 98, 127, 132–4, 136, 141–56, 168, 171, 192–3, 195, 200–2

Teruel, 161, 162, 169, 194
Tevar, 121
Thomas Aquinas, 236
Thouars, 185, 188
Tlemcen, 102, 209
Tojos Outos, 202
Toledo
    bishopric-archbishopric, 20, 37, 136, 195, 243, 245, 246, 247, 249, 254
    city, 9, 11, 15, 88–9, 91, 94–5, 97–8, 126–7, 131–2, 135–6, 136–41, 187, 191, 205, 208–9, 212, 217, 218, 220, 221, 222, 227, 230, 232, 233, 238, 253, 255, 259
    taifa, 5, 6, 7, 11, 36–7, 39–41, 58, 75–6, 80–6, 120, 123, 231
Tordesillas, 29, 79
Toro, 29, 230
Torono, 151
Tortosa, 6, 11, 43, 48–9, 59, 72, 88, 91, 109, 119, 120, 123, 158, 172, 179–80 181, 187, 209, 211–2, 214–5, 217, 218, 224–5, 241, 244, 259, 260
Toulouse, 46, 90, 119, 129, 160, 171, 176, 177, 185, 191, 195, 198, 211, 226
Traba, see Trastamara, lineage
trans-Duero, 39, 79–81, 139–40, 240–1
Trastamara, lineage, 129, 144, 147–8, 152, 192–3, 212, 230, 240
Tripoli, 216
Troyes, 182
Tudéjen, 219
Tudela, 6, 15, 43, 63, 90, 107, 109, 110, 145, 157, 160, 162, 184–5, 188–9, 224, 259, 260
Tunis, 216
Túy, 151–2, 153, 154, 192, 195, 201, 202

Ubeda, 223
Uclés, 97, 126–7, 221
University of Paris, 236
Urban II, 111, 114, 177, 244
Urgel, 46, 48, 72, 116, 117–8, 120, 121–2, 158, 160, 174–5, 185, 215, 218, 260
Urraca I, 51, 90, 96–98, 126–55, 159, 168, 170, 171, 182, 191–3, 201, 206, 230, 243, 244, 247

Urraca Alfónsez, 209–10
Urraca Enríquez, 202
Urraca Fernández, 41–2, 52, 96
Urraca García, 26, 108

Valdorrey, 37
Valencia
  bishopric, 20, 247, 248
  city, 11, 72, 164–5, 171, 217, 218,
    236, 241, 260
  taifa, 5, 6, 7, 11, 37, 39, 58–9, 74,
    80–1, 85, 86–88, 91–2, 94–5, 105,
    109, 112, 116, 120–1, 122–5, 219,
    224–5, 231
Valencia de Don Juan, see Coyanza
Valladolid, 79, 209, 221
Vallespir, 175
Valtierra, 131, 159
Velliti Ariulfi, 42
Venice, 72
Vermudo III, 25, 26, 35, 50
Vermudo Gutiérrez, 77
Vermudo Pérez of Traba, 152, 202
Vezelay, 211
via francigenea, see Santiago de
  Compostela, pilgrimage
Viadangos, 133
Vich, 49, 66, 72, 174, 260
Victor II, 67
Villafranca de Penedès, 177
Villafranca del Bierzo, 259
Viseu, 20, 36, 202
Vivar, 123
Vizcaya, 77–8, 107–8, 185
vizier, 216, 235

War of the Three Sanchos, 40, 44
waterwheel, 8, 29, 33–4, 44, 47

William I of England, 71, 90–1
William VIII of Aquitaine, 75, 90, 108
William IX of Aquitaine, 171, 185
William X of Aquitaine, 187, 258
William of Jerusalem, 189
William of Montpellier, 48, 214
William of Poitiers, 161

Yahyā ibn Ibrāhīm, 100
Yahyā ibn Tāshufīn, 94
Yahyā ibn Umar, 101
Yūsuf al-Muzzafar, 43, 83, 107
Yūsuf ibn Tāshufīn, 82, 84, 88–9, 91,
  92, 93, 94, 95, 101–05, 117, 125, 205

Zafadola, see Saif al-Dawla
zajal, 234
Zaida, 92, 96
Zainab, 101
Zalaca, 88–9, 95, 103, 104, 110
Zamora, 2, 11, 29, 35, 41, 74, 132–4,
  154, 168, 192–3, 195, 197, 229, 230,
  248, 252, 259, 261
Zanata Berbers, 101, 102
Zaragoza
  bishopric, 19
  city, 9, 11, 15, 22, 30, 46, 48, 63, 71,
    141, 145, 158–62, 164, 179,
    184–5, 186, 188, 233, 234, 236
  taifa, 6, 7, 11, 20, 36–7, 39–40,
    43–4, 46–7, 58–9, 74–77, 81,
    83–4, 86–8, 90, 94, 95, 97, 105,
    106–18, 119, 123, 131, 137, 158,
    172, 205, 215, 217, 224–5, 229,
    231, 244, 259
Zīrīd dynasty of Granada, 12
Zīrīd dynasty of Tunisia, 102, 216
Zorita, 81, 97

Lightning Source UK Ltd.
Milton Keynes UK
26 January 2010

149148UK00001B/42/A

9 780631 199649